"*The Language of Man* is founded on a powerful idea: that creativity is not the privilege of a few exceptional minds, but a language that is our natural birthright. **Want to become more fluent in the language of creativity? This hopeful, insightful book will show you how.**"

Daniel H. Pink
New York Times bestselling author, *A Whole New Mind* and *DRIVE*

"**Great books should push readers to rethink their identity and modify daily practices. This is the province of *The Language of Man*.** The reason this is a necessary book for those interested in cultivating their own creativity or leading others is that the author synthesizes ideas from different fields to distill where breakthroughs come from, how to become more open-minded, and what it requires to sit at the edges of knowns and unknowns. **To be honest, the majority of books on creativity rehash the same research and trite, contrived, and appallingly obvious suggestions. Then there is this—mental ambrosia.**"

Todd B. Kashdan, PhD
Author, *Curious?* and *The Upside of Your Dark Side*
Professor of Psychology, George Mason University

"**People are hungry for a connection, for meaning, for a way—their own way—to explore "what could be."** In a word, they want to learn to create. And they don't want a primer on what's already out there, something others too often fail to recognize. **Once again, Larry Robertson digs deeper, almost to the core of what it means to be human, and delivers what we really want.**"

Robert Egger
Author, *Begging for Change*
Founder, DC Central Kitchen and LA Kitchen

"As a book about creativity should be, Larry Robertson's *The Language of Man* is innovative and unique. Wide-ranging and compelling research is just the beginning. It's the author's focus on what creativity is like in actual practice, not just in theory, that makes this book stand out. Robertson does more than help us understand, he helps each of us create. Throughout the book we're introduced to a wide range of truly creative individuals who quickly become personal guides and mentors. Quilting it all together are **Robertson's rare abilities to see patterns, discern simple truths, and tell entertaining and compelling stories**, all of which **make this book necessary and truly enjoyable. *The Language of Man* is a highly recommended, essential read if what you want is to create something valuable and original. And deep inside, you know that's exactly what you want.**"

JJ Ramberg
Host, Your Business, MSNBC
Co-founder, GoodShop

"**Fantastic and extraordinarily valuable. By 'reimagining creativity' as something fundamental to the human endeavor and an innate ability triggered by openness to the beauty and wonder of this world, Larry Robertson elegantly reframes the entire debate about how to foster innovation and genius in us all.** *The Language of Man* turns the discussion of creative and innovative capacity inside-out, arguing that these are not rarified talents of an elite cadre of geniuses, but within reach of if not intrinsic to every human. While he interviews many of the most prominent "cultural creatives" of our era, Robertson's own insights are among the most valuable and far reaching, and his rare gift for asking questions and pursuing the unexplored is bound to release the entrepreneurial and exploratory spirit within us all."

Gary Nabhan
Author, *Cross-pollinations: The Marriage of Science and Poetry*
Co-founder, Native Seeds/SEARCH and MacArthur Fellow

"This deeply original work will probably shatter your most familiar assumptions about creativity—what it is, where it exists, and who is capable of putting it to innovative use. But then again, that's exactly what breakthrough ideas and empowering innovations do. In that sense and in every sense, **The Language of Man is a book about discovery**— not just what the author discovered, but what each of us can discover. Importantly, **it's a book about value, too**: how to use our creative capacity to see value in all its many forms and, more important still, how to use our creativity to seize it. **Rather than discover some trite or stagnant "formula" for creativity, in The Language of Man Larry Robertson opens us up to the mindset and the habit of seeing the possible—something every one of us needs to embrace now more than ever.**"

Gene Kahn
Founder, Cascadian Farms and Small Planet Foods

"Far too often we take our own creative sense for granted or just ignore it. **Knowing how to recognize and verbalize to yourself that you are in fact creative is the first step in bringing it to your world. The Language of Man is a roadmap we all would do well to follow.**"

Darden Smith
Singer, songwriter
Co-founder, SongwritingWith: Soldiers

"Robertson argues that creativity is not magical pixie dust that touches the chosen few but an innate human trait that, like a muscle, either becomes enfeebled from disuse or strengthened and toned if deliberately exercised. This is decidedly a good thing as, **in the current environment, where change is accelerating at an unprecedented pace, the demand for creativity as a survival skill is critical. Robertson's insightful book meets an urgent need to better understand the nature of creativity, how we can all expand our creative capacity, and how this powerful force can be harnessed for good.**"

Diana Wells
President, Ashoka

"For too long we have been led to believe that people are either creative or they are not—that it is an innate talent that exists in rare people and can only be minimally improved. That never seemed right to me. Throughout a career in technology, retail, and consumer products, I have constantly asked myself and my teams: **"Can creativity be taught? Can it be greatly improved? And if so, how and what can we do as leaders to enable this in our organizations?**

"**Larry Robertson answers the first two questions with a resounding yes, explodes the myth of the creative hero, and provides the process to recognize, unlock, and improve the creativity in all of us.** He also delivers great insights on what we can do as leaders to enable this, not just in ourselves but also in our teams. His book will make you reconsider what you are doing and why—and actually enable the innovation that so many organizations seek but so poorly understand."

John Hamlin
Chair, Board of Directors, REI

"**Larry Robertson has written a timely and important book.** We are beset with too much frozen thinking with local, regional, and global crises all around us. We are not taught that creativity is open to "everyman." Robertson's book seeks to teach us how to be far more open, creative, and empowered. *The Language of Man* **makes a critical contribution we all need.**"

Stuart Kauffman
Author, *Humanity in a Creative Universe*
Complex Systems Researcher, MacArthur Fellow

"Creativity isn't just in the realm of a Picasso or a Hemingway or a Steve Jobs, Larry Robertson tells us in his thoughtful book. It's in all of us, as long as we're open to asking questions and thinking outside the box. Broadening our intellectual borders like a cunning fox and putting these ideas into practice like a focused hedgehog is what we're each built for and must do if what we want is our continued human progress."

Tom Bowman
NPR Pentagon Reporter
Edward R. Murrow Award Winner

"I have always been moved by "the power of the story." *The Language of Man* reminds us of the power in each of us to tell our own story and to create. The insights shared brought to mind a still vivid memory: As my grandmother was dying, she pulled me close to her, and in her thick Cajun accent, recited who she was: Hattie, the mother of Elaine, Raymond, and Margie— her story of her greatest creations. Rather than simply explain creativity or tell you how to create, this book offers reasons to feel inspired and the simple power of discovering what creativity means to you."

Lorna Elaine Bourg
Co-founder, President, CEO, Southern Mutual Help Association
MacArthur Fellow

"**In this remarkable book**, Robertson explores the nuances of creative thought and action, arguing that creativity is not the exclusive province of the "genius" or the "hero," but rather accessible to all of us. He urges the reader to be open to creativity, to have the courage to "come to the edge" and take the leap. He reminds us that we are all born with the capacity to be creative, although many of us have forgotten how. In **a joyous celebration** of inquiry and co-creation, he weaves insights and practices developed by creative "guides" into a beautiful paean to creative inquiry, inviting us all to dip our toes into the ocean of the creative process. Ultimately, **[Larry Robertson] has given us all a gift: a guide to finding the ways in which we can develop our own expression of what it means to be human. . . .**"

Ellen Barry
Founder, Legal Services for Prisoners with Children
MacArthur Fellow

THE LANGUAGE OF MAN

Becca —

My very best...
to inspire yours!

THE LANGUAGE OF MAN.

LEARNING TO SPEAK CREATIVITY

LARRY ROBERTSON

daymark

Also by Larry Robertson

A Deliberate Pause:

Entrepreneurship and its Moment in Human Progress

Daymark Press
Published by Daymark Press, Arlington, Virginia.

Cover design and layout by Vanessa Maynard

Library of Congress Cataloging-in-Publication Data
Robertson, Larry

The Language of Man: Learning to Speak Creativity / Larry Robertson

p.   cm.
Includes references and endnotes.

ISBN 978-0-9837574-3-6 (hardcover)
ISBN 978-0-9837574-4-3 (paperback)

Library of Congress Control Number 2016910234
1. Creativity 2. Leadership 3. Innovation 4. Creative Thinking 5. Creative Ability

Printed in the United States of America

Dedicated:

To *you.*

And to *us.*

"Men go forth to marvel at the heights of mountains, at the huge waves of the sea, the broad flow of the rivers, the vastness of the ocean, the orbit of the stars, and they neglect to marvel at themselves."[1]

St. Augustine, ca. 397 C.E.

CONTENTS

REIMAGINING

CREATIVITY

A NOTE TO THE READER

REIMAGINING CREATIVITY

Imagination is something we closely associate with creativity, so before diving into this book, just for a moment, imagine. Picture yourself in the heart of New York City, or any busy urban landscape canyoned by tall buildings and pulsing with human activity. In your mind's eye, what do you see? Chances are you imagine those skyscrapers and the chasms they form. You probably picture a dense traffic of cars, people, bicycles, and buses. Fine-tuning further, you might envision people in business suits hurrying; a fast-peddling bicycle messenger narrowly missing a woman on her phone as she races to be on time for work; cabbies honking their horns and shooting animated gestures at one another; construction workers behind bright orange cones completely engrossed as they jackhammer the street . . .

But do you see the sky?

When asked to imagine an urban scene like this, most people never mention the sky. They know it's there, of course, but it isn't part of their pattern to truly notice or consider it—their habits and routines largely leave it out. Even when asked to picture a rural scene of human activity, the sky rarely warrants mention. Our great tendency is to think first about things known—those elements and patterns of our lives that occupy well-worn grooves.

But if you've ever stood on a mountaintop, experienced the vast expanse of a desert or an ocean, or even climbed to an apartment building rooftop in a big city at night, you know what it feels like to experience the sky and be drawn to it.

Whether we are conscious of it or not, the sky symbolizes the possible and what's yet to be discovered. It's in the sky that we gain a view unencumbered by what already is and catch a glimpse of what might yet be.

Imagined from the broadest view, this book helps you remember to see the sky and, more powerful still, to touch it. First, however, we need to put some language around what that means and what you can expect on the journey you're about to take. Let's start simple.

WHAT LIES AHEAD

Here's a simple truth: Creativity is about the *possible*. More, each of us depends deeply on creativity and for far more than we realize. Most important and powerful of all, creativity is a uniquely *human* capacity that *each* of us possesses—including *you*.

Pause for a moment and take note that creativity surrounds us and the act of creating embodies who we are. The "outputs" we traditionally associate with creativity span the spectrum of human activity— from game-changing physical innovations (e.g., mobile devices or self-driving cars) to new forms of expression (such as performance art or hip-hop culture) to revolutionary ways of doing (think Google or Uber). In every sense, it is our creative capacity that enables us to dream, to do, and to make.

Widen the view a bit more and it quickly becomes clear that the roots of *any* human advancement ever made or imagined—in science and technology, in the arts or government, in social science or healthcare—can be traced back to the seed of creativity. Our existence and our future are inextricably intertwined with it.

I wrote this book to help you understand why creativity is vital to who *you* are and how *all of us* progress. But just as important, I wrote it to help you learn to cultivate your own creative capacity. Our human history, as you will soon see, proves that creativity defines every single one of us. Indeed, if we all understood what creativity truly is and practiced using our capacity for it as a matter of habit, then the many things we need, seek, or dream about would move markedly from the possible to the *tangible*.

What enables all of this is *learning to speak creativity.* You probably don't think of it this way, but creativity *is* a language: the one language common to us all and unique among all living things. Creativity is the language of man. (See Author's Notes: Reimagining Creativity-A.) You were born ready for this language, putting it to use almost from the moment your eyes met the light and you saw the possible in the world around you. But if you are like most, with time you've forgotten this unique capacity. Few of us ever turn its use into our habit. To remedy that, this book will reconnect you with your inherent creative capacity and enable you to develop fluency in this language. Approached with an open mind, what you'll read here will help you contribute *your* verse to the larger "story of creativity"—a story you'll gradually come to see as a richly blended quilt of *all* our individual creative contributions.

What lies ahead of you is a journey but not a sprint. In order to make the most of this journey, I suggest keeping the following in mind.

SUGGESTIONS TO GUIDE YOUR JOURNEY

1. Set Aside Assumptions. No matter who you are, chances are that even in these opening pages you've already made some judgments—about this book, about creativity, even about yourself. Those preconceptions derive from the many assumptions we make, consciously or not. But creativity requires a willingness to reconsider even the most well-worn or deeply cherished assumptions. I urge you to awaken to what yours might be. As one example, if you think you are not creative, put that thought far enough to the side to explore the vast evidence that might lead you to a different conclusion. Or, if you believe you know creativity well, consider the possibility that there is more to learn, different ways to see creativity than the ones you currently know, and endless ways to create.

In a word, be "open"—open in the truest and fullest sense that allows you to go beyond the borders of what's known to you and stay ever open to the new. Openness is central to creativity, and it is your openness that will regulate what you will take away from this creative journey.

least in *theory*. But oddly, and tellingly, few resources addressed creativity in *practice*.

Even when, in rare instances, a resource touched on creativity in practice, it typically failed to offer *insights* gained *directly from practitioners* themselves. More rare still was a resource that went beyond any *one* practitioner or method to look for *patterns* across creativity's many forms and creators. The absence of such insights and patterns led me to the MacArthur Fellows.

In-depth Interviews. To gain a deeper understanding of creativity and a keener sense of the patterns that play out across it, I conducted in-depth interviews with sixty-six MacArthur Fellows. (See MacArthur Fellows in References for a list of those interviewed.) The MacArthur Fellowship is awarded to "talented individuals who have shown extraordinary originality and dedication in their creative pursuits and a marked capacity for self-direction."[2] In short, it honors the doers. It's also the only fellowship specifically awarded for creativity.

Since it was established in 1981 by the John D. and Catherine T. MacArthur Foundation, this fellowship has been awarded to more than eight hundred people. To tap into a variety of generations, circumstances, and perspectives, I spoke with at least one fellow from each year of the award, starting at 1981 and stopping at 2013. (See Author's Notes: Reimagining Creativity-B.) MacArthur Fellows include choreographers and chemists, geneticists and geographers, lawyers and linguists, artists and anthropologists, sociologists and surgeons, biologists and business leaders, and on it goes. Their undertakings span the spectrum of how humans create. Wanting to see how creativity in practice varied by the field or manner in which it was applied, I sought out representative Fellows across this spectrum.

From "Geniuses" to Guides. As I interviewed these insightful practitioners, they unexpectedly became my own personal guides to creativity. Once you read their words and sense the honesty, sincerity, humility, and humanness of each, you'll quickly understand why.

You may find it hard to believe, especially about recipients of an award referred to as "the genius award," but these Fellows are just like you and me with two small but important exceptions: 1) They know each of us is endowed with a creative capacity, and 2) they practice using theirs.

Because of their humanness, this diverse group of seasoned practitioners collectively represents the perfect personal guides on the journey toward tapping into your own creative capacity. You'll be glad they're along to help you reveal what creativity can be for you.

Insight vs. Instruction. As a group, the MacArthur Fellows offer deep and rare insights about creativity—what it is, the forms it takes, where it occurs, what it means, and how it can be used to deliver tangible value. They make all the research come alive and make it relevant. Their fresh insights and the revealing patterns across them will change how you look at creativity. That said, neither I nor the Fellows I interviewed tout themselves as *experts* on creativity. They represent something far more valuable than that; they *speak* creativity.

Their fluency results not from unique genetics, but from continual experimentation. They've cultivated creativity, applied it, morphed it, felt frustrated by it, and been enlightened as well. In addition to being practitioners of creativity, they also happen to be exceptional researchers, business professionals, teachers, and leaders. As such, they offer a wide spectrum of insights rather than any one elusive silver-bullet conclusion. It's by looking *across* their insights that the patterns reveal themselves—patterns you too can use to create.

YOUR JOURNEY BEGINS . . .

As you're about to see, the story of creativity is an incredible one. It is our story, no less than the story of what it means to be human. But the story of creativity is incomplete without your contribution. It's time to learn to speak creativity so you too may contribute your verse.

CREATIVELY

FIGHTING

OURSELVES

CHAPTER ONE

CREATIVELY FIGHTING OURSELVES

How do we begin to reveal the fantastic power that is our creative capacity?

KNOWLEDGEABLE DRIVERS WANTED

Just pause for a moment and you'll quickly see there's a lot to consider—including why we create, what enables us to create, who creates, even what creativity is in the first place. The next four chapters, which together comprise the *Reveal* section of *The Language of Man,* will explore all of this in detail. The purpose of this section is to reveal to you the basic building blocks for understanding creativity, not just in this moment, but ongoing. Creativity is more accurately viewed as a living, breathing, "practice," one characterized by constant motion and perpetual evolution, than it is as a "thing" or even a "recipe" for how to create things. The meaning behind this will soon become clear. But for now, a simple analogy for this section, followed by a story to start this first chapter, help orient us.

Because it's so much a part of our daily lives, we don't often reflect on the fact that the automobile is a fantastic thing. Its ability to cover long distances quickly and reliably is reality-altering compared with how we humans got around for most of our existence—on the power of our own two feet. So advanced have today's cars become that now we look for them to do far more than transport us. We count on them to protect us, entertain us, and even connect us to a myriad of other advancements at the same time they move us from here to there.

But here's the reality and the problem: If we don't understand the equipment itself, we simply cannot tap into the powerful creation that is the car.

Creativity too is powerful. But in a similar way to the car, we must first come to understand the equipment that enables us to create and progress—none other than the creative human brain. Only after we do can we talk about "drivers" and "destinations" or what's possible to discover when venturing out with this remarkable apparatus.

This first chapter of the *Reveal* section delves into how our creative brain came to be, how it works, and how we are capable of either enhancing its power or limiting it—all things we must come to know before creativity can move us forward.

As will become our habit in each chapter, let's begin with a story, one that reflects how we've gotten off on the wrong path and how we might return to a more creative one.

THE DIVIDED PATH TOWARD UNDERSTANDING CREATIVITY

A STUDY IN CONTRASTS

It would be hard to argue against the commonly shared view that Isaac Newton was a deeply creative soul. He's probably best known as the person who helped us understand the concept of gravity. But he also discovered the reason behind the movement of the tides. In addition, he wrote what many call the single most important book of all time, the *Principia* (sorry, *Bible*). The *Principia* established the basic laws of motion from which two and a half subsequent centuries of innovations such as the airplane and the space shuttle have resulted.

Seemingly unbounded, Newton created calculus, designed the first reflecting telescope, and figured out that light is made up of a spectrum of colors among other discoveries almost too numerous to list. His creative thoughts and contributions stretched far beyond the sciences too. Most notably, while Newton is not typically named among the greatest philosophers of the period, he engaged with or influenced the most revered ones—Descartes, Locke, and Hume among them.[3]

Against this backdrop, the following two observations were made about Isaac Newton at the end of his life:

> *"Nature and nature's law hid in night, God said, 'Let Newton be,' and all was right."* – *Pope*

> *"I do not know what I may appear to the world. But to myself, I seem to have been only like a boy, playing in the seashore and diverting myself now and then, finding a smoother pebble or prettier shell than ordinary, while the great ocean of truth lay undiscovered before me."* – *Newton*

These are vastly different descriptions of Newton the person. The author of the first was Alexander Pope. A poet and satirist, Pope wrote this short verse after Newton's death to serve as the epitaph for his tomb. The second account is Isaac Newton himself reflecting late in his life on the adulation his creative achievements had brought and what it all meant. Both commentaries are reflections on a creative life. But more than just describing an individual, these very different portrayals say a lot about how we most often look at creativity and how we should.

BEYOND NEWTON TO "NEWTONIAN"

Pope's words emphasized two aspects of the creative journey, two things that to this day disproportionately shape how we view creativity: the creator and the output. To see why this is so, it's helpful to understand how Pope and others regarded Newton and his accomplishments in the context of their time.

In Pope's tribute it isn't hard to recognize the adulation of a hero. And in his time (and to this day), many considered Isaac Newton to be just that—a heroic, creative genius. But also identifiable in Pope's verse is the symbolism that came to eclipse the man.

Before Newton, the mysteries unveiled by his discoveries were almost universally accounted for by one explanation: God's will. Many considered Newton proof that more precise answers could be found and that man was capable of coming up with such answers— seemingly *without* relying on the invisible hand of the Creator.

When a person not only explains things like why celestial bodies do what they do (including the one we all inhabit), but then goes one better to reduce the explanations to repeatable mathematical formulas, people take notice. Unfortunately, from Newton's great creations people took notice of two things and in the following ways: 1) This creator was unique, heroic even, and 2) his creations offered a template for what we should expect future creations to look like. Pope's epitaph confirms the first conclusion. And unfortunately, whether intended or not, heroic treatment such as this set a bar against which we continue to measure and attempt to identify who is creative and who is not.

The second conclusion was more insidious, even if it was intended to be the opposite. The answers Newton offered appeared attractively concrete, absolute, and best of all, orderly. Why shouldn't all future creative breakthroughs and the creative path to arrive at them be expected to take a similar form (the thinking went)?

The two conclusions quickly solidified into one tenacious belief: The creatives among us are few and heroic, and the way they create is orderly and ultimately arrives at absolutes. How tidy. *Newtonian* thinking is how many came to refer to this reasoning. It was named not for the person but for the attractive facade of a hero and his creations.

NEWTON AND THINGS "NEW"

Looking to "How" not "What." What we see in Newton's own words is something quite apart from the dominant impression of creativity captured in Pope's portrayal. Before looking at Newton's reflection and its possible meaning, the contrast between the two accounts raises this question: *What is it we hope to understand about creativity?*

I offer you an answer to that question, one that too often eludes us when we move rapidly to look for heroes or for orderly answers—the things we often presume explain our desire to understand. What we really want is an understanding of how *we too* can create—any one of us, creating anything, anywhere, anytime. To that end, here's what I believe Newton was telling us: If you want to create things *new*, look at *how* I created and not *what* I created, or who I was.

Insights, Not Idolatry. Despite assumptions to the contrary, Newton never assumed his answers to be permanent ones (and said as much in the *Principia*, the book that laid out his famous "laws" and discoveries) or even that permanent answers were possible. To him, his innovative *answers* were more accurately viewed as *advancements in understanding*—that is, he had advanced what others had done (something he made a point of noting) and he expected that cycle to continue long after him.

The patterns across Newton's life seem to say that Newton understood human beings to be pursuers of two things equally: predictability *and* possibility. He knew and demonstrated we couldn't achieve one without the other; his "genius" was in allowing for both. Less than heroic, he was humbly human.

From a lifetime of creative practice and not just theory, Newton signaled us that his faculty for creativity came from abilities far less superhuman and far more common—play, curiosity, and those instinctive things that any boy or girl at the beach knows how to do. His creative life exemplified that rather than searching for or awaiting *the superhuman*, we ought to practice *the instinctive*, that is, if what we hope to discover is something above the "ordinary"—the smoother pebble, the shinier shell, even the law of gravity.

Newton's own insights direct us toward very different conclusions about creativity and the creative journeys we must individually make. More, they encourage us to peel back those things we think we know about creativity, all the way to their foundation, and to rebuild our understanding of what creativity is and where it comes from.

A BRIEF HISTORY OF YOU

The two interpretations just discussed can be thought of as the **NEW VS. NEWTONIAN** views of creativity and how it takes place. Down one path we pursue a desire to perpetually progress—toward something more or better, and always toward a more evolved answer. Down the other path, we're hoping to find *the* answer, one we can then use to neatly order our lives, our practices, and our expectations. The truth is each one of us is a combination of *both*, new and Newtonian, and our creative journeys are best understood as a perpetual dance between the two. ("New vs. Newtonian" is the first of the "Elements" of the language of man, all of which will be similarly highlighted in the text and summarized in the Glossary of "Elements" in References.)

How did we come to embody these two paths that seem opposed but which Newton and others have concluded are necessary to one another? One thing's for certain: It didn't happen overnight. According to neuroscientist and MacArthur Fellow Nick Strausfeld, "The evolving of who we are and how we create has been gradual and extends back into deep time."[4]

To get a handle on what Nick means, it's helpful to think in terms of the "birth" of our modern selves—in other words, that evolutionary point when we started to think creatively. Researchers from anthropologists to archaeologists, linguists to logisticians have all wondered how humans came to be creative. Though they vary in the details they study, a consensus is emerging across experts and disciplines. Within that common ground, two clear-cut explanations for how modern humans became creative have emerged and fused—one physical and one mental. Together, they paint a picture of "creative you," the you that desires and needs both "new" and "Newtonian."

Let's examine the physical explanation first.

THE PHYSICAL SIDE OF CREATIVE YOU

A few million years ago, two things happened physically to make us uniquely who we are: 1) We stood up and 2) our brain size increased. Scientists tend to agree it happened in that order—bipeds first, big brains next. Both changes eventually contributed in significant ways to make us the uniquely creative beings we are.

Standing Up to Take Notice. Becoming bipeds may have happened due to our ancient ancestors discovering that walking on two legs required less energy than moving on all fours. It may have also been precipitated by the desire to reach for something more (e.g., grabbing food high up in trees) or to see something more (e.g., spotting predators or prey at a greater distance), both also afforded by standing up. Whatever inspired us, standing up and staying up dramatically changed our view and accrued noticeable benefits. For example, the ability to regulate temperature, travel faster, use hands as hands instead of as feet, even work with tools and weapons—all of this and more emerged once we went bipedal. More than that, each advancement gained tended to ripple into others, often with unexpected advantages.

Hard fact or theory, it's fun for us to look at the evidence, notice things, make connections, and speculate on what could have happened. Experts believe our ancestors developed and bequeathed those very habits to us, that is taking note, making connections, and dreaming beyond the obvious. In every way, this shaped who we are and how we create.

Without a doubt, standing upright set us apart from many other animals. But its contributions to making us creative are linked to that *other* point of physical distinction in humans—bigger brains.

Room to Think. Why did our brains get bigger? Several reasons have been speculated: a need for better tools, a need to communicate more expansively with one another, and possibly environmental changes that required adaptation for survival, to name just a few of the more popular theories. In all likelihood, a combination of reasons led our brains to gradually expand in size and develop in thought capacity. But related to creativity, the key factor was this: As our brains expanded, we began to *use* the added capacity and flexibility for more than functional survival.

Built to Connect. To increase our understanding of how our minds are able to create, it helps to know how our brains are built. In modern humans, the adult brain weighs fourteen hundred grams or roughly three pounds, and it holds an estimated one hundred billion neurons. By comparison, a typical domestic house cat's brain weighs just thirty grams and houses only five million neurons. As feisty and smart as cats are (in addition to being agile survivors), our human brains look darn impressive by comparison.

When it comes to taking note, making connections, and thinking in an expanded way, the neurons are the keys—for cats and humans alike. Think of these nerve cells as nodes in an amazingly complex communications network. The number of connections happening in your brain at any one moment is roughly a quadrillion (that's a one followed by fifteen zeroes). The "synapses" in this network are making repeated connections down well-worn neuron pathways all the time. Importantly, their wiring enables the making of *new* connections as well.

It isn't just that there's plenty of allowance in our circuitry for making new connections; our brains actively seek new pathways and fresh *why* this happened—in other words, why our hardware evolved along this path, and what active role, if any, we played in that evolution.

As with every aspect of our evolution, more than one factor has likely come into play. But one answer to why we've evolved into creative beings stands out: *Because the driver of the equipment consciously chose to use it.*

While "the evidence seems to indicate that our power of innovation . . . gained steam over hundreds or thousands of years, fueled by a complex mix of biology and social factors," Liane will tell you that ultimately our creative minds advanced because we began to *choose* to use them, deliberately and creatively.[13,14] We chose to engage and experiment and to ponder what could be—or perhaps what *we* could be. *Choice* was then and remains the difference-maker in moving from creative potential to innovative reality.

We'll discuss choice more in coming chapters, but for now, let's fashion a simple image for carrying all this knowledge and this "history of you" into creative choices of your own.

A SIMPLE VIEW OF YOU: THE FOX AND THE HEDGEHOG

Over time, we have evolved to have a brain capable of thinking in two very different but complementary ways. While one is far older than the other (from an evolutionary standpoint), we are built with and for both ways of thinking. More than that, we progress as a species only when we learn to put both to work together.

In 1953, looking to explain these different yet equally important modes of our thoughts, philosopher Isaiah Berlin borrowed a metaphor captured in this line attributed to the ancient Greek poet Archilochus: "The fox knows many things; the hedgehog knows one big thing." No one knows precisely what Archilochus meant (mysteriously, this was the only surviving line of this poem). Nevertheless, Berlin adopted it as a natural, easy-to-understand reference to the contrasting ways our human brains think.

Meet Your Fox. According to Berlin, the **FOX** way of thinking aligns with what are traditionally considered the core elements of creative thinkers. By being aware of many things, the fox excels in seeing patterns, often across seemingly unrelated sources. He's also good at adapting to whatever comes his way. The fox ventures out, roaming beyond what he knows and often outside of safe, predictable spaces. Because he does, he draws from a wide range of views to generate ideas. When a particular view turns out to be different than what he predicted, he can effectively improvise. The fox actively looks to make new discoveries and connections—and usually succeeds.

Meet Your Hedgehog. The *HEDGEHOG* stands in contrast to the fox and, in many ways, seems the exact opposite. He tends to know one way deeply and hold to it, often fiercely defending it. While the fox operates within moveable borders, the hedgehog is far more focused, formulaic, and fixed in his ways and his thinking.

Political psychology professor Philip Tetlock, who borrowed Berlin's metaphor and made it better known through his research, conjectured that hedgehogs have a strong need to close loops and avoid unpredictability. They not only rely on and defend what's "known," they filter what they encounter (or predict they will encounter) through the known.[15] Being "open" to new concepts for a hedgehog is akin to Henry Ford's version of being "open" when he said his customers could have a car in any color they wanted . . . as long as it was black.

A Bimodal Owner. Tying different ways the human brain thinks to the personalities of these two animals helps simplify the discussion. The images evoked are so relatable that it's tempting to treat the fox and the hedgehog as though they were actual people with singular, fixed personalities. Yet, while you likely know people who tend toward one way of thinking more than the other, *every* human brain is built to operate in *both* fox and hedgehog mode. More importantly, the two mindsets are inter-wired, and each of us relies on a mix of the two to survive, progress, and create.

All that you've learned in this chapter comes together in this metaphor. In the fox and hedgehog, you can see, for example, the free-associating operating mode of the human brain that led to the emergence of human creativity (fox). But you can also see the orderly, answer-driven part that has kept us alive (hedgehog). In fact, when you think of the larger evolutionary lessons, it's hard to imagine how we could have become who we are if we didn't have both fox and hedgehog capabilities.

SIMPLE

TRUTHS

CHAPTER TWO

CHAPTER TWO

SIMPLE TRUTHS

This *Reveal* section of *The Language of Man* explores important elements of the creative journey—the "equipment" (the last chapter), the "land" in which we're traveling (the next chapter), and the "language" that will help us articulate this journey and all journeys yet to come (Chapter Four). All of that is helpful. But right here, right now—before racing off to learn more about creativity—we need to do a "compass" check.

In fact, we're going to establish a pattern of doing such checks throughout *The Language of Man*, what might best be thought of as a pattern of "pausing" to ensure that our understanding is sound. The first kind of pause we'll repeatedly take is with a story at the start of each chapter. The last chapter's Newton story helped make clear that these "starting stories" are meant to do three things: 1) give you a chance to pause; 2) offer you a view outside the immediate topic; and 3) frame the lessons to come in the chapter each begins.

A second form of pause and reflection that will become our habit is even more important—checking in with our guides. Let's do that right now with MacArthur Fellow and gerontological nurse Sarah Kagan before turning to this chapter's starting story. Refreshingly, Sarah gets right to the point about the creative journey and why we need these compass checks.

GETTING TO THE TRUTH

The Limits of Our "Bizarre Construct." "People have a bizarre construct around creativity," Sarah said to me almost immediately in our conversation. "It's a construct we seem to develop without stopping to even think *what* we mean by creativity or even *how* we think or talk about it. I don't know exactly where it comes from," Sarah added, "but my best guess is that it comes from *not* stopping to think."[21]

There's a deep reservoir of insights in Sarah's words, so let's linger and consider them a little more. As we do, notice first that even the small but deliberate act of slowing down long enough to reflect is something we rarely engage in. So eager are we to "get creating" that we miss or misunderstand many of the foundational subtleties that allow the creative process to be fruitful. Typically in that rush to "do," we breeze past the assumptions we've made, even subconscious and inadvertent ones, about the key aspects of creativity and the creative process. Sarah addressed that very point.

"It isn't just that our understanding of creativity is misguided," Sarah continued. "We've formed false impressions about *who* can 'do' creativity as well as *when* and *how*. The mere fact that we *have* should set off alarm bells. Not only do we misunderstand what creativity is, but we also proceed from those false impressions to engage it in the wrong way, or worse, not at all."[22]

Stretch your pause a little further to consider this added insight and you begin to appreciate a subtle force at work, one that carries a tsunami ripple effect. By forgetting or perhaps never even being aware of certain fundamental truths, we permit ourselves the error of barreling forward, never even tapping the brakes, and proceeding with our "bizarre constructs" unquestioned. And then we wonder why we aren't creative.

But worse still, unchecked, those assumptions become our beliefs— beliefs such as: Only a rare few are capable of creating; creativity can only happen in certain places or times; or creativity's value is limited in one or more ways. You can see the wave building, can't you?

So how do we change all this? The answer is rather simple. Take Sarah's advice: pause; rethink; wonder; and repeat often. Let's take a moment to understand the full meaning of this powerfully simple answer.

The Creative Do-Over. Sarah extended her thought saying this: "Every time creativity, or the chance to employ it, comes up we should use it as a cue to *rethink creativity* in the larger sense and reconsider what it *could* mean."[23] In other words, each pause you take to rethink does more than give you the chance to think about "what's next," as in the next big idea you might have. It's also importantly a chance to consider both the meaning and assumptions around "what is," right now. Even if such a pause is brief, it offers a conscious chance to reaffirm what we really know (or think we know).

Such pauses are more than a reconsideration of knowledge; they are a check in on value, a chance to ask: Are we still getting value by continuing to think and do in familiar ways? Frequently the answer comes back "yes." But when we are in the habit of such pauses, we are more likely to be tuned in at those times when the answer is "no."

What I want you to see here is that Sarah's suggestion is simple, but it's also expansive. When she advises we should regularly reconsider creativity, she is absolutely suggesting that we allow those moments to be a time in which to consider "what could be." That part is obvious. But she's also insightfully telling us that the ability to see what could be begins with a reconsideration of what is. What we bring to such moments—what we already have, think, and do— undeniably shapes our ability to see what's still possible. Purposely pausing to rethink and to wonder in the more complete manner, Sarah is suggesting, provides the very catalyst we need to see the next creative breakthrough.

In a way, Sarah is talking about creativity as a growing process, the process by which we grow a breakthrough creative idea. And what she's reminding us is that whenever we grow something we must begin with the seeds, those foundational beginnings without which no fully formed breakthrough or change can occur. The truth is that when it first emerges, creativity doesn't look like the revolution, change, or betterment as we tend to think of it when in full bloom.

What this chapter asks you to pause and reflect on is the fact that creativity's "seeds" start simpler and exist long before the fruit is ready for harvesting. Those catalytic seeds are often so simple and self-evident they are easily overlooked or forgotten. We forget them at our peril. More accurately, if we forget them then the forward-looking ideas we hope for and need are in peril. It's time we rediscover those all-important seeds that form the foundation of any revolutionary idea. A story helps.

EVERY REVOLUTION BEGINS WITH SIMPLE TRUTHS

Forgotten History. When in 1776 Thomas Jefferson took on the role as the leading author of what we now know as the Declaration of Independence, he was taking his fellow colonists and his king on a journey back to seed. The chances are that's not how you think about the Declaration.

The reason you probably don't think of it that way is that when we tell the story of America's birth, we tend to do so in broad brushstrokes. We talk about a colonial David throwing off a Goliath England, the creation of modern democracy, and a baker's dozen of nascent colonies becoming a nation and world power in their own right. Those are the images that dominate, what we might regard as the "creative outputs" that came later. But before all that was the Declaration. And within it lay the seeds out of which everything else grew.

Simple Truths. It's true that the Declaration of Independence was an actual "declaration"—a notification from England's colonies to their king of their intention to strike out on their own. It's also true, but less often remembered, that most of this "letter to King George" was comprised of a long list of grievances by the colonists meant to substantiate that decision to break away. But the heart and soul of the document was something else: a reminder, to the king, obviously, but just as importantly to Jefferson's fellow colonists, of who we are—each of us, colonist and king alike—as human beings.

Take away Jefferson's poetic language and you'll see these seed ideas he used to make his case:

1.   Certain things will always be true about humans and how they progress (as Jefferson chose to highlight them: We're equal, we have certain inalienable rights, and we can and must defend these things);

2. Anyone who forgets these fundamental facts does so at his peril (in this case, King George was that someone); and

3. When one of us does forget (the king), it is the visceral inclination of other humans (the colonists) to point this out, return to seed idea number one above, and then act to make things better.[24]

Our elemental drive to return to these seed ideas, Jefferson was reminding us, is simply that powerful.

To emphasize the importance and centrality of his points, Jefferson chose to call those seed ideas "truths"—what he considered to be the very nexus of all "human events" past, present, and future. He believed that, as much as they might be "self-evident," these truths needed to be spelled out now and then. The broader need for change that Jefferson and his fellow colonists felt in 1776 signaled the perfect time to pause. Certainly they were giving King George pause. But importantly, as they did, they were also checking their own compasses and reaffirming their own truths. In other words, as necessary as these truths were in making the colonists' declaration to the king that it was time for change, reconsidering and reaffirming them was just as necessary to the colonists' ability to make that change and create something new and revolutionary.

The "Simple" Difference. Just think about what these basic building blocks enabled (and still enable). They inspired a ragtag band of thirteen colonies, often at odds with one another, to unite. After the military victory over England, these same seed ideas and the commitment to both nurture and preserve them galvanized those independent states to become a nation. So central were these truths—and so great was that which they catalyzed—that the nation built upon them became synonymous with fresh starts, big ideas, ingenuity, and entrepreneurial spirit.

Following the flow of this positive ripple effect, those core truths, and the example of the United States as a nation anchored in them, continues to inspire people across the world to imagine and reach for their own versions. In many respects, getting started was as simple as taking notice of what was true, putting it to use, and doing as Sarah advised—pausing, then and thereafter, to rethink and wonder.

Yet sometimes even simple things can be challenging or easily forgotten—for anyone, even as it turned out, for Thomas Jefferson.

A Lesson in Forgetting. When we think back on America's beginnings, it's rarely recognized that the Declaration worked because it was a collective undertaking—that is, many people affirming the same simple truths together. One person didn't recognize these truths all on his own; and it took many to rethink and refine their description until it was self-evident and resonant to all.

The Declaration of Independence and its foundational truths were an amalgam. The document itself had a total of five authors; Jefferson was simply the lead author. And as both Jefferson and John Adams (one of those other authors) acknowledged, there was little in the Declaration that hadn't already been put forth by others or in other documents.

Similarly, the "truths" the Declaration reaffirmed resulted in the progressive human accomplishments they did because of the "many"—the many people who stood behind them and the many times those truths were reconsidered. George Washington may get the credit for winning the Revolutionary War, for example, but he did not do so single handedly. He kept returning his soldiers, allies, and fellow colonists to the simple truths for which they were fighting. That, as it turned out, made all the difference. The truth is we all need reminders—to pause and reestablish what's true before we can ever see or seize "what could be."

It's fair to assume that Jefferson knew all of this. But sometimes the memory of just how things get created can fade, even for their creators. To that point, at the end of his life, Jefferson clearly considered himself the *sole* author and creator of the document for which he became famous. He even asserted it on his tombstone as one of his life's three most important accomplishments. It superseded his roles as president of the United States and governor of his beloved state of Virginia, neither of which he asked be noted in his epitaph. (See Author's Notes: Chapter Two.) Oversights or historical revisions such as this can perhaps be forgiven or even understood. But there's something deeper in that historical inconsistency that's worth noting.

As hard as it can be to *remember* simple truths, what's even harder is to *live* by them. While I'd like to believe that in Jefferson's heart he truly believed all *humans* were created equal, his actions (owning slaves and never providing for their freedom) and his omissions (demonstrating that "all men" did not mean "all people") contrasted sharply with what we'd expect to see from someone who actually lived by such truths.

Far from detracting, however, these imperfections make the Jefferson story all the more resonant and relatable. Above all else, Jefferson was *human*. If we look only at his life's "highlight reel," it would be easy (and inaccurate) to conclude him to be an infallible hero or somehow above the simple advice Sarah gave us.

Sarah's advice applies to all of us and always, even to the Jeffersons in our midst. Each role, each moment in life, each new idea or action should serve as our cue to return to our truths. It's in pausing and revisiting them that we discover their inherent power. That's also when we recognize them as the very things that help us create what's presumed impossible. When we tune into such truths—deliberately, habitually—we enable ourselves to create many times over, often grandly, and always wiser than the previous time.

A PICTURE OF CREATIVITY
THAT NEEDS TO CHANGE

Let's merge Sarah's advice and Jefferson's story, using both as a way to begin your rediscovery of your own creative capacity. And let's do that by further widening our understanding of what a pause like the one Sarah suggests we take actually entails.

While they are often referred to by other names, pauses are a valued practice among those we consider to be the most creatively productive. Sociologist and MacArthur Fellow Sara Lawrence-Lightfoot referred to this catalytic creative habit as "allowing for intermissions. In those intermissions," Sara says, "we must do more than just think up new ideas; we must reexamine and reconsider the reigning messages and dogma that want to hold us and our creative thoughts in place." It's this combination of looking ahead but also looking at what might just hold us back that is "precisely what any creative thought represents."[25]

I want to invite you to put that good advice into practice right now. And I want you to do so to "reexamine and reconsider your reigning dogma" around creativity itself. What I'm asking you to do is simple: I want you to paint a picture. Don't worry, I'll guide you as you do and no artistic skills are needed.

WHAT

CREATIVITY IS

CHAPTER THREE

CHAPTER THREE

WHAT CREATIVITY IS

In Chapter One, the "equipment" of creativity (the creative human brain) was the focus. Chapter Two offered two simple, powerful suggestions for putting that unique creative instrument to use: Be on the lookout for Simple Truths, and question the dogma that often keeps you from seeing "what could be."

It's a valuable beginning, but a key question remains: What *is* creativity?

This third chapter of the *Reveal* Section digs beneath the word "creativity." It will help you shift to more accurately regard creativity as a capacity to be tapped rather than a word to be defined. Shedding the superficial layers of our understanding will enable you to rediscover important insights we've lost over time. Bit-by-bit in this chapter, you'll come to understand what creativity is and build a more useful framework for putting yours to use. Here's how we'll get you there.

The Path to Understanding What Creativity Is. This chapter is organized in three separate but interconnected parts. First we'll *deconstruct creativity*. To do that, one of our MacArthur guides takes the lead, Harvard psychologist Howard Gardner. Uniquely, Howard's story gives us a true sense of what it's like to journey back to seed to discover important truths about creativity. His story also introduces us to one particular discovery about creativity that arises time and again and that helps us see more clearly what creativity is—and isn't.

In part two of our exploration, we'll begin to *reestablish common ground*, providing the foundation needed to build a new understanding. We'll do that by coming to understand creativity's most "salient features"—three elements that characterize it no matter where, when, or by whom it's applied.

The third part of our journey finds us actively *reframing creativity*. Here four fresh insights about how to use and individualize this capacity we all share will be added. In combination, this chapter's three parts put you well on your way toward building a creative framework and, with it, your own new way to look at the world. By the time you finish this chapter, you'll begin to see how that framework can grow into something beautiful and powerful.

But first, let's "frame" it all with this chapter's starting story.

Deconstructing Creativity

What's it really like to peel back our understanding and assumptions and look at something fresh, as if for the first time? That's what we want to do with creativity, and it helps tremendously to be able to relate to a story of someone who's already taken that kind of journey. Rather than seeking to emulate how that person went about it, what serves us best is to understand the context in which that individual did so. Before we begin our own reexamination, we want to know: What needs to be reconsidered; what challenges we are likely to face; and the nature of what we might find. We're lucky to have Howard Gardner to help us frame the view.

AWAY FROM "ONE"

Howard is best known for his theory of multiple intelligences (which we'll come back to in a moment). Less well known are the seeds of how and where his influential theory began and its tightly woven connections to creativity.

A Big Idea. As a young post-doctoral student, Howard was part of an ambitious program at Harvard University called Project Zero. Started in the late 1960s and continuing today, Project Zero was originally developed to understand and enhance learning, thinking, and creativity for both individuals and institutions in a variety of disciplines. Its founder, philosopher Nelson Goodman, believed that, until that point in time, "zero" had been firmly established about how human learning, thinking, and creating interwove (hence the name).

Challenges. Like any journey into new territory, Project Zero faced unexpected challenges and the need to constantly pause and reconsider how a new understanding might be created. As one example, while the work initially began with a focus on the arts (in large part because custom said that's where creativity occurred), over time it became clear that, to truly understand and enhance our ability to innovate, the Project needed to include many other sectors as well—the sciences, humanities, and business to name a few. The Project's leaders came to recognize that to evolve their understanding they had to get themselves beyond the strict borders of field or the implicit borders of attitudes about where creativity could and should take place. This border lesson would repeat many times and in many forms.

Even after eliminating the barriers of field, there were still other borders to be confronted, including the surprisingly rigid boundaries of cultural belief. Views on intelligence were a case in point. From the time of Project Zero's inception and well into the years Howard co-directed it (from 1972 to 2000), "intelligence" was widely considered the foundation from which ability and performance, including creative ability, were derived. (See Author's Notes: Chapter Three-A.) There was also a prevailing belief that intelligence could be measured. In theory, went the accepted belief, it could even be measured across all people using a similar test (still referred to as the Intelligence Quotient or IQ test). Even an undertaking as open as Project Zero wasn't immune to the power and intransigence of firmly held beliefs.

Over the three quarters of a century since Alfred Binet created it, the IQ test had defined human intelligence. (See Author's Notes: Chapter Three-B.) Countless theories, modes of operating, and even deeply held institutional beliefs had been built around this view of intelligence—in education, business, academia, and across social mores as well. That meant that in every area in which Project Zero was looking for insights, this theory of intelligence ran deeply. In such conditions, any observations made about learning, thinking, and creating that ran counter to the core beliefs were likely to be challenged if not resisted.

The result was that as much as the Project sought to widen our understanding, in important respects it remained constrained by what we might rightly think of as the view of "one": One form of intelligence; one test; one score; and from these, one implied way of learning, thinking, and creating. Howard didn't think that made sense. Something simply didn't fit, and the persistent feeling of a misfit eventually led him to form this question: *While it would be simpler to conclude that we all learn, think, and create in the same exact way, how could that be possible?*

At this distance, the conclusion imbedded in his question seems self-evident. To anyone who lives and walks, interacts and breathes within the intricate mosaic of the human species, it's clear we do *not* all learn, think, and create in the same way or use a single form of intelligence to do so, period. But within the context of Project Zero, Howard's question presented a substantial problem. It also raised a new question of what to do with what he was seeing and sensing. Should he ignore it, normalize it, or pursue it, even if choosing to do the latter meant arriving at new ideas that broke with old ways of thinking?

Choice. Based on what the research was returning and what he was actually observing, Howard chose to boldly suggest that *many* forms of intelligence existed. More border-flaunting still, he theorized that *all* people naturally possessed *all* forms of intelligence and that each of us was capable of combining and expressing our different forms in highly individualized ways. (See Author's Notes: Chapter Three-C.)

Rather than a new and oversimplified *definition* of intelligence, Howard was suggesting a new *framework* for understanding how humans do what they do. It was new, brilliant, flexible, exciting, and tantamount to treason. After all, what kind of a headline would it make to conclude that no single, simple, cleanly measurable definition of intelligence existed?

But what Howard was suggesting *did* make sense. And while the truth may have been inconvenient, Howard realized that by continuing to insist on a single narrow view, we were holding back our understanding of the very things the IQ—and indeed Project Zero—was supposed to help us identify and comprehend.

Lessons. More than just a fascinating story, Howard's is representative of a number of critically important things about what happens when we seek to learn, think, or create—including, and perhaps especially, when we seek to *relearn, rethink,* and *recreate,* as we are going to be doing in this chapter with creativity. First, it's easy to become fixed in and limited by our assumptions and habits. How people looked at learning, thinking, and creating before Project Zero is one example of this fixedness; how deeply assumptions about intelligence had penetrated society during the period of this story is another.

Second, thinking in an open way can be challenging. Doing so doesn't always result in neatly packaged answers, and staying open requires us to constantly remind ourselves to do so. It takes practice.

ECHOES OF A GROWING CHORUS

A Key Creative Insight. Nearly four decades of research, debate, poking, and prodding have given the multiple intelligences theory a workout. And while some quibble over how many intelligences we have or their exact nature, today few people question Howard's basic insight: *There is no single way in which we learn, think, or create.* And more, we are increasingly accepting that intelligence is just one piece of the puzzle and not the sole or even leading indicator we once assumed it to be.

Building from that broader observation, Howard has further concluded that, like intelligence, "A single variety of creativity is (also) a myth."[31] In his book *Creative Minds: An Anatomy of Creativity,* Howard stated, "It has become increasingly clear that creativity is precisely the kind of phenomenon or concept that does not lend itself to investigation completely within a single discipline."[32] That "single variety" myth, Howard discovered, extends to the ways we look at creativity and try to understand it, in addition to the many ways we attempt to employ it. This particular discovery about creativity is the very insight that helps us to understand what creativity is, and Howard is far from being alone in making and emphasizing it.

Similar Observations by Different Paths. For those who've looked deeply at creativity, their conclusions about it have been remarkably consistent. One interesting example arose in Brewster directly, there is no single accepted description of how it works. Many disciplines touch on it and thus provide peripheral accounts. However, trying to summarize their findings would result in an account similar to the descriptions the blind men gave of the elephant."[38]

Such an open-ended description can be unsettling, whether we're trying to understand consciousness, creativity, or any subject. We want exactitude and the feeling we get when we believe we can delineate clear borders around something. We have an affinity for *definition*—even when all the evidence says there isn't one.

SEEKING A SINGULAR DEFINITION

Our expectation that we must arrive at a *simple, singular definition of creativity* is in fact our biggest block in understanding it. We're trained to think of a definition as a precise meaning, object, or method— something we can count on to always be the same. That is, after all, the definition of definition.

But rather than continue to move in lock step with that habit, let's do something different; let's pause and ask: Is that really what we're after? When it comes to creativity at least, the answer is a rhetorical "no."

As Howard and his Project Zero colleagues sought, we are seeking a greater *understanding* so we can *enhance* our ability to *apply* our creative capacity. That requires moving beyond our current borders and habits to break apart what we think we know and then to reevaluate and reframe.

While there is no single definition of creativity, there are common- alities that exist across all of its forms.

Reestablishing Common Ground

THREE SALIENT FEATURES OF CREATIVITY

Let's add another voice to the chorus of serious students of creativity. Robert Paul Weiner, chair of Liberal Arts at John F. Kennedy

University, has also extensively explored the topic as a writer, teacher, consultant, and practitioner. He reached many of the same core conclusions that Gardner, Ghiselin, Kneller, and Csikszentmihalyi did and by an equally rigorous method.

For his book *Creativity and Beyond: Cultures, Value and Change*, Weiner conducted a comprehensive review of the writings on creativity, but in quite a different way. Weiner looked at a broad sampling of works that included (among other categories) creativity in the arts and literature, empirical psychology analyses of creativity, humanistic works on the subject, creativity games for children, works concerning economic innovation, philosophical essays about it, social and anthropological views, and technical invention and scientific discoveries. From this, he too discerned that creativity was not a one-trick pony. Yet he did find that certain common features were in fact shared in every realm. That's where we'll begin our reconstruction.

Three things in particular—what Weiner refers to as the "salient features" of creativity—are our focus. These same three are consistently identified by others in this book and appeared routinely in my own research. When a pattern confirms itself independently and repeatedly, it's worth paying attention.

Weiner noted the **THREE SALIENT FEATURES OF CREATIVITY** this way:[39]

1. Creativity involves bringing something *new* into being.

2. It is possible *in every domain of human activity*.

3. It is potentially achievable by *anyone*, anywhere.

Thus, creativity is new, anywhere, and accessible by anyone. These salient features provide the fresh new beginning we need.

Most problems we have in understanding creativity generally come *after* these shared observations, when we try to define creativity within the constraints of one of its applications or outputs. When people do, the point and the pulse of understanding get lost. Let's pause and explore what the three salient features actually mean. Doing so will help us understand why they appear so prominently and consistently.

FEATURE #1: BRINGS SOMETHING "NEW" INTO BEING

A Different Kind of New. The "new" element inherent in all creativity is paramount, yet we often miss or misunderstand it. One reason we do is our frequent borrowing of the word "creativity" for other meanings and uses. Here's how the water gets muddy: When someone expresses a good idea, even if it's not new we call it "creative." Being clever is also described that way. Resourcefulness, whatever the degree of originality, is frequently termed creative as well. The collective effect of borrowing the word "creativity" as a synonym for other different terms or using it as a catchall for many transitive meanings is that we lose sight of the core element that most distinguishes it—newness, and not just any kind of new.

"To create is to bring into existence" is how Edward Hirsch, poet, MacArthur Fellow, and president of John Simon Guggenheim Memorial Foundation powerfully put it. When I asked Edward about creativity, he described it as "a defining act. You are bringing something into existence that previously wasn't there."[40]

This is a very different kind of "new"—one that's unequivocally distinct, not partially so. When new takes that form, even just as a possibility, we feel compelled in an unconventional way. More than just novel, creative practitioners consistently describe that this kind of new feels more like a need. Often it's more—the kind of need they're willing to pursue even before knowing what form it might take.

Born of Two Minds. It is this kind of newness and the idea of making it real that naturally speaks to our fox brain. But not only to our fox, and here lies an important nuance. Creativity understood as part of our very makeup isn't only about a new, yet untethered daydream. When we sense the special kind of new associated with creativity, we viscerally want it *to become real*, somehow sensing it as necessary to our progress. Not every thought we have feels this way, but collectively, creative thoughts orient us in that direction—toward something new that results in our betterment and our continuation.

That's where our hedgehog brain comes in. You might think otherwise, but our orderly, rule-honoring hedgehog actually likes the idea of this kind of "new"—something it can order into the tangible and valuable. So while we may automatically relate newness with our fox, the "new" that's salient to creativity fuels both our fox and our hedgehog. It results from a necessary combination of our two mindsets working together. To put a slightly stronger note on Edward's point, this kind of new defines us.

Delving a bit deeper for a moment, what's being described here is what Csikszentmihalyi referred to as the perpetual partnership-competition dynamic between our two mindsets, what he terms our *psychic entropy*. As he wrote in *Flow*, what makes our human thought dynamic so distinct isn't only the perpetual partnership-competition, but that we humans uniquely "weigh possibilities unavailable at the moment."[41]

This is one of the greatest distinctions humans have that other organisms do not—our compasses innately point us toward new.

A Mindset and a Sense. When it comes to "new," most think and speak in terms of *things*. Doing so, however, limits our ability to fully appreciate this central feature of creativity. New doesn't have to be a thing.

"New can be a shift in your entire view about how to create," choreographer Liz Lerman pointed out. "We don't often notice that sometimes it's that kind of new that comes first and later results in an explosion of creative outputs. New can even be *a way* of living in the world, being in the moment in a way that allows you to observe, to express, to bring together something that hasn't been before. I think about new," Liz said, "as a *way to think* as much as, and frankly more than, I do the *things* that way of thinking might produce."[42]

Our subconscious assumption about new needing to be a *thing* is where our understanding often catches like a sweater on a loose nail. Broadening the view, Liz is telling us that "creativity can be creating the *conditions* that allow you and others to think freshly and newly ongoing." [43] "New" is therefore as much a mindset and a sense as it is anything that might result from that mindset and sense.

FEATURE #2: POSSIBLE ANYWHERE

The second salient feature of creativity is that it can occur *anywhere*. It's easy to see creativity in recognized forms such as works of art or innovative technologies. But as Liz's insight hints, the problem is when we allow the creative outputs to begin to define creativity itself. That's when we not only expect "new" forms of creativity to look similar to what we already know, but we expect creative outputs will always (or only) come from the same places.

While creativity can lead to tangible things, creativity itself isn't a tangible to be placed only here or only there. Rather, as Liz noted, it's a *mindset* that's portable and able to exist everywhere simultaneously. Or as Ric Scofidio described it, it's "in motion, as part of an ongoing process, not something you can pin down or label."[44] An example helps, and Gary Nabhan provides a rich one.

Science Meets Poetry. Like many creative practitioners, Gary doesn't find himself tethered to one field, even within the course of a single day. To many, his primary profession is ethnobotanist. But he's equally an internationally celebrated nature writer who has written more than twenty books on a broad range of topics. He's also a farming activist and influential proponent of conserving the links between biodiversity and cultural diversity. There's also the Gary people know as a pioneer in the local food movement, yet one more place where he ports his creative thoughts.

When people describe Gary, they almost always call him creative. But they also tend to define him as creative where they meet him, as if his creativity was limited to a single sphere of activity, subject matter, or thought. Thus, the person who knows Gary as a beautiful poet often has no inkling of what he has creatively done as a botanist to save the ironwood, a tree species in the Sonoran Desert that's threatened (a story we'll expand on later in Chapter Seven). Gary was able to see the ironwood problem in a whole new way. But tellingly, he claims he came up with his breakthrough ideas about solving that problem because he's a *poet*. He beautifully describes this link in his book *Cross-pollinations: The Marriage of Science and Poetry*.[45] It's the breadth of his creativity that makes him creative in any one application.

While we can draw several insights from this example, what's clear is this: Anywhere and indeed everywhere Gary roams, his creativity goes with him, leaving behind remarkable creative impressions within individual projects or fields. As Ric's comment implies, the mindset carries. As it does, creativity can be anywhere.

Gathered "From" Everywhere. Oddly, even in our fast-moving, multi-hatted world, we still categorize each other by single roles—such as a biologist or a bard. The fact that the biologist is also an aficionado of language or jazz or even business doesn't compute. More than the need to openly see that creativity can exist in any of these fields, we begin to realize that it has higher odds of materializing when allowed or better still encouraged to move *across* the many different places we find it. That's another important lesson to learn from Gary.

"After all these years I still have people tell me I need to give up the things 'on the edges' and focus," Gary said with a chuckle. "'If you want to be a good scientist,' they tell me, 'you need to give up that poetry and layman's writing thing.' 'Better still,' they say, 'just be a botanist. Shed that ethnography stuff.'"[46]

Gary knows that his incredible number of breakthroughs have been a direct result of ignoring that type of advice. He continued, "The capacity to think metaphorically, differently, and creatively *within* my science world, or even to understand the value of the thinking that occurs outside that world, comes directly from those different lenses I play with every time I walk into a new space. It's not enough to *see* creativity happening everywhere; you need to *play* with it yourself and in different places—that is, if what you want is to comprehend what's really possible to do with it."[47]

Practice Makes Powerful. Understanding that creativity is everywhere, doesn't just present the opportunity to apply it anywhere; it actually gives you access to the depth of power in this wonderful human capacity. Indeed the potential emerges in reverse funnel-like fashion. Every place you go and every time you discover a new form of it, what starts small only gets bigger. Each new insight into what creativity looks like in another place or through the eyes of another person causes an otherwise limited view to expand. The power potential is literally beyond definition.

The power goes beyond what each of us is capable of seeing and doing individually as well. Gary doesn't just get that he pursues it. "In my work," he explained, "I actively seek creativity not only on my own, but also by bringing together people of disparate skills to interact." The power you sense when you pursue it is almost addictive, in a good way. "Creating with others not only moves me quicker to new ideas, it keeps me open to seeing them in the first place. Even when I'm focused on someone else's work or on something completely apart from work at all," Gary said, "new worlds always seem to open up to me. I actually become more creative just by the exchange. If there's one thing I've learned about creativity, it takes many eyes to see."[48]

We will revisit the idea of collectively leveraging creativity to execute a breakthrough idea in Chapters Eleven to Thirteen. But for now, recognize this: It's by consciously searching to see creativity in its "anywhere" form that our creative capacity expands.

FEATURE #3: ACHIEVABLE BY ANYONE (INCLUDING YOU)

Creativity involves bringing something new into existence. And this can occur everywhere humans are and anywhere they may yet choose to go. But most promising of all, its potential impact can be achieved by *anyone*. That includes you.

Our great tendency is to think of creativity as something "out there" and associated with someone else, someone who appears to have figured out this mysterious, attractive "something." But with just a little deliberate examination, the thin veneer belief that only a few individuals are creative quickly falls away. Even if you think your experience tells you otherwise, this feature is at the heart of the Simple Truth that creativity is the domain of *all* humans, something built into our architecture and existing at the root of life itself.

"Creativity is the ability to think past our experience," said MacArthur Fellow and Blue Ocean Institute founder Carl Safina. "To think past what we know and have encountered and to envision something that doesn't quite exist," Carl said, "is the reason we've progressed as long and as far as we have. It also is the very concept we *all* need to embrace if we want that progress to continue into the future."[49]

To understand creativity requires doing exactly that. Visual artist Gary Hill said it matter-of-factly. "Creativity is what living is. It's not only something each of us is capable of; it is what each of us is meant to do. People are happiest when they are creating—be it in cooking, creating art, anything."[50]

Everyone, everywhere is creative. And the unending drive to put our creativity to use lies at the heart of what it means to be human. But we must remember that even the self-evident can get neglected or become faded if we don't attend to it.

THE IMPORTANCE OF THE THREE FEATURES

New, anywhere, anyone—it has a nice ring to it. That's more than a catchy phrase though. These are features that those who know creativity consistently cite as vital and true. The practiced see them not as "steps" for creating a "thing," but instead as features of a "mindset" necessary to create. And tuning into them is important, not simply to understand, but to fully tap our unique capacity and ensure our continued progress.

In a well-known 2004 *Harvard Business Review* article titled "America's Looming Creativity Crisis," author and economist Richard Florida put it this way: "Creativity is not a tangible asset like mineral deposits, something that can be hoarded or fought over, or even bought and sold. It must be thought of as a 'common good,' like liberty or security. It is something essential that belongs to everyone and must always be nourished, renewed, and maintained—or else it will slip away."[51]

Reframing What Creativity Is

PIECES OF A FRAME

We began this chapter by deconstructing, after which we reestablished important common ground. All of this has been aimed at building a new and more accurate understanding of creativity and, importantly, a framework that any of us can use to apply our unique capacity. We've already been accumulating the basic pieces of such a framework. Learning about our underlying machinery (fox and hedgehog) was part of that. So were the foundational Simple Truths. Just now the three salient features of creativity were added. The advice of our personal guides has also been vital and empowering.

In this final section of the chapter, we're going to add more pieces to the framework. But before we do, let's take a moment to do two things: to revisit why we're even focused on a framework in the first place, and to talk about the right way to think about the unique one we're building here.

WHY A FRAMEWORK, AND WHY NOT A FORMULA?

Earlier, we used the term **FRAMEWORK** as a contrast to its opposite, a formula. As we build a fresh new understanding of creativity, it's worth highlighting the differences.

A Search for What's Not There. Creativity does *not* occur as a formula. If it did, it would inevitably defy the element of "new." It would also be tough for a formula to meet the criteria of applying "anywhere" or be undertaken by "anyone"—no formula can. Thus, a one-size-fits-all formula violates all three salient features at the foundation of creativity.

Focus on What Works: a Framework. A framework has the advantage of providing a *frame of reference* for seeing and thinking (similar to our "map and compass" analogy at the start of the book). A framework offers reminders, guideposts, and options rather than generating static answers. And a framework requires you to do both those things—that is, to see and think. Therefore, using it implies constant and active assessment.

In addition to being guiding, active, and flexible, a framework enables us to *create* formulas and do so powerfully. Yes, we want formulas—*for specific circumstances*. A framework promotes a mindset that recognizes the reality that life requires the *perpetual* creation of new solutions. Once we understand the basics of a framework, we can then use it repeatedly to create formulas and other specific but temporary things we need as circumstances change.

In short, frameworks are forward-looking, creativity-accepting, and creativity-inducing. At their best, they're infinitely malleable. That's precisely the kind of understanding around creativity we are seeking to build. Let's continue building.

How You Should Think About Your Framework. The framework we're building and to which we're about to add is a creative framework. Using the language we already know, it's a framework that must be useable by anyone, anywhere, to create "new" ongoing. That means the pieces that make up this frame shouldn't be regarded as stuck in place, like four pieces of wood forming a rectangular picture frame, for example. The pieces are meant to move. Under different circumstances, some pieces will prove more important than others—but not necessarily the same pieces or for the same reasons. This will all become clearer as we journey, but for the time being, think of your frame and its use as you would **QUILTING**.

Quilters don't become skilled by making a single quilt. Each time they quilt, they use different materials and establish different patterns to produce a new creation informed but not bound by previous works. The salient features along with the many other elements we will be adding to our framework are like the quilter's pieces of material. The framework you're building with them is better understood as an ever-shifting quilt. Keep this image in mind as we now add four powerful insights.

ADDING FOUR FOUNDATIONAL INSIGHTS TO YOUR CREATIVE FRAMEWORK

For our framework to truly be powerful yet flexible, what's needed are insights that not only increase your understanding but also shed light on how to take action. In this section, we'll add four insights whose names signal their purpose and power.

The **CREATION INSIGHT** examines how creative thought and breakthrough ideas occur in that creative brain of yours. The **MINDSET INSIGHT** adds to what we know about our two dominant mindsets (fox and hedgehog) by delving into how "choice" factors in. Building on these, the **LEARNING INSIGHT** examines how humans are *built* to learn and how that innate "architecture" is often at odds with how we're *taught*. Finally, we explore the **OPENNESS INSIGHT** to better understand why crossing borders is vital in levering up our creative capacity and raising the odds of having impact.

THE "CREATION" INSIGHT

How do breakthroughs happen in the first place? What "act of creation" occurs to allow the big ideas to emerge? Once you know what does, how can you influence the incidence in your own mind and world? Good questions, and the creation insight can help address all of them.

The name of this insight honors Arthur Koestler. He first put forth his answers to these questions in 1964 in a book titled *The Act of*

THE "MINDSET" INSIGHT

The intersection of planes happens whether you want it to or not. It's like the way a good joke can automatically flip a switch in your head and make you laugh as you're being entertained. But when you are aware of such intersections and actively seek them out, the odds of your thoughts being creative ones skyrockets. Why? Because as you become aware of the potential of these intersections to produce that rewarding *aha!* breakthrough and actively pursue intersections, your entire mindset shifts. You move away from the strictly "known" and consciously seek out the "new."

Stanford University researcher, author, and psychology professor Carol Dweck has described the shift as choosing to move from a "fixed" mindset to a "growth" mindset. More than just offering a different way to describe that shift, Dweck's insight helps us see how our *choice* of mindset affects our ability to tap into our creative capacity in a larger sense. According to her, mindset doesn't simply affect what we are able to perceive (an intersection, for example), it impacts how we think, learn, and do in total.

Let's examine her ideas and quilt them into our creative framework.

CAROL DWECK AND THE "FIXED" AND "GROWTH" MINDSETS

Here Are Your Options. Carol Dweck is best known for her book *Mindset: The New Psychology of Success*. Its basic message is that each of us, by choice, primarily operates by either a **FIXED MINDSET** or a **GROWTH MINDSET** and, regardless of which we choose, everything else we do gets filtered through that mindset.

The fixed mindset is anchored in the belief that "your qualities are carved in stone."[55] According to Dweck, that means those who choose to navigate by a fixed mindset have concluded that each of us has only a certain amount of intelligence, a set personality, and an unchangeable moral character. For those who choose this mindset, life is about making the most of what you've got within implied limits.

By stark contrast, the *growth* mindset is "based on the belief that your basic qualities are things you can cultivate through your efforts." Those adopting a growth mindset believe that "although people may differ in every which way, everyone can change and grow through application and experience."[56] You might think of the fixed mindset as one defined by firm borders. In contrast, the growth mindset is wide open and borderless. That describes the basics; what are the implications?

Choosing to Stop Growth. In Dweck's view, mindsets are simply *beliefs.* They do not reflect fixed wiring as much as they reflect our patterns of thought and use of our equipment. To make her point, Dweck observed that humans are born with an intense drive to explore and learn; any fears, limitations, and interpretations that modify that initial programming all come later in life. Common observations prove this to be true—infants and toddlers naturally "stretch" in their actions, thoughts, and ideas, thirsting for the "new" beyond the "known." When they encounter failure in their forays, rather than choosing to stop seeking out things "new," they seem preconfigured to absorb the lessons of the experience and to keep growing. Undaunted, they try again until they figure it out. This reflects the nature of our preinstalled software—a strongly balanced blend of fox and hedgehog thinking oriented toward continual growth.

At this early age, we see this growth orientation in more than our actions. Think about toddlers' words and forms of speech. Both are dominantly oriented toward questions and especially the question/word *why.* We don't often consciously note it, but questions themselves have a growth inclination—either confirming the direction we're headed and its value or cluing us into the opportunity or need to change direction. This observation about early life caused Dweck to ask this question: *"What could put an end to this exuberant learning?"*[57] Looking at the population above the toddler age, Dweck observed that the curious, exploring, malleable mindset we start with gets scarce as we age, and quickly. Dweck seized on her own curiosity and pursued her question in earnest.

What she and her colleagues found plays out like a schoolroom curriculum. As we age and learn, especially in formal and socialized settings such as school, we are encouraged toward a fixed mindset. (Considering the teaching environment in most K-12 schools, this observation is easily recognized.) But Dweck noticed that as certain fixed mindset behaviors were modeled and rewarded, many *chose* to allow that mindset to dominate *beyond* the classroom in virtually all they did.

Let's break down this observation into its parts, beginning with a familiar example. Then we'll explore its implications to our own creativity as we age.

A Simple Example: Your Grade and Your Growth. The fixed mindset assumes you either have certain abilities or you do not. A typical classroom setting reinforces this as students are taught to think: "If I get A's and B's, it means I'm not only doing what I've been told to do, it also implies that I'm smart." The converse is suggested as well: "If I *don't* get high grades, I'm *not* smart." Everything in the system and various other signals around young students confirms this, thereby deepening their fixed mindset. But such a mindset *widens* as well, wrote Dweck, forming a broader set of fixed beliefs. Subconsciously, we surmise that the *effort* necessary to achieve *A*'s and *B*'s "is for those who don't have the ability."[58]

Now, you could chalk this up to normal childhood angst. But Dweck's research revealed a more ensnaring effect at work, one that hinges not so much on our learning environment as on the "choice" we gradually make, consciously or not, that enables a *fixed* mindset to dominate over a *growth* one. In the above example, the fixed mindset is at first only being modeled through the grading process, teachers, and peers. But it gradually hones your greater perception—of yourself, of your abilities, and of how you're *allowed* to filter and interact with the world around you.

Follow the thinking accompanying the fixed mindset: "I don't get A's and B's; no amount of effort will change that, so why try?" The flip side of this conclusion is more concerning: "I do get A's and B's, so I'm naturally smart, therefore effort isn't required. *But* if I ever *do* encounter circumstances that require effort," the fixed mindset implies, "that's the signal that I've reached my preset limits."

How Mindset and Beliefs Take Hold. While we may not register it as we pursue report-card metrics, the border-building orientation of the fixed mindset has a powerful negative effect on our creativity too. "In a poll of 143 creativity researchers," Dweck noted, "there was wide agreement about the number one ingredient in creative achievement. And it was exactly the kind of perseverance and resilience produced by the growth mindset."[59] Our classroom example described the cultivation of a *fixed* mindset. That makes it easy to see how it produces the *exact opposite* effect of the perseverance, resilience, and flexibility needed for "creative" achievement above and beyond the performance measures of A's and B's.

As you can probably conclude from your own observations, the fixed mindset is both the one for which humans are most often rewarded and the one that dominates culturally. Referencing best-selling author and *New Yorker* contributor Malcolm Gladwell, Dweck affirmed that "as a society we value natural, effortless accomplishment over achievement through effort. We endow our heroes with superhuman abilities that led them inevitably toward their greatness." It is, Dweck said, as if we conclude that these incredible "artists" across the human landscape simply "popped out of the womb" that way—"Midori fiddling, Michael Jordan dribbling, and Picasso doodling."[60] In reality, what actually starts early in life is our gradual and continuing *choice* to move from thinking of ourselves as naturally creative and growth oriented to something far more limiting. This in part accounts for not having more Midoris, Jordans, and Picassos in our midst, but also for the frequent opinion among the rest of us that we simply lack what they have.

Products of Choice. There's a growing body of research supporting the impact of mindset on our creative ability. There's even more evidence concerning how the conditions around us and in which we learn, grow, and perceive ourselves push our mindset further away from its creative capacity in the absence of counter-forces. Annie Murphy Paul, author of the book *Brilliant: The Science of Smart,* captured the stark trend line. She wrote, "When you ask second graders if they think they are creative, 95% say yes. Three years later, that percentage is cut in half (50%). By the time they are seniors in high school, it's down to 5%."[61] Strikingly, these findings align with Howard Gardner's findings about multiple intelligences. He described our tendency to take the many forms of intelligence we start life with and mute all except one or two as we age and conform. As Howard said, our "other" intelligences don't go away; they just get covered up.

But here's the interesting finding: Despite all the assumptions we make about the power of our teachers, parents, and peers, that "covering up" of our abilities and that shrinking of our belief in our creative capacity, simply can't happen unless we *choose* to allow it. The element of **CHOICE** may just be the most powerful creative finding of Dweck's research.

What Dweck emphasized is extremely important: We aren't only products of our learning environments. We are products of the *choices* we make about the *mindset* we allow to guide how we learn, think, and create. A shift from the wide-open mindset in toddlers to a closed one driven by the belief that we only have so much capacity to learn doesn't result from a natural biological evolution. It's a *choice*.

Even if our environment and how we're taught reward a fixed mindset, no one can make us adopt it; only we control that choice, even when we elect not to make it and allow others to choose for us. People may fall into a pattern of one mindset or the other. But they have the capability for *both* mindsets. The only thing inhibiting the use of both is choice—one on which hinges the effectiveness of your ability to create.

Room to Grow—By Choice. When first hearing of Dweck's findings, it might occur to you she's playing in the hedgehog and fox territory. At a high level, her fixed and growth mindsets seem to align directly. Dweck's work helps us make a key distinction about the hedgehog and fox, the fixed and the growth mindset—that is, when it comes to the choice to create and the actual act of creating, we're not talking about the *equipment*; we're talking about the *driver*.

Regard Dweck's findings this way: To fulfill our potential—including our creative potential—we need to tilt ourselves more fully toward *who we are*. As important as recapturing our growth-oriented fox, it's just as important to note that, according to Dweck, "who we are" is a *combination* of both a fixed and a growth mindset. Our choice of mindset impacts how that mix plays out and where it leads us. And if where we want to go is forward, toward new and continued human progress, we simply must allow our growth mindset to lead. It's another way of saying that, even though a natural hoedown goes on between our mindsets, we have the power to "call" the dance— but first we have to choose to assume that duty.

The school example we used to explain the fixed and growth mindsets yields this additional insight worth noting: If we don't actively choose our mindset for ourselves, then the choice will be made for us—not by our brain as much as by our surroundings. Someone or something has to choose and clearly there's more at stake here than our report card.

ADDING THE "MINDSET" INSIGHT AND THE "YET" FACTOR TO THE FRAMEWORK

While Dweck described her research as being mostly about learning to fulfill our potential, there's something wonderfully implicit in her wording that drives right to the heart of creativity.

For starters, "learning to fulfill our potential" *is* learning to fully leverage our capacity for creative thought. And in Dweck's world, that implies not simply fulfilling our potential one time. It means adopting a *mindset* that drives us to do so *always*.

There's still more packed into her five-word focus of "learning to fulfill our potential." Dweck's choice of the small yet significant word "our" means that, like creative thought itself, the growth mindset is available to *all of us*. But my favorite word of all—one that links the "mindset" insight most closely to creativity—is her word "yet." The following story explains why.

The "Yet" Factor. It's important to emphasize this point: The growth mindset is our forward-looking, imagining-the-possible mindset. It's the mindset fed by that catalyzing seed that is *THE YET FACTOR*—that beginning from which all human progress blooms.

In *Mindset*, Dweck shared a story about new graduate students coming into her program at Columbia University when she taught there. In telling it, she recalled how quickly these historically star performers could be suddenly daunted by the performance of their older peers and the unfamiliar expectations of the program. Dweck wrote, "They look at the faculty with their long list of publications." It's like looking for the first time at a grading system completely foreign to the one they'd trained themselves to adhere to for decades and concluding they weren't capable of or up to the new challenge. "'Oh my God, I can't do that,'" Dweck said they presumed. Then "they look at the advanced students who are submitting articles for publication and writing grant proposals. 'Oh my God, I can't do that'" either, they told themselves. "They know how to take tests and get *A*'s," wrote Dweck. "But they don't know how to do *this*—yet. They forget the *yet*."[62] Alongside it, they forgot the infinite possibility of a growth mindset. We may not all have been graduate students, but we've all been there.

Creativity is about the *yet*. And it takes a growth mindset to see it, experiment with it, shift toward it, and tap into it. Putting it succinctly, Dweck wrote, "The growth mindset is the mindset that allows people to thrive."[63] And embracing it leads to what's commonly referred to as an *aha!* experience.[64] It almost feels as if Dweck was channeling Koestler. To be sure, their insights are part of the same quilt.

THE "LEARNING" INSIGHT

Let's pause and get our bearings.

This chapter titled *What Creativity Is* looks to establish a baseline understanding, one we can continue to build on and use as a framework for creating. From the start, we've clearly stated what we want—to tap into and lever up our creative capacity. A simple definition cannot help us to do that. And it's wishful thinking to believe a formula exists for creativity if, like the fountain of youth, we could only find it. Wisely, we've taken a different path with a different end in mind.

While we began by deconstructing creativity, we quickly built on the common ground of three salient features of creativity—new, anywhere, and anyone. To that, we added the "creation" insight to help us understand *how* and *where* the breakthrough ideas of creativity originate. The "mindset" insight came next and helped us see we can choose to move *toward or away from* breakthrough ideas including what's *yet* to be.

You could say we're taking an approach to understanding creativity that's diverse, dynamic, and distinctive. And according to education innovator Ken Robinson, that's exactly how we are built to think, to create, and most important, to learn. Exploring his observation will help further catapult our capacity to create.

KEN ROBINSON AND A DIVERSE, DYNAMIC, AND DISTINCTIVE WAY OF LEARNING

You might recognize Ken Robinson's name from his smart, humorous, and artful TED Talks on the evolution of modern-day schools. Though Robinson has been dwelling in the education universe for a long time, he's been exploring and discovering in the creative space longer still.

In his book *The Element: How Finding Your Passion Changes Everything*, Robinson described creativity as a blood relative to intelligence. But he wrote that education systems, at least in the United States and the United Kingdom, tend to push "intelligence's relative" to the back of the class when it comes to structuring how we learn. In other words, the environment in which the overwhelming majority of us learn is disproportionately weighted *away* from our creativity-seeking growth mindset. As Robinson has said, "I believe this passionately: that we don't grow into creativity, we grow out of it. Or rather, we get educated out of it."[65]

Here's the familiar part of the disadvantage this learning structure fosters: Typically, we aren't taught about creativity and how to access our creative capacity. But there's a bigger problem with designing education systems and other learning venues *away from* creativity and *toward* a fixed mindset. *Doing so is the exact opposite of how we are built to learn.*

As Robinson has made it his mission to evangelize, humans are built to think and learn in ways that are **DIVERSE, DYNAMIC,** and **DISTINCTIVE**.[66] Think back to those three salient features of creativity, and you'll see a striking alignment between the "new, anywhere, and everyone" features of creativity and these three elements of how humans naturally think and learn. The alignment of these two trios will become even clearer as we examine the pillars of the "learning" insight.

We Are Built to Learn in "Diverse" Ways. The *diverse* element of how we think and learn echoes the findings of others, most obviously Howard Gardner and his theory of multiple intelligences. Everyone has the capacity to think in widely different ways, make connections in nearly unlimited numbers, and create things beyond the limits of what we know or can imagine in any one moment. But Robinson clued us into the reality that because of the infinite possible connections to be made, the paths and outputs for how

create the environment and enable *yourself* to learn in a diverse, dynamic, and distinctive way is a choice, indeed a responsibility that lies with *you*.

It would be easy to miss Robinson's insight given its context of schools. Schools and public education policy is simply where Robinson has chosen to *apply* his insight and shape his own creative approach. Robinson is clear that the environments in which we learn and operate can help or hinder us in our journey to discovering our creative selves. He and others advocate that environmental change should be happening at the societal level. And that would be great, wouldn't it? But what he's *not* saying, and what would be a mistake to conclude, is that we ought to sit around and wait until the bigger environment shifts. Quite the contrary.

If you read and listen to Robinson, he clearly believes that embracing *who we are*—which is to say, how we learn, must be everyone's modus operandi and our individual responsibility if we want to discover "new" and understand creativity. "There's a wealth of talent that lies in all of us," Robinson said. Therefore, "All of us, including those who work in schools, must nurture creativity systematically and not kill it unwittingly."[77] And that starts with how we learn.

THE "OPENNESS" INSIGHT

Have you noticed that the insights you're gaining in this section come from sources you probably didn't expect? Odds are you'd never heard of Arthur Koestler before, and while you might have heard of Carol Dweck or Ken Robinson, chances are you associated them with psychology or education rather than creativity.

Creativity means a willingness to go beyond the borders of what's known to find the insights you need to understand and use it. (There's a lesson right there.) These wise minds you're learning from here help you do that. Notice that as they illuminate some of its most fundamental elements, they aren't screaming out definitions or answers for what creativity is or how to be creative. Instead, their astute insights reveal the openness that's required and an understanding that only comes when you embrace that openness.

Many assessments of creativity are driving for a hard and fast answer and toward achieving fixed outcomes. Sure, eventually you want a tangible outcome. But more accurately, you want to understand how to get tangible, worthy outcomes *repeatedly*, by adapting what you know to any circumstance. You seek to understand *where* and *how* breakthrough ideas of any kind occur so you can orient yourself toward them and make them real. Inevitably, you learn best through practice, so that's where we turn for our fourth framing insight—to a practitioner who lives "openness."

LIZ LERMAN AND HIKING THE HORIZONTAL

Any one creative *idea* might be bound by time and circumstances; *creativity* however is not. It flows and shapeshifts over time and as circumstances change. In a word, creativity depends on openness.

So as you build a framework for creating, it must be one that's open and flexible enough to be applicable not just in this moment but in any future moment. There's no doubt that an effective creative framework is one built for **THE LONG VIEW**.

Sometimes even when we believe we are walking a creative path we have to let experience re-teach us the openness lesson. The separate but similar experiences of three Fellows in the world of dance serve as poignant examples. One of these Fellows, Liz Lerman, has developed an open mindset she calls **HIKING THE HORIZONTAL,** which offers us a lasting image for keeping this openness insight forefront in our creating.

When Creativity Isn't Creative. Like Ken Robinson described about education, "professional" dance resides in a well-established, entrenched world that's not easily changed. Surprised? So too were Liz and MacArthur Fellows Martha Clarke and Elizabeth Streb. At very young ages they were drawn to dance and the environment that, from the outside looking in, seemed to promise openness and the chance to create. Dance *is* creative. So all three were surprised to discover that the field of dance was not.

To give me, as an outsider to that world, a sense of what she was talking about, Liz described a "hierarchy" that exists in dance and indeed, she believes, exists in the arts in general. At the top is *high art*, the presumably important elite forms. In dance, think of Baryshnikov, premier league, diva dance. It's a sanctioned form, born of sanctioned schools, reviewed by sanctioned peers, all of whom *define* high art.

The formal dance training Liz, Martha, and Elizabeth received taught young dancers that *adhering* to this well-defined high art was both the goal and the measure of one's creative ability. More, its *prescribed* outputs were the only ones worth pursuing, they were repeatedly told. This struck each of them as not only odd, but also counter to what they each sensed, hoped, and believed creativity to be. What if they favored another form of dance, or what if they had their own ideas? But any different dance form, said Liz, was considered something closer to *low art*. And low art was generally viewed not only as unworthy of pursuit but of little value.

To put yourself in their ballet slippers, you might ask, "Does this mean that if Michael Jackson's *Thriller* dance video[78] garners more than 317 *million* views (which it had as of 2016), it would not be considered creative or of high value simply because it's not a sanctioned form of dance?" This kind of thinking just didn't make sense to any of them. And as Liz, Martha, and Elizabeth all separately realized, such rigid rules effectively meant closing their minds and the door to anything they might create that fell outside the borders of the sanctioned.

Try to imagine it for yourself: Here they were in a world actually *labeled* creative, and yet *where*, they wondered, was the openness that had attracted them? And *what*, they each asked themselves, should they do next?

The "Choice" When Confronted With Borders. Within such constraints, a high art dance piece becomes hard to describe as creative. As Martha put it, "It's a bit deceptive if not dishonest to call it 'creating' if ultimately everything you're 'allowed' to create has to pass through someone else's rule book."[79] Dance in this way is only "a *product* of creativity," Elizabeth concluded—and even that point could be argued. "You can choose to conclude you're being creative by rearranging the existing parts to produce a surface variation of the same thing," Elizabeth told me, "but that's more *reinterpretation* than it is creativity in the fullest sense."[80]

Confronted with an environment of constraint, not of creativity, these talented women faced three options: 1) stay within the borders and confines they were being taught; 2) respect the borders and leave them unchallenged, but leave dance; or 3) view dance and indeed creativity as open and borderless and, in the spirit of Sarah Kagan, rethink and then redefine creativity anew. To our collective benefit, they each chose the third.

Trading Borders for an Endless Horizon. Once they made their choices, they each had to develop a "mindset" that would guide them. Moving past the borders someone else had set was freeing. Yet without a sense of direction and a guiding compass, it would be hard to "make" anything of value. That's where mindset and the practice and habit of cultivating it come in.

Liz described the mindset she evolved this way: "Imagine turning this [prescribed hierarchy for creating] sideways to lay it horizontal. That way each of the poles," the high and the low implied by a hierarchy, "exerts an equal pull and has an equal weight."[81] Rather than simply come up with a ranking of her own of what qualified as creative, Liz did away with the ranking altogether. Instead of creating a new set of fixed rules, she flattened the rules and assumptions, making it harder to assert the conclusion that creativity took only one form or resulted from only one way of creating. When she did these things, not only could no single way of thinking, learning, or creating rank higher or reign superior to the rest, but each *new* way she encountered offered an opportunity to learn something new and see differently.

What Liz created was a mindset of perpetual discovery. She chose, as she put it, to abandon the hierarchy and "hike the horizontal." The result was that each time she approached a new possibility, this flat, borderless, endlessly open horizon allowed her to *adjust* her frame and mold it anew to the "possible in each new moment" and furthermore, to whatever might be necessary to make that possible "tangible." The effect was powerful and the creative potential unbounded.

The Boundless Rewards of a Creative Mindset. Liz told me that her open mindset about dance and about creating shaped a new way of being, seeing, and doing in every sense. To this day, she creates not by formula but by framing creativity as an ongoing journey. And as she "moves between the poles"—places, experiences, people that provide inspiration and insight—she's proactively creating *intersections*. That's when the "known" and "new" collide, each time catalyzed and amplified by Liz. More than choosing, she's perpetually molding an environment and a perspective necessary to create freshly all the time, one that not surprisingly is diverse, dynamic, and distinct. Hiking the horizontal isn't just a creative mindset, it's a practice of perpetual growth—in total an amazingly productive way to frame the view of what creativity is.

What's been the result? This revolutionary artist was among the first to bring video and technology into dance pieces. More, she has unconventionally incorporated her audience and non-dancers into her dances—senior citizens, scientists, factory workers, and war veterans. She has, in other words, found a way for dance not simply to be *viewed* but to be *shared*. Further breaking with "tradition," she has staged her performances in places not typically associated with dance or creativity—including shipyards, office buildings, and even in the Large Hadron Collider at CERN (really). In so doing, she has moved creativity itself beyond any prescribed borders that might otherwise limit it. Her pieces personify the *definition* of "new, anywhere, and anyone."

At the same time, they don't; hiking the horizontal doesn't have such "defining" borders. Instead, its defining trait is openness—the most powerful "theatre" in which to dance.

ADDING THE "OPENNESS" INSIGHT TO THE FRAMEWORK

Liz wrote, "Hiking the horizontal became my shorthand for a whole series of behaviors, practices, and beliefs that I have been working toward for most of my life. At its essence are several concepts."[82] Note in the following summary not only how much these concepts reflect the openness insight but how remarkably aligned they are with what you've learned about creativity:

1. "Allow for multiple perspectives . . . in hiking the horizontal, many ideas can coexist."

2. "Make the walls permeable."

3. "Find a way to respect something that lives at the end of the spectrum farthest from where you are comfortable—the respect has to be authentic, but it doesn't have to be uncritical."

4.   "Name where you are on the spectrum at any given moment."

Reinforcing this, Liz told me that hiking the horizontal is the term she "currently" uses to express a deep running philosophy that's central to her creativity. I like that; even her name for her framework is fluid and open.

Her creative framework is powerful in another sense because it actually describes an ancient dance—the dance of our minds, between our fox and our hedgehog, where who leads and who follows is most accurately seen as horizontal, not hierarchical. The *pictures* Liz can create *within* that framework represent what can come from using such an open framework or any framework seeded from the same basic elements of creativity. The use and outputs can even inform the framework, but they do not replace it any more than they fix it in place. This essential insight about openness is what allows Liz, just in her seventies, to continue being creative in her work.

Speaking to the power embodied in the openness insight, Liz wrote, "When it comes to ideas, a hook is not enough. It is more like casting a net. I throw my ideas in a broad and loosely knit construct that includes stories, questions, and histories both personal and public. Then I wait and listen. Eventually I gather in my net to see what has happened to this data and begin to discover what 'catch' matters in this place, to these people. Then the next round of the conversation begins."[83] This is hiking the horizontal—this is creativity in action.

"DEFINING" CREATIVITY

New, imaginative, innovative, relevant, or *meaningful*—some combination of these descriptors appears in most attempts to "define" *creativity*. They often show up beside such words and concepts as *the ability to transcend, a state of flow,* or *passion*—all attractive concepts, each open to interpretation.

Across formal definitions is a clear effort to come up with a description that encompasses *ideas* as much as *acts*, a *capacity* as much as an *output*, a *way* as much as an *environment* that nurtures a way. The creativity many are attempting to define is one capable of *bringing* something new into being as much as it allows *thinking* about things in new or fresh ways.

After a while, one gets the feeling we're searching for a magical formula with wings that would allow us to fly effortlessly and from peak to peak. Rather than mechanically persist, we should pause to wonder: Are we clear why we're even after a definition in the first place and what we hope to *gain*? Is it knowledge? A truer understanding? New ways of seeing? Is it perhaps even something more?

PAUSING TO STEP BACK AND SEE THE FRAME

As we've journeyed to discover what creativity is, we've stepped outside the implied borders of our subject—into humor, the psychology of achievement and success, the way we're taught in schools, and even into dance—each time to get a different view. Each sub-journey was a kind of pause to reconsider creativity. Again let me briefly offer you that kind of pause, this time by stepping into nature, one of the most creative forces of all and one of which we are an integral part. After this pause, I'll "define" creativity for you.

Author Edward Abbey once stopped to consider a beautiful rock formation in the canyons of Utah known as Delicate Arch, noting the many ways of "defining" it. "Depending on your preconceptions," Abbey wrote, "you may see the eroded remnant of a sandstone fin, a giant engagement ring cemented in the rock, a bow-legged pair of petrified cowboy chaps, a triumphal arch for a procession of angels, an illogical geologic freak."[84] He could list countless other things, each a new interpretation shaped by the practicality of one's personal lens and patterns. Or, Abbey suggested, we could take a different view, seeing this wonder as "a frame more significant than its picture."[85]

In seeking to understand what creativity is, we'd be wise to borrow Abbey's advice. Here, too, the *frame* is more suggestive than any *picture* it might contain.

Pushing beyond definitions in a way Edward Abbey would have admired, Jerome Bruner wrote in *On Knowing: Essays for the Left Hand*, "There is good reason to inquire about creativity, a reason beyond practicality. Practicality is not a reason but a justification after the fact. The reason is the ancient search of the humanist for the excellence of man."[86]

We humans are increasingly capable of far more than outcomes in the finite sense. We're after something bigger, something lasting, something more fully reflective of who we are. But remarkably, we manufacture many rings of barriers to our own perpetuation.

What you've already seen across explorers of creativity—Koestler, Kneller, Ghiselin, Dweck, Weiner, Watts, Robinson, Lerman, and Gardner among them—is that they believe strongly in looking at both creativity and humans across a broad expanse. Insights that lead to progress and perpetuation lie *there*, rather than in singular outputs, ways, or times.

When Robert Paul Weiner wrote in *Creativity & Beyond*, "To a considerable extent, world history is the history of creativity,"[87] he was in search of this bigger meaning behind what creativity is, and he was signaling us that we ought to be after the same thing. Instead of limiting ourselves to one way, we need to understand creativity as a perpetual dance between interpretations and applications. Better yet, we need to dance down into permeable rubble the walls that suggest that one narrow interpretation reigns over all others. Only then can we can fully realize our excellence and perpetuate our history. It follows then that we need a fresh perspective in understanding our creative capacity.

SIMPLE TRUTH:

CREATIVITY IS

THE LANGUAGE

OF MAN

CHAPTER FOUR

SIMPLE TRUTH: CREATIVITY IS THE LANGUAGE OF MAN

DREAM OF A COMMON LANGUAGE

Much has been revealed to you in these last three chapters—elements, insights, and Simple Truths that will all prove essential to your creative journey. In the broadest sense you can now say that you know about the equipment, the importance of steady compass checks, and even understand more clearly this land of creativity in which our journey is taking place. Now it's time to understand how you'll bring narrative to it and to your dreams—it's time to understand creativity as our common language. But first, a story.

THE GIRL AND THE GAP

Education visionary Ken Robinson has done several TED Talks, each wildly and justifiably popular. His most acclaimed one, viewed by more than thirty-seven million people as of this writing, is titled "Do Schools Kill Creativity?"[88] In it, he told the following story.

A little girl is sitting in the back of her grade school classroom. The focus of the day is a drawing lesson. Having let the children loose to draw, the teacher becomes aware of the enthusiasm and concentration with which this girl tackles the assignment. It's completely opposite to her typical behavior. So the teacher wanders over to see what she's drawing. Unsure, the teacher asks. The little girl looks up and says, "I'm drawing a picture of God." A bit taken aback, the teacher quickly and confidently objects. "No one knows what God looks like," she says. And the little girl replies, "Well, they will in a minute."

Play back through the scene of this unassuming and powerful tale. A young girl is drawing a picture of God, something her teacher implies no one can do because no one knows what God looks like. To the teacher, this is an unbridgeable gap—that distance from what she knows to something her experience tells her cannot be known. But to the girl, there is no gap. The distance, if any at all, is a matter of a little time. What is "not to be" for the teacher is "about to be" for the girl.

I love this story. It's simple, yet it conveys so much—most obviously about the gap between those firmly in touch with their creative capacity and those out of practice. It's also about the means necessary to cross the gap. On one side sits the teacher, on the other, the student. Here is the discipline; there is the dream. Here: rules; there: the borderless possibilities.

And yet despite the apparent gap, a common language lies between the two—one that's more about *use* than *structure*, more about a flexible frame than a precise picture. The value of this language is derived from *meaning* more than method. At a certain level, the language's power resides far more in the metaphoric than the literal.

While the teacher in this tale sees the limits of this language, the girl senses that this language's character is precisely the source of its influence. Age is forgetful and cautious; youth simply knows.

Creativity can feel like this: the gap, the extremes, and the puzzlement in between. At times, that gap can seem enormous. But closing the perceived gap is as simple as having the right language to communicate across it *and* the confidence to know you're built to do exactly that. *Anyone* can do this.

Somewhere inside you know this, you just need someone to draw you a picture to help you remember that you do.

THE MINDSET OF A COMMON LANGUAGE

Creativity is a language, powerful and universal. But calling creativity a language may initially present a mental hurdle. After all, it doesn't take long to reach an age when we come to hold certain impressions of language.

In the same timeframe in which our beliefs about language narrow, we often acquire an expectation that we need to *see* before we *believe*. Sensitive to those tendencies, this chapter offers you a bit of what we *need* (proof) before we go on to what we really *want*—to speak creativity with fluency.

We'll begin by first examining language itself—its potential, its limits, and more fundamentally, what it is, what it does, and how it gives us leverage. Only after we understand language at its foundational level can we put creativity to the test and ultimately prove it *is* a language. And we'll do just that as we help you *see to believe*.

On this part of the journey, we'll not only gain an appreciation for this remarkable ability often taken for granted, we'll form a base for seeing how we can go about regaining fluency in the language of man.

WHAT ARE YOU SAYING?—THE POTENTIAL OF LANGUAGE

Have you ever truly considered what language *is*? Unless you are a linguist or a writing teacher, you've likely only noted what language *does* and, in that sense, what it does for you *directly*. To open up the view, let's have a look at the power of language.

THE MANY POWERS IN LANGUAGE

At the most fundamental level, language is a powerful form of *communication*—for your thoughts, desires, ideas, even your feelings. In every sense, it's a mark of *identity*. The language you speak and how you use it conveys a great deal about who you are.

Language is also a grand form of *expression*. We ordinarily think of it in the spoken sense, but it can also be expressed in sounds, motions, or symbols, written and otherwise. Even nature has a language in its rivers and streams, oceans and winds, seasons and shapes that tell the tuned-in observer a lot. (See Author's Notes: Chapter Four-A.)

In these ways, language is a *currency* through which value can be conveyed and created.

Communication, expression, and currency all emphatically convey its power, and yet language is far more. Consider the following points as proof.

A Multifaceted Ability. In humans, language represents a unique cognitive ability to *learn*. Languages can be spoken, signed, encoded, touched (Braille), symbolized, written, whistled, or rhythmically sounded. And each method of expressing language can transmit complex and textured messages and data. Related, at least for humans, language isn't only a method of communicating but of recording and representing as well, thus giving it a critical role in our history. More important still, language enables us to build on the value we create with it and carry it across time. In that sense, language is an unrivaled *multiplier*.

More than a Swiss army knife jam-packed with distinct tools for learning, the elements of human language can be combined in an infinite number of ways to form textured *meaning*. In other animals, the capacity to express and think is primarily genetic. It appears to most often take form as a finite series of utterances with what appear to be built-in, limited, and fixed meanings. But in humans, the capacity for expressing meaning goes much further than a primal toolkit.

The human capacity for language is exceptionally adapted to weaving our myriad forms of expression together. More, it allows for elements of social interaction to constantly and dynamically shape language and its meanings. Most distinct of all, human language allows us to do all of these things in a *forward* mode. Quite literally, we can think and communicate things that don't even exist but could—the imagined, the abstract, and the hypothetical. This is truly distinct and so powerful that it amplifies all the other capacities human language embodies.

Wide Open to Possibility. What you might already be able to see from the preceding description is that human language is an *open* system. This, too, makes it formidable and ripe with possibility. To the best of our knowledge, other animal languages are closed, which means a limited number of possible things can be expressed.

By comparison, humans bring intentionality to language and that intentionality constantly shapes its use. That open nature enables us to first express and then materialize those things we can imagine but are yet to be.

In the human form, language is *malleable* and as varied as those who use it. As a small but telling expression of the range, it's estimated there are six to seven thousand languages in existence worldwide today. The most practiced isn't English either, as many Westerners might assume. It's Mandarin Chinese. (See Author's Notes: Chapter Four-B.)

But the suppleness goes further still. In addition to our core capacity for language, we humans create our own derivations within specific languages to fulfill individual or group needs. The broad spectrum includes variations for communication within a certain culture or geography. It can include subsets of industries—for example, the sub-language programmers use to develop apps for a single type of device in a single operating system. In effect, the permutations of human language are so great, they feel impossible to even calculate with accuracy.

Undeniably Indelible. Language in humans is believed to be *innate*, not a capacity possessed by "the few." Its potent possibility offers equal access. Typically, a human child is capable of communicating fully by age three. Indeed, the capacity for language is deeply rooted and central to why we've survived and thrived to this point.

It's believed that language originated with the earliest hominids as their world, their groupings, and the size of their brains changed. Ample proof exists that humans started writing about eight thousand years ago. Going further back, 17,000 years ago, there's evidence of our ancestors using all major representational techniques including painting, drawing, engraving, sculpture, ceramics, and stencil. These were applied both in a standalone mode and in highly complex works of art and communication. It's possible that language precedes even our official categorization as humans, with some scientists concluding signs of use going back 350,000 years or more.

In her book *Reason for Hope*, primatologist Jane Goodall provided context for the elemental role of language. As someone who values and acknowledges the capacities of all animals, she still pointed out that "we, and only we, have developed a sophisticated language."[89] There's meaning in that statement far beyond an impotent conclusion that humans are superior.

Referring to humans, Goodall explained, "For *the first time in evolution*, a species evolved that was able to *teach* its young about *objects and events not present*, to *pass on wisdom gleaned* from successes—and the mistakes—of the past, to *make plans* for the *distant future*, to *discuss ideas* so that they could grow, *sometimes out of all recognition*, through the *combined wisdom* of the group. With language," Goodall said, "we can ask, as no other living beings, those questions about who we are and why we are here."[90] (I've added italics for emphasis because each italicized thought is a formidable inflection point.) Goodall's comments help us conclude that human language truly is powerful. More than that, it's imbedded in the blueprint that *is* the human being, and it's vital to our ability to see and seize the possible.

THE MEANING AND USE OF LANGUAGE

Take note that Jane Goodall wasn't referring to any one human language—not English, nor Swahili, American Sign Language, or any of the thousands of other bounded languages humans use to communicate. She was pointing to human language at a fundamental level. What is human language at that fundamental level, what purpose does it serve, and how does it fulfill that purpose? The best way to understand is to explore what most agree to be the four elements of language and their roles.

LANGUAGE'S FOUR ELEMENTS, THE FLUID AND FIXED

Language experts concur that all languages boil down to these elements: *meaning, use, sound structure,* and *grammar structure.* (Technically, those four elements are known as semantics, pragmatics, phonology, and syntax. But unless you "speak linguistics," these terms might as well be Mandarin.) One important but often overlooked thing to note is that two of these are fluid (meaning and use) and two are fixed (the structural elements of sound and grammar). Their nature, as well as the emphasis and attention we give each, has a significant impact on the degree to which we are able to leverage any language's power.

Consider, for example, the element of **MEANING**. This element reminds us that any word, symbol, or part of language can be imbued or associated with a particular meaning. But there's more to it. The associated meaning of a word is *fluid,* allowing it to change with setting, use, person, or idea. In fact, so open and fluid is *meaning* in human language that it can actually *affect* the setting, use, person, or idea in *reverse;* it isn't just defined by those things.

Think, for example, of the device we call a phone, or even of the word "phone." That thing we used once upon a time to simply speak to someone voice to voice has now become something we use in countless ways beyond voice communication. It functions as a medium for playing games or doing work, watching videos, storing photos, sending emails, surfing the web, and so much more. We don't often think of the "call" function of the phone as representing anything more than a single "app" on this now ubiquitous (and mobile) device. Our use of phones has completely changed the meanings of both the word and the device from what they were for more than a century.

Calling upon the "learning insight" of Chapter Three, you could rightfully describe meaning in human language as diverse, dynamic, and distinctive—and in that sense, a natural and even necessary facilitator of creativity.

The other fluid element defining language is **USE**. As a critical partner element with *meaning,* use provides the context that shapes the significance and relevance of a certain word under certain circumstances. Meaning shifts and evolves according to usage. Stone carver and MacArthur Fellow Elizabeth Turk offered an appropriate example through her use of the word "creativity" and the resulting meaning.

"Creativity," Elizabeth said, "is usually thought of as an *additive* process. But *I* think of it just as much as a *reductive* process, deconstructing its meaning each time I create to possibly find something better."[91] To more fully understand the power and range of language's fluent elements of meaning and use, just for a moment let's pause and play out Elizabeth's insight using her "language" of stone carving as a case in point.

FLUIDITY IN MEANING AND USE: A CREATIVE EXAMPLE

When Elizabeth considers a block of stone she might carve, she rarely selects the block with the idea of what she wants to carve already set in her mind—that is to say, she doesn't begin with meaning or use predetermined. In other words, she doesn't begin with the plan to carve a "David" and then seek the rock from which to extract him. For Elizabeth, most often, the stone block comes *before* the idea. As much as she is the creator and even has her own subject preferences and styles, Elizabeth says the *stone* conveys to *her* what it's capable of, and then she and the block engage in an exchange from which her use of the stone and its meaning are derived.

While it's accurate to describe what she's doing as "constructing," in the bring-forth-and-build sense of the word, that is an incomplete description of how Elizabeth creates. To create something new, Elizabeth understands, she's also "deconstructing"—bit-by-bit taking not just grains and chips but meaning from the stone. In her language, Elizabeth's interpretation of meaning and use derives from a diverse, dynamic, distinct, and indeed perpetual back and forth—precisely the kind of creative reconsideration for which Sarah Kagan suggested we must strive (Chapter Two). It's this version of meaning and use that shapes something wondrous for Elizabeth— as it does for any of us. If her approach were completely rule-bound and structured, the result would eventually be something less.

No matter in what form we articulate it, meaning and use are malleable, changeable, and multidirectional—even if at times we regard them as otherwise. It isn't that structure doesn't play an important role, including in language, but its role is to support the meaning and use sought in any one moment. "Nothing," we might say, "is written in stone." In language, therefore, to regard *use* or *meaning* as fixed or formulaic is to risk crushing the elements that make this unique human capacity a mighty force.

THE STRUCTURE OF LANGUAGE

Along with meaning and use, language is typically described by its structures, often disproportionately so. In part, structures tell us how to organize and, seen as guidelines, often enhance the more fluid elements of language—all of which are both positive and necessary. But more often than not, we regard structures in language and elsewhere as fixed—solid, reliable, and permanent in nature. When we do, structure can inadvertently restrict meaning and use. Here's a tangible example.

When I was in college, one of the school's key dormitory buildings wasn't a building at all—it was a set of trailers, or mobile homes. The structures had been lowered to the ground to give them a permanent feel, but had you peeled back the siding surrounding each, you'd have seen the wheels were still there, ready to be called into action. Entering as freshmen, all of this was explained away as *temporary* housing. That sounded a bit odd when we learned in the next breath that this "temporary" housing had been there over a decade. More ironic still, nearly twenty years after I graduated, these impermanent structures still stood, flaunting their temporariness.

Like those dorms, many structures have a way of becoming more fixed than we intend when we first establish them. Even when the foundational assemblies themselves outlive their usefulness, the *surrounding* structures we establish around them—tradition, process, use, and habit—can make them hard to remove. (Recall the fixedness that Howard Gardner and Project Zero encountered with intelligence and the IQ.) Languages are not immune to this problem.

ICH SPRECHE KEIN DEUTSCH – THAT'S "GERMAN," RIGHT?

Years ago, I set out to learn German. The instruction I received almost exclusively focused on grammar, vocabulary, sentence formation, and pronunciation—in a word, my instruction was in *structure*. Yet while I could use what I'd learned to convey meaning among my classmates, this training hardly prepared me for tapping into the meaning and patterns of use among speakers *outside* the classroom.

For example, beyond the formal rules, German speakers in general have a habit of blending many words, truncating others, or skipping over some entirely. They do so if they think the meaning is implied or if new and better meaning can be made. Rather than being isolated, this is accepted practice. In other words, while in the formal teaching of the German language structure dominates, in reality there's a natural and purposeful tendency among users of the language to bend or even break the structure if it's believed new or increased value can be gained. And indeed this makes intuitive sense.

The flip side of this practice, however, is just as interesting and instructive. Once new meaning and use have been established, *new* structure tends to follow, and yet while well intended, its effects can often be narrowing. Presumably the new rules around use *enhance* communication. But the creators of the new or additional layers of structure rarely focus on the fact that these additions also have the effect of *limiting* communication to a user group that tends to grow smaller with each new layer. My wife, for example, has been fluent in German since childhood, having grown up in the United States learning German and English in parallel. But when she went for a time to Germany from the U.S. (adding structural layers rooted in geography) to work in business (which added an industry layer of language) and to work for one particular company (a corporate cultural layer), she initially felt like she'd entered a foreign land whose residents spoke an entirely different language. Communication took place through a highly nuanced mesh of different language rules, words, and structures that while productive in their limited setting, were in fact limiting to all but those within that subset group of "German" speakers.

The point of this example is that humans will always seek out opportunities to expand meaning and use. It's also true that once we arrive at something valuable, our natural hedgehog tendency is to support and even defend the value created, most often by creating structure of some sort. There's a natural logic, even a benefit in doing so. But what's disadvantageous even if unintended is when the value equation becomes *flipped* and structure, rather than supporting meaning and use, becomes the focus. Structures, which are inevitably temporary, should serve rather than restrict meaning and use.

CROSSING THE LANGUAGE BARRIER
TO REACH CREATIVITY

Of the six thousand-plus languages left in the world today, a full third of them have fewer than a thousand native speakers. As a result, many languages are approaching *dead* status, a term used to describe still-known languages spoken only in special contexts. Many *past* languages—far more than those that exist today—have already become extinct, meaning their use and users no long exist. Linguists believe that, of the languages currently in use, up to 90 percent will have become extinct by the year 2050. Not just dead, but dead and gone.

What does this tell us about language and why it exists? At the very least, the implications snap us to attention. But to what should we attend?

Certainly we could respond at the granular level by trying to preserve individual languages and the meaning they uniquely express before they are lost, a noble and even important thing. But more powerfully, we can return ourselves to reflect on what language in the larger sense enables—meaning and use—and ensure that in any language we don't lose sight of these priorities. Perhaps the best way for doing so is to collectively embrace a universal language alongside those many more finite languages we rely on, one that offers context and continually calls us to attend to value.

Language is an undeniably powerful human capacity. Its greatest power is that it allows us to formulate, express, share, and make real what our creative minds imagine. This cannot be forgotten. But in reminding ourselves, author Marilynne Robinson asked in her essay "Beauty," "Why must we lapse into French or Greek to speak of an experience that is surely primary and universal?"[92]

Building on Robinson's thought, there's tremendous value to be gained by turning our attention toward rediscovering that *primary, universal language* that's capable of *producing* French and Greek, and Picasso's *Guernica,* and the iPod, and microlending, and a dazzling array of other derivations from our creative minds: *creativity.* But before we do, let's address the matter of proof—proof that creativity is a language.

THE MATTER OF PROOF

Revving Up Both Sides of Your Brain. Climate scientist and MacArthur Fellow Peter Huybers described creativity as a dynamic in which "*believing is seeing* as opposed to *seeing is believing.*"[93] It's an important insight in at least two respects. First, Peter was telling us what creativity actually *is*—a leap of faith of sorts; an initial absence of reliable structure, templates, or rules to follow; a trust in a gradual unfolding with good odds of revealing something new. That message is one repeatedly echoed by Peter's MacArthur peers and all those who speak creativity. But second and equally honest, Peter was acknowledging the default mode most of us are trained for and quickly fall into: *Prove it to me first before I believe and proceed.*

In the context of creativity, we want what it promises, of course, but most often before we pursue it, we demand tangible assurance that the path is clear and straight. In a similar way, you may want confirmation that creativity *is* a language before committing to learn to speak it. Fair enough. To appeal to our hedgehog desire to "see" first, let's use what we've already learned about language to give creativity a test. But as we "kick the tires," let's also engage our fox and think more like Peter suggested.

DOES CREATIVITY DELIVER ON USE, MEANING, AND OTHER CRITERIA?

Use. A language is something that allows you to communicate. But a powerful language, a human language, allows you to communicate in more than a basic way. It lets you share your thoughts, desires, ideas, and even your feelings. More robust still, a truly powerful language functions as currency, a means of trading, translating, and transferring value from one human to another.

To be valuable, such a language must enable us to build *with* it and *on* it while remaining capable of carrying knowledge, history, ideas, and experience across time. Thus a truly valuable language gives its users the capacity to express in a *forward* mode—to literally think and communicate about things that don't yet exist but could.

Rather than just being valuable to conceptualizing "what could be," a commanding language must also be useful to the process of making the possible real. That requires it to be a language that can be used by more than a handful of people and across whatever other boundaries might otherwise separate them.

I submit that creativity meets the stated criteria of *use* as a language— but it does much more.

Meaning. A language must also be capable of allowing us to form *meaning* with it ongoing. Note the distinction: It's the capacity to *form* meaning *continually* that matters, not just to forge it once and preserve it. Creativity doesn't simply *meet* this test; it *embodies* it. Plus its foundation in "new" is implicitly forward moving. And creativity's additional pillars of "anywhere and anyone" remind us this language allows *any* of us to create our own meaning with it.

A language's power for expressing meaning is greatest when it is an open language based on a more fluid structure capable of and even dependent on change. As a language, creativity is unique in this respect. Because it's a language that always prioritizes *meaning* and *use* over strict structure, it allows us to tap into our fullest potential and to progress—in this moment and in future moments.

"Details" With Purpose. Fine. We've noted that creativity meets the broad criteria of a language. But what about the *specifics*? What about *words* and the *structures* needed to put a language together in a usable way?

Recall Peter's comment and then recognize how we've been trained to think about languages—that is, to catapult quickly forward from the *meaning* and *use* that makes us want to speak a language in the first place, to demand the *how-to* of the structure and the rules for using it. As novelist Ray Bradbury once warned, "The intellect is a great danger to creativity because you begin to rationalize and make up reasons for things, instead of staying with your own basic truth— who you are, what you are, what you want to be."[94] Creativity is concerned with those basic truths; the how-to is situational and malleable.

More than just situational and malleable, creativity is personal. As a language, it connects you with your *own* basic truth, that essential feature Bradbury highlighted. Its "structures" must always enable that, but that doesn't mean it is without structure.

Elements. In the language of man, the "words" are encompassed in the *elements*, the "terms" and the concepts you're discovering as each new layer of the story of creativity is revealed to you. Think of "fox and hedgehog," "hiking the horizontal," "border crossing," and "new, anywhere, anyone" as a few examples of elements you already know. These are more than words; each element integrates *ideas, concepts, insights,* and *truths.* (See the Glossary of "Elements" for a summary.)

As you've seen, elements don't come wrapped with hard and fast rules for how they can be used, combined, or reshaped. That said, there is a framework to the language of man that provides a reliable means by which you can direct the elements, communicate, and form ideas to guide you to creative outcomes.

Structure. What's powerful about the elements isn't limited to their meaning. It also extends to how you put them together for use. Typically, a "structure" isn't something that's flexible; but with the language of man, you dictate its form and use as the situation calls for you to do. More than a flexible feature of this language, it's a *requirement* that the structure stay fluid. If every time you put your creative capacity to use you pause to reconsider what creativity is and what it might do, inevitably the way you structure the elements will have to shift. With each new use, you actively rediscover the incredible versatility in structure, use, and meaning the language of man offers.

These language elements may be different than the ones you've encountered in other languages (different, for instance, from the grammar, vocabulary, sentence formation, and pronunciation I was taught when learning German). But it's in their difference that the leverage, value, and universality of the language of man are found.

All of this is absolutely true. You just might have to "believe" it first to "see" it.

The Language of "You." As you learn the language of man, you're actually learning to be you again—fully, fluidly, and phenomenally. It's hard to do that if, in "speaking creativity," you insist on approaching this language as you do other languages.

So what do we do about that? Poet Richard Kenney offered wise insight. He suggested we think of language as we did when we learned it as children.

"Language as we're taught language," Richard explained to me, "language with all its structures and formalities, rules and rights and wrongs, tends to make categories *for* us. But we start life in quite the opposite way. As children we direct language and not the other way around," Richard reflected. "Somewhere along the line we yield and let language direct us. We don't think about that or language much most days; we just follow the rules we're given. Imagine if that weren't the case."[95]

We can feel a chilling familiarity in what Richard described. We know we end up doing the opposite of what children do when first learning to communicate. A gap follows.

As children, we think about meaning and use *first*—that is, about how to perceive and express ourselves as we figure out how to open up the world around us. To a young girl, for example, the structure and rules bear importance only as they serve her quest for meaning. The rules become relative. And when they fail her, she simply changes them or abandons them. Watch any toddler shortcut the rules by using single words in place of full sentences, or employing objects, hand signals, and facial expressions when words won't come or don't fit. Doing this is instinctive.

So as you reignite this ability and begin to speak this language, proceed childlike. Follow your instincts. Lean toward *meaning* and *use*. Don't think of doing so as looking to kill your rule-oriented hedgehog. Rather, think of it as putting your hedgehog in the proper context without allowing it to become your overlord. And when your fox and your hedgehog blend to guide *how* you create, this language of creativity will serve as the incredible tool it's meant to be.

CLOSING THE GAP

As we complete this Simple Truth—that creativity is the language of man—and wrap up the *Reveal* Section, let me leave you with a thought and an image.

The thought is this: You already have a greater understanding of creativity than you did a few chapters ago. Through the elements and by revealing how they form a language, you're on your way to using your creative capacity as never before. The gap is narrowing between what you've come to believe is possible and the true possibility of what you can do with your creative capacity.

As you'll see, the next section of *The Language of Man, Render,* moves rapidly forward, taking what you know and showing you how it can be used to discover those breakthrough ideas we all desire. By the end of the *Render* section, you'll know more than just where to find that "space" where breakthroughs come from; you'll know how to create it.

For the image: Let's return to stone carver Elizabeth Turk and a "visual" of what *use* and *meaning* look like in action.

BEYOND THE GAP

Carving Out Your Own Meaning. "I'm very intrigued with the idea of creativity," Elizabeth said to me. "Not just what it means, but what we can make it mean."[96] I could almost hear the gears in her mind moving as she played with the idea. And in her beautiful works made of stone, I'd already seen where that play could take her. But that's the beautifully sculpted ending of the story; let's begin with the stone.

To most people, a stone is a stone is a stone. In their eyes, solid rock is solid. Permanent. It is as it appears and as we are taught it to be. That's the message most of us accept, "fixing" it in our minds.

But as you read earlier in this chapter, Elizabeth doesn't think about things that way. When it comes to creativity, she told us, most think of it as an *additive* process. Yet she thinks of it equally as a *reductive* one. Elizabeth's instinct tells her that meaning is malleable, and that leads her to hear another message entirely from the stone, one quite apart from what the rest of us believe to be immutable.

To Elizabeth, the stone is what Stu Kauffman would call an **ENABLING CONSTRAINT.** Be it a seemingly solid form of matter, a long-standing belief or law, or a way of doing things, we are prone to swing in the direction of regarding our myriad "borders" as fixed. But when Elizabeth looks, she sees where aspects of the constraints can be taken away, reduced, and opened into something that's powerful, moving, and meaningful.

Elizabeth sculpts and lives by the sea, a place where fluidity, impermanence, and possibility are always part of the fabric. As she works with materials that appear permanent, to Elizabeth there's a precariousness apparent as well. This stone carver sees her work as the challenge of pushing what appears solid to the edges of collapse. *Meaning* and *use* are forever testing their constraints.

The results are stunning if not unbelievable. Looking at them, it's hard to remember that Elizabeth's beautiful works begin as stone. Examples: Stone shaped into ribbons you'd expect to see on a Christmas package or around the waist of a flower girl skipping

down the aisle at a wedding. Stone transformed into wings and
Celtic knots or impossibly intricate shapes that look like the delicate
skeleton of a beautiful alien insect or the secret inner workings of a
dandelion. (See Author's Notes: Chapter Four-C.)

Honoring the Cycle. As Elizabeth knows, the ability to speak
creativity comes from recognizing and honoring the whole process—
learning, speaking, and creating—and not any one outcome. It's
the *cycle* of readying, revealing, rendering, reconnecting, returning,
and then readying to do it all over again that gives the language of
man its depth.

Such important truths are easily forgotten, and Elizabeth knows
this too. To remind her of this cyclicality in the language of man,
Elizabeth has developed a ritual. After long months of sculpting
and creating magnificent outcomes, she takes each piece from her
workshop down to the seashore. Next, she carries the piece gently in
her arms to the surf line. And then stunningly (at least to the rest of
us), she places it in the turbulent and unstructured breaking waves.

In a sense, she is taking her beautiful, hard-earned creative
outputs—her ostensible absolutes—and consciously bringing them
back to that edge where "known" meets "new." The waves could
easily toss one of these delicate works the wrong way, breaking it and
"deconstructing" months of labor and love. *Or*, Elizabeth believes,
she might learn something new from the ritual, perhaps observing
what the waves do and allowing that to suggest what to do next with
her chisels. When she's ready to engage creativity anew, it's possible
that even in the broken pieces of a sculpture there's inspiration for a
new design waiting to be seen.

Even just by moving out of her studio space, she creates the
possibility that the construction of a seashell she happens upon
might provide a new breakthrough idea to pursue. In all these ways,
her creative practice is open, expressive, meaning-rich, malleable,
forward-looking, and formidable—the very things a powerful
language should be.

As with the language of man, it's the *meaning* in this image of
Elizabeth's practice and what just happens to be *her* approach to
"speaking creativity" that matters most. As we move forward to
develop our own fluency, our aim isn't to render her same work or

follow her example to the letter, as though she were our language tutor. Her example reminds us to always seek to define and heighten our meaning and use of this language in everything we undertake—drawing a picture, teaching a class, even looking at things we assume to be solid and absolute.

When creativity is the language through which we filter the world and project back what we see, remember, or imagine, then suddenly a stone isn't just a stone.

WHERE

BREAKTHROUGHS

COME FROM

CHAPTER FIVE

WHERE BREAKTHROUGHS COME FROM

This book unfolds over five sections. The first section got you *Ready*. The section you just read helped *Reveal* the basic building blocks for understanding creativity. Across both sections we began to establish a powerful framework. It's time to start seeing what it means to use that framework to *Render* those breakthrough ideas so emblematic of creativity.

The proper starting point for doing so is to understand **THE BREAKTHROUGH SPACE**—the place where those big creative ideas occur. It seems obvious that we want to know what that space is, how to find it, and how to access it. But we'll go one better.

In this *Render* section, you'll learn how to *create* that breakthrough space. Here's the path you'll follow in the next four chapters to render the breakthroughs you seek. . . .

This chapter focuses on identifying and defining the breakthrough space. Think of it not as the *recipe* for creativity but the *kitchen* in which you'll cook up creative ideas many times over. The next chapter, Chapter Six, builds on that knowledge by giving you insights to put yourself in that space more often, thus raising the odds that breakthrough ideas will come. Chapter Seven provides fundamental "tools" you'll need for cooking up ideas in that breakthrough space. You'll quickly discover that when their use becomes your habit, these tools are stepping stones to a mindset that enables you to produce breakthrough ideas not one time but endlessly. Then, to wrap up the *Render* section, Chapter Eight reveals the *one thing* that drives humans forward to create in the first place—something both obvious and surprising.

Paying attention to the breakthrough space and how to tap into it will help you understand your creative capacity like never before. But to increase the odds of that happening, it's vitally important to have the right mindset for this part of your journey. Establishing that mindset starts with keeping this goal in mind: *You want to be able to render the breakthrough space for yourself anytime, anywhere.* And that means applying your creative capacity as a habit rather than an occasional occurrence.

To set the tone for the entire *Render* section, I want to tell you a story that takes it all in. It also happens to be the story of a remarkable even if little known woman, Yoshiko McFarland. For a moment, just focus on that. The lessons and relevance of this story to where we're headed in the next several chapters will soon reveal themselves.

AN OVERLAYING MINDSET

First Impressions. Yoshiko McFarland was born in Japan on December 7, 1941. (Only later did she come to know the date's significance in America's history as the day Pearl Harbor was attacked by the Japanese.) As she wrote, her first "impressed memory" was the burning of Osaka at night in February of 1945.[97] She was only four years old. For nearly twenty-four hours, 247 U.S. aircraft dropped 1,733 tons of napalm, incendiary and other bombing ordinance on the city—something it's fair to say would leave an impression on anyone.[98]

Logic would dictate that these were some disheartening beginnings. But Yoshiko's impression was different than we might expect. Instead of horror, anger, or hatred, these images—coupled with the connection she eventually made between these two events (Pearl Harbor and Osaka)—planted a hope-filled seed in her mind. It came in the form of this question: *How could I come up with a way to make connections across the gap between people and cultures?*

It's a remarkable thought until you realize that it came from, as in Ken Robinson's story, another "girl" casting her gaze beyond the "gap."

A Matter of Habit. The circumstances of her childhood presented ongoing challenges. As a fatherless child in wartime and post-war Japan, Yoshiko knew poverty. Anything she wanted or needed, she had to create herself using branches, wood pieces, stones, bits of cloth, whatever she found around her that others had cast aside.

It was more than "things" that Yoshiko learned to connect and create. Many of the cultural touchstones and traditions of her family and ancestors had been destroyed during the war. Adding to that, the constant moving around and scraping to get by that her family had to do could easily have snuffed out any remaining meaning. Yet Yoshiko used her childhood patterns of play—gathering a scrap here, augmenting a remnant there—to piece together stories and meaning and a sense of who she was, and even what she might yet become. This habit is the very thing that fostered her creativity and framed the way she thought about everything in her life. Such habits are hard to break and rewarding to live by.

Building a Creative Framework. As she came of age, Yoshiko continued to take notice of "promising pieces" and to hone her "quilting" skills. She studied interior design, was influenced by Taoism, met a unique batik artist and became one herself, staged one-person exhibitions, wrote essay series for newspapers, and narrated a television history program. Within each new medium, she sought to bring value and meaning sown in other places and for other purposes while creating new and blended meaning. Each experience was an exercise in bridging a gap and each informed the others. In fact, everything she created told of a "mixing" that's sometimes literal but more often conceptual.

How Yoshiko went about learning, creating, and doing could easily sound chaotic to those whose habit is to remain within set borders and follow prescribed ways. But to her, a logical system emerged across the many lands she journeyed into and out of—one representing, as she described it, "a thick overlay of talents, wisdom, input of labors, and supports accumulated for years."[99] It's something we'd recognize in our own journey, not as a formula but a creative framework comprised of many elements. Hers was a flexible, ever-evolving framework, too. It's not surprising therefore that, out of the use of that framework, she came to conclude that, "Creation is born by binding together," a characterization not unlike how many MacArthur Fellows describe creativity.[100] It is indeed each new "possibility" of creating that dictates and drives the framework's form and use, not the other way around. Her overlay system is most definitely logical, but it is far from limiting.

Earth Language and the Building of a Greater Story. Even this short summary of her journey reveals Yoshiko's creative framework to be ever evolving. What anchors it and centers its logic is that question formed at the start, one she has continued to return to: *How could she make connections across the gap between people and cultures?*

Of course each individual exploration and creation is meant to answer that question; but Yoshiko felt she could go further. *How,* she asked reframing her question, *could the overlay system itself be shared so* anyone, anywhere *could use it to make connections and bridge the gaps?* As she put it, she began to seek a way that all she had learned could be "flexibly tied together . . . like a quilt to wrap the world in peace."[101] Her answer was Earth Language.

Sharing a Creative Framework. Yoshiko described Earth Language (EL) as a kind of reform—a new "space" with new and flexible tools intended to support a different way of thinking and communicating. That's at the high level. But EL is also an actual language, a universal one, intended to be flexible enough to be meet Yoshiko's 'anyone, anywhere' criteria.

Made up of seventy "base" written symbols (lines, circles, arcs, and common picture-like characters), EL's foundational components can be combined, "pluraled," and layered in infinite ways to express ideas and meaning. As one powerful example, in EL a circle with a simple arc above it (as if the circle had a hat) is the symbol for "brain." At least, that's what the symbol means in "noun" form. But as a verb, the same symbol can mean "to think," "to consider," or even "to raise a question" (as in "to make the brain work").

Noun or verb, *this* symbol's meaning is an overlay of *other* symbols, each with their own components of meaning. For example, the *circle* symbol signifies the "world" or a "globe." But in Yoshiko's design of EL, that same circle is also imbued with the idea of "something substantial" or the "main thing," depending on how it's used or "combined" with other symbols. Similarly, the *arc* symbol in EL, when drawn rainbow-like, embodies the ideas of "time," "nature," and "motion." Yet when that same arc is flipped top to bottom into the shape of a smile, it means "the creation of something by a human." Yoshiko's EL is a language emphasizing shared meaning and use, with its structure remaining ever flexible.

Crossing a Border. To see Yoshiko's Earth Language as simply another output of her creative ways would be to sell it short and miss its greater value. More than a culminating expression of *her* creative habit, Earth Language is a metaphor for a framework and a mindset needed for anyone to speak the language of man. You'll come to understand this more as our journey continues. But right here and right now, her story already offers a helpful frame of reference even just for understanding where breakthroughs come from.

Keep in mind these elements of Yoshiko's story—the need for meaning; questioning and noticing as a matter of habit; seeing and venturing across borders; and seeking to intersect seemingly disparate pieces into new, larger, and more valuable wholes. In this chapter, you will come to know these elements intimately, each of them necessary to create the breakthrough space. The point of sharing this particular story isn't to suggest that you should replicate what Yoshiko did, but simply to see EL as one manifestation of a vibrant creative framework that facilitates breakthrough ideas.

It's time to move into the breakthrough space. To do that, learning from Yoshiko's example, we'll let three questions guide us:

Who sees breakthroughs and why?

Where do they look?

As they look, what are they after?

The balance of this chapter will be organized in three sections, one each around these questions. Within each of the three sections you'll find stories that teach you about the breakthrough space, and better still, take you into it. By this chapter's end, you'll have answers to these three questions and be well-versed in how to use *our* universal language—creativity—to create *your* own breakthrough space anytime, anywhere.

Who Sees Breakthroughs?

It's tempting to conclude that certain people have a built-in advantage for breakthrough ideas. But it's not true. There is no lucky strain in the gene pool, no personality type, and no economic background or educational advantage that sets people apart in this respect. Certain habits and mindsets do, however, lead to a far greater incidence of breakthrough ideas. The *practiced noticer*, the *luck maker*, and the *deliberate pause taker* reflect such habits. Because they do, people who practice these habits have the highest likelihood of seeing breakthroughs.

Let's consider each to see why and do so by beginning with a story.

THE "PRACTICED NOTICER" SEES BREAKTHROUGHS

Taking Notice. A rich and underused word, the strict definition of a *noticer* is *someone who takes notice* as in "she was a careful noticer of details." But more subtly and powerfully, a **PRACTICED NOTICER** is *a person who becomes aware*. The distinction between the two is the difference between simple fact checking and *perceiving the possible*.

Though the *concept* itself wasn't new to me, I first heard the *word* noticer while listening to a talk by Ken Burns. He's the prolific documentary filmmaker who has created such penetrating visionary works as *Baseball, The Civil War, Jefferson, Jazz,* and *The Roosevelts*.

Burns is widely regarded as deeply creative, genius even, and there's no argument that his work has changed the landscape if not the definition of documentary filmmaking. But as with Yoshiko and EL, it isn't what Burns produced that offers us needed insight into where breakthroughs come from; it's how he goes about doing what he does. Burns is a practiced noticer. To get a good sense of how and why practiced noticers see breakthroughs more than most, it helps to spend a little time understanding what Ken Burns does, how he does it, and why he used the term "noticer" in his talk.

What Noticing Looks Like to Ken Burns. Ken Burns sees the subtleties in things most people take for granted. He becomes aware of patterns, many sitting out in the open for all to see, yet ones that have somehow been missed by others. Here's an example.

In his groundbreaking film *The Civil War*, Burns highlighted a now iconic photograph of a group gathered for Abraham Lincoln's inauguration. The picture is a grainy group shot and not even a remarkable one at that. It's why before he made *The Civil War*, the photo was only known to a few historians.

But in it, Burns noticed something more. Slowly moving from a wide view of the group, Burns gradually magnified his focus to a single face among several hundred—a face we've looked at a thousand times elsewhere but never seen in the *larger* context of a "person," his "history," even his thoughts, dreams, ambitions, and biases. Burns took us into the photo and to that one face—the face of Lincoln's assassin, John Wilkes Booth, as he stands eerily in the back of the crowd watching his future target sworn in as president. Suddenly, this blasé old photograph took on a whole new significance. It connected moments across years and meaning across the borders planted firmly in our minds around these people and events. Simple noticing led to a breakthrough.

A Habit of the Mind and What It Can Reveal. What makes Ken Burns stand out isn't his skill as a filmmaker or his ever-growing catalog of films, all of which are undeniably impressive. It's his practice of noticing, not an ability some have and others lack the capacity for. *Anyone* can notice. But because it's his *habit*, once he begins to take notice, he sees lines, expressions, head tilts, clothing textures—an endless array of details that normally don't draw more than a passing glance from others.

It's practice that yields Burns the added ability to *connect* the things he sees to one another, noticing what fits, what's valuable, and what's new. When you hear Burns describe his practice, you can tell it doesn't just take place when he's working. It's part of who he is in every setting. Noticing so consumes his way of being that you can sense that he doesn't only notice with his "eyes"; he notices with *all* the senses. Sound and texture, even taste and scent seem considered. Thus, his films are an eye-opening rendering of his skill as a noticer and of the connections he makes.

While Burns' ability to notice is remarkable, more extraordinary still is his ability to awaken it in *us*. Noticing isn't just something he *does*; it's become the foundation of how he *communicates*—the central component of his "overlay system" as a filmmaker that he, like Yoshiko, seeks to pass on to us. And so his films don't just show us what he's noticed, they show us *how* to notice and make us want to do it ourselves. Astutely sensing that hunger, years ago Apple Inc. added the "Ken Burns Effect" to its video software iMovie. It gives users a tool to create a similar effect of scanning and weaving together images and the ability to move in and take notice. Of course, you'd have to buy an Apple device to get that particular tool, but the real power of noticing comes at no cost at all. You already own that equipment. To awaken it, all you need is *practice*.

Practice Makes Perception. It's easy to look at someone as accomplished as Ken Burns and conclude that his kind of noticing is the exception to the rule. As if to embolden the myth, when I first heard Burns use the word *noticer,* he was lecturing about three other accomplished individuals featured in his films: Thomas Jefferson, Frank Lloyd Wright, and Mark Twain. These three could appear like a club of creative geniuses. But the point of his talk wasn't to push the status of these individuals further above the rest of us. Instead, it seemed clear Burns wanted his audience to notice something we normally wouldn't about them. It's something shared and at the heart of why they were capable of the breakthroughs we've come to know them by, something far less exceptional or grand than what each did with it.

But first Burns set about shaking up our default way of thinking about these men. As if to make clear there were no special genes or special traits they alone shared, he began his talk by pointing out how completely *different* Jefferson, Wright, and Twain were from one another. A Renaissance man and founding father (Jefferson), a tradition-shattering architect (Wright), and an iconic writer (Twain), each living ages apart from one another couldn't be more different, right? By placing them side by side (as they're not normally considered), Burns forced us to reconsider what we saw. Only then could we come to understand the one thing that *did* connect them.

Having awakened us to a new way of seeing, Burns offered, "Mark Twain was an enormous *noticer,*" a person for whom "the ordinariness of life and things and events had mystical possibility."[102] Since he'd already made parallel observations about the other two, his comment caused the gears in our heads to lock in to this new connection. Suddenly we could see that, along with Twain, Jefferson and Wright were also enormous noticers, the difference being that their noticing had taken place in different settings from Twain's and from each other's.

Though their life paths had varied widely, this shared habit of noticing could be traced to each individual and also to the seeds of each of their many creative and diverse accomplishments. That was *their* confluence. But as he spoke, Burns was making the connection between what *they* did and what *we*, his audience, might yet do. And the connection was a simple and subtle piece of advice: Practice taking notice.

Burns was certainly allowing that Jefferson, Wright, and Twain "appeared" to be of a higher order—*beholders*, even *percipients*. But by shifting our focus, through his well-honed craft, Burns was allowing us to see that they simply employed more practiced noticing. It was a seemingly elite level owed to nothing more than the practice, the habit, and the mindset of noticing.

Each individual he described had formed a habit of seeing distinctions, connections, and possibilities in the world around them. This, Burns was saying, had played a significant role, perhaps the most important role in enabling them to conjure up the grand ideas they pursued in the world—ideas that forever changed the lives of Americans and the world at large. But what Burns was really doing, I believe, was employing his own practice once again. He was drawing our attention to that "face in the crowd" as if to say "this person" could be the *next* to have the breakthrough idea that changes us all. For everyone in the audience that night, the face was our own.

The Truly Grand. Exceptional. Genius even. That's how these three "creative icons" Jefferson, Twain, and Wright *appear* to us and how we *speak* of them. It's also how we describe the things they did. But *all of it*, even the outcomes, began with something far simpler, far more common, and far more important: the *practice of noticing*.

As Burns pointed out in his talk, "All of us are in the business of ideas."[103] That's true, but this statement risks being slightly misleading. We like ideas, but we also care about what endures. *Lasting impact* is what we want, remember, and build on. It's what allows us to progress from one idea to the next. We want the staying power that allows the idea generation to be iterative. It's the practice of "noticing" that enables that idea engine. Therefore, to find the breakthrough space, we need to be practiced noticers.

THE "LUCK MAKER" SEES BREAKTHROUGHS

As Luck Would Have It. Many people think the breakthrough idea isn't a matter of mindset or noticing or any other insight you'll learn about in this chapter. Rather, they insist on believing that breakthroughs result from pure luck. If you happen to adhere to this view, you might find the longstanding science behind luck eye-opening.

Yes, you read correctly; there's a science behind luck that reveals what it really is, and years of data substantiate its findings. And those findings reveal that the old adage is true: *Luck is made.* So too are breakthroughs and indeed the space in which they occur. And looking at the luck maker's mindset helps us see why.

Science Over Happenstance. Among the most recognized experts in the field of luck science is British professor Richard Wiseman, author of *The Luck Factor* and a researcher in this area for more than two decades. As Wiseman wrote, "Luck is not a magical ability or a gift from the gods. Instead, it is a state of mind—a way of thinking and behaving."[104]

Despite the truth, Wiseman says (and perhaps your own observations confirm) most people both talk and think of luck as something floating around "out there" waiting for the lucky person to happen upon it. Two additional common but false beliefs are that "luck happens to some more than others" and when it does, "luck happens in lightning-strike fashion." For more people than you might think, these beliefs are knit closely to their impressions about creativity and who ends up being creative as well. To others, however, the whole lightning-strike thing is symbolic of our collective misunderstanding of creativity. It can literally make them shudder (and you'll meet one of these people shortly).

Impressions aside, the findings of Wiseman's rigorous experiments argue that luck can be influenced and even created. Behind our ability to do these things is a mindset, one that aligns with and expands upon the mindset of the practiced noticer.

Principled and Practiced vs. Just Lucky. Wiseman boiled down his observations about lucky people to **FOUR LUCK PRINCIPLES**, four habits that when practiced result in a higher incidence of what many deem luck.

The first principle is that lucky people *create, notice,* and *act upon* chance opportunities across their lives, the habit of which results in things that make them *appear* unusually lucky. Put simply, they are good noticers. And because they're in the *habit* of noticing and have experienced that luck follows such noticing, lucky people tend to spend a lot of time purposely thinking about what they notice and considering what it could mean.

Rather than noticing something for its face value, they think about "what could be made" from what they notice. It's a pattern connection similar to that of Ken Burns, but with a very forward orientation. You could say lucky people *perceive potential* by not simply noticing what's there but sensing what *could* be there. That potential becomes the driver that leads them to *act*. The action often takes the form of playing with their ideas and teasing out the nuances. But it also results in actively choosing to put themselves in *more* situations where they're likely to notice *other* things. As they act in this way, they have a tendency to convert what they notice into "opportunities"—ones that arise out of nowhere and appear *lucky.*

The second "luck" principle Wiseman found is that lucky people *trust their intuition.* Intuition and a close and practiced connection with it are often attributed to creative people as well. Their "gut" says something's possible in what they see and tells them it's worth checking out. Because they trust their intuition, they're willing to *go toward* this hunch of theirs, even when it's unfamiliar or outside their comfort zone. As Peter Huybers noted about creative people, lucky people also are willing to *believe* before they *see.*

Wiseman's last two principles about so-called lucky people are related. The third principle is that lucky people *expect good luck.* And the fourth and final one is that when they encounter *bad* luck, *they turn it into good luck.* As you read these observations, be careful not to dismiss them as positive thinking psychobabble. They yield something fundamental to your ability to tap into your creative capacity.

As humans, *what we expect* has a great deal to do with *what we actually see and do*. (In Chapter Three, Carol Dweck's growth vs. fixed mindset research conveyed this same insight arrived at from a different path.) Expecting that something lucky or good or breakthrough will happen isn't a *guarantee* that something will actually happen, any more than positive thinking is a guarantee of only positive things occurring. But this misses the point—and the insight.

What Wiseman saw in "lucky people" and Dweck observed in people with a "growth mindset" applies to creative thinkers as well—that is, all of them have a forward-moving orientation. They fully expect that the universe of possibilities is constantly expanding, that their minds are similarly capable of expansion and growth, and that because their overall "tilt" is *forward leaning*, the eventual discovery of something better is inevitable. In other words, so-called lucky people believe that good things come not to those who are patient but to those who pursue.

Lucky people notice breakthroughs because they have mastered the Burns Effect—turning what appears as still photos into stirring moving pictures. Like Ken Burns himself, lucky people don't possess anything you don't have too. The distinction comes with awareness and practice.

THE "DELIBERATE PAUSE TAKER" SEES BREAKTHROUGHS

Alongside the question of *who* sees breakthroughs, you might be wondering *where and when* do those who speak creativity become aware of breakthroughs? The answer is deceivingly simple: in deliberate pauses. You might know other terms that feel similar and offer overlap—inflection points or transitions, for example. But the expression **A DELIBERATE PAUSE**, like the term *noticer*, speaks of far more than we might assume. And to be sure, those who take them see more.

A POWERFUL TOOL FOR: CREATING

In my 2009 book *A Deliberate Pause: Entrepreneurship and its Moment in Human Progress,* I described the dynamic this way: "A deliberate pause is a conscious moment in which we open our minds and ask, 'why are things the way they are?' and wonder aloud, 'how could life be better?' It is a natural and uniquely human inclination" to think in this way. "It's also the critical factor that sparks fresh ideas and is seized on . . . to catalyze seismic changes—ones that allow humanity to progress."[105] Without a doubt, the pause is "where and when" we become aware of breakthroughs.

As we first learned from Sarah Kagan in Chapter Two, at a minimum, pausing creates an opportunity for us to check our creativity compass. Deliberately doing so reminds us not to assume that the way we travel, the place in which we do it, or the reward we expect will remain constants. But more than simply checking in, pausing deliberately and often allows you to become *aware*. And when you are aware, you just flat out see more.

Pausing isn't hard, but it's an action easily skipped. When you skip it, you miss the possible—be it a possible opportunity or even a possible threat. When on the other hand you practice pausing, you see that the deliberate pause becomes a powerful, nuanced, and highly effective tool for creating.

A POWERFUL TOOL FOR: CONNECTING

So far, we've described the pause at the individual level. But as you'll increasingly come to understand, creativity is most often a collective undertaking—even at the most basic level of getting others to see what you see.

Consider the environment in which MacArthur Fellow Steve Goodman seeks to create. Officially, Steve is a conservation biologist with the Field Museum in Chicago. His goal, however, has been to preserve a rare and highly threatened ecology half a world away in Madagascar. While Steve may have grand visions of protecting the country's habitats, he knows Madagascar as an island nation belongs to many others, perhaps least of all to him. Thus, to actually take hold and bear fruit, whatever creative ideas Steve might have for protecting its habitats must serve *others'* needs and fit *their* visions.

Drawing on our quilting analogy, Steve is but one contributor to the larger fabric. It's not uncommon for bright, creative people in one place (say Steve in Chicago) to dream up a breakthrough idea (saving a rare and fragile ecosystem) that they imagine being realized somewhere else (in this case, Madagascar), and then to go to that place assuming it all will just unfold as imagined and according to plan. Steve is keenly aware that the ecosystem he wants to protect is part of its own larger quilt—the entire country of Madagascar and anyone who touches or is touched by it. More, his idea to protect that ecosystem is only a single conservation idea among many, and conservation itself is but one way to use the land. In this context, Steve's big idea and his power to see it realized can feel quite small. Even the greatest breakthrough ideas meet with this kind of challenge; it's the rule, not the exception. With your big creative idea in hand, you might just charge ahead into frustration and wonder later why your creative brilliance never materialized.

A habit of pausing is one of the best ways to see this reality before it becomes a foregone conclusion. Pausing is also a valuable aid for navigating the path to realizing the creative idea as it inevitably changes. But equally important, pausing represents a tool for connecting. It can serve not only as a powerful means for seeing how others view things, it can act as the seed that helps grow an environment in which to create *with* others. In this regard too, Steve's creative practice and deep experience stretching over two decades serves as a wonderful example.

A POWERFUL TOOL FOR: CREATING CULTURE

Steve has recognized that pausing is powerful in a multitude of ways. Because of its versatility, pausing has become the modus operandi for his conservation team's work in total. "Among those of us who've done this for a long time, we focus first on pausing to observe and appreciate where we are," Steve said. "What inhibits our progress, even our ability to think in new ways and see better approaches, is doing things too quickly, rushing progress or working too hard to define the outcome," said Steve. This doesn't just apply to how they manage the here and now; it doesn't apply only to the current team members either. Rather, it's what they strive to instill as part of an ongoing culture. "That pausing," Steve noted, "is central when we recruit and train others."[106]

Pausing isn't just central "philosophically"; it's integral from the very first step Steve and his Madagascar colleagues take with new recruits, a first step that often surprises those joining. "First we send them out to observe and appreciate where they are."[107] They are put in the environment that Steve dreams of saving, but they aren't instructed or trained to observe in a certain way. There's no structure or rules to adhere to—no memorizing, no defined goals, no lectures on how to do this, no best practices taught on how to save that. New participants are simply invited to go to the place and see what they see. As much as they may learn about themselves or the rare ecosystems to which they go, through this practice, they are learning to take a deliberate pause.

Contrasting his creative cultural way to what he described as more typical, Steve referenced previous experiences in the United States. "In the States, we rush to act and produce the data and outcomes 'yesterday,'" Steve said. "In Madagascar, we prioritize the *understanding*. We want understanding in a holistic sense. So we've built a process that reminds us to stop and think about that often."[108] More than planting creative ideas, Steve, like Yoshiko McFarland and Ken Burns, continually builds a shared creative framework as a priority.

Referring to his use of the pause culturally and ongoing in Madagascar, he said, "It's not only the natural environment of (the Madagascans') country we want them to observe and absorb, or even our ideas about conservation. We want to place them in a position and mindset to sense *'FIT.'*" This is something Steve feels the practice of pausing deliberately tunes you into. And what does he mean by fit? "The fit with their lives and their dreams; their own fit in the natural world and in the world at large; the fit between their efforts to protect their world and what doing so offers back to them—these are the obvious things," Steve said. "But the *concept* of fit itself is the real prize."

Fit is how you see what's working and what's not. It's what thereafter catalyzes creative thinking. It's how you see your vital role in it all. He said, "It's an ability that can be ported anywhere you dream or create. You just have to make room to see it."[109] And fit—or misfit—can only be recognized if you consciously pause.

It would be impossible not to notice that Steve described an entire environment and way of being that's been deliberately built around the pause. In so doing, he's made it clear that the practice of pausing isn't just a reason those who use it see more breakthroughs. It's key to the entire creative process and all who contribute to it.

CREATING SPACE THROUGH THE PAUSE

The Pause Fits—Everywhere. While Steve's story is an emphatic affirmation that we should pause if we want to be creative, you might wonder if the insights he reveals about deliberately pausing are too extreme to apply other places? If anything, the reverse is true: The extremes of Madagascar prove the versatility and resilience the pause can bring. Or as Grammy-nominated composer and MacArthur Fellow John Harbison rhetorically asked, "What creation of any value can be produced in a culture that doesn't have pauses in it?"

While the "raw" world gives us ample opportunities to pause and progress, our typical internal programming, even our societal messaging, often muffles those signals. Pausing isn't built into our programming. We have to train ourselves for it. And we must do so not just because it's a good habit to form if we want to be more creative, but also because the world around us *demands* pausing. As John said, "Frequently the world around us is asking us to stop and attend to the many specific signals that are so clearly out of the flow—the very signals we most often wave off. But it strikes me that rather than being just an option, we *need* to be interrupted and not just carried along with the flow. We need to be jostled out of the immediate. We need to create space. Failing to do so is growing into a new and radical problem we grossly underestimate."[110]

We often assume it's hard to find the time to pause, yet even the smallest pause can make room for more. In fact, the very space we need in order to take a pause is actually created by our practice of pausing. Think about the first thing Steve invites his trainees to do—to go to the space in which they think they want to create and then simply notice. This is less a suggestion to take more time and more a suggestion about how to use time. The more they take notice in places they already go, the more the pause becomes part of their natural flow. Bit by bit, slowly and gradually, each pause makes room for others. They layer on top of one another a little at a time. As they do, they quilt together into what feels like bigger pauses, ones that inevitably result in bigger understanding and a bigger space in which to create.

Back to You. As if extending the thought, Susan Meiselas told me, "Creativity means creating space. In that space, what's perhaps most important and conducive to creating is being able to respond to instinct."[111]

"Creativity relies on instinct," Susan said. "But even knowing what your instinct is begins first with trusting yourself." Only when you learn to trust yourself can you fully tap your creative capacity. Only by knowing your instinct can you notice in a way that helps you experience that sense of something valuable and worth pursuing. But here's the wondrous, iterative power that is the pause: It is *both* the "space" Susan and others say we need for creating *and* the place where we come to trust ourselves and know the nature of our instinct.

Your creative capacity remains raw until you choose to shape it. So does the breakthrough space—until you choose to actively create it. Trust is what solidifies these things and pausing brings that. It's a cycle, a circular path that nurtures itself every time you walk it.

Where Do They Look?

At the beginning of this chapter, we established three questions and then explored a rich overlay of insights into the first: *Who sees breakthroughs?* What you didn't read was something like "Joe sees breakthroughs" or "Picasso sees breakthroughs"—no names, professions, or levels of fame based on some elusive ranking of individual people or what they create. Instead, you've discovered that people who have certain deliberate habits—noticing, "making" luck, pausing—are those who consistently see breakthroughs and with more frequency than most. This good news means *you* can do this, too. But it's just the first step in helping you understand *where* breakthroughs come from. Which brings us to the second of the three questions: *Where do they look?* What follows isn't simply an answer to where those who seem to disproportionately see breakthroughs cast their gaze; it's unwavering advice about where *you* need to start looking.

LOOK IN THE "ADJACENT POSSIBLE"

Surprising as it may sound, the most productive place to find breakthrough ideas is right next door. It's a place Fellow Stu Kauffman calls the "adjacent possible," a telling term we'll explore in this section. But first let's talk about where good ideas really come from.

WHERE GOOD IDEAS "REALLY" COME FROM

When we think about creativity, we often think about big ideas—those groundbreaking, progress-enhancing, life-changing ideas we secretly wish *we* had thought of. Our impressions about big ideas are most often formed in reverse. From a hindsight view, we see the size of their impact and attribute a similar scale to how we imagine the idea must have been born. To come up with the telephone, the Internet, democracy, or other innovations that have contributed to human progress in a lasting way, we tell ourselves that the idea maker must have been hit in the head by a lightning strike of an idea.

But when you talk to the humans behind such heroic tales and look at the facts behind all such creations, you see something far more like David than Goliath. That's what Steven Johnson set out to prove in his book *Where Good Ideas Come From*. What he concluded was that good ideas and innovations slowly ripple across time rather than occur in enormous rogue waves appearing from out of nowhere.[112] He wasn't merely speculating either.

Across centuries of human history he meticulously cataloged a consistent pattern of innovations that gradually revealed themselves in steady cycles and not, as we so often think, in single grand moments. Johnson found the biggest innovations emerged one small idea at a time, slowly linking and layering in a vast web of intersections that, seen in the rearview mirror, only look like one big idea.

That misconception laid to rest, it makes one wonder, as Johnson did, when it comes to creativity, more than just looking for the wrong *thing* (breakthrough ideas occurring all at once), could we also be looking in the wrong *places*? And to confirm his suspicion, one of the insightful people Johnson turned to was Stu Kauffman. Stu, a prolific creator across many fields, was emphatic in his answer—stop looking so big and so far away. He told Johnson to look in **THE ADJACENT POSSIBLE**, and when he did, suddenly Johnson had a named source for the pattern he'd seen across human creation and innovation. Let me share with you what Stu told Johnson and me.

UNDERSTANDING THE ADJACENT POSSIBLE

As he explained to me, Stu has come to understand that big ideas are the product of a journey, one that begins and continues to unfold through a habit of exploring things "nearby." That nearby can be mental or physical. But in our conversation Stu used the more physical analogy of crossing a large stream to convey the insight.

The Place We Can Reach. Stream crossing begins with small exploratory moves. In fact, Stu pointed out, sometimes when you come to a stream your first thoughts and actions aren't even about crossing. From my own childhood I know this to be true: Arriving at the edge of an unknown body of water, my pressing interest was to play and explore. But whether you intend to cross or not, it's widely known that no one who makes any progress ever just hops to the middle part of the stream or jumps immediately to the opposite shore.

Thoughtfully considered, you already know how it works: We look for the next closest place to where we are—a rock, a log, or a sandbar—in other words, something within our reach and onto which we can step. Bit-by-bit, often moving backwards or sideways, sometimes combining rocks into a pile, or turning rocks and logs into a partial bridge, we begin to consider ways to cross.

Stu will tell you that we arrive at big ideas in the very same way and for very good reasons.

Why We Go and Should Go There. First, what's adjacent is *right there*, so in one sense, why not explore it? Second, because it's right there it's also far less intimidating than some place beyond our view. Effort and fear are both major inhibitors to creativity. Exploring what's adjacent helps us overcome both. With one foot in the "known," stepping into what's new yet still close by feels more like extending our walk in the neighborhood to add a new block, and less like how we feel when we think of climbing Mt. Everest.

A third reason we come to our edges, psychic and physical, is that instinctually we know that what's adjacent is also at the border of the "known" and the "new." In Chapter Three, Arthur Koestler made clear that creativity lies there. We are naturally drawn there because we sense that place to have the highest odds of giving us those *ah!*, *aha!*, or *ha ha!* breakthrough feelings. It may not be conscious, but our standard-issue software attracts us to the adjacent possible.

On top of all of this, looking in the adjacent possible for breakthrough ideas makes sense for a fourth and far more important reason: *History proves it to be the place where breakthrough ideas actually come from.* And that's exactly what Stu Kauffman and Steven Johnson have been saying from the start. If you want to increase your odds of arriving at a breakthrough idea, look in the adjacent possible.

WHAT THE ADJACENT POSSIBLE CAN LOOK LIKE

Bookmark the adjacent possible insight in your brain for a moment, pause, and consider this example from my conversation with architect Ric Scofidio. His story not only helps us understand where big ideas come from; it poignantly reminds us of where they do not.

Today's Forecast—No Lightning Strikes. What's immediately obvious about Ric is that he cares deeply about the *idea* of creativity and the *power* of creative thought. He also believes in the importance of *deepening* and *sharing* our understanding of creativity. His view of creativity as a perpetual learning isn't just talk and theory; Ric *lives* this belief.

While an award-winning architect in his own right, Ric credits his most successful projects to the practice of collaborating with others, including his business partner and wife Liz Diller. From everything they say, write, and do, it's clear that for Ric and Liz, creativity is a shared exchange—of insights, ideas, lessons, and credit. Reflecting that, they were awarded the MacArthur Fellowship *together*, a rare exception to the individual recipient rule.

However, I almost didn't get the chance to benefit from Ric's thoughts because he absolutely did not want to talk about lightning strikes. To put it mildly, he doesn't believe that breakthrough ideas come from out of nowhere, in a flash, unearned. And they aren't the result of "dumb luck" either (as Richard Wiseman would concur).

But so prolific is the belief in lightning strikes that most times when people seek out Ric to talk about creativity, it's lightning strikes they want to discuss. After assuring Ric I wasn't seeking to discuss the weather, he thankfully agreed to share his insights born of experience and observation, not rumor and myth.

"Creativity takes an enormous amount of going through ideas," Ric said. "Sorting. Refining. Discovering. Challenging. Tuning in and tossing out—and most often with all of this occurring in the mundane. It's the process of going deeply into something that will eventually be rewarding. But having a single big idea happen in a flash is nonsense."[113]

It's Not Just Where You Look But How You Look. Already you know a lot about Ric's creative practice: His creative ideas don't happen in an instant. Many of his best creations result from an exchange with those around him. Creativity for Ric isn't something he "knows" in the permanent sense. Instead, it's a lesson and an ongoing exercise—his ability to create results from an enormous amount of sifting and fine-tuning, which is usually unglamorous.

The one word that comes to mind for me to summarize this is "gradual." If Stu were to describe how Ric creates, he'd likely say "adjacently." All that sorting, refining, challenging, and fine-tuning Ric does happens gradually, but it also happens close by. He creates right where he resides.

Still on the whole we persistently resist Ric's advice that this is the surest way to create. In fact, wrote Steven Johnson, "We have a natural tendency to romanticize breakthrough innovations." We imagine "momentous ideas transcending their surroundings, a gifted mind somehow seeing over the detritus of old ideas and ossified tradition. But ideas are works of bricolage; they're built *out of* that detritus."[114]

Don't let Johnson's choice of a few uncommon words throw you off. *Bricolage* is the French word for *tinkering*. *Detritus* is the stuff thrown away, *the overlooked*, the things around you at the edges of your world and just beyond. You'd miss them if your creative habits were other than what Ric and, indeed, everyone you've heard from described.

Seeing Big Isn't Magic. As unglamorous as it may sound, it's this pedestrian practice of Ric's that begets big ideas. The High Line project that Ric, Liz, and their partners conceived is one wonderful example.

Before Ric and company, the High Line was nothing more than a near-century-old dilapidated raised railroad track spanning twenty blocks in the heart of New York City's west side. For more than three decades, none of the tens of thousands who walked by the abandoned elevated train tracks could see them as more than an eyesore. In other words, this "detritus" was immediately adjacent to the citizens of lower Manhattan every single day, and yet they couldn't see the "breakthrough" in it that Ric and his partners did.

What Diller, Scofidio & Renfro (Ric's partnership) saw was a raised paradise of walkways and gardens, fountains and performance areas—an urban park like no other. And that is what those abandoned tracks have become. It's why the High Line is now a destination for Manhattan locals and tourists alike. When you stroll its pathways, walk in its water features, and lounge on its sculptured part-art and part-respite benches, it's easy to think of this idea as inevitable—as if lightning had struck. But as big as it was and beautiful as it has become, until Ric came along, others just couldn't see it.

What explains this? If it wasn't lightning striking him or some magical ability of his, how did he see what others did not?

Ric answered these questions by explaining not how his team formulated the High Line idea but how he renders creativity every single day.

A Matter of Habit. "I don't believe in prescriptions," Ric said about how creativity works for him. "I don't believe in the universal way." One can imagine others who might say with conviction that a freight rail track is forever a freight rail track. Prescribed. End of story. But Ric said, "It's more about raising a series of questions. You have to be inquisitive, not just an absorbing sponge.

"Pieces don't just fit; you have to discover their intersections. It is the process of asking and exploring, not just receiving and moving forward on a flat, unchanged line. Eventually," Ric said, "things move you forward, or they don't. And even when they don't, it's telling you something. Both asking and exploring move you forward *if* you are tuned in enough to see it."

The path to creative insight is far from a straight-line undertaking. It's not even a line at all. There's no universal way. It's an exploration, like picking your way across a stream—a stepping stone here, a fallen tree there. If you take Ric's advice, you get more creative by getting in the habit of looking for those stepping stones.

Independent of any one project, that's what Ric does. Metaphorically, he picks up stones in the shallows, turns them over, even tosses a few new ones in the stream of possibilities. He's not specifically in search of a path but he's always open to one emerging. By the time someone asks him what to do with an old, rundown elevated freight rail track, he's already seeing ways to bridge the gap between an abandoned line and the High Line. And he does so in ways most others can't—not because he's specially equipped, but because he's constantly using his equipment; not because he can leap tall buildings in a single bound, but because he spends a lot of time walking around and through the ideas and things right outside his building. And because he's always playing with the possibilities around him, he's in the mindset to take what others consider huge leaps to a big idea. That's how an old railroad track became a beautiful garden path.

MORE POSSIBLE THAN MEETS THE EYE

The adjacent possible is a neat concept in part because it's simple. But Ric's story ought to hint that there's more to it than the simplicity of being able to step into this space and explore one little step or question at a time. Steven Johnson described an even larger potential this way: "The *adjacent possible* is a kind of shadow future, a map of all the ways in which the present can reinvent itself."[115]

That makes the adjacent possible sound big, perhaps even formidable. Well, it is and it isn't. As Stu described it to me, the adjacent possible *is* right there—in your mind and in the world around you. And part of it *is* made up of things you know plus new things that have existed nearby and simply gone unnoticed. You can access and play with it all just by being willing to put your toe across the line and see what you might find.

That's the simplicity of the adjacent possible. But as Stu described it, a funny thing happens when you do put your toe across the line. "As soon as you go into this space of possibility, you do more than access things that were *already there and possible*. You actually create *more* possibilities."[116]

This is where the adjacent possible becomes mighty in your hands, capable and worthy of inspiring respect from even the most hedgehog-minded. You can sense this added level of creative power in the way Ric's day-to-day practice bloomed into a big idea like the High Line. But to make this idea of creating more possibilities clearer, let's examine an example from Stu's own creative practice.

THE ADJACENT GETS BIGGER: THE SANTA FE INSTITUTE

Seeing the Possible. Stu Kauffman was one of the early collaborators at a place called the Santa Fe Institute (SFI). The story of how SFI was created goes something like this. Several scientists working in academia but in different departments realized a pattern. They noticed that whenever they ventured across the borders of their departments and into one another's spaces—for example, the biologist into the chemistry department or the neurologist into philosophy—they frequently encountered new ideas and gained new insights. More, they observed that, on the whole, they were seeing a higher number of breakthrough ideas this way at the same time they were seeing a decline in big ideas within the silos of their own departments. Exploring beyond their prescribed borders, they sensed, could bring forth more new ideas, while at the same time revitalizing their home fronts.

Excited by this and realizing that many of their colleagues elsewhere were having similar experiences, they lobbied their institution to promote a breaking down of walls between the departments. This wasn't a proposal of anarchy. Instead, it was a suggestion to their institution to encourage the practice of looking next door to expand how they thought, learned, and created.

The Possible Rejected—Now What? The answer from the higher ups at their institution was unambiguous but not uncommon. The presidents, provosts, and deans considered this "simple idea" to be threatening. To them, it embodied a risk to how these institutions functioned. "No" was their answer.

As it turned out, the scientists' colleagues at other institutions were making similar arguments that were met with the same response: No. Interestingly, the administrative powers-that-be often understood the potential the scientists saw, but they couldn't see beyond their own models and ways of doing things to change. "Borders are borders," seemed to be their conclusion. "Just go back to your lab and come up with a big idea." But the scientists knew doing that would be like farming in desert sands after having discovered the rich soil adjacent to their labs.

How did the scientists respond? They chose to *believe before they saw* and took action. Knowing and believing in the potential of the adjacent possible, they left to create their own breakthrough space, and the Santa Fe Institute was born.

Creating "New" Space. "Those early years at SFI were the best example of the kind of cross-border exchange that leads to truly breakthrough ideas," Stu shared. "We all borrowed from one another in this wonderfully co-creative environment where 'possible' was always right around the corner and all you had to do was leave your desk to find it."[117]

Like Ric's approach but on a larger organizational scale, at SFI there were no set paths for how to cross the streams. More often than not, even the agenda and expectation of outcomes weren't set ahead of time. As their pre-SFI experiences had suggested, developing and playing in the adjacent possible became their focus.

It paid off. Together, these explorers of the adjacent possible spawned and continue to birth huge breakthrough ideas across disciplines, minds, and methods. Reflecting on this and mirroring Ric's comments, Stu acknowledged, "None of us could have done what we did alone. We borrowed from each other, just like improv comedy."[118]

The adjacent was not only in their experiments but also in their experiences and indeed in their culture. Perhaps most rewarding, even surprising, was that the biggest breakthroughs came not from the "known" space of combining one another's knowledge territories (as in, "You know chemistry, I know geology, let's see what we can make from the pieces we already know"). The biggest breakthroughs resulted from the "new" space—one created when, by stepping into the adjacent possible, they *expanded* it. The breakthrough space came, in other words, from that "shadow future" Johnson described— something that became tangible and expanded every time someone explored it.

Tangible Outcomes from the Possible. The Santa Fe Institute is well known to those who believe the next big breakthroughs in science will come not from *within* any one sector but from the *intersection* of fields. When such areas of understanding intersect, the result is far greater than 1 + 1 = 2. More often, it looks like 1 + 1 = 11. Not only did the breakthrough *space* become tangible; so did the actual *outputs* derived from it.

In *The Medici Effect,* Frans Johansson described one wonderful example at SFI in which a France Telecom R&D engineer casually met an ecologist at an SFI seminar. The ecologist specialized in studying insects such as bees, butterflies, and ants. As Johansson described it, "They talked about, among other things, how ants find food."[119] Can you imagine the setting? Perhaps the two were sitting at lunch and knew the basics of what one another did. Seeing ants crawl across the ground, the telecom engineer may have simply said out loud, "I've always wondered how ants find their way to the picnic so quickly," to which the ecologist would have replied, "Well, that's easy" and offered the answer from his known territory. After a quick "wonder" outside of their separate spaces, they "wandered" into a new adjacent possible, and here's what happened.

The telecom engineer walked away from the conversation with new insights that, as Johansson said, would lead ten years later to "helping petrol truck drivers plan their routes through the Swiss alps." From a simple foray into the adjacent, he saw "a powerful computing metaphor" in the ecologist's explanation of how ants prioritize paths as they work together.[120] When he returned to his own world, he started applying the seemingly distant ideas from insect research to routing data in telecom networks. The ideas spread, not only from ecologist to engineer, but from the engineer's work at France Telecom to a new company he founded. From there, other companies across the globe heard about the idea and jumped on it. Eventually, a whole new area of study known as *swarm intelligence* was born—all from a lunchtime stroll in the adjacent possible.

Swarm intelligence is playing a major role in global telecommunications, cloud computing, and "big data" management. A willingness to drift into the adjacent possible created a whole new world of opportunities. It's but one more example proving Stu's observation that the adjacent possible is rich with opportunity for breakthrough creativity and infinitely expandable.

VALUE IN WHAT'S "POSSIBLE"

There's an insight present in all of these examples and interwoven into the wisdom shared by everyone you've just heard from: If you want breakthrough ideas, you shouldn't go into the adjacent possible expecting anything more than a chance to open your mind to possibilities. The adjacent possible won't always be the *adjacent tangible*, just as breakthrough ideas aren't always viable in their first iteration. Yet going to the space immediately around you is among the best ways to exercise your creative capacity. It's fertile ground for shaping how you think in addition to what you see. Going there often affords fine-tuning, not to mention fun. And as you do, you're gradually creating the space in which creative ideas have the highest likelihood of breaking through.

That's why Ric and Stu and the folks at SFI go there as a matter of habit. This story from Ric reinforces the point *and*, fittingly, expands the view of what's possible.

When I talked with Ric, I asked him, "What is your favorite project of all the ones you've done? Which was your most creative?" Having seen the High Line, I thought it might rank up there for him. I also knew his firm had been selected to design the Institute of Contemporary Art, the first new museum to be built in Boston in a hundred years. Maybe this was his favorite project.

But Ric named a project few know about and one we can't see because it doesn't exist—a house so magnificent, it brought his firm a lot of press just in its *anticipation*. He called it the house that no one built.

"The house went into construction and then the client had to pull back," Ric explained, not an ounce of regret noticeable in his voice about the unwanted ending to his favorite project. Indeed, in this house, he'd innovated new ways of thinking about materials, new ideas about how people don't simply fill a space but live in it, and a "bricolage" of countless "little ideas" that Ric knows will someday contribute in some yet unknown way to something "big."

"I don't live in the past," said Ric. "The fact that the house itself wasn't realized doesn't bother me at all. The very act of thinking about that design, of what it could be, was in itself a completion for me. It was vastly rewarding."[121]

For Ric, the many ideas conceived around this project affirmed his creative habit and the possibilities that habit can yield. There's no question in Ric's mind those ideas have already seeded other ideas elsewhere—just as other ideas long before shaped the ones that went into the house. *Those* rewards exceeded any other "tangible" that could have come from the project's continuation.

"Great thoughts don't materialize in one form or assume one kind of value," Ric said. "Most often the ideas seed and resurface elsewhere, if they're good and if they're meant to last. The process and the constancy of pushing the edges of your world out—*that's* the most important thing. It's so terribly valuable to the creative process that I'm sometimes more disturbed by things like the High Line that become permanent, including the way people think about them. I prefer to think about the power of the possible, of the flexible, and of the forward movement that *could be*. That's what gets me up every day."[122] It's also what keeps creativity alive and humans moving forward.

LOOK "ACROSS BORDERS"

Where do those who see breakthrough ideas look? That question naturally follows once you know *who* sees breakthroughs. The first part of the answer to "where they look" was "in the adjacent possible." Part two of the answer has been showing up regularly throughout *The Language of Man*. Here we make it official and expand our understanding: The people most likely to see breakthrough ideas look *across borders*.

Every journey into "new" requires crossing the borders that surround your "known" zone. This zone is defined by everything you're already aware of that drives your actions and thoughts. You'll find countless examples of **BORDER CROSSING** throughout *The Language of Man* reminding you that to create anything new requires moving outside your known zone. But in this section specifically dedicated to it, we'll connect border crossing with the breakthrough idea itself.

To do so, let's once again turn to your personal guides for the insights we need. Pat Churchland provides an excellent example with which to frame our understanding of border crossing as a key element of creativity and in creating the breakthrough space.

THE TROUBLE WITH PAT

Temptations Just Across the Border. Before Pat won a MacArthur Fellowship and was officially declared creative, she would say that people didn't take much notice of her. She described herself as "just a philosopher, way up in Canada."[123] And she was a *woman* in philosophy and in *academia*, something her MacArthur peer Rebecca Newberger Goldstein described as "not to be considered a worry" in the male-dominated worlds at that time.[124] But Pat was about to become a worry, a problem, *and* an inspiration to a whole new field of study. By border crossing.

Speaking with Pat, one gets the impression she has always been a border crosser. It's just that her doing so didn't garner a lot of concern until, as she said, she got fed up with her chosen field of philosophy and its rules, conclusions, and accepted answers. As Pat told me, "I felt there were answers being accepted there [in her field, among philosophers, and in the academy] that didn't fit, that didn't cover sufficient ground. Somehow there had to be more. And once I found it, I wasn't quiet about it—something I later came to understand people expect you to be about anything new or provocative."[125]

To try to address the shortcomings in *philosophy*, Pat began to explore neuroscience. *Neuroscience?* Yes, neuroscience, a systematic study of the nervous system. It was a field that, until a few non-neuroscientists like Pat started exploring it, was effectively separated from philosophy by firm borders. In fact, the borders of the two fields weren't even regarded as adjacent to one another. She chose to disregard that memo.

Pat thought that the questions and ideas being explored in neuroscience actually overlapped with those in philosophy. "But that wasn't what people in philosophy were looking at," she explained. "So to them, pointing out what I saw was a wrongheaded problem."[126]

Temptations Within. For Pat, what everyone else was *examining*, what everyone *accepted*, and what people in her field *agreed* they ought to be looking at—the known—was to her like a hitting a wall. Worse still, it was boring. She was frustrated. And even when she tried to put her head down and play along, the voice kept coming back: *This doesn't fit! I'm uninspired. Tell me again why I should keep flinging myself against the wall? Maybe instead I should leap that wall, or take a pickax to it, or . . .* Too often we mute such voices. Yet, they can be tenacious communiqués from our fox brain to move beyond our known zone.

Environment always plays a role in amplifying the voices we hear. Often it turns up the external ones, the voices that say, "Don't rock the boat." But the ironic twist for Pat was this: "Nobody expected much of me way up north in Manitoba and perhaps also as a woman in academia," she told me. "So, what the hell?" What the hell indeed. The voice inside her won out. As it did, the implicit barriers softened. In total, these things she allowed gave her "the freedom to follow the impulse."

INITIAL LESSONS IN BORDER CROSSING

Border crossing, practiced as a habit, soon becomes a textured tool of creativity. So let's pause a moment and appreciate the basics of border crossing Pat has already shared with us.

Taking Note of Border-Crossing Basics. First, while border crossing can sound like a physical act, it is more accurately an act of the mind. Philosophy and neuroscience, for example, shared a crossable border for Pat because she let her mind put those two topics side by side—as simple as that. So in a sense, the borders you can cross are innumerable, and your mind is the only border patrol allowing or disallowing exploration.

A second lesson gleaned from Pat's story is that many different things can trigger border crossing. For Pat, those included boredom and gumption. But the most important factor is "fit"—that sense both of what *didn't* fit (in Pat's case, the current answers and rules of her field) and what *might* fit (the possibilities she sensed in neuroscience that intrigued her).

There's a third lesson in Pat's story: Sometimes, it takes a "what the hell" conclusion to just get going and cross over.

A Different View of Borders: Porous, Impermanent. Acting on your "what the hell" conclusion isn't as hard as you might think. Ultimately, borders are *indicators* around the "known." Very rarely are they permanent, even if feeling content with our patterns leads us to regard them otherwise.

With the right mindset, borders can be porous, even erased. In *A Deliberate Pause,* I referred to these edges and boundaries, rules and stated limits as **CHALK LINES**—what entrepreneurial thinkers, just like creative thinkers, have a visceral tendency to walk through.[127]

Though they may appear permanent and serve us well, even sometimes for long periods, borders result from the variables that create them in the first place. The fact is all variables shift. Time, mindsets, environment, knowledge, and the people who weave those variables together into tangible things do not sit still for long. When variables inevitably change, so do the relevance and value of the borders they helped to define.

Borders are both tricky and sticky because going beyond simple acknowledgment to actively embrace their impermanence inevitably means one thing: change. On the one hand we like the idea of progress and betterment. But we are equally aware that change means letting go of the security of the status quo. It also most often requires effort. When we think about such sacrifices, our borders get stickier and it's harder to think about breaching them—even when we clearly sense better things lying just beyond these chalk lines. The truth, however, remains: All borders are temporary.

THE RIPPLE EFFECTS OF BORDER CROSSING ON YOU

Let's assume that, like Pat, you begin to cross borders. What happens next? More specifically, what's the risk? And what happens to "who you are" as border crossing becomes your pattern?

Border Crossing and Risk. We know that, to many, borders are firm and absolute, not to be trespassed. Not surprisingly, to those who heed borders, the risk is in the crossing. To those who form the habit of crossing them, however, the greater risk is in *not* doing it.

This is a hard concept to embrace for those not used to exercising their creative capacity. I encountered this while researching risk for *A Deliberate Pause*. Entrepreneurs are people who follow their gut. So when, like Pat, they reach a point when every fiber in their body is telling them good stuff lies "over there," the risk calculation for them flips. They see this possibility as "something they sincerely believe could make the world better," and they experience *a feeling reaching to their very core* that they have **NO CHOICE** except to pursue what they see and make it real.[128]

MacArthur Fellows make similar references when describing both the creative path and the reactions and interpretations of others to their choice to take such a path. Those *outside* tend to see the undertaking as excessive risk-taking; those *within* it see it as relative, calculated, and necessary. This absolutely critical distinction contributes to why so many never even allow themselves to come to the edges of their borders even just for a look, let alone cross the line. (Chapter Ten explores this in greater detail.)

"No matter what the circumstances," Pat said, "these have always been keys for me: The desire to do—to actually pursue and explore— and the feeling of freedom that comes with such actions. I tune into and follow those signals. This is especially true when I sense that what's being done isn't cutting it," she continued. "There's a sense of 'rightness,' even of inevitability, and of necessity in going beyond the boundaries of 'right now' to seek something better. Trusting those feelings has always been my difference maker."[129]

Knowing her own truths—the *same* truths other practitioners who have created lasting impact have discovered—has resulted in Pat's breakthrough contributions to a field she helped create, neurophilosophy. More important, being loyal to her truths added to her sense of *who* she is.

The Change that Occurs When Border Crossing Becomes Your Habit. Feeling a misfit that has you considering a border crossing might be thought of as a Phase One. Crossing because the risk of not crossing is greater would then be akin to a Phase Two. Phase Three is the inevitable pushback you get from those who defend borders or abhor change. But at some point after those initial phases, at a point when border crossing becomes habitual, a new phase—even a new state of being—often emerges.

"What I saw *out there* changed what and how I saw things in my *own* field," Pat said. "But looking back, it was changing me, too. [My peers] were angry, maybe even a bit threatened. I was NOT—shall we say—accepted. But for me it wasn't limited to the professional. My way of seeing in total no longer fit the molds. Peer pushback aside," Pat concluded, "I knew that returning to where I'd come from wasn't an option."

Describing the unfolding of the path to new possibilities, Pat made this comment: "I discovered that in a sense I cared, but I really *didn't* care." Notice the initial feeling of dissonance in this statement. But peeling back the layers of her observation renders a rare insider view of what happens when border crossing moves beyond an act to become a creative habit.

For Pat, the more she crossed the borders, the more she realized how deeply she cared about discovering things "new" that represented a better fit than what was "known." She found that whenever she did this, *everything* made more sense to her. She found greater meaning, newer meaning, deeper meaning. She felt alive with a sense of increased value to be gained and shared. Habitual border crossing sharpened her as a "noticer" in such a way that each time she border crossed, she wasn't simply more adept at noticing. She was more skilled at noticing what mattered most and able to sort that from the detritus. Her sense of what she cared about became her filter for finding the gems.

At the same time, an equally strong feeling struck her about *not* caring what others thought about her. It wasn't that she didn't care about those people; it was that she had gained a sense of herself in relation to them and for what would allow her life to move in the direction of her insights. The importance of the old borders and old ways of thinking became relative and, without question, less constraining. (If you pause for a moment, you can sense the link back to what Susan Meiselas taught us about instinct and trust in oneself earlier in the chapter.) In this dynamic, we learn that meaning drives us to pursue our hunches, execute our ideas, and press on through all the headwinds we encounter. And the more meaning there is, the better and braver border crossers we become.

Change and Your Role in It. One last subtle insight here is that border crossing symbolizes the fact that we each change. Creativity happens to be the most exciting expression of that reality. It begins when you come to the edges of what you know, perhaps just to peer over. But it continues when you cross over your edges—maybe just to satisfy your curiosity. Even as something incredible and powerful is happening, you're opening to the possible. And when you do, as much as you may see new "things," you simply begin to "see" differently.

In that moment, you are no longer who you once were.

Border crossing isn't just an interesting exercise; it's a transformative practice. It engages you as an active participant in the inevitable change that happens to all of us.

Famed co-discoverer of the DNA double helix and an early mentor to Pat, Francis Crick, used to remind her of two important things about creativity and border crossing. The first was that anything new you try—anytime you think or do something in a way that rocks the boat—people are likely to regard you at best as "just fooling around," and at worst as a threat.

But second and more important, Crick would remind Pat that staying true to her gut and not only to the roles and rules of her life or her field was the only way to know *who she was* and *who she might yet be.*

What Are They After?

We know *who* sees breakthroughs—noticers, luck makers, and those who habitually take deliberate pauses. We also know *where* they look for big ideas—in the adjacent possible and across borders. But to peel more layers of the onion, we need to understand this: *When they look, what are they after?* The answer is almost self-evident: They look for **INTERSECTIONS**.

CREATIVE PEOPLE SEEK INTERSECTIONS

It would be appealing to say creative people seek intersections because they've read about Arthur Koestler and the intersection of the "known" and the "new." But the real reason they do is far more compelling: They've learned through experience that intersections are the most productive source of breakthrough ideas.

What's interesting about this insight is that it's an old one that's not broadly shared. For centuries, humans have known about the power of the intersection and actively pursued it. For proof and for fun, let me share a more than 500-year-old story reminding us that, as humans, it's our nature and our need to intersect. Indeed, it's the truest way to create and progress.

As often happens at intersections, get ready for your thinking to shift.

A MOVEABLE FEAST

Picture This. Imagine with me for a moment and consider this question: Why would you invite sixty *different* guests to your home for a sit-down dinner *every night*? I know, it's an unusual thought. But while we're imagining, let's press the image and assume the guests were mostly strangers to one another. And picture that you yourself, the host, knew little more than the names of some of the guests before they arrived.

Imagine them also as guests speaking more than one language, some foreign to you. Then visualize each guest coming from different occupations, which among other things means they probably have distinct ways of thinking, valuing, and even creating.

Now, with the image of this mysterious menagerie gathered around your dining table, ask again: *Why would you ever consider doing this?*

If you were Lorenzo de Medici in fifteenth-century Florence, your answer might be one word: *intersections*. If you're looking for an entertaining dinner party full of surprises, it would be interesting to create intersections among guests who share different ideas, knowledge, and dreams. But, if what you really want is to create things that move society or humanity forward, then creating those intersections is more than entertaining; it's a necessity.

Catalyzing Intersections. Lorenzo de Medici, who lived from 1449 to 1492, was a consummate border crosser. The time preceding his era had been a centuries-long period of creative and intellectual darkness. During these Middle Ages, virtually all exploration in the Western world—in the arts, the sciences, and beyond—came to an abrupt halt, precipitated by the collapse of the Roman Empire. Here and there in the century immediately before Lorenzo's time, some of the knowledge that had been shut away all those years began to slowly seep back into Europe and other parts of the former Roman Empire. But it exploded into view in the late fifteenth century, especially in Italy, and particularly in Florence—and in no small way because of Lorenzo.

Lorenzo wasn't only a border crosser; he was a *CATALYST*. He gave spark to what many around him hungered for, whether they could put the name *intersections* on it or not. They hungered to know of each other, to share ideas, and to open up their worlds—to converse, learn, and create. Their urge was elemental.

We'll return to Lorenzo's story shortly. But within the outline offered by his tale, let's talk more specifically about *intersections* and what we can expect to find there.

INTERSECTING OBSERVATIONS

Running Interference. Especially before we become practiced at finding and leveraging intersections, it's important to realize they can at times look like the opposite of what we seek. It's easy to mistake an intersection for *interference* because they're in fact two sides of the same coin. Both are a place of "collision." In one case, however, the collision triggers an "Oh, wow!" while in the other, it's more like "Oh, damn!"

While it's true, as Howard Gardner told me, that "frequently, creative breakthroughs occur at the intersections of the different ways we *do* things or even the different *things* we do," that's also the problem with them.[130] We tend to establish boundaries around our ways and things. Our hedgehog makes sure we do in order to keep us on track and make us efficient. Among our hedgehog's tactics for assuring this is to establish warning signals to indicate when a boundary has been crossed. When the rules aren't being followed or the process slows down, like a referee our hedgehog blows the whistle and yells, "Interference!"

Having order and a warning system are good things. But balance is what moves us forward. If our brain is tuned only or primarily to look for interference, how likely do you think it is we'd see the intersection as the breakthrough Howard described? Would it even be something positive? The question is rhetorical; the answer is "not likely."

Even being able to *see* intersections requires us to tune ourselves into allowing for their possibility in the first place. More than that, we have to develop the ability to regulate between *interference* and *intersection*, for one doesn't get very far without the other.

Not on Any Map. Susan Meiselas described creative intersections as "things coming together that aren't normally associated."[131] She pointed out a challenge that naturally accompanies an opportunity— that is, even when you're tuned in, intersections and breakthroughs are still sometimes hard to discern.

"The intersection is a place where our understanding of what to do and how to do it is opaque at best," wrote Frans Johansson in *The Medici Effect: What Elephants and Epidemics Can Teach Us About Innovation*. "The possible" has *at least* two sides. As Johansson wrote, "An intersectional idea can go in any number of directions." But he added, "We don't know which one will work until we start trying them."[132] Think of it this way: If we *knew* precisely what we'd find at the intersection or could predict which intersection the big idea would come from, then the idea wouldn't be *new*.

The possible "bad" news? We won't find a giant map pin at the intersection of two ideas with a note attached saying, "A good idea can be found here." As obvious as the point may sound, just stopping our search for map pins increases our odds of noticing the breakthrough idea.

But the "good" news is this: The more practiced we become at opening up to intersections, the more we reach a level of perception that allows us to quickly spot the worthwhile intersection over the interference. It's not just the best way; it's the *only* way.

"Since we cannot rely on past experience to devise a perfect execution path," Johansson wrote, "we must rely on learning what works and what doesn't."[133] Johansson's point, echoed by many MacArthur Fellows, is that skill in finding the intersections that yield breakthrough ideas results from practice and from learning what does and doesn't work. It's not a perfect plan, path, or formulaic "do this, get that" set of actions. It's sheer doing, with awareness and the expectation of continual refinement.

In short, we have to make a habit of placing ourselves in spaces like this and purposely going where intersections are likely to happen.

Using What You Know. We already know a lot that can help us fine-tune this habit. Among the applicable lessons, Ric Scofidio taught us not only to sort and refine, test and toss out, but to purposely make these a part of our practice rather than regard them as things we are only forced to do if our plans fail. Ken Burns would suggest we overlay Ric's advice with practiced noticing. That would mean engaging in sorting not for sorting's sake, but instead as a kind of purposeful play where we consciously look to discern what's different this time from the last, or to see what might meaningfully connect that once did not. Pat Churchland would add that, if we develop a sense of the kind of things we draw meaning from, we can improve the precision in distinguishing opportunities at the intersection and even become more adept at targeting the kinds of intersections most likely to yield value. These are but a few examples of how to fine-tune at the intersection.

As we learn what works and what doesn't, our comfort in experimenting increases profoundly. And as it does, inevitably a creative mindset emerges, one that supersedes in value any map we might long for to tell us precisely how to create.

The Meaning of Life. Here's something interesting to pause and think about: Though we may at first feel discomfort there, the intersection is a natural zone—for humans and for all living things. That's true no matter how much your hedgehog tries to tell you otherwise.

Gary Nabhan was one of several Fellows who referenced an almost biological need for intersections. "Ecologists have a term for this mixing across the edges of our known worlds," Gary said. "They call them *ecotones*. Basically, they are transition zones where life intermingles, not in a conscious way but in ways born of exposure and experimentation. Things get tried there. Life intersects, on purpose and by accident. The stuff that works lasts while what doesn't work doesn't last."[134]

It's not only Gary's words that are noteworthy; it's the fact that he lives by them. The man himself is a perpetual intersection. "That's where I live," he told me.

Gary is one of the most creative people you may ever meet. Who Gary is and what he does simply can't be pinned down to one field, thought, or creation. Remarkably, he's also creatively prolific in *each* of his many worlds—biology, poetry, the local food movement he helped create, and an uncountable list of hybrid worlds in between these and other worlds he inhabits. The secret to all of this? Intersections.

"Working between cultures and fields—and even just having friends I collaborate with who do things beyond my own discipline—these things push me forward and allow me to see," Gary told me. He expanded this thought in his book *Cross-pollinations*, writing, "Cross-pollination," another term for border crossing in search of intersections, "is not merely a metaphor but a requisite for sustaining the diversity of life on earth. It is a survival necessity for certain organisms, the only way they are able to continue their legacy."[135]

People, Gary suspects, may need this more than any other species—not for purely biological reasons but because our brains have evolved to depend on this kind of intersection to create and to move us forward. (Think back to the evolution of the mental side of "creative you" in Chapter One as taught to us by Liane Gabora.)

It may feel as though Gary's comment has us drifting toward bigger thoughts than we're used to or want right now. But consider that Gary's message about life and intersections resonates in our lives every day, even if we don't consciously take note of it. As Dov Seidman wrote in *How: Why How We Do Anything Means Everything*, "No matter what our specialty, achievement in the twenty-first century dramatically depends on our ability to thrive in a system of connections more vast, more varied, and more exposed than ever before in the history of man."[136] Though Seidman writes and consults for a business audience, he makes a remarkably similar observation to Gary's coming from the world of the sciences.

Each is saying that life and human progress are all about intersections and the connections that occur at those intersections. Therefore, rather than being the *exception*, intersections are the *norm*. The future is critically linked to our ability to sense and see the intersections. And when we choose to tune in, we do far more than survive.

Yet as apparent as all of this may sound, humans typically don't act in the direction of the obvious. As evolutionary biologist and MacArthur Fellow Dan Janzen said in Gary's book, "What escapes the eye is the most insidious kind of extinction—the extinction of interactions."[137] While our technology and our conversations give the impression that we perceive ourselves as experiencing *more* intersections, are we in fact becoming *less* interactive and *less* oriented toward them? It's an important question to address, but hold that thought—at least until after dinner.

A RENAISSANCE AT DINNER

The Medicis played critical roles in facilitating intersections between people who might have otherwise spent most of their lives apart. Because they did, the Renaissance—the reawakening of human minds and spirits—played a catalytic role in shaping the modern world.

In no small way, the Renaissance and its rebirth of human potential created the fertile soil for what later became the Reformation, the Enlightenment, the Industrial Age, and every subsequent period of human progress right up to our own time. With that in mind, let's return to Lorenzo and his dinner table in Florence to experience an intersection and learn why they are at the heart of the breakthrough space.

Seeking Points of Intersection. During their lives, Lorenzo de Medici and his father Cosimo spent considerable time and money recovering manuscripts that had largely been lost to the Western world during the Middle Ages. When the manuscripts fell out of the public eye, so did the broad knowledge they contained about science, math, art, the heavens, and the expanse of the earthly world. Gathering them back together was the first step toward returning what had been lost. But sharing knowledge of these ancient insights and finding ways to create new insights seems to have been Lorenzo's greater agenda.

As Miles J. Unger wrote in *Magnifico: The Brilliant Life and Violent Times of Lorenzo de Medici*, during his life "Lorenzo had amassed one of the greatest collections of manuscripts in the world, turning the two hundred he had inherited to over one thousand at the time of his death."[138] This was certainly one reason why the Medici palace and Lorenzo himself were natural draws for explorers of all types, from artists to adventurers to intellectuals. Unger described the wide range of people who gathered there collectively as freethinkers— "those of a speculative and daring cast of mind."[139]

But what gave life to all of the possibility in knowledge and people gathered at his home? Lorenzo not only sought to converge "a vanished body of knowledge" but to instill "an attitude toward life that embraced the world and man's glorious destiny. . . . For those like Lorenzo—driven, ambitious, confident in their own abilities, the ancient texts," and the environment Lorenzo established around them, "contained a revelation of man's potential to shape the world. . . ."[140] Lorenzo gave his guests a chance and a space in which to intersect.

By all accounts, Lorenzo embodied two wonderful states of thinking: He was open-minded and a humanist. He saw bounty in breadth. He realized the power of intersecting ideas, views, and ways of doing.

And he actively encouraged the same in those around him. He believed in the unique power of man to think, create, and advance toward betterment. His dining room seems to have epitomized the man and the intersections he sought.

Far From "Tabling" the Thought. Household records of visitors to the Medici's home offer a sense of the dining room in Lorenzo's palazzo. Using such references, Irving Stone in *The Agony and the Ecstasy* imagined how Lorenzo's orientation toward intersections might have come to life around his dinner table. Unlike the rest of the palace, which boasted one of the finest, most eclectic collections of art in the known world, the dining room held not one single work of art. "The panel frames and lintels were done in gold leaf, the walls in a cool cream color, quiet and restrained."[141] No sculpture. No bookcases holding manuscripts. Not even a single nail in the wall to hold one of the Medici's priceless paintings or tapestries. And yet the room was full of intersections.

"There was a table across the end, seating a dozen, and down both sides at right angles to it, two more tables formed a U, seating another dozen inside and out, so that no one was more than a few slender gilt chairs from Lorenzo and sixty could dine in intimacy."[142] Clearly, the focus of both the room and the dinners was the guests and their intersecting conversations.

Visitors changed nightly. They came from within Florence, across Italy, and indeed from around Europe, the Middle East, Northern Africa, and more. They were royals and sculptors, religious leaders and military men, poets and men of medicine, explorers and scientists, professors and merchants, monks and philosophers—no one quite like the other.

As Stone painted the mix, he imagined the maestro figure of Lorenzo within it, writing, "He speaks in turn to some thirty or forty guests . . . he enjoys all these people, the noise and talk and fun. Yet at the same time he sits down with a hundred purposes in mind, and rises with them all accomplished."[143] With Stone's descriptions, it's easy to imagine what it was like for Lorenzo or any participant. Open. Deliberate. Noticing. Connecting. Stepping into one intersection, then another, then back out again into their own lives—expanded.

Indeed, Lorenzo was more than a facilitator or observer. A full contributor and "a creative figure in his own right," he maintained a deep "closeness to and active collaboration with some of the most creative spirits of the age—artists like Botticelli, Verrocchio, Leonardo, and Michelangelo and writers like Luigi Pulci, Angelo Poliziano, [Niccolo Machiavelli], and Pico della Mirandola, who regarded him as a colleague as well as a patron."[144] Though it's the "man" we think of, it was the intersections catalyzed *around* Lorenzo that led to powerful human change.

Robert Paul Weiner wrote of this period in *Creativity & Beyond,* noting, "The awareness that heretofore unknown things might be discoverable was a fundamental impulse to creative efforts and the understanding of creativity."[145] That's why, for me, this ancient story is fresh, representative, and a memorable way to carry the intersection.

Lorenzo wasn't (as some have cast him) a god. Nor was he (as his detractors portrayed him) a bit player in this great human movement. Both go beyond the point anyway. Rather than looking for a hero or a villain, the point is to see ourselves. Lorenzo created a space that opened the minds of others to the possible, leaving plenty of room for results to materialize in countless forms. He was, in short, a human being drawn to intersections. Just like you.

PAUSING TO TAKE IN THE VIEW: LESSONS LEARNED

Three guiding questions have not only increased your understanding of where breakthroughs come from; they have also taken you into that breakthrough space. They are:

Who sees breakthroughs and why?

Where do they look?

As they look, what are they after?

What has our exploration and the insights it yielded taught us? To answer that, let's return to the analogy of quilting—a good one both for learning to speak creativity and for understanding where breakthrough ideas come from.

In this chapter, we laid out a broad field of "elements" of the language of man, among them *the practiced noticer, the deliberate pause, the adjacent possible, border crossing, intersections, meaning, catalysts, chalk lines, no choice,* and now *quilting.* Like pieces that go into making a quilt, some are new while others have been repositioned and expanded. Bringing them together quilt-like not only helps us understand creativity in a new way; these individual elements revealed are slowly growing into language.

Notice that you've taken no big leaps to reach this more enlightened state. You've been building the breakthrough space. It's putting these pieces together and using them as a matter of habit that creates the space in which you are most likely to encounter breakthrough ideas.

As valuable as all of that is, our journey into the breakthrough space of creativity yields one bigger insight yet . . . purposeful accidents.

REFLECTIONS FROM THE BREAKTHROUGH SPACE

The final insight of this chapter puts all you've learned into context. For me, it was an insight that slowly came into focus over my conversations with the Fellows. By beginning with a few thoughts from them, I hope to let it sink in for you in a similar way.

Doodling to Get It "Write." Consider how Richard Kenney described his creative process to me. "When I am writing, I'm not thinking about the fully formed poem at the end. Often, I'm not even thinking about poetry at all. It's more like doodling," Richard said.

"Yet it also feels like serious play. In the moment, it won't be tied to large-scale questions or specific focal points, or even directly to work efforts. It's more that a word or phrase or image—perhaps something as dissonant as a sneaker in a terrier's mouth—leads me to places where I didn't know I was going. It's not writing to an end; it's a process concerned only with exploring. The surprise and delight and indeed any grand result come as a conclusion unforeseen."[146]

Richard's description of the creative process isn't an outlier; if anything, it's representative. In *Art & Fear,* David Bayles and Ted Orland wrote this about the creative process: "What's really needed [to create] is nothing more than a broad sense of what you are looking for, some strategy for how to find it, and an overriding willingness to embrace mistakes and surprises along the way."[147]

In one respect, comments like these might register in the mind as *interferences*. "How," you might ask, "can I possibly explore, advance, and create in such looseness?" No talk of plans, big goals, defined outputs, or even clear direction leaves our hedgehog screaming to us to resist. But when such comments occur in a pattern, it's time to consider them not as dissonant interference but as intersections of experience.

"Music" to the Ears . . . and the Brain. John Harbison brought me to the same crossover. "Creativity," he told me, "is often made to sound clearly useful or practical. But I find I have often been interested in a lot of things [for which] I couldn't tell at the time what the use was or was going to be." With a backward glance, John laughed knowingly and then told me, "I'm taken with the idea that the things I was interested in at such times were not immediately practical. In those moments, I always somehow knew that the blocks could be assembled even if I couldn't yet guess how. It's play," he concluded.

And this play has become his practice, too. "I liked to mull and play and see what can be made out of the unobvious. It's like being at the edge of some body of transformative knowledge working to tune the dial into the signal. When you play at that, rather than becoming obsessed by the question of 'where will this all lead?' it allows creativity to become far more a mindset then an act or an output. And inevitably, such play expands the fertile ground from which the best ideas always come."[148]

You can see more than a pattern building across these Fellows. You can see a commonality in how they think about breakthroughs and perceive the space in which they often occur. John and Richard demonstrated that, but so did Gary, Pat, Stu, and other Fellows you met in previous chapters. There's a vital insight emerging across them. But before we describe that insight, let's hear from one more Fellow—award-winning novelist Joanna Scott.

A "Novel" and Powerful Insight. When I asked Joanna about creativity—not just what it *was* or how *she* used it but also how she communicated it as a professor teaching others—she shared many thoughts. But one particular reflection stood out as stitching together what others had said.

"On the one hand, I don't know and have never known what enables creative thought," Joanna said. "But I can tell you this—it often feels *accidental*. Still I know with certainty that I'm enriched by exposure to inspired human expression—going to museums or cracking an interesting book or feeling transformed by theatre. These are the things I consciously chose to do, not because I'm trying to create but because they give meaning to my life. When I do them, I *know* something will come of them. Sometimes it's truly breakthrough. But each time I choose to do such things, exactly what will come matters far less."[149]

It struck me that Joanna would allow for experiences such as these on *purpose*, even though the exact meaning was likely to unfold by *accident*. As she spoke, I realized she was describing the same dynamic so many others had: Breakthrough ideas are the result of **PURPOSEFUL ACCIDENTS**.

PURPOSEFUL ACCIDENTS

To me, the purposeful accident represents much. It's emblematic of how we must think about the breakthrough space. It's telling about how we can best mine that space. But separate from the breakthrough, it embodies the idea of what matters and not only to creativity: Bigger than that, it's rooted in what matters to us individually.

The purposeful accident summarizes the ongoing cycle this chapter refers to. When you look back over these lessons of "who" sees, "where" they look, and "what" they hope to find, you may be able to discern that cyclicality.

Indeed, each new foray into the breakthrough space brings you back to the beginning. You notice new things all over again; you're compelled to cross borders to explore those things. I feel certain you can play out the rest. It's a circle that's drawn and redrawn ad infinitum.

If you step back and consider this, it's possible to see it like a drawing of an actual circle. Looking at it that way, imagine that it represents a huge target zone—the *breakthrough space* come to life, made and remade one circumnavigation at a time.

Though the details will vary by person, time, and circumstances, the cycle is clear. So is this lesson: The more you travel this circle's path, the more you begin to see that what your creative mind searches for with *purposeful* intent is unveiled to you most often accidentally, but not in the way we most often think of accidents as random and unwelcome. Like Richard, John, and Joanna, you build an ever-increasing degree of *trust* in the cycle, one that is far from accidental or untethered. Each return *deepens your understanding.* And consciously or unconsciously, you know that engaging this cycle and this space where breakthroughs come from—and allowing for all of that to unfold, gradually—is what it means to be human.

Curl up in the warmth of that quilt of ideas and let's explore the Simple Truth about *why* breakthroughs come.

SIMPLE TRUTH:

OPENNESS IS

WHY

BREAKTHROUGHS

COME

CHAPTER SIX

SIMPLE TRUTH: OPENNESS IS WHY BREAKTHROUGHS COME

GRAND CANYON MOMENTS AND WHY BREAKTHROUGHS COME

In 1540, Don Garcia López de Cárdenas went in search of a great river. He was sent by his boss, the famed Spanish explorer Coronado. If the rumors were true and this river could be found, it might give the conquistadors easy passage out of the North American desert southwest and into the lands of gold they sought.

As he searched, Cárdenas eventually met members of the Hopi tribe. Yes, they said, they knew the great river and could take him there. They led him to the rim of the Grand Canyon and pointed across its incomprehensible expanse and far into its mile-deep bottom to a tiny ribbon of blue—the mighty Colorado River. Cárdenas couldn't see it. He was looking right at it, but to his eyes, it wasn't there.

Encouraged by his men who argued they'd come this far anyway, he sent a scouting party from the rim into the canyon and toward the distant blue thread. Despite being confident they'd easily reach their target, the canyon proved so incredibly vast that Cárdenas' men had to turn around early. But they got close enough to see that, indeed, the Hopis were right. An immense river lay at the base of the canyon.

The scouting party returned to the rim and told their leader what they'd seen. Emphatically, stubbornly, Cárdenas demurred. "There can be nothing more than a stream," he persisted. Having seen it with their own eyes, his men tried to explain that even with the good view he had from the rim, the scale of the canyon, its rock features, and thus the river were far bigger than Cárdenas assumed. To help him comprehend, they pointed at a distant rock spire and told Cárdenas that, while it appeared to be small it stood even higher than the massive Catedral de Santa Maria de la Sede back in Spain. Reaching 344 feet into the sky, the cathedral was one of Europe's tallest buildings of that time. Still, Cárdenas waved them off.

Within days, Cárdenas abandoned the search and headed back to confidently tell Coronado there was no great river to be found. In his journal, he barely even mentioned the canyon, one of the biggest, most iconic natural wonders of the world. It was as if he couldn't see any of it—a natural feature so massive it can be seen from space. Running right through its center was a tiny blue thread just as magnificent. (See Author's Notes: Chapter Six.)

The more I've studied creativity, the more I've come to refer to this as a **GRAND CANYON MOMENT**. It's an instant when an entire world of possibility lies at your feet, when you can be in active search and have every incentive to find something grand, and yet you don't see it.

These moments happen all the time. Such opportunities can result in good things, including breakthrough ideas, but they can just as easily result in missed opportunities. One thing's for sure. You can influence the outcome, but to do so, you have to be truly open. Being open is *why* breakthroughs happen.

EXPLORING OPENNESS

If you're to see anything new, exploring in an unknown world doesn't just benefit from **OPENNESS,** it requires it. In some respects, openness is an easy concept to embrace. It isn't difficult to comprehend that if you only look at things the way you've always done and only expect to see what you've always seen, anything else, including anything new, is likely to get screened out, overlooked, or ignored.

But truly being open is far more nuanced. To be open, your thinking must be malleable. Your measures and definitions of success must be flexible, sometimes even reconstructed. Openness in the creative sense implies, as George F. Kneller noted, "a tolerance for conflict and ambiguity, a lack of rigid categories in thinking, and a rejection of the notion that one has all the answers. It is in a sense," Kneller wrote, "a childlike quality, for the young child is a natural explorer and experimenter who embraces every new experience with open arms and an open mind and who constantly 'creates' with thoughts, with words, with pencil and paints."[150] True openness is the fullest expression of believing before seeing.

There's wide agreement among writers, researchers, and practitioners of creativity that openness is central. In this Simple Truth chapter, we'll investigate this confluence of opinion, but we'll also explore evidence that openness is equally central to who we are. Later in the chapter, we'll take what we've learned about openness in theory and look at it in practice with several of our guides. The goal of this exploration is that you'll do more than nod in passive agreement. Instead, it will get you to open up and understand more fully what openness is, how it results in ideas emerging in the breakthrough space, and how *you* can become more open.

A Tenacious Theme—The Evidence for Openness

"Openness" and "creativity" share a common encumbrance—they are both words so familiar that we take little time to understand their meaning. But given a closer look, the evidence is overwhelming that, rather than just being a new age cliché, openness is elemental to creativity, to who we are, and to what and how we create. As we explore each of these themes, you're encouraged to see openness in a different light.

THE EVIDENCE IN CREATIVITY

"Open" Everywhere. There may be a little déjà vu as you hear openness emphasized as important. First of all, you've seen it throughout *The Language of Man*. Though we may not have called it out explicitly, you already know countless ways in which openness fuels creativity. Openness gives us confidence to cross borders into the breakthrough space. It enables us to notice the intersection over the interference. And as we learned in Chapter One from Liane

Gabora, it's also the mechanism that lets us rapidly shift from "now" to "then" thinking and back again, allowing our fox and hedgehog to dance together out in the open. And openness is the underlying engine fueling Carol Dweck's growth mindset—you get the idea.

But openness appears other places with notable consistency as well. It seems someone is always rediscovering it and reawakening to its value. We talk of technology platforms being open so more people can add to their design and the ideas of many can be melded into one. We refer to the value of open economies in which the free market can reign, better products and services can be brought to bear, and value can grow. We're even told in leisure activities such as yoga and meditation that openness is the ultimate goal.

Regardless of the era in which it's "rediscovered" or the field or circumstances in which the rediscovery takes place, those who pause and take notice conclude openness to be not only *present* in creativity but *fundamental*. Individual examples stand out, but it's too easy to treat them as exceptions.

To more fully appreciate the importance, it's best to scan the universe of examples and conclusions to look for a pattern. Thankfully, George F. Kneller gave us a running start by doing just that in *The Art and Science of Creativity.*

An "Open" and Shut Case for Openness in Creativity. Kneller was a consummate researcher and writer in the academic sense of both words. He was the kind of scholar that those who need to "see before they believe" trusted. Far from anecdotal or speculative in drawing his conclusions, Kneller was hedgehog-like. He scoured human knowledge and undertakings to understand creativity.

Rather than rely on one or a few fields, Kneller drew extensively from education, psychology, anthropology, mathematics, medicine, sociology, the arts, and the humanities. What we might call an "open" approach he regarded as "thorough."

His matter-of-fact approach was scientific, precise, and dry. And through most of his book, the language reflected that. He'd lay out the facts and accumulate the data behind them. Only after doing that did he draw evidence-supported conclusions. With great care, he made sure his readers saw that, as different as the many areas he examined were from one another, important conclusions across those fields proved to be remarkably consistent. More than any other common conclusion, Kneller overwhelmingly found *openness* to be regarded as vital to creativity.

Opening Up to a Bigger Finding. Kneller's research provides us with a helpful survey of evidence about the role of openness in creativity. But it's clear that Kneller's appreciation for what he discovered ran deeper still. At times when he writes about openness, it comes across less like a finding and more like an "awakening." He concluded that creativity, because it relied so heavily on openness, represented "one of those rare meeting grounds of science and art that give practitioners heady glimpses of each other's business."[151]

Kneller came to conclude not only that creativity relied on openness but that creativity itself represented openness *come to life*. He stressed the importance of creativity not only as a "topic of study" but as a "place"—one similar to the breakthrough space, a rare, border-free environment between fields and ways of thinking. Kneller even wrote of openness as a mindset stating, "Creativity is the ability to remain open to the world."[152]

Beyond what we might learn from one another or how we might advance in our fields, Kneller was saying that creativity, with openness as its foundation, is our means of continuance in an ever-changing world. It's a big statement but far from an overstatement. And while Kneller may or may not have been aware of it, he was describing something backed up by the evidence of how we humans even came to be.

THE EVIDENCE IN WHO WE ARE

Kneller's research looked at examinations of creativity spanning no more than a century or two. But the evidence of the centrality of openness turns up in research elsewhere and traces back to the beginning of modern humans. Experts from anthropology to psychology generally agree that in the Middle-Upper Paleolithic era between 60,000 and 30,000 years ago, humans began to consider openness important and for reasons beyond day-to-day survival. Not coincidentally, this was a time when there appears to have been "an explosion of creativity" and "an evolution of our means for transforming this planet" and not simply existing on it. Liane Gabora has called this period the *Big Bang of Human Creativity*.[153]

The Big Bang of Human Creativity. Today, most are aware of the value of being open but tend to regard it as a choice. Yet many believe it goes deeper in our make-up, regarding it not simply as a choice but as a core function and need. The pull to a more open mindset was at first a result of use—that is, the more we opened up to the power of our bigger brains through simple experimentation and trial and error, the more we became aware of the power *within* our brains. Every time we used that power, our brain's physical structure and wiring further evolved so that what we might once have called the "option" of an expansive view became the default "function" in how we operated. Liane and others believe that once we came to rely on that open capacity, we actually *became* more consciously creative *and*, it's fair to say, more dependent on creativity and the openness on which it is based.

The archaeological record from this big bang time provides an abundance of proof in the tools, art, and hints of language our ancestors left behind. So impressive and rapid was the boon of our openness, it's easy to see why we easily forget the actual years involved and believe in moon-leap creativity.

But regardless, one thing springs forth from our evolutionary record: Humans aren't just open by *choice*; we're open by *nature*.

Our Place in the World. Looking at the evidence, we can see that the facts speak to more than our "physical" links to openness. As much as our "equipment" design has evolved to favor openness, our "software" design appears to have done so as well. And while looking at this evidence can lead to heady thoughts, examining it provides a window into the range, power, and importance of openness in *who we are* and *what we do*.

Among those who've pursued this line of thought, psychologist E. G. Schachtel argued that openness wasn't simply *important* to human adaptability and ingenuity; it was fundamental to *being* human. "Schachtel maintained that creativity resulted from openness to the world," but he also believed that "man *needs* to be creative [and open] . . . because he needs to *relate* to the world."[154] (Emphases added.) Schachtel's observation was expansive and can be more fully appreciated in the following way.

There's an acknowledgment in Schachtel's comment that, in our evolution, humans have uniquely developed an awareness of the world around us. We understand that the world around us is in constant flux. While at first we used this understanding simply to adapt and survive as the world changed, Schachtel is pointing out that eventually we wanted something more. We wanted not only to *exist* in that changing world but also to *explain our place* in the dynamic of that changing world. It became our fundamental need "to see things in their fullness and in their reality," far beyond our immediate needs or in terms that only went so far as to explain what the world could give us to satisfy our own self-interest.[155]

Let's not lose sight of the fact that, while Schachtel was talking about the "bigger thoughts" of our place in the world and what it means to be human, he made his observations within the context of creativity. His expanded thoughts take us beyond the immediate task of understanding creativity and figuring out how we can most productively create. Is that important for us to do as well? Even the pragmatic George Kneller thought it was important. He gave Schachtel's insight more than passing reference in his survey of creativity. And then Kneller pursued these bigger thoughts, suggesting we ought to be equally open to Carl R. Rogers' even grander view of openness and creativity.

Defined by Openness. Rogers saw humans as more than adaptively successful creators who needed to explain their place in the world. He regarded them as contemplative, aspirational beings. "Creativity," he declared, "is self-realization, and the motive for it is to fulfill oneself."[156]

Be open and stick with this thought for a moment more.

Rogers' view takes our discussion of openness and creativity to an entirely different level. Rogers agreed with Schachtel's observations, but he believed there was still more to be gleaned about *why* we are open and *how* it impacts us. To Rogers, there is a conscious purpose to our openness, which is to leverage our open and creative nature in order to *define* ourselves. That means to not just survive, not just evolve, not just understand our place in the world, but to become the fullest expression of who we are. "In this sense," Rogers wrote, "a person is creative to the extent that he fulfills his potentialities as a human being."[157] Being open and creative was, to Rogers, how we come to understand what it means to be human.

Open to the Evidence. Perhaps when reading statements as profound as Rogers', your inner skeptic perks up. Good. "Fit" is a highly individualized judgment. The goal here isn't to get you to agree with Schachtel's or Rogers' views; it's to present the evidence so you can discern your *own* truth. It's another reason to appreciate Kneller and his work. Reading Kneller's book, you get the sense he too was a skeptic—one not easily sold on big ideas or big claims. He did, in fact, point out there were many "stretch" theories of creativity to be careful of.

But trust in Kneller—at least trust him long enough to be open to the possibilities. To him, those who pointed to the role of openness in creativity and beyond (including Schachtel and Rogers) were on to something.

THE EVIDENCE IN HOW WE CREATE

It should be abundantly evident that openness is a part of *who we are*. But how does it link to *how we create*? More precisely, how does openness result in the breakthrough idea?

To get at the answers, let's return to Richard Wiseman's research on "lucky people"—those individuals we perceive as more likely to run into breakthrough ideas and opportunities—and see what his studies say in the context of openness. And let's refine our questions and ask, "Does openness actually increase the odds of creating breakthrough ideas?"

"Principled" Openness. A luck researcher with a fitting last name, Wiseman has consistently found that what people call "luck" arises from that so-called lucky person having an open mindset. It's not a stretch to say that openness created the luck, the opportunity, and even the desirable outcomes lucky people seem to encounter disproportionately to others. Wiseman showed us why.

In his research, Wiseman found a high correlation between people who discovered new opportunities or tapped into new forms of value and those who were open in their thinking and actions. When open, these individuals were far more likely than others to experiment with new things and persevere in their experimentation.[158]

More important yet, Wiseman found that because openness wasn't a "thing" they were willing to try but a "way of being," so-called lucky people also increased their incidence of encountering the "new" and "rewarding."[159] Baseball provides a good analogy. Baseball players who take more "at bats" are more likely to see their batting averages rise than those who have fewer appearances at the plate. When openness pervades how we think and what we do, the likelihood of a "home run" automatically goes up.

Carrying that thought further, Wiseman also discovered people with an open mindset were likely to *see things through* to a successfully realized idea (the "perseverance" part of his findings). Openness, it turned out, wasn't only what led those he studied to see new things; it was also what kept them sticking with such opportunities until one of them produced the unique *outcome* people called lucky.[160] The creative significance is worth stating: *You need openness not only to "see" but also to "deliver."*

Although Wiseman wasn't directly studying creativity, his findings align with research about creativity. Specifically, he found that three factors consistently drove the discovery of new ideas and new opportunities: 1) a willingness and habit to venture out, 2) a relaxed attitude, and 3) an openness to new experiences.[161] All three shout the same conclusion: Open! Open! Open! Without openness, you might say, you're out of luck.

Openness in the Balance. To some, openness feels *too* open—too undefined, in need of a few inviolable, predictable rules. So when you hear the first part of Wiseman's findings, you may have trouble buying in. But that's only if you misinterpret these insights to say you need to turn off your hedgehog completely to be open. That isn't the message here. It's one of balance, of *opening up your fox more* while not turning off your hedgehog.

Wiseman's studies show that so-called lucky people tend to engage in highly purposeful ways. They consciously orient themselves *toward* outcomes. ("Hurray!" says your hedgehog.) But they aren't only preoccupied with determining where those outcomes will come from or what they will look like. ("Hurray!" says your fox.) When

For Sandy, viewing the Baja and Sonoran Mexico terrain from a low-flying airplane wasn't only magical; it was mind-opening. The span of seeing distances too great to connect on the ground in a single view or even a single day, afforded her the chance to make connections that could be made no other way. Even early on, something told her this perspective from the air held within it a way she could help others break through the borders in their minds and in their lives.

But while the feeling was strong and undeniable, the form it would eventually take was still unclear. It took that unexpectedly failed flight with the photographer for Sandy to "see" it.

During the flight, the photographer seemed nonplussed. That was hard enough for Sandy to believe, but it was his comment on the way back that shot through her when he quipped, "Well, I got something *good enough* for the client." "I was so angry," Sandy told me, still incredulous, "I turned to him sharply and said, 'That isn't going to cut it. We're going up again.'"

In that instant, Sandy saw that it was more than being up in the air that made her "see"; it was her child-in-the-woods practice of knowing how to "look." The photographer, she realized, lacked that knowledge. As much as his job was to see, he was locked into the frame of his camera's viewfinder and bordered up by the assignments he was hired to do. In an instant, Sandy sensed it was her *mindset* and a different way of *being open* that was grafting onto the wide-open view from the plane. Like a jazz musician in an fMRI machine, she improvised a unique interpretation of the world laid out below her. In that moment, Sandy knew she not only had to take people up; she needed to help them *open up*.

Paying Openness Forward. So she established Environmental Flying Services (EFS). The goal of the operation was to help anyone she took up—conservationists, biologists, local and regional business people, even political leaders—reach a perspective they couldn't climb to on their own. Rather than benign parental neglect, they needed direct exposure to what they were missing.

Soon, a whole range of people were learning the value of this open view. For example, Sandy's service has allowed conservationists to view species migrations that, before EFS, they didn't even know took place. She has enabled political leaders to observe population and species interactions—human, non-human, and blended—that the ground experts were either unaware of or assumed had been greatly reduced. But once they were rediscovered, they revealed rippling value and shifted policy mindsets.

From monk devil ray migrations and whale shark breeding grounds in remote areas of the Sea of Cortez, to prairie dog and hummingbird observations on the mainland, EFS and Sandy have sought to transform what the so-called experts see. But just as valuable and yet perhaps unexpected, Sandy and EFS have caused biologists, business leaders, and bureaucrats to open up and *see one another*. In this way, she transformed her open view from a personal skill to a viable business and from a teaching tool to a bridge builder.

An Ongoing Practice. What's particularly remarkable about Sandy's openness is that it is unceasing. The evolution of EFS is a great example. Getting folks up in the air was truly important and paid forward the lesson of openness countless times. But it wasn't enough for Sandy. It didn't take long for her to realize that even though unintended, her service came with the assumption that those with money could partake of it but those without could not. Believing it was vital that *everyone* had the opportunity to "see," Sandy changed EFS' business model to match her creative vision. Today, her passengers pay only for fuel; she relies on donations and grants to keep her company, her plane, and herself going. Without ignoring the need to be in the black financially, she isn't letting money limit her vision. For Sandy, it's all about gaining and giving an ever more open view.

THE "WIDE VIEW" OF OPEN— RUTH DEFRIES

Asking Bigger Questions to Open Up the View. It isn't only Ruth DeFries' job as an environmental geographer at Columbia University that challenges the mind to open up and think bigger; it's the question she's pursuing.

"I've taken on a very *big* question," Ruth said chuckling but in a tone of complete seriousness when I interviewed her. "*How is it that humans are a species that dominate the world through, of all things, excess production of food?* The answer is part 'amazing planet' to be sure.

But then there's ingenuity. Even just to conceive of the idea to do what we do, it's remarkable. Where does that come from?" Ruth wondered. "How do we do what we do? And why is it at times our *undoing*? All of that is the human part, beyond the amazing planet we inhabit."[166]

What Ruth described isn't the way most of us regard food, is it? But that's the starting point from which Ruth's own exploration opened up. That big *human* part—the "idea" to do what we do with food— that's the part she's working to figure out. The rest of us are just eating (or starving, in some cases), never thinking about the ripple effect it has. But the more you learn about Ruth's work, the more you realize that the expanse of her view is so open and wide, the horizon starts to curve back on itself.

Sensing More. Ruth is a pioneer in the science and practice of remote sensor monitoring. What does that have to do with exploring her question about humans dominating the world by producing food in excess? "It's an idea that came to me," she said, "while I was at home with the kids." Ironically, her big *open* question actually occurred in a space that was *confining*, something her mind clearly didn't accept. And then she opened up even more. She asked how she could seek answers to her big question without going out of the house and into the field. I quickly got the impression that Ruth's then-now thinking switch is always flipped to "open."

"My *'aha'* connection was to use remote sensing to enhance what I could see. It occurred to me that remote sensing would actually empower *anyone* studying the environment to be in many places at once. From a data and observation standpoint, they wouldn't be restricted to one locale." Her idea became even more creative and valuable when she said, "When you can move around unrestricted to get answers, you can't help but put it all into a bigger context."[167]

The sensors she's speaking of can do jobs it would be difficult (if not prohibitive) to do with humans as the onsite "equipment." Sensors can monitor climate, soil dryness and changes, and countless other indicators that go into growing food, and they can do it all on their own. Of course, humans can observe those indicators directly. But they can't do it as accurately, broadly, constantly, or cost-effectively as sensors can, and humans can't possibly be everywhere at once either.

"Using sensors," Ruth said, "we can see a more complete picture, in the moment and over time, including things we weren't previously able to capture. The world begins to look more whole, more complete. And with that data, we not only learn more ourselves; we can share what we know with more people—from those on the ground farming and using the land, to those in government and public policy. Interconnecting this data and the insights unique to these sources, we are understanding more fully how we do what we do and how we could do it even better."

In Ruth's world, the view isn't the only thing that's open and wide; it's also the quilt of ideas and the people piecing it together.

STAYING OPEN WITH A PAUSE

I've said repeatedly that pausing deliberately is crucial to understanding creativity. Let's do that now to widen the lens and ask a bigger question: *Why does Ruth's work matter—to Ruth and to each of us?*

Certainly the specifics of what she does matter. She assesses earth's habitability under the influence of human activities—from actions that seem clearly destructive, such as deforestation, to those that appear positive, including farming the land to produce food.

That part is important, but what matters most for Ruth is the same thing Sandy and countless others habitually do. *They look at the world with an open mindset and an orientation toward how that world could be better by opening up our minds.* Thus, openness isn't only a commonly observed *element* across the observers and investigators of creativity; it's a common *practice* among the creators themselves. For that reason most of all, Ruth's example matters greatly.

Since we're in a pause and lest you think the "Sandys" and "Ruths" of the world are infallibly open, I add this truth: *Every* view, even the most open one, has a strong inclination to narrow as time and knowledge grow. Each view will narrow, that is, if it isn't regularly and consciously *opened up*.

Notice that Sandy had to "reopen" her view to see that EFS' goals and business model needed to change for EFS to keep expanding the value of its core idea. Ruth shared her own example, putting her humanness fully on display. She said, "I'm a bit of a control freak. When I'm creating something important, particularly something I started, I want people to be responsive and committed. And I want them to value what I see, even as I try to help them see it on their own and in their own way. But," she added, "I've come to know that, just as often, I have to remind *myself* to be open to styles and views that aren't my own."[168]

Ruth has discovered that opening up to other views actually allows her to get her own views out there, accepted, and embraced. More valuable still, it helps her shape better reasons for bringing her ideas to life—reasons quilted together from many people and not just Ruth. One important takeaway is that openness needs pauses too. It's easy to get stuck in our thinking and believe that openness and pauses only benefit our hedgehog. But always it's a balance. Even our open-minded fox needs a pause, a check-in, and reconsideration in order to see the possible.

A PHILOSOPHICAL CHOICE TO BE OPEN—REBECCA GOLDSTEIN

Let me share one final example of openness through the experiences of Rebecca Newberger Goldstein.

Sometimes when our mindset is open, we emerge with more than a new idea; we come forth with a flipped view. Across my MacArthur interviews, I smiled at the frequency of examples I encountered of a **FLIPPED VIEW** derived from the pursuit and practice of an open mindset. This included my conversation with Rebecca. So dramatic was her flip that it's best appreciated by taking a step back in her evolution to see where her story began and how it might have turned out differently.

Convergent Beginnings. "I was trained in a rigorous form of philosophy," Rebecca explained when we spoke. "I loved it from the start. I was relatively young. I had been successful quickly. I was on a desirable track and in an area (philosophy) that was the epitome of wisdom, something I felt was a person's ultimate goal."[169] What interfered with this wunderkind storyline? Life.

"I was hit with two very big changes in my life," Rebecca confided. "My father died and, soon after, my daughter was born. What didn't fit, and it surprised me, was that my education failed to reveal the wisdom I needed in the intersection of those two events. I didn't know how to define what was happening or even what I was seeking. But I clearly knew I lacked the answers."

Some context here helps. Rebecca is a philosopher. Philosophy is the study of the fundamental nature of knowing, of reality, and of what existence is all about. It is, quite literally, about *knowing the answers* (or so the approved definition says). This wasn't only Rebecca's area of work; it was her *genius*. "Here I was, this so-called 'whiz-kid' in philosophy," Rebecca told me, "but I didn't know how to answer the key questions." For her, those questions were:

Why does a loved one die suddenly and get taken away, and the next moment a new life appears? Why does it feel the way it does, and what does it all mean?

These were the kind of questions that floated up in Rebecca's mind, layering question upon question so thickly, that at first she tried to brush them away just to "see." But the answers that would have allowed her to do that simply did not come. The questions, the feelings, even the idea that the way of thinking she knew and trusted so well couldn't provide satisfactory responses, weren't even on her radar screen of possibilities at that time. Given her meteoric rise on a single path, this was a mind-numbing admission to her. But that's precisely when things started to open up.

I was listening closely to her story, even trying to predict the ending, when she said the unexpected. "I think that is one of the most potent forms of creativity. I wasn't looking for it, but in that moment, I found my entrée into one very powerful source of new ideas and new ways to see." In that action of admitting that *what she knew and how she operated* wasn't complete enough, a wide-open space started to form, one she previously didn't think existed.

Unprofessional Questions and a Flipped View. As Rebecca described it, "Suddenly, I was asking the most 'unprofessional' sorts of questions—ones I would have snickered at in graduate school. 'How does all this philosophy help me deal with the brute contingencies of life? How does it relate to life as life *really* is?' I wanted to confront such questions in my writing," Rebecca said, "in a way that would insert 'real life' intimately into the intellectual struggle. In short,

I wanted to write a philosophically motivated novel." That's not a typo. This academic philosopher said *novel*.

As you hear Rebecca's story, you're witnessing a view flipping. A certain life path set in place (Rebecca's early rise in academia) in a sector built on knowing with certainty (philosophy) collides with the reality of new variables entering life's calculus. Suddenly and insistently, something didn't fit. But rather than ignoring this gut feeling, Rebecca turned toward it.

As she did, even more questions—"unprofessional" but vital questions—arose. They were the kind her peers in the academy advised her to wave off. Yet they were precisely the questions she couldn't ignore. "They allowed me to think in a way that totally surprised me but also opened up something bigger, something remarkable," Rebecca said. "It was like finding there were two wholly different parts of me, as if those two big events and the questions I allowed myself to ask linked those parts of me." Imagine how much Charles Limb would have loved watching the resulting light show on Rebecca's fMRI scan!

The first step in flipping her view was as simple as being open to new questions and ready to pursue them. Just entertaining these questions she hadn't previously allowed had her seeing from fresh vantage points outside her known world. As venturing into the adjacent possible will do, her world began to expand. The added layers of openness also helped Rebecca evolve a more refined sense of what mattered to her and what she cared about. It was just as Pat Churchland described of her own increased sharpness brought on by a willingness to expand her view. Also, like Pat, others told Rebecca not to cross the borders she was crossing—in essence, not to open up—and implied she was doing so at her peril. But her new and more open view, flipped to its core, indicated otherwise.

We could say that, like Pat, she knew what she cared about and perhaps what she no longer did as well.

No Looking Back from the Breakthrough. As interesting as what Rebecca found was what she felt. "'What is the central element to living a human life?' I knew intellectually and professionally that was the ultimate question [of philosophy]," Rebecca said. "But I had lost the feel." It's remarkable how the nearest and smallest of questions can connect to something bigger and tune us in to whether the feeling or meaning still exists.

For Rebecca, this question of *what it means to be human* was big in two ways. First, it's universal and Rebecca recognized it. She also recognized it as the question that had been her starting point and the reason she'd pursued philosophy in the first place. But she came to see it in a different way, with different options for seeking answers, just by giving herself permission to explore.

"I felt the need to get back to where the answers, even the question came from. I not only had to *understand* but to *navigate*. I had professional skills, but I needed a way to handle the question in personal terms. Yet, to write a novel seemed crazy in the context of my training." Crazy to others too, perhaps. But Rebecca's view had flipped irretrievably as she noted, "I never wrote another journal article again."

To academics, journal articles are the lifeblood of their careers. Publish or perish. One thing was clear; no one in the academy would have advised that advancement would come by writing novels. But as Rebecca explained, "I lost interest in the concept of one way forward. I had tasted what it felt like to surprise myself— out there, in the open, where you don't know where the direction or the answers will come from next.

"*That's* creativity," she exclaimed. "It's perpetual openness and everything that comes with it. In that space, you're confused, surprised, and sometimes shocked. But you like it. And you let it keep coming. I now find that even when I want a certain project to be fulfilled, even when I'm deeply invested in it, I drop it if it lacks that *feel*, that life-giving vitality. That's a hard concept, but it's a constant gift."[170]

Rebecca went on to write ten books, six of which were novels, three nonfiction, and one a collection of stories.

A Life-Giving Feeling. Until you've walked up to the line, crossed it, seen something new, and stepped into the promise of the adjacent possible, it can be hard to understand the attraction of stepping into the open. But the draw can be so strong, you'd do the kinds of things Rebecca has done and likely never look back.

Rebecca described a feeling shared by many about creativity. That feeling goes far deeper than a simple affinity for the experience or a rush in those moments of creative breakthrough. It often emerges for the first time when people sense a lack of fit. They feel it when the "unprofessional" questions arise and can't be ignored. They feel it as they step into the adjacent borderlands, beyond the known and accepted. They certainly feel it when those big ideas break through. And they feel it whenever they sense they've gained insight into what it means to be human. They feel it throughout and with each added opening.

OPENED UP TO CREATIVITY

Be it in our personal lives or our workplaces, in our societal patterns or our measures of value, creativity and staying open are often outliers. Odd, isn't it? Something that's so centrally human isn't typically given room to exist, let alone thrive. Something that's been the reason for our progress is often the very thing we fear and crowd out.

Nineteenth-century British philosopher John Stuart Mill once observed, "The perpetual obstacle to human advancement is custom." Yes, we get comfortable. We find something we can rely on and act as though we can stop time to make what works in this moment a perpetual, permanent fit. We do these things . . . and then we don't.

As much as human society is filled with rules, human history is rife with border crossers bending and breaking those rules wide open. Curious souls, they feel a lack of fit and can't get that out of their hearts or heads; they feel restricted in ways they can't abide or explain; they sense something better is out there; they are human and aware; and in both deep and surface ways, they wonder at the question *what does it means to be fully human?*

In telling us his conclusions about the art and science of creativity, George Kneller wanted to be sure we didn't just quickly glance over that point and move on. He shared psychologist Carl Rogers' observation that this desire to forge beyond what we know in any one moment is "man's tendency to actualize himself, to become his potentialities."[171] In other words, we open up over and over and over again to become who we are.

But even setting aside that big picture view of *who we are*, both Rogers and Kneller believed these inclinations—to be open and to seek what could be better still—as "the mainspring of creativity." We return repeatedly to our creative capacity to see, as Rogers put it, how we might "expand, extend, develop, or mature" *what we have* and *who we are*.[172]

If you open up a little, you're sure to see it.

THE

PATTERN AND

POWER OF

QUESTIONS

CHAPTER SEVEN

THE PATTERN AND POWER OF QUESTIONS

The point of this third section of *The Language of Man* is to learn what allows us to *render* the creative thought or, more precisely, the breakthrough idea we view as the product of such thinking. Fittingly, we began by focusing on the "place" where creative ideas are born—what we've come to know as the breakthrough space. We've learned two key lessons that stand above the rest: 1) the breakthrough space is a place we create and 2) openness is the key that unlocks it. Now it's time to build on those insights.

You may have discerned a pattern in learning about the place where creative ideas are born. Everywhere it seems there have been *questions* posed formally and informally. And it seems every time you've heard from your guides, their insights and journeys are laced with questions. More than a *pattern*, questions have undeniably been rendered as a *power*.

To amplify this insight, let's begin with a story.

TUNED INTO INQUIRY

Singing a Different Tune. The room was filled with 150 skeptics: entrepreneurs, educators, scientists, leaders—all participants in an intense four-day "experiential" classroom. We were seated stadium-style in a large auditorium ready to learn about entrepreneurship—at least that's what every promotional message about this day had led us to believe. So why was the guy at the front of the classroom carrying a guitar saying, "We're going to *write a song—together!*"? The "what the . . ." and "oh, sure we are" and "not me" responses were audible.

But there stood Darden Smith, singer, songwriter, and now friend, confidently telling our group that a) we *would* write a song, b) even the most skeptical among us would have a hand in its creation, c) contrary to the whispers, it wouldn't suck, and d) it was completely relevant. Yes, doing this would relate not only to entrepreneurship but to *everything* we did. As the session began, the scoffing and griping quickly turned to guarded giggles. Here's what happened. . . .

We *did* write a song. Together! Granted, few of us jumped in at the start. After all, we felt overshadowed beyond our own recognition by the roles we played before we entered the room and by the worlds in which we played them—business, academia, science, the arts. We had answers, and we had inhibitions. Both were limiting. But by the end, we were nearly climbing over the desktops to participate. And as promised, the song did *not* suck. But what actually happened that led to that song's creation proved far more chart-topping.

"Questioning" Creativity. Imagine taking a *direct* route to songwriting. Unsurprisingly, it would begin with the end in mind. We want a song; therefore, diligent doers that we are, we would get down to it post haste—humming perhaps, throwing out lyrics, dreaming of record deals—all things we unconsciously assumed led to the desired outcome. But that wasn't where Darden took us. In fact, at first we wondered if he even cared about the outcome.

"What was your favorite part of growing up?" he asked us. Say what? Did he just ask us about growing up? *"What does a rainstorm feel like?"* he wondered next. Come again? Heads tilted, eyebrows and noses scrunched up as we stared back at him in disbelief. *"How long does it take to get beach sand out from between your toes?"* For nearly fifteen minutes he kept the questions coming. Soon we found ourselves shouting out answers.

We weren't songwriting; rather, we were wondering, remembering, and playing. As we answered his questions, he jotted down individual words and images *in his own notepad*, not up on a whiteboard for everyone to see as expected in a classroom setting. *What's he writing down?* Before long, without consciously deciding to, I found *myself* writing things down—purposefully but to what end was still unclear. I was no longer thinking about what *he* was doing; *I* was doing. I saw others following suit—smiling, giggling, completely inattentive to the clock or the outcome. They were tuned into their questions.

And then someone in the second row shouted, *Hey look! There's a pattern!* Really? A pattern linking the freedom of growing up and window-shaking thunder and the tenth of a second before hot summer sand glues to your inner pinky toe and . . . oh my gosh, there *was* a pattern! But my pattern and the shouter's in the second row weren't the same. Wait a second; *her* pattern and *my* pattern made another *new* pattern entirely, someone else pointed out. And we were off—songwriting.

Questions Taking Center Stage. That day, Darden Smith did something remarkably and powerfully simple: He brought questions to the forefront. Commonly, we send our questions to the background. It's not that we never question. But our unconscious tendency, according to David McRaney, author of *You Are Now Less Dumb,* is to question mainly out of necessity. We do it occasionally and in a rote and momentary way. And even when we *do* question, our great tendency is to "move on without skepticism if the question . . . gets resolved in a pleasing way."[173] That's the most typical way we question because, not surprisingly, it confirms what we already think we know to be true.

Darden was vividly demonstrating that we tend to lean toward the comfort zone of existing answers—that is, if we don't have a habit that causes us to pause and consider the alternatives. There's a conflict in our custom, however. While we like the comfort of answers and the sense of protection and permanence they give, such boundaries also make us chafe. This is who we are—beings constantly wondering about *what could be* even as we value and defend *what is.* The insight here goes far beyond our basic makeup.

It's an elemental truth that to "think creatively," as George Kneller put it, "we must look afresh at what we normally take for granted."[174] It's a good thing we have a built-in mechanism to turn to—that is, asking questions. What Darden was teaching was the importance of bringing it forward.

OPEN TO QUESTION

A questioning mind is a human mind. And the habit of questioning plays a greater role in creativity and human progress than the narrow ways in which we typically treat inquiry. This chapter will help you understand the role of questions and show how to make the most of them in developing your creative capacity.

As we dive in, though, *be open*. Challenge yourself to rethink what it means to question. For instance, is a question really what you think it is and if it's not, how does that affect its use? How do questions and answers relate to one another? Could it be you're missing the significance of both? What does it mean to take inquiry beyond your individual use and make it a powerful part of a culture? Exploring these questions will reveal the pattern and power of inquiry in creativity.

Once we've considered each in a broad sense here in this chapter, we'll then look at three diverse but interrelated examples of what can happen when the question comes first. One involves a fourth grade classroom, one takes us to the edges of "dance" (and reality), and the third finds us in the world of business.

Near the end of the chapter, we'll explore eight question types that offer a powerful and versatile beginning to creating your own unique inquiry toolkit. Consider them a gift from your guides. Finally, we'll look at a surprising and intimately "human" aspect of this vital element in the language of man: the *gift* of inquiry.

Challenging Questions

We begin our exploration of the power and pattern of inquiry in creativity with arguably the most foundational question of all: What exactly is a question? It's not something we typically pause and consider. But how we understand what a question is has a powerful ripple effect into how we use questions and perceive the answers they allow us to generate.

WHAT'S THE QUESTION?

INQUIRY AT THE EXTREMES: WAY VS. WORDS

What exactly *is* a question? To some, it's a *tool* for eliciting information. How that tool is used can span extremes. On one extreme, a question can be used to probe something unknown and for which clear answers do not yet exist. Albert Einstein's use of inquiry serves as a good example. One of his driving questions that eventually led to his famous theory of relativity was this: What if I could ride across the universe on a beam of light?[175] It's a safe bet that no one had asked such a question before and also that, before Einstein did, there was no ready answer. But when a question is pursued tenaciously, answers—even unexpected ones—do come, as they did for Einstein (e.g., E=MC2).

And then a strange thing happens that marks the *other* extreme in how we use the question as a tool. When we like an answer, get used to it, and build other knowledge around it, sometimes our questions become a way to *reaffirm* an answer. "What would it mean if you could ride a beam of light across the universe" becomes fused with the answer "apply Einstein's theory of relativity and you'll know." And when this fusion happens, the true power of a question gets muted. When this happens, rather than explore with a question, we memorize a relationship—*that* question gets *this* answer.

But what if there were a different answer to the question "What is a question?" There is, and this is it: For some, questions are a *mindset*.

Some people just plain think in questions. "I've asked questions so often over the last thirty years that the grooves of the habit for me are like rails for a train," said tropical insect biologist and Fellow Phil DeVries.[176] A life-giving perpetual opportunity for discovery thrives in the asking and Phil knows it. To him, it's like a heartbeat; if inquiry isn't present, he's as good as dead.

That said, it isn't *everyone's* practice, way, or mindset, and Phil knows that as well. "I irritate the world by saying, *'It's not that simple, guys'* when the answers are too familiar, too threadbare, or come too easily. And then I barrage them with questions—ones that demand proof, even of the proven. They often get pissed, but I don't think their deepest frustration is with me."[177] Perhaps their frustration is with *their* own answers to the question itself: *What is a question?*

NOW THAT'S A CHALLENGE

Phil believes people inherently know the "question" is the fulcrum for anything good. But questions by nature are *challenges* of two different sorts. One form of challenge is that, like working out at the gym, asking questions takes effort, especially if you're out of practice. As with any ability or muscle that's underused, when suddenly called on, our capacity for inquiry can be slow to respond, even resistant.

But the other challenge is the kind that Phil described he often receives from his peers who are out of the practice of inquiry. For those who use inquiry only on occasion or in rote or narrow ways, questions can be regarded as a pain. At the extreme, they can even be interpreted as the active effort of the person posing them to disrupt things or slow them down.

Pause and look at where you are in our exploration of inquiry. You'll see that coming up with a simple answer to the question "what is a question" is itself a challenge. Already there are more answers than we usually take note of: e.g., it's a tool for eliciting answers; it's a stimulus to the imagination; a question can also be a way to reinforce your answers; and it's a challenge, either of remaining adept in using questions, or a challenge to the status quo. But undeniably, there's at least one more answer: When questions become a mindset, they're at the root of where good ideas come from.

POWER IN A MINDSET

Looking back over what you've already learned about creativity, you can see that questions must always be in your mind as you take the creative journey. Here are a few examples to prime your memory pump: Questions are what arise when, like Rebecca or Pat, we feel something about what we know or how we do things just doesn't fit. Questions are what lead us to cross borders in search of new information, new ideas, or even just a different view. Questions cause us to reconsider the pieces of what we know and whether or not they might be quilted together in a different way. When questioning is our mindset, all of these are in play.

Inquiry is central to a mindset oriented toward the possible. Inquiry helps you become adept at making new connections and formulating new ideas. If you pause to think about it, inquiry actually shapes your creative capacity in total.

For a moment, be like Yoshiko McFarland and overlay that observation about *a mindset fueled by inquiry* onto the Simple Truth of the *power of openness* from the last chapter. Picture what it could mean to your creativity when the two are combined by imagining what creative thought must look like for Phil.

Besides his work in insect biology, Phil is an accomplished photographer, jazz musician, university professor, author, and documentary filmmaker. What kind of answers might come rolling back if you asked this jazz musician about the "biology" of jazz, or asked this biologist about the "rhythm" of insect lifecycles? When they're part of a person's mindset, questions shift perspective, habit, and possibilities. Worlds merge. And the scope and potential of the adjacent possible that forms is unquestionably breakthrough.

Inquiry as a mindset doesn't only take you into new realms or reveal new findings; it transforms your way of being. In the process, it transforms the territory itself that your questions seek to understand. The power of the ripple effect is truly astounding. Seeing all of this, you can't help but conclude that there's more to a question than meets the eye.

THAT'S THE ANSWER—RIGHT?

All of these eye-opening observations about *questions* aren't intended to minimize the importance of *answers*. We need answers if we are ever to materialize our ideas, create the tangible, or extract value. But we can't leave it at that. We must understand two important things about answers to get to the results we desire: 1) Answers are temporary, and 2) they are part of a greater cycle.

To the first point, answers by nature are temporal and not meant to last. They're built out of the specific circumstances and variables that produce them, thus serving those exact variables and circumstances. When those things change, the answers linked to them often must change. And this leads us to the second point: Questions not only evoke answers; those answers—when seen with an eye toward *what's next*—naturally beget more questions.

Questions and answers are two aspects of a larger cycle far more important than either of the components. Within that cycle, it's the questions that move us forward—from one answer in one time to ever-better answers that ensure we'll get to our future. In this cycle, questions clearly help us to make new discoveries and arrive at new and better answers. But they also test the answers we already know for their ongoing validity and value. It's the cyclicality of this dynamic by which we not only create, but also progress as a species.

A LARGER CYCLE

The basic conclusion about the interconnectedness of answers and questions and about the power of inquiry in our human progress is fairly self-evident. But an example serves us well. To get a sense of this call-response-call cycle of questions and answers, Gary Nabhan explained how his creativity seeks a perpetual cycle of inquiry rather than singular outcomes. "This strange cycle of inquiry is a derivative of how I explore the world," he told me. "More than some formal designing of a question on paper or outlining of the answer sought, I start simply by always trying to stay tuned into the 'exception'—something apart from the pattern I've come to know or rely on. When I encounter it, my habit is always to question the 'rule,'" Gary said.[178]

Wanting to make sure I understood, Gary continued. "Questioning the rules—even the rules of my own thinking, discoveries, or habits—isn't an exercise in malice or rabble rousing for its own sake. Exceptions can mean many things, and it's my job to figure out what each exception tells me. Is it an error in how we do things or understand? Is it an opportunity? Or is it simply that I was moving too fast when I saw it and it's the exception itself that ought to be questioned? No matter what, it's questioning that flushes it out and allows me to keep discovering the 'best possible.'"

Like Phil, Gary's inquiring mindset goes with him; it isn't just part of his practice where he resides. "The very same thing happens when I'm learning about areas that are brand new to me," Gary said. "Once I get to know a culture, a circumstance, or an idea, I question what experts and casual observers are telling me to see if it satisfies the big questions. Of course I study what the great masters have seen or said; ignoring those insights would be foolish. I just don't stop there; that would be equally foolish.

"Questions are my navigation tool and the way I go about playing out what I'm sensing—what feels wrong or right to me. What I do and know in a larger sense—in the important sense, in the creative sense—comes from *feel*. The questions help me gain clarity and feel. They help me find what works. Without a doubt, they enable me to create. It's a deductive cycle, one I find myself constantly returning to."[179]

Often, we think of questions as the *means to an end* with the end being the answer. But Gary suggested there's more accuracy and power in understanding both questions and answers as part of the same cycle. He's in good company.

ECHOING THE CALL TO QUESTION

In my conversations about creativity with MacArthur Fellows, I was surprised to hear more than a few references to the groundbreaking work of Nobel Prize-winning Japanese physicist Hideki Yukawa—a person who was born at the start of the twentieth century and died nearly thirty-five years ago. Why all the references to him? Yukawa was a peer of Albert Einstein's, and his work in physics, like Einstein's, helped shape his field. But his name came up with Fellows in a variety of fields from geology to choreography—and it did because of Yukawa's observations on the criticality of inquiry.

Though working in a field predominantly guided by precise laws and practices, Yukawa realized that advancements in physics came from somewhere other than the hallowed knowledge and laws of science. It was his constant questioning and the accumulation and sorting of provisional answers that served as important stepping stones from which to advance. This realization was so important to him, he wrote a book dedicated to sharing that insight.

In his beautiful journal-memoir *Creativity and Intuition*, Yukawa described what he knew to be a deep truth in discovery and creativity. He wrote, "Without some contradiction within, there can be no study; that, indeed, is the essential nature of study."[180] While acknowledging that contradiction, confusion, and even delay can result from testing the borders of the known and accepted, Yukawa advised that questioning should not be avoided but pursued. His observations and experiences told him empathically that, without the purposeful dissonance of questions, no new insights or human advancement could occur. *Nurturing* questions rather than *avoiding* them was to Yukawa the catalytic seed for both intuition and creativity.

While at some level Yukawa's observations may seem obvious, his book comes across as a clear expression of his belief that somehow the obvious was being overlooked. At times, his book feels like a plea to his colleagues to embrace a more questioning mindset. Reflecting on his own life and accomplishments made across cultures, generations, and fields, Yukawa humbly made clear it was only his simple habit of inquiry that set him apart. For me, it is equally telling that this is the message he chose above all others to advance his legacy in the twilight of his career.

By comparison, Yukawa's call to awaken to the centrality of inquiry was gentle. Mathematician, biologist, historian of science, poet, playwright, and inventor Jacob Bronowski was more blunt. "Ask the impertinent question," Bronowski said, "and you are on the way to the pertinent answer."[181]

Regardless of the delivery, the message that continues to echo across time and creative practitioners is that asking questions is a tool to be employed more than once in a while. Asking questions is our duty, even if it means ruffling feathers or appearing "unprofessional" in doing so.

Asking questions defines creative exploration and leads to breakthrough ideas. What's more, such ideas continue to arise through a *cycle*—that is, one where a question leads to an answer followed by a questioning of that answer to yield still better answers and a return back to inquiry, ad infinitum.

WHAT'S THE CULTURE?

To be sure, thinking about questions in a new way is challenging at the individual level—how each of us sees inquiry and shapes our own unique practice. But it becomes even more complicated at the cultural level, especially when we want the culture to be a creative one. Complications aside, the importance that people like Yukawa and Bronowski place on inquiry implies a need for us to reconsider the meaning and the role of "the question" both individually and together.

This begs a new question: How do we think about *shared* inquiry? Obviously, we can't assume we'll all just agree on the same curiosities and thus ask the same questions. That's not realistic. Sure, we might share the same environments, experiences, and underlying mental equipment. But given that we think differently from one another, how might we face this challenge of sharing and collectively embracing inquiry? Is there a creative way to do so?

Just as no fixed set of questions exists, there's no set way to develop a culture of inquiry. Using a *framework* approach, however—much the same way we're developing fluency in creativity—proves most effective. MacArthur Fellow Deborah Meier's "five habits of the mind" provide an excellent point of reference for shared inquiry, yielding insights about how we can frame it for ourselves.

A QUESTION OF FRAMEWORK

Deborah Meier operates in a challenging world for a questioning mindset: education. Public education systems often place a premium on answers and develop structures around the so-called "right answers" in an effort not only to direct how to *teach* but also how to *think about learning*. Like turning the proverbial aircraft carrier, organized education doesn't change direction easily or quickly.

As Ken Robinson described in Chapter Three, schools typically resolve to teach certain subjects and in certain ways. They then measure by specific metrics in hopes of getting uniform results. It can take a long time to figure out the best ways to do this. Because it's challenging as well as time consuming to question how things are done in education, schools, school districts, and even education policy, we often default to the operating assumption that "what is" is what's best—or at least good enough. (I smile wryly recalling that when I started to teach my MBA course in entrepreneurship at Georgetown University, a wise insider warned me: "We were established in 1789 and we like it there.")

But whether we like it or not, knowledge, the content to be learned, and the best ways to teach it keep changing. So do the students and real-world expectations of what they can, will, or must do with what they learn. It follows that education needs to regularly be reassessed. More important, if we are to educate in ways that leverage how humans are actually built to learn, then *what* we teach and *how* we teach must be dynamic, diverse, and distinctive.

As someone who's earned the sometimes-celebrated, sometimes-unloved title of "education reformer," Deborah is acutely aware of this. Throughout her career, she has created new schools and education models that have changed how many Americans look at education. Yet, even though she has successfully led education reform (including the "small schools movement" she catalyzed), she cares most about imbedding in the thinking around education a deep-seated acknowledgment that *how we teach* must continue to evolve. All of this, of course, is only possible when many people think, create, and work together. So Deborah and her colleagues have devised a framework they call **THE FIVE HABITS OF THE MIND**. It's an approach meant to enable thinking in a reform-minded way to always be possible. It's also intended to allow that thinking to be shared. And tellingly, it's a framework founded on five questions.

THE FIVE HABITS OF THE MIND

Clarity from the Start. "The schools I work with," Deborah shared, "are driven by the five habits."[182] The overarching "habit" is the commitment of Deborah and her colleagues to question. Whenever something isn't working, whenever an opportunity arises, even whenever someone new is introduced to the dynamic, questions are brought to bear. And the first question always asked is this: *How do you know what you know?* Explaining the purpose of this question, Deborah said, "We never assume 'the facts' as givens."

To get the feel for the power of the five habits and their related questions, and for this first question in particular, remember a time when you were new on the scene—a new employee, a new student—in other words, someone arriving at a place where things are known, agreed to, and where the "this is how we do things" mantra dominates. When you arrive in such a place, what typically happens? You're *told* how things work. Rarely are you invited to ask questions. Never are you encouraged to ask the kind of questions that go right to the heart of why everything works the way it does, how that came to be, or if it still makes sense to do things that way. These are the very things the first habit is meant to upend. Habit one of the five habits opens up the process and the culture for everyone, new and old, to reconsider why "what is" is.

Turning Toward What's Telling. That first habit and question is followed by the second: *Is there a pattern?* Remember Gary's description of his own creative process? After he takes note of something, he looks to see if what it tells him is a pattern or an aberration. In either case, he's looking to home in his brain on what the importance might be.

The second habit does the same thing for Deborah and her teams. "What anyone whose paying attention learns," Deborah said, "is that good, bad, or just plain different, patterns are telltale. When you see them, you're on to something, either the seeds of a problem that needs attention or the beginnings of an idea that must be pursued."

Letting Creativity Enter and Be Shared. She continued the description of this culture of shared inquiry by telling me, "Then in one or many forms, we ask the third question," one that helps move them toward building a "what's possible" answer. "That third question is flexible, but it always begins with: *What if . . . ?*" Deborah told me. "The 'what if' question is almost playful. It's like a permission to explore, toss in new ideas, or toss aside old ones that are holding us back. But it always amazes me that asking 'what if' also has a calming effect."

Strange, isn't it? When we talk about change or ask about a different way of doing things, we expect people will get their guard up and shut down conversation. Deborah's view is that the problem lies more with the "expectation." When that expectation dominates, it leads cultures away from the habits Deborah's approach seeks to form. In contrast, within the five habits approach there's a shared knowledge that the questioning isn't accusing. There's also an understanding that no matter what happens, everyone shares responsibility. The five habits offer insight, options, and a choice: We can all just live with what we've got, or we can all work together to figure out a better way.

The third habit doesn't simply allow that there might be a better way. It acknowledges that the search for a better way isn't a perfect process. "Your first observations and even your first ideas are not always your best, even if they're the ideas you've built the entire program around," Deborah said. "There's something human in asking 'what if'; some simultaneous release of the tension built around protecting an old way, mixed with a release of ideas about new ways that might just be better."

Commitment to the Questions. Reflecting on the first three habits, Deborah explained, "As 'what is' gets reopened to question, better ideas invariably get generated. But even when the current way of doing things proves sound, the questions you allow yourself to explore invariably lead to more good reasons to stick with what you've got. But, no matter what answers we get back from the first three questions," Deborah continued, "we always ask the fourth question: *Is there another way of looking at it?* No. Matter. What."

This question reminds people that ongoing inquiry matters, even when the answers seem clear or remain the same. Such a habit shapes a natural framework within which value, the need to change, and big ideas can be more clearly seen—*and* realized.

The Value in the Answer. Rounding out the habits, Deborah made clear that none of the initial questions nor any of the "pilot" answers mean a hill of beans if they aren't tied to a deep and objective consideration of value. It's value not as it existed before questioning started and not simply value as it could be, but value *in total* that Deborah says must be reassessed. She was describing value of a form that can be seen, felt, and recognized by many, not one. That's the kind of value that the five habits remind us to seek. And *that's* the goal of the creative pursuit—generating something real, something tangible, something that matters *long term* to many people.

The value element is precisely why the final question and habit of the mind is: *Who cares?* "If you forget to ask that one," Deborah said, "all is for naught."

The lesson here? Opening up possibilities through inquiry increases the odds of strong, valuable results, ones people care enough to make happen and that have impact. And here's a wonderful irony: Despite our initial assumptions about the complexity of shared inquiry, making the five habits a cultural process actually *increases* the likelihood of creating something valuable and better than what we often so ardently defend.

Framing a Mindset—Why All the Fuss? Deborah called these questions *habits*—that is, habits of the mind. Calling them so is in part to send a signal to you that these questioning habits are not to be checked off or walked through mindlessly as we sometimes do with questions. The overarching goal of the five habits is to stimulate a way of thinking and being.

You might ask, why such emphasis here? Why all the fuss? Can't we simply make the point and move on? Well, actually no—not before inserting a pause to appreciate the distinction and to learn from Deborah's depth of experience with shared inquiry.

As much as Deborah advocated *new* habits, we humans have tenacious *old* habits that become strikingly sticky (oversimplifying, finalizing, and institutionalizing, to name a few). An example comes from what many have tried to do with the questions behind the five habits. As Deborah explained, "A lot of people who have seen what we've accomplished by filtering ideas through the five habits have translated them into *statements*, not questions."

"For example," Deborah demonstrated, "the question *who cares?* becomes a statement about relevance, as in *'This program serves the needs of the community'*—a statement in which questions of *whose* needs, *why* those needs exist, and *how* and *why* the current program best addresses those needs are simply lost. Offering a further example, Deborah explained, "The question, *How do you know what you know?"* frequently becomes an oversimplified edict of *'here's the evidence.'"* Deborah acknowledges that at first this can all seem subtle, even nitpicking. Unnoticed and unattended however, "The habits simply disappear and so does the spirit of the questions.

"And outside of education, or the five habits themselves, to not attend to such signals, misses the opportunity *and*, I think, the need," Deborah concluded. "People need to question, and they want to feel they can. The power of questions is that they are *active*. When the mode is active, there are many ways to see, to come at a topic, and to discover. Creativity is ongoing and questions allow that."

their own individual visions, I will have done them a great disservice. I'm just a facilitator," he said. "The students run the Game. I have no say in how they handle [the crises and questions]."[191]

Hunter knows what matters to him, and now he's allowing his students to figure that out for themselves. It's a remarkable way to teach, certain to produce results that, while being diverse, dynamic, and distinct, might actually lead to world peace—or other fourth-grade achievements.

A Habit Proven to Work. Should you want to rush to call Hunter with his thirty-five years of observations an outlier, note that teachers of other games with similar "world play" features have made the same observations. As Michele Root-Bernstein, a researcher of imaginative play and games, concluded, "The relative freedom of the children to invent outside and beyond the lesson plan [allows] the learning to be more than an exercise" and instead "to become a vision."[192] She wrote, "Children reach for the creative synthesis when they enter the imaginative moment and discover something new and non-prescriptive about themselves and society."[193]

And the word from the frontlines is that it doesn't take as much as you'd think to get such an environment going *outside* a classroom. For Hunter, it's as simple as pointing his students toward their curiosities, their caring, and the task of coming into their own. Even with the implied "urgencies" World Peace asks them to grapple with, John emphasized the game is about "slowing things down until we have within us the strength and courage to find the best and truest answer instead of settling for an easier, quicker one along the way."[194] Be it one, five, or five hundred questions being asked, this implies that the habit of inquiry is key and, more than that, *meaning matters*. It's the difference maker. And in the final analysis, how to get to meaning is all in the questions.

EXAMPLE TWO: PEERING OVER THE EDGE TO SEE THE POSSIBLE

Warning: Breakthroughs Ahead. If you thought the power of questions was limited to poking at the edges of the known looking for incremental shifts and advances, MacArthur Fellow Elizabeth Streb can set you straight. For Elizabeth, questions help give shape and power to an entire way of thinking beyond her career as a choreographer. Equally, they act as the accelerator in an ongoing journey, a means for pushing things further to see what's possible. When you talk with Elizabeth or witness the results of her inquiry, you start to wonder, "Just how far can a question take you?" Such thoughts aren't an exaggeration; they're a warning.

Almost at the start of our conversation, Elizabeth offered, "I've collected many questions over the years. We (the team at STREB Lab) ask them and push them with our minds. And then we try them out and put them to the test. The questions and answers overlap and build on one another. The unceasing cycle stokes the ideas and the wonder."[195] At first glance, this sounds like the same cycle of questions and answers others have described. But note the nuance: She *collects* questions like *assets* in her arsenal for capturing the possible. And like Hunter's classroom, *questions define the environment* at STREB Lab and the culture of wondering, and stoking, and *adding* to the well-considered stockpile. But Elizabeth is saying more than that.

Approaching the Edge. "Every question is the act of going to the edge and peering over," Elizabeth explained while hitting the accelerator. For her, the edge is not a flowery metaphor but a matter-of-fact explanation of what she does. That is, she constantly goes to the edge of what she knows and even to the edges of the questions she asks, then she peers over, inquires deeper still, and leaps.

It's almost a necessity to understand what Elizabeth does to see how far she pushes the power of a question. Though trained classically, she's a self-described "extreme action choreographer, developing a form of movement that's more NASCAR than modern dance, more boxing than ballet."[196] Really.

To give you an image of her work product, picture a group of performers swan diving off a twenty-foot high platform (the height of a two-story house) to land on a thin gym mat—except they don't come out of the dive; they land not on their feet but in that horizontal position they left the platform in. *Why?* Is it some trick they're trying to pull off (maybe for the last time)? Not to Elizabeth. This is one of the questions she's trying to answer: *Can humans fly?* She suspects they can. (For the link to a live-action example of Elizabeth's work, see Author's Notes: Chapter Seven-A.)

What the . . . and Why? Now, try this one: Imagine a similar group of movement specialists lying on the floor fanned out in a circle, with their feet meeting in the circle's hub like the human version of the spokes of a wheel. Take this image three-dimensional and visualize a huge steel I-beam hanging above the hub of this human wheel from the ceiling. Its length is extended out horizontally to the edges of this human circle, right where STREB Lab's members have their human heads.

Now, in your mind's eye, start that steel beam rotating. As it does, picture the humans-turned-spokes alternately lifting themselves up and down in sit-up fashion. They move into the path of that spinning beam fractions of a second before and after the I-beam whips by just inches away. Faster and faster it goes and so do they. Each is dropping his or her head out of the way precisely in time to miss being smashed by one end of the beam, then raising their head back up over and over again. The motion becomes so fluid, it appears seamless—no up and down, just motion. After the gasps and "wow!" reactions, it's hard not to ask *why?* (Perfect! You're asking questions too!)

Inquiry Switched "On" and Diving Deeper. For Elizabeth and her team, it's less about an answer than about a quest. They seek to figure out how to move the human body in a single fluid motion, up and down, back and forth, without steps and stops. To understand why Elizabeth thinks it needs to be figured out, we have to return to questions.

Like all of us, Elizabeth was born questioning. But rather than taper off her inquiry, she ramped it up. As it turned out, learning to dance in the classic sense was a fertile breeding ground for her questioning. "How could dance be what classical teaching said it was?" Elizabeth asked. When she looked at the varied styles and significance of ancient dance among humans, it seemed hard to picture dancers tens of thousands of years ago doing what she was doing when she first began in traditional ballet. "Would they really be 'at the bar' in a sterile white dance studio watching their reflections in a mirror?" Elizabeth asked, repeating the questions that changed her view. "Is that what dance meant to them? Were their moves learned staccato-like, broken down into this turn and that dip and pieced together to attempt to look like real movement?" To Elizabeth, it didn't only seem unlikely; it seemed unnatural.

Dance to her was a derivative and an expression of something larger—of figuring out what the human body is capable of. "When you watch most dancers," Elizabeth offered, "they go at a medium speed—not fast, not instant acceleration, and always with lots of pauses whereby dance moves are treated as *separate* from one another."[197] It was intriguing—and until she said it, I'd never thought about dancers putting together a series of steps rather than making a single move. I thought I understood, until Elizabeth said, "That spurs me to ask, 'If you changed all that, could you fall *up*?'" *I'm sorry, what?* Elizabeth's questioning mindset far outpaced my simple Q&A approach.

Inquiry on the Move. Questions and quests like these moved Elizabeth out of traditional dance and into the study of *motion*. She isn't as much a choreographer as a brilliantly combustible mix of scientist, extreme action hero, philosopher, innovator, and mathematician—someone who happens to know about dance too. So when she looks at a typical dance, she sees stutters, pauses, and breaks in movement that the rest of us miss until she points them out. While we're thinking, "Huh! She's right," she's already off and asking, *Why isn't dance more like true motion? What exactly is the human body capable of? Can it fall up? Can we fly?*

I know, I know. Your brain might be experiencing a mental discord at these questions. But that's precisely the point. Elizabeth uses questions to take her beyond the edge of her comfort zone and into space yet to be explored.

Her mind moves through this kind of questioning almost as fast as her STREB Lab cohorts move through the air. The freeing result is a willingness to break traditions, rules, and classical movements to see what else can be created or discovered. To Elizabeth, it isn't extremist; it's necessary and effective—like letting fourth-graders loose on the intransigent problem of world peace. It's only the unfamiliar audacity to push questions this far that briefly feels extreme.

"I'm not interested in reinterpretation," Elizabeth told me bluntly. "Experimentation and innovation allow me to go down to the deepest part of movement to figure out what still can be. If creativity can be defined, that's what it is to me. But then again," she quickly added, "if it can be defined, it probably isn't creativity." With this,

Elizabeth is no longer talking about dance and perhaps not even about motion. Instead, she's talking about human potential.

Moved to Ask. Watching what STREB Lab does (which I encourage you to go online and do) is to see Elizabeth's way of questioning come alive. More than that, it awakens a new way of questioning in yourself. At first when you watch one of her creations, you might think you're seeing something circus-like. Then it feels like science fiction come to life—human bodies intermixed with bodies of machines. But wait! No, it's something else. Gymnastics? No, not gymnastics, but *what* then?

The fact is you can't hang what they're doing on a familiar peg in your mind. You find yourself entranced by the grace of their motion, and your mind jumps to conclude this must be dance, right? But then instantly, it's questioning and changing and telling you emphatically, "This is something else entirely." These are thoughts and "answers" you'd never imagine because they come from a habit of questioning that few engage in—a habit in which the questioning never stops and the answer serves to inform the next question and the one after that. At least this is how Elizabeth asks herself a question—and if you're open, she spurs the same possibility in you.

"To ask a question about an answer that's usually viewed as being so unquestionably true that it doesn't occur to you to even *ask* that question . . . and then to see if any little light goes off . . . that's what it's all about." That's how Elizabeth described creative inquiry. "It's asking what others call the absurd question to understand how much more there still is to do, to know how far one can go, to deeply understand, to challenge, to reveal. It's a habit of pushing deeper, of feeling that 'what is' is not enough, that it's not time to call it final. It's about exploring what could be, and what *we* could be."[198]

EXAMPLE THREE: QUESTIONING YOUR ASSUMPTIONS

After reading this far, has your perspective regarding inquiry been challenged or brightened? Of the MacArthur Fellows you've met, it's wonderful how they represent a breathtaking cross-section of human pursuits—public health, neurophilosophy, and architecture equally with musicology, poetry, and dance. Within and across those pursuits, they push beyond the edges of accepted knowledge and familiar approaches not because they are genetically rare, but because they practice using their creativity, and that's where it takes them. As they do, they're pushing the limits of their capacity as well. In both cases, inquiry fuels the push.

But take yourself outside of their fields (and even your own field) and think about this: The mindset of inquiry they collectively point to—and the possible discoveries they've experienced can come from it—is precisely what's expected from leading businesses, institutions, and world leaders of *every* type, isn't it? If humans can find insights for business or global leadership in the study of movement, energy, and the potential of the body, why *not* look there?

I pose these questions because it would be easy to see the word "choreographer" or read about the extremes to which Elizabeth pushes the "field of dance" and dismiss both as having little relevance to your world. Pause and take another look . . . because Elizabeth represents a powerful pattern across human endeavors and over time that has a direct bearing on what *you* do—no matter what that might be.

Why, Why, Why, Why, Why. When Elizabeth shared with me what she does and where questions fit in, I told her it reminded me of Toyota in the 1980s and its *5 LAYERS OF WHY* (the 5 Whys, for short—not to be confused with the five habits but equally powerful and noteworthy). She was intrigued but not necessarily surprised to hear Toyota compared with dance and movement. What surprised her more (and it might you as well) was to learn the role that a habit of questioning had played in Toyota's ability to become a world-class manufacturing company.

In the 1980s, Japanese manufacturing led by Toyota was (to be blunt) handing U.S. manufacturers their backsides, competitively speaking. The Japanese appeared marvelous and the Americans mediocre. In Japan, this was the era of just-in-time manufacturing and a production process that allowed *any* employee—from the top to the bottom of company ranks—to literally stop the presses. That meant that if *any* employee discovered an error or spied an opportunity for improvement, they could call for a pause in operations—a pause to question. Theirs was a business culture deeply imbued with inquiry, a concept Western business leaders at the time thought absurd, destined for chaos, and anything but "best practice."

In their 1985 book *Kaisha: The Japanese Corporation,*[199] James C. Abegglen and George Stalk, Jr. described the nuances of this time and how Westerners had still to learn about the fluidity of "best" answers. Desperate and curious American business leaders eventually turned to this and other books for an explanation of Japan's business superiority. But Abegglen and Stalk's central finding—the 5 Layers of Why—went largely overlooked. (Westerners assumed they'd understood the "techniques," but they missed the source of those techniques: A culture and habit of shared inquiry.)

The belief that turned into a "cultural way" and helped Toyota become a juggernaut success was this: Asking the question *why*, deeply and repeatedly. Toyota believed it was the way to reveal what was actually true and to find true value. More precisely, Toyota believed that by asking *five layers of why*, the real problem or true opportunity would be discovered. This insight is credited to Sakichi Toyoda, founder of Toyota Industries and often referred to as the "King of Japanese Inventors." An example will help you grasp what the Toyota company saw and others missed.

The "5 Whys" at Work. In practice, triggering of the 5 Whys would begin with a problem such as a car not starting: (1) *Why (will it not start)?* was the obvious first-layer question to ask. And the first-layer answer would come back like this: *The battery is dead.* This initial layer of "why" might or might not resolve the issue in the short run, but it sheds little insight on why the problem came about to begin with. So using Toyoda's method, we'd persist and ask: (2) *Why (is the battery dead)?* Answer two: *The alternator is not functioning.* *Ah!* Not knowing this might have resulted in either a new battery being installed unnecessarily or it working briefly but soon repeating the same fate.

Toyoda's method implies there's more. Elizabeth Streb-like, the 5 Whys insist on going deeper. So the third question might be this: (3) *Why (is the alternator not working)?* Looking beyond the obvious provides more texture toward getting this answer: *The alternator belt is broken.* Now the question becomes: (4) *Why (is the belt broken)? It's beyond its useful life and has not recently been replaced.*

At this level of the 5 Whys, we sense the problem being more than a one-time fluke but something systemic. So we peer past what had been presumed the "edge" of understanding—the battery, the alternator, the broken belt—and ask: (5) *Why (for crying out loud) wasn't the belt replaced before it broke, causing the alternator to fail, the battery to die and most important, the car to cease functioning?* Well, we conclude, *the vehicle is not maintained as recommended.*[200] *Ah!* or if you prefer, *Aha!*

By level five, our problem and any good ideas for addressing it look infinitely different than when we started. So too would any solution arrived at by this method. More than the solutions, with the steady use of the 5 Whys, a habit is forming. It's a culture-wide habit of questioning and then considering answers beyond the immediate ones. The result? Better questions still: *What if we changed our maintenance policies and how we communicate with our customers?* Now we're getting somewhere.

Depth Check. While a question could be taken to even greater layers of depth, Toyota found that five was typically the number of "whys" needed to get to the problem's root and well beyond the obvious. The 5 Whys took them past surface questions and pat answers to examine processes, assumptions, and (eventually) possibilities for change. Watching a pattern unfold, Toyota saw that going deeper revealed added value, often intangible and unseen, and it allowed them to anticipate problems as well as fix them.

As often happens, the culture of inquiry that developed around the 5 Whys became the place in which entirely *new* ideas and insights were born. Though it began as a solution to a manufacturing challenge, a habit of inquiry gifted Toyota an even greater reward: Its own breakthrough space.

Today, the central idea of the 5 Whys is reflected in countless business best practices, including Total Quality Management, lean manufacturing, and Six Sigma. Yet the method and its powerful ability to spur creative thinking fit anywhere. Like Elizabeth, Toyoda developed a practice of asking a question in situations in which the answer is viewed as being so unquestionably true that it doesn't often occur to anyone to even ask the (obvious) question, *Why?* Without asking—indeed, without the mindset to do so deeply—it's unlikely the proverbial "light" will ever go off that would reveal a better response and perhaps even a breakthrough idea.

The Power in Every Questioner. Realizing the power of the question doesn't make one person better than the rest; everyone has this inherent capability to ask questions. Toyota fully appreciated that and built a culture around it, one in which *every* person was deemed capable of taking part and bringing value. STREB Lab has done that too. As Elizabeth's and Toyota's different examples show, people use that capability of questioning in different ways and to their own creative ends. It isn't the case-specific application or the format of the inquiry that returns the value; it's the practice. And, as both examples demonstrate, when that practice is shared, the effect isn't just reinforcing; it's amplifying.

Every questioner in *every* field and setting matters. We have a tendency to segregate who can question and who can create by *rank* (the CEO but not the secretary) and *return* (profit but not raw human potential). But inquiry is a capacity we all share. The value comes in the mindset and the use. "I don't move buildings or feed the masses," Elizabeth bluntly acknowledged. "But every day I wake up and rationalize how what I do makes the world a better place. The questions drive that. It's about working on questions to understand what is benign and what is not, what is visible even if hidden, and what is not yet seeable. Questioning becomes something you *enter into*, not something you *do*—like flying versus falling. The richness of that experiment in the extreme is infinite. When I create, I plum from there."

Believing deeply in the power of what she does, Elizabeth is forever striving to share it. No, she's not trying to make everyone a student of motion or an extreme action hero, but she's setting an example for what human potential can yet do. As she said, "I want audience members to walk out saying, 'I can do what is scary in *my* world.'"

There's insight in all of this talk about inquiry that widens the lens out to creativity and what questions help us do. Elizabeth regards what she and her team do as "changing our sense of wonder—our view of what's possible. We aim to preserve a sense of wonder, both keeping it awake and reawakening it, stretching it," Elizabeth told me. "It's bringing in (or bringing back) that sense of urgency around movement, around being human. People need to be interested in their own questions," she added, "and not seek answers or approval too soon. You have to learn to become, and learn to shepherd your ideas."[201] That's when *your* creativity kicks in.

Any questions?

Just Asking—Eight Powerful Forms of Creative Inquiry

We have revealed important insights about questions and established the beginnings of an understanding that's often lost when considering inquiry. These have everything to do with gaining fluency in the language of man. But as we've repeatedly learned, eventually it comes down to *use* and *you*.

It's time to expand your toolkit and show you just how easy it is to develop an inquiring mindset.

FINDING THE RIGHT QUESTION

Someone once brilliantly observed that it's not the answers that are the difficult thing; it's finding the right question. When you find a good, crisply formulated question, they said, it's almost like pulling on a fishing line . . . you can keep going and going until you finally pull up something surprising. How do we go about finding such a question?

Across the many applications of creativity, certain patterns appear in the *types* of questions asked that consistently lead to a valuable end. The eight "framing" question types that follow are good examples. I've chosen them for their ubiquity and proven productivity, and also because each is simple and straightforward.

Rather than providing an instruction manual, the idea is to offer you clay for sculpting your own unique habit of inquiry. For each of the eight types, I offer a brief description and an example or two. In the end, shaping them to your own sense of style matters most, but the examples offer important insights and points of reference.

These question types can be borrowed, morphed, combined, and personalized to the circumstances, person, or needs. In total, they'll help you develop a wide range of thinking "tools" central to creativity—"observing, imaging, abstracting, recognizing and forming patterns, empathizing . . . dimensional thinking, playing, modeling, transforming and synthesizing."[202] Ready?

QUESTION TYPES

1. Unprofessional Questions. Rebecca Newberger Goldstein introduced us to the first question type, one echoed by many other Fellows. "In the course of grieving for my father and glorying in my daughter," Rebecca told us, "I found that the very precise questions I'd been trained to analyze weren't gripping me the way they once had. Suddenly, I was asking 'unprofessional' sorts of questions . . . ones I need to ask to insert 'real-life' intimately into my intellectual struggle."[203]

As we've seen played out by people like Pat Churchland, Phil DeVries, and Elizabeth Streb, *UNPROFESSIONAL QUESTIONS* are best thought of as those "explorations into the assumed." They arise in those moments when the environment and culture around you has drifted disproportionately toward a hedgehog view of things (i.e., a belief that there is one right answer), while your fox senses something more. So, against the suggestions of the status quo and the urging of others, you ask what you most fear asking.

In Rebecca's case, she decided not only to question the accepted answers of her profession, but to go further and break through the sanctioned lines of questioning as well. While doing either was openly regarded to be unprofessional, she believed such inquiry and the new thinking it stimulated would lead not only to new answers but also to better, deeper, different, and more satisfying perspectives.

"I'd been told probing this way was a bad career move," Rebecca confessed. Pat Churchland, you might recall, was told much the same, and not in a kind way, when she blurred the lines, conclusions, and questions typically separating philosophy and neuroscience. "But," Rebecca said, as if speaking for all those whose questions broke rank in search of something more, "I didn't listen. I was on fire." That "on fire" factor is vitally important and easily overlooked.

Asking the unprofessional question isn't an act of outright and thoughtless rebellion. Rather, it's driven by a deep sense, a gut feeling, that something else is still to be discovered. Unprofessional questions asked in this thoughtful way are the type Hideki Yukawa and Jacob Bronowski were referring to. Bronowski described them as asking what to others seems impertinent to get to what's relevant and revitalizing. He considered doing this to be the "essence" of discovery. When the unprofessional question is rooted in such intent—that is, the intent to discover something better, something pertinent, something that might move us forward—"rebellious" shifts to "right-minded."

That "gut feel" quality is a further sign of rightness. Rebecca sensed she'd receive far greater understanding and rewards by pursuing her unprofessional questions—even if she didn't know quite what form those rewards would take. Deep inside, she knew that, whatever it was she sensed was "out there," she had no choice but to explore. In other words, in the absence of proof or guarantees, she had to trust that feeling, that value appraisal that told her there was more still to be gained. As she put it, "You don't throw something like that away for a piddly career move. You walk *toward* it."[204]

2. Questions of Fit. Rebecca's unprofessional questions were sparked by a sense that something didn't fit. Those answers she'd relied on for so long felt unsatisfactory, incomplete somehow. The pieces just didn't fit neatly anymore. This is a familiar trigger point for some of the best questions you can ask, unprofessional or otherwise, if you want to break through.

You might recall that Rebecca described the period in which her thinking shifted as a time when she'd "lost the feel" for her work, for the answers she'd relied on for so long, even for how to question. But she hadn't lost her ability to sense that something wasn't right. Somehow, no matter what else is clear or cloudy, we never seem to lose the capacity for those kinds of feelings. The creative distinction comes in the choice to turn toward such feelings and investigate them. When we do, **QUESTIONS OF FIT** rise up.

Questions of fit take many forms. Sometimes they take the form of a direct probing of the way things are—something as neutral as Deborah's "how do we know" question, or as "unprofessional" as Phil's "that's not how it works, guys" approach to investigation. The common denominator in questions of fit is that they are targeted at what their name speaks to: Trying to understand both why things don't currently fit and how they could. Fit questions are the verbal and thinking form of working on a jigsaw puzzle—examining the scattered pieces before you, then finding the corners and edges that frame a new picture.

"This wondering, this search for fit," Fellow Elaine Pagels reflected, "is the very thing that makes us human."[205] The "fit indicator," as she called it, isn't only common; it's innate to everyone. But if that's true, why doesn't that "sense" we share translate more often into questions of fit?

I'd suggest there's a natural gap between *feeling* a misfit and a *habit* of forming and pursuing questions based on it. Those who use their creative capacity distinguish themselves because they consciously *tune into* fit while others only *take note* of a misfit and then move on. Tuning in triggers our natural inclination toward inquiry. It also helps us get good at solving puzzles.

Once you start to question fit, inquiry and creativity naturally take off. It isn't a far leap to ask "unprofessional" and "what if" questions or to dig to ever-deeper layers of why. Other forms of inquiry typically and naturally follow. You begin wondering about a misfit and soon find yourself seeking a *better* fit.

The way I've described questions of fit, you may get the impression that such questions are mild, less in-your-face feeling than, for example, unprofessional questions. But it's important to recognize that, like their close cousin, questions of fit aren't always easy or immediately popular. The reason is obvious: Questions of fit *challenge*.

Johns Hopkins epidemiologist and MacArthur Fellow Lisa Cooper knows this well. Early in her career Lisa noticed that although the healthcare resources around her (and of which she was a part) were by and large excellent, certain patient populations didn't always benefit from that level of quality. Pat answers such as "That just happens sometimes, Lisa" didn't placate her. For Lisa, something didn't feel right. It wasn't that such patients were being consciously excluded from care, but what they received wasn't equal. Staying with her questions, Lisa quickly realized that the unique needs and circumstances of patients in these populations weren't well understood by healthcare professionals. In turn, the patients didn't understand their options. There was truly a misfit.

But when Lisa pointed this out and said it needed to change, people balked, to say the least. Viewed one way, Lisa was simply saying, "There's a problem and I think I see a way to solve it." But the other side of that view led many to hear what Lisa was saying as, "What you're doing isn't good enough and you need to change."

"Each time I sensed a disconnect or a better possibility, I recognized the complexity, but I still felt compelled to ask out loud, 'What can we do differently?'" Lisa told me. "The opposition at times was immediate, sometimes open and other times behind the scenes. But," Lisa said, "I kept thinking about why I do what I do, and I kept seeing ways to do it better. There just wasn't any question about working to make that happen. But that was me. What turned the tide to eventually change how we cared for our patients was tuning others into their *own* sense of fit. I did less telling, more asking. Suddenly we were talking about what fit our mission and vision—as a department, as a hospital, and as a profession. At that point there was a 'collective' sense, and we began asking how we might make things better."[206] Well, would you look at that—the questions had come full circle.

3. Self-Interview Questions. We know that questions of "fit" and "unprofessional" questions allow us to look *outward* in new ways. Doing so assumes a certain *inward* clarity. The fact is the creative journey must enhance our understanding of ourselves relative to the things we imagine or discover. "Sometimes you have to interview yourself to recognize something of use or importance," Liz Lerman pointed out in *Hiking the Horizontal*.[207] To name this question type, I have adopted her wording and call these **SELF-INTERVIEW QUESTIONS**.

Creativity is an exploration of the unknown. Some ideas work; others do not. The one thing you can know with reliability is *who you are*, and self-interview questions get you there. So how do you use these questions to gain creative clarity?

Right off the bat, challenge your latent assumptions about the meaning of "interview." You don't have to dress up for this kind of interview. And the only one asking and answering is you. Don't think of the "self-interview" as asking questions with rote, predictable, résumé-like answers, or even as pursuing questions with answers that can be covered in a single interview. And most important, remind yourself there's no judgment at the end of a self-interview (or at least there shouldn't be).

Bringing self-interview questions into your inquiry toolkit is like tuning into yourself and listening to the signals you naturally give off about fit and possibility.

Once you get past your assumptions about the meaning of the word "interview," you'll quickly discover this kind of noticing and reflecting is actually the easy part of using this form of inquiry. A bigger hurdle is turning it into a habit.

We rarely take time to ask questions of ourselves: *what we think, what we desire, why we want what we want, who we are, why we do what we do, whom we do it for, or what all of this means to us.* Without a sense of these "W" queries, however, it's hard to confidently build up from what we know and link it to a something new out there. Koestler's intersection of known with new *requires* that we're aware of what we know. How could that not include self-knowledge?

Self-interview questions remind us who's driving our innate creative equipment. To be effective, the driver and the equipment must be in sync. Such fine-tuning is an ongoing process. Maria Chudnovsky described it as "perpetually adding to, removing from, and refining what you know. Of course you have to guess along the way," Maria added, "but in some sense, this is precisely how you learn to refine, to discern, and to create."[208]

Self-interviewing is a gradual awakening, not an all-at-once knowing. It's an "adjacent" kind of query, not a moon leap. And because it is all of this, it works best when it becomes your habit.

One more thought to guide you: Pause and consider the notion that self-interview questions are a sign of being interested in *yourself*, just as you are in the things you want to imagine, discover, or create. As Richard Kenney told me, "It's setting up a psychology in your own mind. With it, you set up the template for the creative dynamic and its necessary interaction with others and the world around you."[209]

4. Missing Questions. Missing questions are one of my favorite types. And the story behind **MISSING QUESTIONS** not only tells you why they earned this name, it explains their meaning in a way you'll not soon forget.

The story, attributed to the Roman philosopher Cicero, goes like this: A stranger was visiting a Roman temple. Proud of the temple, its god, and especially the power presumed to be embodied in both, its caretaker sought to impress the visitor. To do so, he showed the visitor a painting of a group of sailors said to have been faithful to the temple's god. Because of their faith, the caretaker said, they were saved when their ship was taken down in a storm. Rather than asking questions about the sailors who had faith, nonplused, the visitor asked the "missing question": Where was the painting of the sailors on that same ship who had faith but were *not* saved?

Reflecting on this story in his best-selling book *Stumbling on Happiness*, Daniel Gilbert wrote, "Scientific research suggests that ordinary folks like us rarely ask to see the picture of the missing sailors."[210] Creative thinkers would say it's because most people aren't in the habit of thinking about the missing questions.

Consider missing questions as the most direct path to flipping your view or, at the very least, expanding it. They take you out of the accepted "picture" (represented by the caretaker's view) and cause you to wonder, "Is there actually a full *gallery* of pictures to be seen?" Missing questions change your view of the accepted answers too.

Come back to your own world. How many examples can you think of where you don't pursue the missing question and simply accept the answer? Here are a few primers to help you think:

Politics: I hear your critique of the other party and your opponent, but what's *your solution* beyond getting yourself elected?

Corporate: I understand who you are blaming and that you've asked that person to step down, but how will you keep the *problem* from happening again?

Education (channeling Deborah Meier): I'm clear that, as an administrator, you want all students to do well on the standardized tests so you encourage teachers to teach to them . . . but help me out here: How does this benefit the *students*?

It's not that we never consider the missing questions but, like fit, rarely do we pursue such questions and rarer still do we make them our habit. But such a habit is the mechanism that creates exchanges, solicits evidence of understanding and proof of value, generates new information, challenges stale ways of doing, and most important, reveals possibilities for a better way. At the very least, missing questions ought to be put in our toolkit and maintained well.

It shouldn't surprise you that missing questions offer one of the most direct paths to breakthrough ideas. More than border crossing, questions of this sort are often border busting—at once moving into new territory to explore while directly confronting the value of defending old turf. At times, they actually allow you to *form* the intersection of "known" and "new" rather than simply stay open to it.

Musicologist and MacArthur Fellow Susan McClary described her "missing questions" habit this way: "What I listen for and often hear are the *anomalies*, the things most others miss or conclude are simply unimportant 'mistakes.' That's when I ask myself, 'Am I going to normalize that like everyone else, or hit 'em upside the head with it?' When I dig into the part that's being missed," Susan said, "it can't help but inform. And sometimes, it reveals. In all honesty, my most creative discoveries have come from the part that's missing or being missed."[211]

Susan's way of asking the missing questions exposes a subtle but vital observation not to be overlooked if you want to use missing questions (or any type of question) to amplify your creative capacity. It's a matter of *choice*. As she stated it, even as the missing question forms in your head, another question is always hot on its heels—so are you going to "normalize" or pursue? Or, as Cicero might have put it, are you going to accept what the temple keepers tell you is relevant, or are you going to dig into what's missing to see how it might reshape the story and the lesson? Within that choice, the missing question either becomes relevant or another chance to ignore your gut.

Everything about missing questions invites a flipped view, something central to creativity. It's a mental version of walking across the borders that naturally frame your view and then turning around to look back on your world and asking these questions: *Does it all still fit and make sense from this angle? Or do I see something missing, maybe even something new, possibly better?* It's a way to avoid what author and mythologist Joseph Campbell called "the sin of inadvertence, of not being alert, not quite awake." He believed that, with all of mankind's gifts, his greatest fault was failing to stay awake and remain willing to reconsider. (See Author's Notes: Chapter Seven-B.) We could also describe this fault as not being in the habit of taking note, questioning, and asking ourselves what's missing.

5. Portraiture Questions. To no small degree, we've been taught that every question asked should eventually be paired with a single, right, matching answer. Indeed, many aspects of our lives reinforce that belief. But when the goal instead is to create something new, we want the questions to open us up. That means asking good questions isn't enough. We have to place our questions and what they tell us in context. That's where **PORTRAITURE QUESTIONS** come in.

Portraiture questions take their name from Fellow Sara Lawrence-Lightfoot's methodology of panning out the lens to take in more of what's going on. (Later in this chapter, you'll hear from Sara and later in the book you'll learn much more about portraiture.) Portraiture questions are *framework* questions; they function to set anything you see or consider in context.

You're already familiar with a few examples of portraiture questions. They include Deborah Meier's five habits of the mind, Toyota's 5 Whys, even "missing" and "unprofessional" questions can function as portraiture questions. Each pushes away from the formulaic one-answer-equals-one-response structure and allows you to consider whatever you're looking at in a wider scope. Each type pushes you to think in context, to consider relevance, impact, and even "return"—that is, what you get back minus what you put into the effort. By contrast, when you operate in the mindset of censure of other possibilities (especially when trying to create), you don't shut out only those other possibilities; you inevitably shut out *reality*.

Portraiture questions don't simply put you back in touch with other *things* you might not be considering; they help link you to other *people* and what they are seeing and considering. Like their namesake, portraiture questions are acts of *co-creation*. They acknowledge and honor that big ideas are a layering and weaving and sorting of many smaller ideas, not all of which are likely to be your own.

Similarly, portraiture questions lead you to understanding what *others* think and extending the invitation to them to create alongside you. It isn't just the possibility of what they might bring to your big idea that makes you do this. It's the reality that if they don't feel a sense of ownership, then their commitment to making the idea real never solidifies. (For two familiar examples, think back to the dynamic around Deborah's Five Habits and how she and others collaborate to reform education, or about how John Hunter's fourth graders work together to solve world peace.)

MacArthur Fellow and founder of Legal Services for Prisoners with Children Ellen Barry described this kind of contextual and co-created inquiry as another level of opening up. "A lot of creativity is about opening up ways to talk to one another," Ellen made clear. "In that comes the chance to ask more questions and to *think* in expanded ways that lead to better and better answers."[212]

As I listened to Ellen, I couldn't help but think about the challenging borders she's had to cross to gain rights for incarcerated parents and their children. "Prisons are the third rail," Ellen said of a place and context often perceived as "fixed." It's also a topic that's hard to think about differently because it's almost taboo to touch. "But creativity is needed there too," Ellen said. "While creativity around social justice is not something people immediately recognize, social justice is absolutely an area that *requires* and is *enhanced* by creativity." The question is how to insert it.

To successfully do what she does, Ellen asks portraiture questions. One question at a time, the old frameworks through which people view prisons and prisoners are taken apart, re-examined, and reconsidered. The conclusions that seemed obvious in a "thought-stagnant" world look different when they're opened up. Ellen has consistently found that new ways to put the pieces together and to see naturally rise like a phoenix out of this type of questioning.

Ellen described it this way: "When you're in a particular field or defined by a particular role, it's easy to believe everyone knows and accepts certain things. The implications in social justice are even greater. You can easily become fixed in your views. That said," she continued, "I'm constantly struck by the value of a fresh look and amazed at how a simple question can act like a little window offering a view not previously considered. Sometimes that window is internal—prisoner-to-prisoner, prisoner-to-correctional staff. Other times it's external—a simple question previously unasked causes those who regulate prisons or the taxpayers who fund them, or anyone who's never thought about what might be different to suddenly pause and consider what *might* be.

"The bottom line is this: If you can't open up the conversation, then you can't help but bound your creative possibilities. Without the little windows, the only ideas likely to come forth are the formulaic kind. Questions create those windows."[213]

Portraiture questions powerfully get at what Ellen described because they move us from a "what-driven" view to a "why-driven" view. Here's the difference. If our habit is to think, "That's *what* we've always done" or "*What* do I get at the end of this effort?" we're in a "what-driven" mode. But when all is said and done, we care far more about "why." *Why* do we want the outputs of the current way of doing things? *Why* does what we have right now represent the greatest possible value we could have? *Why* exactly do we do and think the way we do?

We think the answers to "what" represent value. But it's the answers to "why" that allow us to define and create value in the first place and expand it with time. (More on this in Chapter Thirteen.) Asking portraiture questions is the key to understanding this; it helps get us to the value we seek.

6. Depth-Check Questions. Having a framework view gives you room to step back, so let's do that now. Some of the thoughts elicited by the types of questions discussed so far—unprofessional, fit, self-interview, missing, and portraiture—can be heady ones. While some people think big thoughts often, many do not. And while such big thoughts and questions are enormously beneficial, sometimes they aren't. That's why it's important to regularly ask questions that check the depth at which you're operating. **DEPTH-CHECK QUESTIONS** help you gauge *where* you are and *why* you're seeing what you see. They also signal when you may need to *change* depths to get the larger frame back in focus.

I credit Liz Lerman with leading me to designate these as depth-check questions. In *Hiking the Horizontal,* Liz described her own questioning mind as sometimes being in the "shallow" and other times in the "deep." An image of swimming in the big neighborhood pool during the summers of my youth immediately came to mind.

"I think both ends of a spectrum like this are useful and valuable," Liz wrote. Tracking with her comment, I thought of how, on certain days at the pool, no one could drag me out of the deep end. That's where I'd dive in, go deep, and challenge myself by testing how long I could hold my breath at the deepest point. But other days, lolling in the shallow water fit my mood and my needs better. "It is good to have the ability to move among these possibilities with ease, skill, and an unembarrassable outlook," Liz concluded.[214] Why? Because swimming the depth range is how we weave and weigh meaning.

Creativity that has impact is akin to using the "whole" pool, not necessarily in one swim or even one summer, but over time. To the point of "different depths at different times," it is, in fact, impossible to swim in both the deep and shallow ends at the same time. But it's just as true that somewhere in the mix, the extremes overlap with no clear line of demarcation. So even when you're in one end, you're aware of (perhaps overlapped with) the other.

What you experience at each extreme is quite different. That's why exploring both the deep and the shallow is important. What you experience at each end influences how you see *everywhere*. On any particular day, your swimming skills are more or less attuned to playing more proficiently at one end, even if you possess the skills to swim in both. But over time, the richest experience—the fullest understanding of this fluid space—comes from spending time at both ends, not only one. Balance again.

Liz wrote, "I learned over a long period that meaning is wonderful but sometimes it isn't."[215] I love the honesty of that insight. You'd think it applied mainly to the deep end and deep questions. It's natural to think that when you go deep, you'll find the meaning. But Liz is pointing to a more valuable insight and a better rule of thumb. There isn't just one place where good ideas imbued with meaning and value can be found. You have to be willing to swim around and be open to questions as you do.

I like how Maria Chudnovsky added to the insight, one as true in her world of math as in Liz's world of dance. "Usually there are a couple of big questions that everyone in the field is trying to solve," Maria said about math's deep end. "But if you sat at your desk and tried to solve only those, you'd never get anywhere. You have to chip away or spin off to carve a path. Those smaller efforts, at times taking you way off to one side and seemingly away from the point, eventually connect you back to the big questions. They can also help you *shape* those big questions or form more meaningful ones. Regardless, the process of questioning is never static."[216]

Deep to shallow. Shallow to deep. Ultimately, making meaning and achieving a lasting impact is a blend of both. What helps you to see that meaning and materialize it requires continually checking your depth.

A Word About the Last Two Question Types. The first six types of questions were ones that appeared often in my research and conversations. For example, almost every MacArthur Fellow had a knack for asking "unprofessional" questions as part of their larger habit of inquiry. The remaining two question types are a bit different. They are intended to give you a flavor of just how nuanced and effective questions can get once creative inquiry becomes your habit.

As their skill in using inquiry to fuel their creative process rises, people tend to develop powerful questioning forms uniquely their own. And in the end, that's precisely the point. How you use the creative element of inquiry—just as how you come to use *any* of the elements of the language of man—must eventually become a unique expression of *you*.

Both "reverse metaphor" questions and "change-the-W" questions represent how diverse and personalized creative questions can become. In addition, they're both unique and powerful in their own right and worth a look.

7. Reverse Metaphor Questions. In both his book *Cross-pollinations: The Marriage of Science and Poetry* and in my exchanges with him, Gary Nabhan often mentioned the power of metaphor in his creation process. While he's among the most vocal, others share a belief in the value of "injecting one idea or thing into another" to see what new might come from it. This conscious act is a version of Koestler's idea of intersections happening in unexpected ways and toward novel ends.

A metaphor is a way of speaking that transfers the aspects of one thing to another. *Thinking* in metaphors can tap the same power of transference but in ideas. Gary puts an added twist on this taking it one powerful step further.

As strongly as he feels the use of metaphor can be in revealing new ideas, he believes the **REVERSE METAPHOR** explored in the form of a question is an even more potent means by which a new view or idea with breakthrough potential emerges. So when he finds a good metaphor, he flips it to see what else he might see—and then he asks himself questions.

A simple example goes something like this: If the metaphor was "the hospital was a refrigerator" (as in, the place was really, really cold), Gary would reverse it to consider "what would it mean if the refrigerator was a hospital?" He flips the metaphor around to see if it might tell him even more. "Often," Gary said, "I need to run the thinking in both directions like that, to see if the interesting observation truly reveals a breakthrough idea or maybe a pattern I've missed. Sometimes," Gary admitted, "an interesting observation is only that."[217]

In our simple example, calling the refrigerator a hospital brings up a full range of new associations beyond cold: A place for food, a machine, something you ought to clean more often than you do, perhaps. . . . Gary would probably notice all of these as being relevant. He might think, if the refrigerator *were* a hospital, would that mean we'd design it with separate "wards," each with unique equipment, to be used by different "patients," or in the case of a fridge, different household members?

At first glance, it may be hard to see reverse metaphor questions as little more than play without a point. And Gary fully acknowledged this practice can result in wackiness. But that's precisely the explosive value of the questions raised through the reverse metaphor.

First, it shifts your rote thinking. Once Gary arrives at a good metaphor, his hedgehog brain wants to lock into that idea and build it out. But by choosing to instead first reverse it, before he allows it to lock in, Gary forces his hedgehog into a pause even before the cement sets on the value of the original metaphor. This results in a second benefit: It allows him to poke holes in and test ideas and assumptions he's creating in his head. By asking a question that reverses the meaning, he sees more critically, more creatively, and therefore more clearly.

Still skeptical? Not a problem, because to Gary's way of thinking, there's a benefit to asking this type of question even when it doesn't directly produce a better idea or more clarity. While many times it reveals something unexpected, uniquely valuable, and truly breakthrough, sometimes the pause it gives his brain is value enough.

A favorite example of how using reverse metaphor questions can produce a breakthrough came as a result of Gary's quest to find out why ironwood trees were disappearing from the Sonoran Desert around the Arizona-Mexico border. To explain the mystery, Gary had to understand his baseline by knowing how much ironwood was out there in the desert. He began by making his own observations and supplementing them with what others had seen. Strangely, the results contrasted markedly. In short, he saw *more* trees than others did.

Gary's immediate thought was, "Man! Their research is colorblind!" And while he may have meant it as an off-the-cuff remark, it occurred to him to "flip" the thought. Suppose the research (and researchers) *were* colorblind; . . . might they be seeing something different than non-colorblind people could see?

In reverse metaphor fashion, he rounded up two groups of colleagues—colorblind and not colorblind—and sent them into the desert to count ironwood in the exact same area. Sure enough, because ironwood trees camouflaged themselves near other protective plants, the trees were more visible to those who *were* colorblind than those who were not. (In case you're wondering, Gary is colorblind. That's why he saw more trees in his initial surveys.) This insight allowed researchers to not just look *for* ironwood trees in a different way, but to look *at* them differently as well.

Gary has developed a simple, accessible form of inquiry. Just flip the tool you're already using, metaphor or otherwise, and see what results might surface. This habit works like a two-way mirror—from one side you *reflect;* from the other you *observe* and *see through.* The resulting *blended view* raises possibilities that would have otherwise gone unnoticed and unconsidered.

8. Change-the-W Questions. Sara Lawrence-Lightfoot's co-authored book *The Art and Science of Portraiture* references the philosopher Nelson Goodman and his 1978 essay "When Is Art?"

Just by sharing the title of his essay, Sara and co-author Jessica Hoffmann Davis allude to one of the most versatile, creative, and revealing question types I've come across. I call it the **CHANGE-THE-W QUESTION**.

Look at Goodman's essay title and ask, *What's wrong with it?* Really, it's only "wrong" in the sense that it's not what we "expect." We fully expect the question *What is art?*—a deeply entangled prompt leading to an equally knotted argument. But asking *When is art?* causes an unexpected chain reaction. We tilt our head (literally and figuratively) at wording that diverges from our expectation. When we do, we pause at least long enough to sort things out. In that instant, we're already on the verge of thinking differently. We just need to give ourselves a push into new thinking, and "changing the W" is an easy way to provide that push.

Like Gary Nabhan, Nelson Goodman has employed a form of metaphor in his question as well. We don't associate the word "when" in this question with the typical thoughts we have about art. So in exchanging "when" for "what" in the question, our brain rejiggers ideas and transfers associations from one mental file to another. Intersection!

As Sara wrote, "Goodman dismisses the determination of what is art and what is not art as a most frustrating initiative . . ." and "instead redirects his inquiry into the aspects objects display *when* they are functioning as art."[218] That sly devil. With the change of a *single word*, he's torn down the walls prebuilt to limit discussion, and he's taken us across the border into new lands. It provides a chance for a new exchange and entirely new ideas. Not only does this "slight of hand" shift the entire focus of the conversation and its meaning, but he suddenly has us thinking about the *process*, not just the *output*.

There's nothing fancy here. And *you* can ask this type of question as well as anyone. Changing the W, in fact, may be the easiest of all the question types to experiment with. You know the options like the back of your hand: *Who? What? Where? When? Why? How?* You're so comfortable with them that, long ago, you learned to overlook that one sibling begins with an *H* instead of a *W* and you like her anyway.

Using this type of question is as simple as taking the question that occurs to you for reasons of fit, framing, depth, or a sense of something missing, and then changing the first word. Doing that could shift everything.

IS THAT A QUESTION?

So wise are we becoming about questions and creativity, let's consider this question before we leave the discussion: Does questioning have to take the form of a question? The short answer is: *No.* The five-layers-deep answer looks like this: It doesn't because it's not really about the *question* anyway; it's about the *mindset infused with inquiry*.

Several MacArthur Fellows made a point of saying that a question doesn't always take the form of a question, and others agree. "Sometimes, and probably more often than we realize, the important questions roll around in our minds for a long time before we act on them," wrote Bayles and Orland. "Sometimes, in fact, they sit there for a long time before we even realize they're important."[219] And in that period of incubation, the questions may not first appear as questions.

For photojournalist Susan Meiselas, questions weren't consciously seen as her driver. "I'm not sure I'd frame it as questions," Susan said about her creative unfolding. "My thought process is more visual. The visual thinking and sorting defines my flow rather than a question."[220]

Though she was speaking about questions in the traditional format with words and a question mark, it's clear that questions have always been there for her, a fact that quickly seeped into our conversation. As I took my own deliberate pause to let her meaning soak in, Susan confidently continued, "Of course, there *are* questions that come from an encounter with a subject or a setting, but I follow what's happening in the moment. I don't stop and ponder. I'm too busy doing."

Fair enough. As Susan and others made clear, a question need not be something that garners undue attention or cogitating. But when they occur—and at whatever speed they enter then exit our immediate focus—questions give us an opportunity to take a conscious pause so we can *absorb* what's been done and seen before we start "doing" all over again.

To Susan, the value isn't in pondering at length. Though the question is absolutely present, it's processed so quickly that it's rarely noted as a question. Because much of her work takes place in war-torn countries where women who think as freely as Susan aren't always valued, this rapid-fire approach is understandable. In her young career, she's been kidnapped more than once and narrowly escaped death several times. Such dynamic circumstances are hardly the environment in which one thinks about the formal *act* of asking and answering questions. You could say Susan's work often forces her to swim quickly at the wading end of the thought pool; war simply doesn't allow frequent deep dips into inquiry. But that's only part of the story. . . .

When given the chance to pause, Susan sees the connections between the smaller questions quickly asked and answered during each assignment. Unexpectedly, she's seen them quilt *across* assignments too.

"In a recent retrospective, I did step back and focus on larger questions," Susan acknowledged. "For perhaps the first time, rather than considering a single assignment, I thought about my practice in total. Clearly, that's the point of a retrospective. *What were the common threads? What questions had I considered along the way, even imperceptibly? What led me from one kind of project to another?*" Susan was realizing this almost as she said it to me.

"So rather than presenting a series of objects, I tried to link the photos across the years to see the progression," she said. In addition to challenging herself, she was also being challenged by the exhibit's curator to ask big questions and take deliberate pauses to consider them. They were, in a word, co-creating. That resulted in finding deeper meaning, and the mechanism for mining the depth was inquiry.

"In choosing the pieces and trying to link them, I avoided saying 'I like'—as in 'I like this subject' or 'I like to shoot this way,'" Susan reflected. "Because I did so, I saw progression—the challenges I'd set for myself, and how I moved through and between them. I described my meaning or what things had in common or how patterns came to be. The curator saw them too and prompted me further with questions."[221]

For Susan, pushing herself to see patterns was empowering and, from that, "chapters" emerged in her creative story to that point. She continued, "What that means for coming chapters or even right now is hard to say. *Do the past patterns influence?* Maybe. *Will there emerge other leaps and shapes and patterns still unknown?* Undoubtedly, but who knows for sure?" Sounds like a lot of good questions. . . .

Liz Lerman provided an added observation to Susan's story. She pointed out that we often *disguise* questions even if we don't mean to. Offering an example, she commented, "If you are a child or a young adult, noticing frequently takes the form of complaining. It took me a while to see the connection between that internal crankiness and a method of inquiry."[222] Child or not, we've all drifted into this dynamic; we just didn't know that when we did, we were drifting toward a question.

Not surprisingly, Liz has built a career out of her questioning mindset. The questions are in the forefront for her now, but she says matter-of-factly, "None of these realizations started as questions. They all started as complaints, opinions, awareness of discomfort, internal monologues looping around in an obsessive brain. It took a while to figure out that by changing the tone and letting my sentences end with an upward tilt, I could actually get back to the material at hand and go to work. Inquiry became liberating."[223]

Again, tapping into our creative capacity is less about the question than about the questioning nature of our mindset. Good questions simply help to lever up what's already innate. To make the link, sometimes we have to call it out—or perhaps have it called out for us. "I want my audience to *lean forward* into my work. I want their *heads to tilt*," Liz said about the familiar signals we give to indicate we're beginning to wonder.[224] Liz knows that when her audience does these things, the questions are no longer hers alone.

If you lean forward and let *your* head tilt, I think you'll see what I'm talking about—without question.

THE GIFT OF INQUIRY

WONDERS NEVER CEASE

When I began my conversations with MacArthur Fellows, I had many questions in mind. Among them, I asked about the role of questions themselves in each individual's creative process and the importance of questions to creativity overall. But I couldn't have predicted the extent of the pervasiveness of questions in the creative practices of every person I spoke with. "The deepest aspect of creativity is finding the question," Stu Kauffman said, reflecting a sentiment that permeated my interviews. "A question is the deepest mystery and the very thing that drives you forward into the unknown."[225]

But most surprising was the degree to which the Fellows sought to *gift* this grail to others. The gift of inquiry took place in classrooms and labs, in communities large and small, in public and in private. And it happened professionally as well as personally. The idea of gifting the power of inquiry wasn't solicited by me; it simply surfaced. In each case, the stories and the tone in which they were shared moved me deeply. My interview with Sara Lawrence-Lightfoot is representative of this point. It was a powerful and ultimately beautiful conversation.

"In my family, there was this 'way,'" Sara began.[226] Then she paused briefly but perceptibly. I could "hear" her reflecting on the clear impact this "way" had had on her. It was similar to feeling I could "hear" in Susan's voice her ability to "see" the questions in her creative process as she described it to me.

"There was this constant interest in asking questions. Good ones. Not necessarily the kind of questions that had clear answers, but questions *judged as good* when they opened up possibility and the opportunity of pursuing knowledge," Sara continued. Clearly, for Sara and her family, this was more than inquiry. It was a way of thinking, communicating, exploring, and connecting with one another—in short, a way of *being* in which inquiry was central.

A validating story came to mind for Sara as she talked about this. Sara said, "My parents had a practice. On your birthday, you could ask one question you really wanted to get the answer to. For my siblings and me, they became *burning* questions, *building* ones.

Sometimes they would build over a year before we got that big opportunity to ask."

Picture a question *so* valuable, it was considered a *gift* just to ask it. Ponder the mindset and the way of being that could spring up around such a ritual.

Sara related a story about something she overheard her father say one evening. He made the comment to close friends ("comrades in the struggle" Sara called them, referring to her parents and her parents' friends). Together, they were seeking to make an impact as young black professionals in the 1960s. "I heard my father call himself a *feminist*," Sara told me. "When I heard him say that word, it felt *dangerous*, ominous. Two weeks later, I had my eighth birthday and asked about that comment. It led to a whole deep conversation and eventually to a way of being for me."

PAYING IT FORWARD

As I listened to Sara, I recalled similarities in my growing up years. Questions weren't only a gift in my home, they were an expectation—something we trained for each day and especially at dinner. While in most families parents assume the role of questioner, in my family, my parents (my father in particular) wanted questions coming back at them. My brother and I weren't only expected to contribute; we were expected to *question*—to think, to dig in, to understand, and to build on what we heard in response. Each subsequent question we asked needed to be headed somewhere.

To this day, my father has a reputation as the guy at social gatherings who finds a person to talk to—*one* person—and spends the entire event asking him or her questions. Rarely are they run-of-the-mill inquiries such as *What do you do?* or *Where do you live?* Most are unexpected such as *What do you remember most fondly about growing up?* and *Who was the biggest influence in your life?* These are Darden Smith-like questions. Layers of questions follow his first, each tailor-made from the person's answers—a sure sign he's exploring and listening. His "quarries" most often come away feeling as if, often for the first time, someone genuinely wants to *know* them. They also feel they understand themselves better as a result of considering the questions they were prompted to answer.

For a long time I thought this came from the "lawyer" qualities in my dad. But over time, I've come to appreciate it's the *human* qualities in him—a man fully in touch with the remarkable power of a question. As Sara concluded in our conversation, "The most important thing is the question you are asking—the methodology, the results, the impact. Everything follows that. It's a person's mindset."

Just as my parents used questions with me, my wife and I do with our two children—at dinner, on hikes, when traveling, even when driving around town. It's clear that Sara too has assimilated questions into her life and her work. It's also evident she has absorbed the desire to share this gift with others, to pay it forward.

FRAMING THE VIEW

As noted earlier, Sara is the creator of a research approach to sociology called Portraiture. Sara's method is unique, in part because it looks at every available aspect of a person's world and "inquires" how each element shapes them. Consider it a framework view, one that's deeply tied to questioning.

Unlike most sociology pedagogy, portraiture is a two-way exchange. Think of it not as an analysis but as a *conversation,* one in which the flow of questions, answers, and observations is multidirectional. You ask, I ask, we discover and create. Together. It's inquiry coming "full circle" in the fullest sense.

Using this method, the presumed research *subject* is more accurately called a *participant.* As Sara says, portraitists (i.e., researchers employing this method) don't only listen *to* a story; they listen *for* a story. The story that's ultimately told is one of co-creation, which is a remarkable departure from the typical outsider-looking-in way of telling stories about others. In effect, the two-way portraiture process opens up a broader view—precisely what inquiry is meant to do.

But at some level, a "model"—even one as exceptional as portraiture—can sound all theory and academic, can't it? The true gift of inquiry arrives when you witness that it's infused your whole life. Sara's story about Agnes conveys a beautiful example of that.

RIPPLES BACK

One way Sara has shared her insights has been by writing books. As each is published, she typically goes on a book tour to talk about it. "When I'm on the road speaking," Sara said, "the audience is more diverse [than at home or at work at Harvard]. Who they are and why they're there isn't always clear."[227] While the purpose of these tour events is primarily for the author to share her insights, Sara allows ample time for questions from audience members. Not all speakers do this—maybe due to lack of time or a fear of opening up or as a result of viewing their role as only sharing *their* answers. But this is not Sara's approach.

When Sara concluded her remarks at one particular event several years back, she opened up the conversation to the room. No one immediately raised a hand, but as people got ready to leave, one woman in the front row raised hers. The woman wasn't dressed like everyone else there. She appeared more ragged and slightly unkempt. Sara had a feeling she'd seen this woman somewhere before. Was it at a previous event, Sara wondered, or had it been on the sidewalk outside? Sara wasn't sure, and it was hard to tell what letting this woman ask a question might bring. But allowing questions matters to Sara—after all, she knows that inquiry is a gift.

So she called on Agnes (as Sara later learned the woman's name to be). Agnes said, "You know, professor, when you began describing your book, I thought, 'I don't understand a word this woman is saying. Why am I here? What is she trying to tell me?' Then I said to myself, 'Agnes, just relax and let the words fall over you.' I did just that and I'm here to say you are saying something profound." With a feeling of amazement clearly lingering, Sara then told me what Agnes said she saw in Sara's work. "Agnes told *me* exactly what I was saying. And she asked me questions I hadn't thought about, or at least not in the way Agnes thought about them." Inquiry isn't just a gift; it's a gift that gives back.

A CLOSING THOUGHT—OR IS IT "OPENING?"

"In the most profound sense," George Kneller wrote, "to be creative is to fulfill oneself as a person."[228]

Ultimately, each of us individually—Sara, Agnes, me, you . . . all of us—must choose to be who we are. When we do, we catalyze a ripple effect. We step across borders. We open up to the possible. We think about why things are the way they are. We imagine what could be. In all of this, we are, as John Hunter put it, *in the process of becoming* as we search for answers to the biggest question of all: *What does it mean to be human?*

Inquiry is a gift, and if we're smart, we unwrap that gift. If we're smarter still, we re-gift it. When we do, sometimes someone out of the ordinary steps up to reveal her *own* questions and her *own* insights and, in the process, yours are transformed too. Remarkable. In this way, asking questions can become an invitation to play and a collective creation with ever-greater returns.

But you never know until you ask.

SIMPLE TRUTH:

THE HUMAN

QUESTION

DRIVES US

CHAPTER EIGHT

SIMPLE TRUTH: THE HUMAN QUESTION DRIVES US

Questions are a fundamental element of the language of man, springboarding us across borders and into the breakthrough space where we render the "big" ideas. The form, range, and use of questions are limitless.

But one question unites all inquiry in the realm of creativity—the "human question": *What does it mean to be human?*

THE HUMAN QUESTION

Full disclosure: There's some depth to the human question and therefore to this chapter. But as James Nestor wrote in *Deep: Freediving, Renegade Science, and What the Ocean Tells Us About Ourselves*, "the deeper we dive the more pronounced [our] reflexes become."[229] And that's just what we want—to strengthen our creative reflexes. Dipping into the "deep end" to explore the human question, one of the richest topics in understanding creativity, is an important way to do that.

If you're not typically a deep-end swimmer or thinker, fear not. This chapter simply puts a critical first toe in the water, beginning with a story to get you in the proper frame of mind for swimming. For now, sit for a moment on the edge of the pool and "watch" this TV spot for the Apple iPad. Relax. I'll paint the picture for you. . . .

ONE BITE OF THE APPLE

In early 2014, Apple Inc. launched an ad campaign called Your Verse, the hub of which was a ninety-second video spot infused with the voice of actor and comedian Robin Williams. (See Author's Notes: Chapter Eight.)

Williams' distinct, soothing baritone stitches together a breathtaking album of images: a busy marketplace; a cathedral-like entryway; skaters at a hockey rink; kids walking in the woods; a deep-sea diver below the sea's surface; an offshore wind turbine above that surface; a marching band warming up; a rock concert seen from the first row; the cockpit of a rescue helicopter; a woman dancing; storm chasers beneath a developing tornado. In total, the Apple spot provides a Technicolor sampler of the human fabric.

Once the images have unfolded and your mind has begun to fathom what you see, Williams' voice warmly oozes in to guide you deeper. "We don't read and write poetry because it's cute," Williams said. "We read and write poetry because we are members of the human race. And the human race is filled with *passion*." He pauses, deliberately, and then continues at a swift pace. "Medicine, law, business, engineering—these are noble pursuits and necessary to *sustain* life. But *poetry . . . beauty . . .* romance, love—*these* are what we stay alive *for*."[230] And in a short twenty-eight seconds and only fifty-five words, you feel your pulse quicken. He's already got you.

Williams' siren-like voice hums like a vibration deep inside. And there's something more you're hearing—something with a familiar ring. It's the sound of a question forming, one that Apple knows each of us identifies with: *What does it mean to be human?* The visual feast offered is so rich, it would be hard to come up with a single answer to this question. And Williams has made the options for answering richer still—pointing us to something deeper (poetry, passion, beauty)—things we might not have brought to mind as our first thought, but once he's said it, we find ourselves saying, *"Yes."*

As the ad continues, Williams quotes a Walt Whitman poem[231] that ponders human existence and worth. "O me! O life! Of the questions of these recurring," Williams breathes. "What good amid these, O me, o life?" he asks. Now the questions aren't simply implied; they're at the forefront. And they're big. *Why am I here? Why do I exist? Why bother?* They seem unanswerable. But Whitman has an answer, and the creatives at Apple know the power behind the answer to *any* question lies within it.

His answer: "That you are here—that life exists and identity. That the powerful play goes on, and you may contribute a verse." Translation: Each of us, each living being, is a statement of *existence* and more. There's *identity*—not simply existence but *expression*. And it's not one line, one act, or one performance that defines our identity or completes our expression of it. It's the rippling of many expressions, ours and those of others, across a *powerful play*. For Whitman, every individual represents a matchless statement of being. And each life is part of a powerful play that goes on *because* of us—magically, masterfully, confusingly, rapidly, perpetually.

You are here and play a part, passively or actively. But the true wonder is that *you can contribute a verse*—a powerful, creativity-laden verse. And when you do, life exists. So does identity. Yours.

Even without Whitman and Williams and Apple, you know this to be true: *Your thoughts, your actions, and your creations matter.* They matter for what they can do and for what they might manifest, yes, but also for the expression they give to *who you are* and to *what it means* to be human.

Brilliantly, Apple calls forth what you know and feel deep within you, even if you don't often stop to consider it. Williams repeats Whitman's answer a second time—"that the powerful play goes on, and you may contribute a verse"—to signal you, to reignite you, to push the cycle forward once again. And then, he pushes you forward directly into this question: "What will *your* verse be?"

SWIMMING CREATIVE WATERS

Why would Apple put out such a big question in a ninety-second spot ultimately meant to sell iPads?

Within the context of the hundreds of messages bombarding us each day, this appears to be unnecessarily risky. Think about it: Most ads *tell* us; this one *asks* us. More, it asks a big, deep question: What will *your* verse be? Crazy? Yup—crazy like a fox.

Here's what's brilliant about the Your Verse spot: Apple knows that you not only can handle going deep, but you're also drawn to it. The company isn't afraid of what this big question might negatively do to iPad sales, even though this question resides in the *deep end* of our cerebral sea. Apple isn't worried because the question also dwells in the *shallow* end of our thoughts and actions. It lingers in our day-to-day activities and the in-between depths as well. It may perhaps go unnoticed, but it's undeniably there because humans are on earth to contribute a verse—and we know it, consciously or not.

EXPLORING THE HUMAN QUESTION— JUST A TOE IN THE OCEAN

All of this asking, knowing, and creating is part and parcel of what I've come to call **THE HUMAN QUESTION**. In conveying this Simple Truth, I plant this thought: Being consciously aware of the human question may be the most potently effective means you have for maximizing your creative potential.

Let me say this clearly and emphatically: The human question drives us—it's a pure and simple truth. It's also, at least at first, a big thought to get your mind around. How big? Well, as big as an ocean.

Creativity *is* ocean-like, and the human question opens a window to the scope of possibility. That's both attractive and overwhelming, as James Nestor's description of the actual ocean conveys. "The current exploration of the ocean," Nestor wrote, "is the equivalent of snapping a photograph of a finger to figure out how our bodies work. The liver, the stomach, the blood, the bones, the brain, the heart of the ocean—what's in it, how it functions, how we function within it—remains a secret, much of it hidden in the dark sunless realms."[232] Considered this way, the human question can feel equally attractive and repelling.

When we push back from this question, we do so in part because it's complicated to talk or even write about. Anytime we pick up the human question and wax philosophic about it, we risk sliding into the limitations that strip it of its power in the creative process. We do so by trying to be emphatic in our answers. It's then we risk implying, even if unintentionally, that there's one way to look at this question, whatever that way might be. Once down that slope, we too easily get into a quagmire about its value.

But it *is* valuable. And the human question repeatedly surfaces when creative practitioners talk about how they do what they do. My goal here is simple: To invite you to put your toe in the tide line of this vast ocean, nothing more. Your goal is to become *aware* of how the human question helps you explore this vast ocean that is creativity. So as you read on, I suggest you try "being" Isaac Newton as he described himself earlier, "playing in the seashore" seeking something beyond the "ordinary" while recognizing that "the great ocean of truth" will always somehow remain undiscovered.

Better still, be like my daughter Ella. As big as this question seems, move forward toward it and be newly aware of its role of creativity. Go a bit further still and resolve to wade in and give the human question your consideration more often. Play with the idea—just as Ella played with the idea that the tide isn't as ominous and off-putting as it might at first appear.

For now, I offer this small enticing bite of the apple. Consider it your own ninety-second spot.

THE PATTERN BEFORE US

DO YOU SEE IT?

One of the most compelling reasons for calling attention to the human question is the pattern you may have noticed across the Fellows' descriptions of creativity. To jog your pattern-recognition powers, here's a flashback to a few of their comments:

> *"There's something human in asking . . . about new ways that might be better."*   —Deborah Meier

> *"What's the central element to living a human life? That's the ultimate question."*   —Rebecca Newberger Goldstein

> *"Creativity is about preserving a sense of wonder at all, both keeping it awake and reawakening it, stretching it. It's bringing in or bringing back that sense of urgency . . . around being human."*
> — Elizabeth Streb

> *"This wondering, this search for fit is the very thing that makes us human."*   — Elaine Pagels

Besides these examples, similar references were made by visual artist Gary Hill, neurophilosopher Pat Churchland, conservationist Steve Goodman, stone carver Elizabeth Turk, ethnobotanist Gary Nabhan. . . . Are you seeing a pattern?

Consistently, those who openly practice creativity make the connection between creativity and the human question. They don't merely acknowledge creativity as a human *ability*. Instead, they see it as *defining the search* for what it means to be us and *reflecting the effort* to manifest answers to the human question.

THE PATTERN ALL AROUND YOU

The MacArthur Fellows aren't the only ones pursuing the human question; they just happen to appreciate its link to creativity more than most. The prevalence of the human question around us in itself should give us pause to consider the meaning and power of its role.

Putting a different spin on it, *You Are Now Less Dumb* author David McRaney suggested that "all humans eventually reduce every confusing element of life down to two questions: Where did we come from and why are we here?"[233] It's interesting how McRaney used this observation to point out that *all of us*—not a special subset of the population—have similar questions rolling around in our heads. It turns out that McRaney, a self-described psychology geek and award-winning author, is one of countless thinkers who have referenced the human question and its derivatives.

To offer a slice of evidence, while this book was being written, sociologist Brené Brown was tearing up the TED Talk series with her message captured by the title of her best-selling book *Daring Greatly*. The core of her message was to help us realize "what we know matters, but who we are matters more."[234] She said it's incumbent on each of us—simply because we're human—to dare greatly and realize that we are meant to, need to, and even equipped to seek out the answer to *who we are* as humans.

About the same time, an article appeared in the *Washington Post* by science writer Joel Achenbach titled "5 Big Questions Still Stump Science."[235] He pinpointed overarching vital questions including: *Why does the universe exist* and *what's our place in it?* His siren call reminded us not to complacently conclude we've got it all figured out.

To solidify his point, Achenbach observed that even those all-knowing scientists doing a lot of answering for us are still searching for answers to *what does it mean to be human* kinds of questions. Likely, they always would be, he concluded. Start looking around and you'll undoubtedly see examples of your own. And if you take an unhurried moment to think about it, you realize McRaney, Brown, and Achenbach are right: The human question is all around us and continues to call us forth.

HOW "OTHER" QUESTIONS FIT INTO THE HUMAN QUESTION

We might not give such questions grand treatment; we might not even consider them consciously. But we've all asked a version of the human question at some point—in traffic, in a place of worship, at the end of a hard day, when a new life comes into the world, when a loved one dies. We ask a thousand "other" contributing questions too, each infused with nuance from our view of the world, our personal needs, and our individual level of comfort with questioning. It turns out that, instead of tackling the human question head on, all those "other" questions often prove to be the key to gradually chipping away at the human question.

GETTING BENEATH THE HUMAN QUESTION TO INFORM IT

Though we most often consider them separately, the many contributing questions we pursue in our lives powerfully quilt together. Even when it's unconscious, the answers we arrive at to any one question inform the rest. All of our Q&A merges naturally into *how* we learn and think as well as *what* we do and *why.* Because it does, we often perceive the process as little more than day-to-day learning, thinking, and doing. Yet it's all part of the more encompassing question of *what it means to be human*—whether or not we consciously pause to think of it this way.

Asked directly or involuntarily, our individual questions involve us in the *same search* that creative practitioners consistently refer to. Sometimes we even recognize our other questions as "touching the edge" of the human question. But when we do, our tendency is to pull back from the insight. Why? Well, first of all, the human question can feel *enormous*—like the ocean.

Second, when it's encountered, we reflexively consider it to be like other questions and assume the human question has *an* answer. That's precisely where we can get frustrated, confused, or put off. There simply isn't a single answer.

Rather than move back from the edge of the human question, we need to move in and "pull apart" this question as well as our assumptions about its answer. We can then understand it more accurately for the role it plays in our lives. Only after that can we bring it all back together again to see its power.

To see both why and how this happens, let's turn again to our MacArthur Fellow guides.

SIMPLE YET POWERFUL "OTHER" QUESTIONS

"Big" questions aren't typically the ones that feed our daily thoughts; it's "other" questions that do. I wondered if such questions could be the kind that *inform* the big questions. So when I interviewed the MacArthur Fellows, I didn't ask them if they pondered the human question. Instead, I asked this: *Are there certain questions that keep resurfacing for you?*

With this question, I didn't expect one universal answer. The diversity in background of this MacArthur group alone would argue against that. In many respects, the only thing the Fellows have in common is having had the same fellowship bestowed on them. Their fields, their generations, their backgrounds, and their resulting priorities and beliefs couldn't be more different. And yet *every one of them* offered up a single question that guided them.

Here's a sample of their recurring "other" questions:

"How do we keep shifting to a new way of being?"
—Bill Drayton, social entrepreneur

"Wouldn't it be cool if . . . ?"
—Heather Williams, animal behavior biologist

"What is it about the 'lie' of fiction that we seem to need or at least be attracted to?"
—Joanna Scott, author and professor of English

"Where is the resonance?"
—Carol Levine, family care specialist

"How can I change the way we think about this?"
—David Rudovsky, civil rights lawyer

"Why is danger profound?"
—Elizabeth Streb, choreographer

"What are we after and how are our current views and language limiting our ability to get there?"
—Gary Nabhan, ethnobotanist

"How can I weave the light into the dark?"
—Lynsey Addario, photojournalist

"How does nature do this and how does nature know?"
—Michael Marletta, president, CEO, Scripps
     Research Institute

"Is this really so?"
—Nick Strausfeld, brain evolution scientist

"Why isn't this more fun?"
—Pam Solo, arms control analyst

Now, pause for a moment and consider this: When an arms control analyst says she's driven by the question of *why isn't this more fun*, doesn't it make you wonder where that question takes her? Even more intriguing is the fact that Pam Solo *returns* to this question—but why? What's the nature of its *ongoing* power? Where does it lead her or what does it connect her to? When nuclear winter always lurks in the background of Pam's work, it can't possibly mean what it seems on the surface. It must point to something *bigger*.

Would Pam link her question directly to the human question? From my conversation with her, I think she would. But her answer doesn't even matter. You see, what Pam, and Michael, and Bill and the rest are doing is adding to the human question one individual question at a time. Each of their questions renders more depth to the human question itself. And the act of looping back around to revisit their driving question is one of refinement, layering, and reconsideration of what they know and what they still want to know.

Here's something else they appreciate: Everything they learn and share through such questions—every level higher they build in their own understanding—takes *all of us* closer to understanding what it means to be human. So when what they *know* gets infused into what they *create*, we all gain value from their contributions to the human question.

POWERFUL, NOT ALL-POWERFUL

These "other" questions shared—and the insights revealed about why these Fellows ask them—are awe-inspiring. But they are not all-powerful, even to the MacArthur Fellows themselves. No one portrayed these questions as being forefront in their minds every day or all the time. That said, each was fully aware of their presence and the ongoing role they played in helping them hone their creative capacity. The questions were part of a larger mindset of inquiry, and that questioning mindset was one part of an even larger *creative* mindset.

All of your guides know as well that there is no secret "right" question to be discovered and then asked. The umbrella-like nature of the human question represents the entire fabric of *who we are* and *how we create.* Its influence and power are best understood when we see the asking and the resulting action of any one question, asked by any one person, as part of a quilt of inquiry. It's a quilt made up of countless sub-questions that reflect *who we are* as individuals and, when combined, as a species. Conclusion? Smaller questions that are consciously and repeatedly asked are the real secret to plumbing the human question.

THE HUMAN QUESTION MUST BE ANSWERED BY YOU

After talking about the role of questions with MacArthur Fellows for nearly two years, I inevitably heard many moving and wonderful stories of how they've individually addressed the human question. Yet this elemental truth remains: *The human question must be answered by each of us, individually.* The method of asking, like the answer itself, doesn't take a singular form. By knowing that, you already know something powerful about creativity and how to tap into it.

Here's an equally important truth: No matter who you are, if you don't consciously seek out your own answer to the human question, others will do it for you. That would be *your* mistake, for it's harder to think creatively and for yourself when you rely on others to provide the answers.

The problem isn't in the kind of answers that others would provide; it's that the answers themselves aren't what matter most in the creative process. (Are you seeing a pattern?) Rather, the power is in *active engagement*—the *act* and the *asking*. It's the only way to develop *your* version of the *creative* mindset, and *that* mindset is what it's all about.

Think back across *The Language of Man*—the growth mindset; a framework mindset; an open, border crossing, questioning, deliberate mindset—and you'll see we're quilting a *creative* mindset. Where does the human question fit in? When *you* engage it, the human question does more than add to your creative mindset; it *amplifies* it.

Each of us not only "does" things in our own way; we "explore," "answer," and "create" in individual ways as well. If we do these consciously, all that "border crossing," "noticing," and "breaking through" accumulates. But when we progress one step further still and consider all of this in the context of the human question, all those "elements" begin to quilt. That's when we see things differently. That's when we sense something larger. And eventually, that's how something beautiful emerges.

It's all part of finding your own *expression* of what it means to be human.

EXPRESSIONS, NOT ANSWERS

"Applying algorithms to creativity is like biochemists trying to formulate the chemistry of love," Twyla Tharp wrote in *The Creative Habit*.[236] It's a good analogy to keep in mind when considering the human question. Still it's helpful to sense the range of answers the human question will bring.

Here, to make the human question (and Tharp's analogy) relevant to our journey, let's revisit two Fellows—Rebecca Newberger Goldstein and Susan Meiselas. Building on what you already know about them, we're able to place the human question into a familiar context.

As you might recall, the styles of these two women couldn't be more different. In that regard, their contrast punctuates the lesson that exploring the human question requires finding your own expression rather than formulaically pursuing it. In their distinctive ways, their stories also emphasize how the pursuit of the human question is ongoing.

"FEEL" AND "ORIGIN"

Rebecca is a philosopher by training, and because of that, she puts the human question squarely in the forefront of her thinking—that's her style. She stated it this way: *What is the central element to living a human life?*

Most of us, however, aren't philosophers or likely to put the human question center stage in the way Rebecca does. But the more important lesson—and what makes *her* story stand out—is that even with the human question firmly in mind, at one point she "lost the feel" for it. Sometimes asking it is not enough.

When her father died and her daughter was born, Rebecca *was* asking the human question, but initially she did so because that's what she'd been taught philosophers were *supposed* to do. In fact, she'd been taught more than the question. She'd been taught the accepted *answers* to the question—all of which was fine . . . until it wasn't. When her life changed quickly and dramatically, she realized it wasn't the actual *answers* she needed. As she said, "I felt the need to get back to where the answers, even the question, *came from*. I needed that not only to understand but also to navigate." It became the difference between *knowing* the question and knowing *how* to question.

As Rebecca described it, "Exploring the questions of life involves *push* as much as *pull*. So as much as you might feel yourself pulled to the question of what it means to be human, sometimes you have to *push* yourself directly back into the storm to maintain contact with the feel and the meaning. The back and forth is perpetual, even if by degrees. One can even experience pain in pursuing this question; to say otherwise would be disingenuous.

"People try hard to get over an experience and don't stay with it long," Rebecca elaborated. "But to me, that unsettling is both the key and the magic. It has to be there in anything I do. Similarly, if you're not tied to those feeling and thinking centers of your brain, you simply don't think well or conceive fully. If what you seek to find is something new, deep, meaningful, and lasting," Rebecca said, "there's no other way than to acknowledge this. *That's* the central element of living a human life."[237]

How *you* choose to engage this exploration—the push and the pull, the unsettling and the magic—can only be *informed* by Rebecca's insights. *Your* experience, *your* feel, and even *your* results will never be the same as hers—thankfully. If they were, the collective understanding of what it means to be human would be lacking *your* unique insight.

But as you proceed on your journey, Rebecca's insights become helpful compass readings. They include the importance of feel, the need to stay in the practice of asking, the tension and uncertainty that can accompany inquiry, and that tension's vital role in revealing meaningful answers.

SOUL-REVEALING IMAGES IN THE REAR VIEW

As direct, present, and beautiful as Rebecca's expression is, it's rare to place the human question up front. In contrast, Susan's story showed how this question can be considered at the end of cycles and even in reverse. Her style is just as discerning as Rebecca's.

Recall that Susan said within any single photojournalism assignment, she didn't consciously pursue a higher question or its absolute answer. But when she allowed herself to look back across the assignments and the soul-revealing images she'd created, she saw clear questions being pursued, even if subconsciously. In hindsight, she saw patterns.

For Susan, seeing those patterns served to record what she'd already seen, created, and learned. But those backward-looking questions also told her what had yet to be done; they framed the view ahead. Even though she wasn't thinking about them all the time, questions amplified the possibility, value, and meaning attained *and* yet to be discovered. Across all of this and in her own way, she was addressing what it means to be human.

The tangible component in both Rebecca's and Susan's stories is individual expression. In the end, it's the true power in the human question. It calls us to express *our* version of creativity. And when we become aware of the dynamic dance between the human question and our creative thoughts and actions, we can more fully tap into our capacity.

LESSONS FROM THE DEEP DIVE

We began this dip into the human question with James Nestor's description of the ocean, so it seems fitting to let him bring us full circle.

Nestor's fascinating book *Deep: Freediving, Renegade Science and What the Ocean Tells Us About Ourselves* explored something we'll likely never feel tempted to do: Hold our breath and, without assistance from scuba tanks or air lines or anything else, drop a hundred feet into the ocean and stay there.

Fascinated with this phenomenon, Nestor wanted to know how freedivers did this. So he began asking questions, and the answers he got from a whole range of experts were basically summed up in this response: "You just dive; you just get in the water."[238]

Just as the ocean sounds too *big*, to Nestor this answer—to just dive in and try it—sounded way too *small*. How could just trying something a little reveal the big "secret?" But then he paused long enough to see the pattern and the wisdom. Across all the practitioners he talked with—the ones who knew freediving from the inside rather than speculating from the outside—Nestor finally realized he had been hearing the *same* message. True, all of them expressed their answers in their own unique ways; but after pausing to consider them, the answers wove together.

In the same way, I invite you to pause and see that this lesson applies to exploring the human question as well. As Nestor wrote, "There was no shortcut, no rulebook, no secret handshake, no specialized equipment or diet or pill that would get me there. The secret to going deep, they all seemed to be saying, was within each of us. We're born with it."[239] All we have to do is start to explore it.

You were born programmed to pursue the human question. If you want it to help you explore the ocean-sized possibilities of creativity, all you have to do is dive in. The Simple Truth is that's the only way to know what Your Verse will be.

THE MYTH

OF

GENIUS

CHAPTER NINE

THE MYTH OF GENIUS

Deliberately take note of how far you've come.

You now know more about creativity than most and, chances are, far more than you did at the start. At this point in your journey, be clear on this: *There's nothing you've learned that you cannot do—from switching between your fox and hedgehog at will, to creating the breakthrough space, to using questions to reveal breakthrough ideas.* Like everyone, you began life with the same factory-issued creative equipment. And by now you are well aware that the "pie chart picture" of creativity in Chapter Two is a false one: There's no genetic lottery dividing the world into one wafer-thin slice of people who are creative, with the rest of the pie made up of those who aren't.

Rest assured, you are *Ready* to create, know how to *Reveal* the space in which creativity thrives, and can *Render* breakthrough ideas with effectiveness.

Building on that, the goal of this fourth section of *The Language of Man* is to *Reconnect* you. At one level, the next four chapters will reconnect you to ideas you've only just come to know but in new and expansive ways. This section will also reconnect you to certain truths long forgotten or previously misunderstood. But at another level, a connection will increasingly be made to those "others" who play a pivotal role in your ability to turn your big ideas into actual, tangible power—a truth instinctively known but easy to lose sight of when the creating is taking place at the individual level.

All this reconnecting serves the two primary goals established right from this journey's start: 1) to deepen your *understanding* of creativity and 2) to get you *using* your creative capacity effectively as a matter of habit.

It's fair to say that at this point the basics of your understanding are in place. To get you using your creative capacity, however, requires two more things: removing certain impediments that frequently stop people in their creative tracks (this chapter and Chapter Ten) and adding further insights that make your ability to use your creative capacity even stronger (Chapters Eleven and Twelve). In combination, the lessons of this section will *Reconnect* you at an important, deeper, and actionable level to your creative capacity.

There's a certain "genius" that comes to you once you become aware of these added lessons and are capable of using them to overcome the impediments to creativity. But by using that word, I risk closing the door to what you are capable of—a door you've been working hard to swing open.

Here's a story that explains why. . . .

FINDING GENIUS

BEHIND GENIUS

The Who, the What, and the When is a collection of essays and letters about "legendary [creators] in the arts, politics, science, and technology."[240] This book teased readers by featuring sixty-five iconic names including Walt Disney, Alan Turing, Harper Lee, and Watson and Crick. What did they all have in common? They were well known and widely considered to be creative geniuses. *But* they had *something else* in common, and this is what led to the book's unexpected premise and content.

On its surface, *The Who, the What, and the When* is a compendium of historical facts and biographical trivia about these individuals. But it's more accurately described as a collection of *admissions*. Instead of recounting the popular myths that shroud each of these "creative geniuses," the sixty-five essays tell of parents and spouses, peers and partners who played vital roles in cultivating that "genius." Benefactors, friends, and mentors also had a hand.

Coaches, stand-ins, rivals, lovers, even the human race at large were all credited by these famous figures as having served up examples, ideas, challenges, revelations, hard-won lessons, and simple but valuable encouragement. All of these were needed, not only to keep these "heroes" moving forward in their creative journeys but to power those "light bulbs of brilliance" hanging over their heads.

The upshot? Not a single "hero" created alone. And the lesson? That lone ranger image—the rogue genetic outlier with that "extra something" or presumed "X-factor" others don't have—is a hindsight myth.

When we hail these heroes and recount their mythologies, we think we are celebrating a conquest. But in reality, we're most often shoring up an impediment, for this idea of genius stands as one of the biggest hurdles to our ability and even willingness to tap into our creative capacity.

Whether intentional or not, we associate genius with rare individuals. Genius, in other words, equals some*one*, not some*thing*. The fantasy of the glorious heroic genius—someone above all our human faults, foibles, and shortcomings who accomplishes things we could only dream of—sets up a border that often comes to be regarded as impenetrable and an ideal implied to be out of reach. *Regular people*, the myth conveys, can't get there.

Ironically, those so-called heroes tell us such a border doesn't exist. Nothing, they claim, separates them from us. That's a claim worthy of a deeper look, so let's check in with our guides.

TOWARD YOUR GENIUS

When I first reached out to MacArthur Fellows, as much as they were eager to speak about creativity, they hesitated about doing so as part of "the MacArthur pool." It wasn't because they aren't proud to be a part of that group; most certainly they are. But there's a mystique around this award, its secretive nomination and selection process, and its accomplished recipients; it's one that years ago led a journalist to dub the Fellowship "the genius award." The label stuck. And fellowship recipients have been living down that mythological moniker ever since.

None of the sixty-six Fellows I spoke with thinks of himself or herself as a genius. In fact, many went out of their way to tell me they were not. Hammering the point further, their peers and families, the people who know them best, don't think of them this way either and willingly remind them from time to time. Ellen Barry, for example, told me about her six-year-old daughter who put Ellen's mythical status quickly into context by agreeing only to call her "*mommy* genius."

But unease with the label is simply emblematic of the larger concern your guides share. They worry that the whole idea of genius is holding back our individual and collective understanding of *what creativity is* and *why all of us must use our capacity for it.* Interesting, isn't it? Something we might misconstrue as the goal (being placed on a pedestal and called a genius) is unexpectedly identified as a root problem.

So in this chapter, we'll address head-on the myth of genius to discover what it really is and learn why we've lost sight of its true origin, meaning, and universality. We'll also go behind the hero myth—one closely linked to the genius myth and equally limiting to our creativity. We'll look at how the journey to heroism actually unfolds—the good, the bad, and the after story—and how the truth about that cycle can inform us about the creative journey. You'll come to understand that, rather than being *above* you, these geniuses are *just like you.* What a simple, powerful truth.

TRUE GENIUS

To understand why the label of genius is both distracting and limiting, let's consider the history of genius and the origin of the word. Journeying from its point of origin to the present can be unexpectedly empowering in helping you tap into your own genius.

ANCIENT ROOTS

GENIUS, both the concept and the word, originated with the Greeks and was spread by the Romans. To its originators, *geni* meant "an element of the soul." Both cultures viewed genius and creative capacity not as separate abilities but as a single intertwined capability of *every* human being. Any point of distinction arose only between those who had *engaged* their geni and those who had not.

To the ancient Greeks and Romans, "genius" was a manifestation of something innate materialized by will, effort, and practice.

The ancients also saw genius as diverse. Rather than playing out in a prescribed way, it was believed to uniquely take form according to the individual who brought it out. No common metric existed by which a person's genius could be ranked above or below another person's. In a similar way, genius was viewed as something that could happen in any field or human undertaking. In short, this original view of genius makes it clear that *anyone, anywhere* could create something *new, distinct, and inspiring.*

Unfortunately, the idea of genius lost its way with the fall of the Roman Empire. It wasn't that humans suddenly misplaced their creative capacity. Instead, when the culture that had nurtured this ancient view of genius collapsed, so did the cultural priority of tapping into it. The period after the Roman Empire and before the Renaissance has been called the Dark Ages. While historians argue about the suitability of the name, there's no doubt the priority of the human capacity for creativity took a backseat to basic existence during those uncertain times.

THE REBIRTH OF "GENIUS"

After centuries of dormancy, the term "genius" was reborn in northern Italy in the late 1400s. This marked the start of the Renaissance, a term that literally means rebirth, resurgence, and recovery. During this period, human ingenuity once again blossomed after a prolonged dark winter. So incredible did the resulting creative outputs appear that people needed a word for what they were witnessing.

Just imagine what it must have been like to be part of this humanist revolution. Within a few decades, the known world leapt from near total absence of original art and literature, invention and new ideas, to a sudden explosion of all of these. Many of the greatest creations mankind has ever seen were born during the Renaissance. Consider alone those who congregated in or traveled through Florence, Italy, to the home of Lorenzo de Medici (as described in Chapter Five)—Michelangelo, Leonardo da Vinci, Brunelleschi, Botticelli, and Vespucci among them. In addition, the ideas and insights of countless other minds, including Shakespeare, Columbus, and Gutenberg, were pouring in, weaving into a bright new collective "possible." It would be difficult to live in that time and place and not to sense the electric atmosphere. Even today, this period in human history boggles the mind. It certainly did for Giorgio Vasari, who brought the word "genius" back into use as a way to capture what he was seeing.

In his now iconic book *Lives of the Most Excellent Painters, Sculptors and Architects*, published in 1550, Vasari was the first to use the word "renaissance" as well (at least in print). His use of that term was clear, but in reintroducing the term "genius" to the world, Vasari was much less clear. Did he mean it to refer to the creative *outputs* he was witnessing—Michelangelo's *David*, Leonardo's *Mona Lisa*, or Botticelli's *Birth of Venus*—or was he instead referring to the *creators* themselves? Perhaps he was referring to a shared *capacity* that these individuals had embraced? Both Vasari and the historical record are imprecise.

What's clear is this: Regardless of his intention, the word that originally described a *universal* capacity soon came to be seen as a designation bestowed on a select few.

GENIUS AND CREATIVITY COME APART

As used by the Greeks and Romans, the concept of genius carried a message of unity and ubiquity. It emphasized the value, even the necessity, of interaction with others in bringing out one's individual genius, along with the universality of the capacity. But post-Vasari, the word "genius" increasingly came to mean something "solo" and "superhuman." When it did, a slippery slope started to form that eventually led to our current confusion around the word. Indeed, it has led to an unintended decoupling of the idea of genius from creativity.

First the historical highlight reel, then the slippery slope . . .

Trying to Predict Genius. People were captivated with the kinds of individual heroics Vasari highlighted and, before long, some wondered if it were possible to *predict* genius. Could we identify the *exceptions* among the populace, and perhaps even pinpoint the exact sources from which human greatness was likely to come? Seen on a sliding scale, the question became far more hedgehog than fox, and it profoundly shaped the trajectory of how genius came to be regarded.

In the late 1700s, German philosopher Immanuel Kant made a push to substantiate the idea of a genius as an exceptional person. Kant proposed establishing "indicators" that, in theory, people could look out for, test, and track. He came up with two: a genius was 1) "an individual creative thinker" and 2) someone who produced works both "original and exemplary." All one had to do, reasoned Kant, was find proof of both and the "genius" label could be bestowed. (See Author's Notes: Chapter Nine-A.)

In addition to seeing creative genius as exceptional, identifiable, and measurable, Kant (and those who built on his views including Arthur Schopenhauer and Bertrand Russell) saw genius as closely tied to one's superior intellect or intelligence. Rather than taking its place as a separate observation, this view resulted in a trend toward the belief that intelligence was the *source* of creativity, and even a proxy. That shift eventually proved to be a tipping point in the whole idea of genius and its relationship to creativity. Out of that history, a slippery slope took shape.

Sloping Away from Creativity. Let's do a quick review: Vasari celebrated an explosion of human creativity and breathed new life into the ancient word "genius." Unfortunately, he sparked a new meaning as well: genius = heroic individual performing heroic feats. People were smitten with the suggestion enough to try to find ways to identify, even predict, these heroes in our midst. That meant they had to find a way to identify, measure, and test for genius— which presented at least two problems. First, they had to arrive at a common "factor" that could be measured and tested to identify the exceptional person. If that could be done, then second, they had to figure out how to qualify and judge the genius' work as "original and exemplary." Here's what happened next. . . .

Addressing the first problem was a toughie. Creativity proved hard to pin down. It clearly varied in form and by field. In short, it didn't conform to a neat and singular measure. So those committed to fixing creativity in place turned to intelligence hoping to find greater success and precision. Granted, at the time they had no measure of intelligence either. But they must have assumed as intellectuals that intelligence was something they knew well enough to figure it out—at least more easily than creativity.

Addressing the second problem—judging genius—only took the quest further down the slippery slope. What better (and easier) way to identify "original and exemplary," the thinking went, than by direct comparison to things already *known?* This included the works of art, the theories, and the other discoveries they'd already agreed were genius. And who better to judge excellence in any particular field than one's peers and the field's leaders, right?

Do you see the problem? The desire to narrow the idea of genius to certain individuals and certain fields and by way of certain recognizable filters, all contributed to cutting away the true meaning and value sought. Simultaneously, our understanding of creativity was cheated by intelligence becoming its substitute. In short: *While searching for the fox, we put the hedgehog in charge.*

The hedgehog would establish the rules by which the fox could play and even the criteria by which actions could be judged fox-worthy. As hedgehogs will do, the search for things "new" was forced to pass the test of looking like things "known." Rather than seeking to strike a balance and push back on our hedgehog, the thought leaders pressed on to form ever-narrower concepts of both genius and creativity.

REIMAGINING GENIUS

This narrowing of our understanding of creativity and genius rapidly picked up steam after Kant's era. Within a short hundred years of his proposal, we went from hoping for some kind of measure to a hard-and-fast score: the Intelligence Quotient, or IQ. Thus *intelligence* formally became a proxy for *genius* and even for creativity. (See Author's Notes: Chapter Nine-B.)

Here's the irony: All of this began with a desire to understand creativity. Yet over the totality of this history—from Vasari to the present—the insights that might have yielded that understanding were progressively lost under a heap of hedgehog-like good intentions.

The situation begs this question: Does "genius" even mean anything in our modern use of the term? Perhaps a more valuable question is this: What *could* it mean if we returned to its original meaning and linked it to creativity?

Before pursuing that question, let's untangle one more cloudy concept deeply intertwined with the word "genius"—the idea of "hero."

TRUE HEROISM

For many, there's a strong connection between our modern impressions of genius and our ideas about heroes. Heroes are assumed to be exceptional and apart. We simplistically think of the hero as the one who figured out how to do something the rest of us could not. In the most basic sense, we conclude that heroes are smart, "ingenious" in some way, and single-handedly produce their "original and exemplary output." Even if we don't call the hero a genius in the same breath, we tend to give heroes and geniuses the same treatment. So, to fully clear away the impediments that keep us from seeing that those so-called creative geniuses are just like us, we need to address the hero myth as well.

For clarity, let's turn to the person most often connected with the idea of the hero, Joseph Campbell.

A HEROIC JOURNEY

An American scholar, author, and mythologist, Joseph Campbell identified a pattern across human storytelling he called **THE HERO'S JOURNEY**. He first described it in 1949 in his seminal work *The Hero with a Thousand Faces*.

Campbell's premise was that, while the "faces" we attach the word "hero" to might shift with time, the storyline does not. In fact, said Campbell, the journeys that "heroes" take are all remarkably similar.

Hero stories have existed as far back as written tradition. These stories extend even further into humankind's oral traditions and likely trace back to the beginning of humans themselves. The hero's tale seems almost as universal as creativity. Indeed, the two are closely linked. But also like creativity, we tend to forget and thus fail to understand the true story of the hero.

Campbell believed the hero's story was instructive as our human story. He noted there were many parts to it, some of them less than heroic, and that all journeys were circular—that is, heroes learned or created, failed or triumphed not once but many times over. As Campbell realized, many of the steps in this deeply human journey are most often overlooked when we praise heroes.

Stepping through each of them as identified by Campbell, not only helps to unravel the mythology, it tells us a lot about the creative journey itself.

HUMBLE BEGINNINGS

The first step, Campbell observed, was that a hero's journey always begins in the ordinary world. Heroes aren't heroes when they start; they're ordinary folks. The central characters of hero stories share the same environment, history, and customs as those around them. For all intents and purposes, they are "completely normal" except for one thing: When would-be heroes look out at their worlds, they have an undeniable sense that *something doesn't fit*. That alone isn't what makes them unusual. What sets them apart is that they can't ignore the misfit. They are unable to turn away from what isn't right, what could be better, or whatever form the misfit may take. And because they can't, they are eventually propelled into their journeys—and into all the trouble and glory that follows.

Campbell determined that heroes-to-be are remarkably human, including their initial desire to *ignore* the misfit and stay with what they know. Commonly, heroes at first do exactly that: They try to ignore it, at least until circumstances no longer let them do so. Campbell refers to this point as the *call to action*.

How the hero handles arrival at this point and inevitably heeds the call often isn't heroic. Rather than grabbing for the glory, most often the central character hesitates, sometimes indignantly so. (Think of Liz Lerman's description of how the questions she eventually pursues begin as complaints, agitation, and even grumpiness.)

As Campbell described it, in some sense heroes actually *refuse the call*. They fear the unknown. They are warned away by their peers and seriously consider those warnings. They sense the implications of what calls them—leaving the land they know, figuratively and often literally. Usually some event (think: Rebecca Goldstein's father's death alongside her daughter's birth) or an experienced mentor (think: Francis Crick for Pat Churchland) plays a role in encouraging heroes to trust their gut and go forward. It's as though they need reassurance. We all do.

THIS IS A TEST

Eventually, these heroes *cross the threshold* (in Campbell's parlance), committing to engage the unfamiliar in the pursuit of something better. In "the language of man," we call this *border crossing*.

What happens next might be called a series of tests. For example, friendships and allegiances are tested. Patience is tested. Ideas new and old are tested. And the meaning of all things in the here and now—rules, goals, leadership, value—is retested for validity and relevance.

As heroes undergo this process, they invariably start to see things differently and make new connections. Over time, they find new approaches and ultimately forge a new path to a better way. Rarely is the process quick or easy; there always seems to be an unfolding. And it typically comes through the interactions of "the many," not solely out of the mind or superhuman abilities of "the one." This is the hero-shaping stuff we often filter out in favor of a *"they must have been born that way"* conclusion.

Reflecting this gradual awakening, Campbell actually identified *twelve* stages or steps that comprise the hero's journey—four times as many as the three stages of "genius, victory, and glory" often used to summarize the hero's story. (See Author's Notes: Chapter Nine-C.) It isn't until about three-quarters of the way through those stages that heroes gain their rewards and events start to make sense.

It's worth pausing to acknowledge that we most often think of heroism and reward as almost automatic, that by being the hero, the inevitable reward comes fairly quickly. But Campbell found that the reward doesn't even show a glimmer on the horizon until far into the hero's trials and tribulations. So much for light bulbs, lightning strikes, or overnight successes.

APPLY, RINSE, REPEAT

Too often when we retell the hero's story, we wrap it up after the "she wins the day" part and close the book. But studying the actual stories created over thousands of years and across thousands of "faces," Campbell concluded that, just like no journey happens overnight, no quick, clean wrap-up exists either. In essence, there's a story after the story. He called it *the road back*.

Heroes can't live at the zenith forever; they must return from the land of victory and glory. Not unlike soldiers coming home from a victorious battle, they must reintegrate and arrive at a new order for doing and being. And also like soldiers, the task is rarely easy. This balancing occurs in the final two stages of the journey, the *resurrection* and the *return with the elixir*. In the resurrection, the hero is symbolically tested again. Most often the test calls for more sacrifice and more "death" and "rebirth" of ideas *after* and *because of* the "victory." (The elixir may be important, but it's not a cure-all.)

Here's where the lesson comes in: With each heroic idea or act, a reshuffling occurs. When it does, there are naturally new feelings of misfit, which can cause us to reengage our curiosity and creativity all over again. Heroism, Campbell observed, is a circular journey.

HERO MEETS GENIUS

Here's what has become clear: Despite our modern treatment, it's the ancient meaning of genius—something everyone possesses and something deeply intertwined with creativity—that has value to us. More, when we truncate the heroic journey to the erroneous shorthand of "genius, victory, and glory," we lose valuable insights about the journey—ones we need for our own journey whether or not we regard ourselves as heroic. Yet history shows it's far too easy to lose such insights.

Bringing our discussion full circle allows us to make this connection: When we declare someone a creative genius, we run headlong into the hero problem of seeing a false "them" and "us." We discount our own sense of fit or misfit and ignore the call to action we hear. The more we do this, the more we "lose the feel" and forego the chance to write our own creative story.

If you get up close to those so-called heroes and creative geniuses, you'll find the reality of their lives reflects a *complete* journey with all its ups and downs. More than that, you'll find the central characters are far more human than heroic. In fact, they're just like you.

JUST LIKE YOU

"True heroism is remarkably sober, very undramatic," said tennis champion Arthur Ashe.[241] He always had a way of quickly laying bare the truth. We're ready to do the same.

No doubt, the people we call heroes and their stories inspire us. But we have far more to gain from their stories as real people than we do from the partial tales of their exceptionality. With our rediscovered understanding of genius and the hero's journey, we're ready to actually "hear" what our guides have to say about all this.

Through their candidly honest ways of speaking about creativity, the MacArthur Fellows show us what it's like to be a "creative genius." Hint: Arthur Ashe's words were prescient.

REAL PEOPLE

"My favorite line about the MacArthur Fellowship came from my son," professor of law, medicine, and psychiatry Sylvia Law said chuckling. "He was about six years old when I got this award. Five years later, the Fellowship ran out. When it did, my son said, 'She's an ex-genius now.'"[242]

As much as praise and attention abound when one is crowned a "genius," so do plenty of reminders about where one actually stands. To that point, Steve Goodman shared an experience that happened within hours of receiving the award. "When I got the Fellowship, a friend sent me an article by a past Fellow that said, in short, 'you're just another human being; this business of genius is just words and marketing; get over yourself and get on with the work.' It's a strange thing," Steve reflected. "For a moment, somewhere in your mind, you think you are someone special. And then you realize pretty quickly that's just rubbish."[243]

Rather than a legion of superheroes, poet Richard Kenney described the Fellows he'd met over the years as "people you know, people you see every day, title-less people. Most were good at what they did, and it was outwardly evident what they did mattered a great deal to them. But in most other ways, they were just people like you or me and reflective of the whole range of the rest of us. Most seemed like my friends back home."[244]

Rather than being exceptions, Sylvia, Steve, Richard, Ellen, and all the rest are just like us: human. Regardless of age, gender, accomplishment, notoriety, background, or field, the MacArthur Fellows simply represent "the whole range of the rest of us," as Richard so wisely put it.

With that clear, let's look more precisely at *how* the Fellows are just like you in the creative sense. Specifically, we'll examine the kinds of things and feelings they encounter, the very things that could hold us back from using our creative capacity. Seeing their humanness and gaining a sense for what they do in such circumstances helps get us going and doing as well.

THEY HAVE FEARS, GET STUCK, AND FEEL DOUBT

It's easy to look from the outside in and think, "Those creative geniuses are so bold. Like a supremely confident Jackson Pollack standing on a blank canvas throwing paint, they do what they do with complete ease and a knowing sense that success is around the corner." That's a load of creative . . . myth. They fear, falter, and have misgivings like any other human being.

"I have been over my head many times," Richard stated candidly. "I've been in situations in which I had to invent everything around me—what I knew, what I had to work with, even who I was in that unfamiliar setting. Part of it was thrilling. But then there are all the nagging feelings and haunting fears—*What if I can't do it? What if I can't pull it off? What if I can't finish?*"

Richard wasn't portraying these as false fears one has to get over, either. Remember, creativity is a capacity, not a promise. "There were times," he said, "when some of those fears came true, though never nearly at the scale I'd allowed my mind to imagine." And even those downsides proved valuable. "Sometimes it's the education of going through the experience that counts, even if it doesn't produce brilliance."[245]

Still, some hear this refreshingly honest report from the front lines of creativity and imagine that folks like Richard, even with their fears, must be less affected than others. Presumably, they're better equipped than the rest of us. They may face fears, people conclude, but they start with unique abilities so their fear is unwarranted, right? Wrong.

Looking across the landscape of the creative, *Art & Fear* authors Bayles and Orland tried to shake us out of any "excuses" not to engage. Using the word "art" as shorthand for the creative act, they observed that "while geniuses may get made once-a-century or so, good art gets made all the time. Making art is a common and intimately human activity, filled with all the perils (and rewards) that accompany any worthwhile effort. The difficulties art makers face are not remote and heroic, but universal and familiar."[246]

Maria Chudnovsky concurred. "Unfortunately, it's hard to get out of the valleys in this cycle that is creativity," she said. "Because those are the places where you doubt yourself. The downside of creativity is that it can be hard. And it's fickle. It's difficult to demand oneself to be creative on command and on deadline."[247] Just as practiced creators don't get a waiver from this cycle, none avoid the fear, the perils, or the peaks and valleys of the cycle either. Ever.

The words of choreographer, playwright, and photographer Martha Clarke stick in my mind when thinking about pushing beyond fears and self-doubts. "I trust my instinct," she said, referring to a hard-earned level of comfort she's found by tapping into her creative capacity. It's a comfort honed through countless cycles of fear and doubt, and it's imperfect. Showing her humanness, she added, "I'm ninety-eight percent right about my feelings . . . or maybe it's ninety-seven percent." She trusts the creative *process*. And yet she doesn't try to extract guarantees from it. Even as she increasingly comes to know the nature of her instincts, she acknowledges that the often-frightening element of the unknown never goes away.

"Sure, I make mistakes and still question," Martha said about the waves that define creativity in actual practice. "You go from excitement and joy to doubt and dissolution, to difficulty and suffering, to that tipping point when what you desire starts to emerge, usually in ways you didn't expect. Creativity just isn't steady or predictable."[248]

THEY PUSH THROUGH FEAR TO ASPIRE AND DREAM

While fear of failure, rejection, and the unknown each factor into the "powerful play" (as Whitman described it), fear is moveable, malleable, or meager when compared to what can be gained by going *beyond* fear. But how do so-called creative geniuses bridge the gap that moves them beyond fear to create? Stu Kauffman offered several deceivingly simple yet vital insights.

The first thing Stu is in the habit of doing to push through fear and the stumbling blocks along the way is to wonder—"to simply allow myself to 'go there' and imagine," Stu said.[249] I love this insight, and I can't help smiling every time I think of Stu saying it. He was laughing when he did. Rather than being an insight we've missed, he's pointing to an insight we forget: *The very things that help us create are also the things that help us get unstuck—wonder, imagination, and the allowance for both.*

Too often it's as if something so natural to our fourth-grade selves becomes herculean to our older selves. "In the professional sense, it can feel whacky," Stu admitted, offering a clue why we forget or avoid wonder. "But as unprofessional as it often seems, I've always felt that allowing myself to wonder is fundamental to any kind of progress— to any idea that might move me from wherever I'm standing and toward something better still. It's the difference between dreaming up and dumbing down."

As Carol Dweck and Richard Wiseman both pointed out, we can adopt a mindset that "good things come to those who wait," but invariably, time proves they do not. All of us dream and aspire. The only difference between people such as Stu and those who never stumble into breakthrough ideas is that—like all creative practitioners—he *acts* in the direction of his dreams.

Such actions begin by simply allowing yourself to wonder. And here's a subtle but key insight: It's not bold and swashbuckling; it's simple, incremental wondering—an invitation you give to yourself to "play" with the idea of what could be.

This idea of "play" matters. In fact, failing to see wonder as a form of play is a silent but deadly killer of creativity. (We'll return to this in a moment.)

THEIR BRILLIANCE ISN'T ALWAYS
RECOGNIZED BY OTHERS

Just because you push past your fears, or wonder as a habit, or even arrive at breakthrough ideas, doesn't mean you can assume everyone else will come along for the ride. People have a tendency to look in hindsight at a brilliant creative outcome and assume it's always been considered brilliant. But the experiences of the MacArthur Fellows tell a more truthful story.

Susan Meiselas described a pattern she experiences when pursuing new ideas. Looking backward at the pattern, she said, "Once I saw the path forward, I had enormous difficulty explaining to those around me where I was, what I saw, and how we could make it work."[250] Joseph Campbell might say that, when trying to describe a new idea and persuade others to move in its direction, it can feel like you and your audience speak different languages. In fact, you do.

Even though we're all *capable* of speaking creativity, most of us aren't in the practice of doing so. So there's often a gap between practiced creative thinkers and their unpracticed audiences. As Susan knows, a whole new level of creativity is often required to close that gap and have an idea received. She's not alone.

In Fellow Lorna Bourg's work of bringing ideas and resources to rural communities in the South, she constantly experiences this natural tension. She put it bluntly, "There are people who feel creativity or even a new idea is going to mess up what they know. They already know what to do 'right now'; they know how to work the ways of this moment perfectly well, thank you. To ask them to accept a new idea, or to come together to create newness of their own, or even to remember how they created what they have now, is too great for some, especially at the start when none of it is yet tangible."[251]

Creativity is not precision; it's practice. It's not an unveiling; it's an unfolding. This rings as true when sharing ideas with others or encouraging them to have ideas of their own as it does when it's you alone imagining what could be.

Even when creativity becomes a practice, a mindset, part of one's natural rhythms, it doesn't mean smooth sailing will follow forevermore. Remember, every hero had to come down from the summit to face the realities on the ground, seek balance, and prepare to repeat the whole process again.

This isn't a discouraging tale so much as it is a natural part of the story to creating anything new or better. Through a practiced, creative mindset, "the bridges find a way to construct," as Lorna put it, closing the gaps between people and ideas, amid new ways and old. "If these bridges begin with something people truly believe to be better, and if those ideas are deeply rooted in their *own* vision, they don't just close gaps, they make inroads. The possibilities begin to show up in *their* minds and as a result of *their* work. That's what brings others forward and allows people and their ideas to connect.

"But before that connection happens," Lorna said, "there's often terror, confusion, and deep misunderstanding. No idea is so great as to avoid that. This tension has to be grappled with. And the 'idea people' can't push, especially if they're coming from the outside of the group they want to benefit. Sometimes they can't even be the ones to lead, even if the whole idea started as theirs. Others must add to the bridging. People have to decide for themselves."[252]

Listening to Lorna, you get the idea that, rather than figuring out a way to persuade others to embrace your big ideas, the process is about helping one another's fluency in a common language. That fluency applies not only in speaking that language but in using it—in the act of creating.

Creativity opens us up to the possible. The flip side is that it opens us up to differences in how we communicate our creative ideas. That's the challenge all of us face—whether we call ourselves geniuses or not. But it can also be the reason the idea ends up succeeding.

THEIR UNFOLDING IS GRADUAL

What's the downside of creativity? It's hard. And as Maria Chudnovsky said, "It's difficult to control or demand oneself 'be creative *right now*,' in this moment, on command, and on deadline." There's no trick or special dispensation so-called geniuses have to make the creative process easier for them than it is for you or me.

Plain and simple, the process of seeing new opportunities and having breakthrough ideas happens gradually for all of us. "It happens in steps—steps toward a new habit," said Ernie Cortés. "It's a shaping of the bold, the thoughtful, the attentive, the engaging. It's not an overnight epiphany. It's a formation process. It's iterative. It's ongoing. Creativity is a 'never done' kind of work."[253]

By now, this message shouldn't be a surprise. Still, we are human. Socially, technologically, and even mentally, much of the human race seems to accept the false notion that everything—even creativity— happens in an instant. "We have become a society that needs a twenty-second hit," Ric Scofidio said, reflecting his frustration with the myth of genius and the belief in creation by luck. It's what led him to express his concern that "We are becoming more *receptors* than *creators*."[254]

And there it is in a nutshell. Creativity doesn't function in a three-second sound bite, nor can it be spelled out in a 140-character "tweet." Yes, we may *spread* creative ideas through quick-hit mechanisms, but we don't *create* them there.

"It's discipline too. You have to ride through phases of joy and difficulty in creating," [255] Martha Clarke added. And, ultimately, it's habit and mindset.

"I ask questions of the strangest kind," Stu said about how he keeps his creative capacity fresh and vibrant ongoing. "I've found as I allow myself to wonder that somehow one thing leads to another and another, and creativity reveals itself, just more slowly than we tend to think."[256]

Unfolding gradually isn't bad. As any hero's story would convey, the reward isn't only the breakthrough idea but the journey itself. Said AIDS and family care policy specialist Carol Levine, "To feel that you can affect others even in a modest sense along the way is an enormously powerful catalyst to keep engaging the creative process—its lows along with its highs."[257]

THEY HAVE A NEED FOR PLAY AND WONDER

A minute ago we touched on the importance of play. More than important, play, as it turns out, is vital. Humans are the only animals that, as adults, *need* to play. It's where and how we learn in our early years; it's also how we're built to continue learning as we mature. And to learn, we have to imagine ideas exist beyond what we currently know. When we play, we engage in wonder; and when we allow ourselves to wonder, we are at play.

As children, we may have had a stronger grip on our imagination than today because we used it more often and more freely back then. Yet in adulthood, we still "play." We picture ourselves making that diving save playing beach volleyball at the family reunion, or catching the errant foul ball at a big league game without spilling our pricey soda.

Believe it or not, it isn't that far to dream bigger "what if" dreams *if* you allow yourself to practice the habit of wonder. But to get there, you have to stick out your neck a little, like stepping up to the plate for the very first time as a kid learning baseball. That can be scary, yet "whenever people stick out their necks, there emerges a believability," said Lorna. "One step builds on the next. Bridges link others together. Suddenly, the impossible becomes inevitable."[258]

"Every one of us carries pipe dreams," fisherman and conservationist Ted Ames told me. "Even if things don't go in that direction, we still carry them and somehow, somewhere, we can't help but bring our dreams back out again and again. That's where the fun comes in."[259] Creativity *allows* for that "bringing back out again" and it also *requires* it. All this happens more easily when creativity becomes a habit of play.

CREATIVE PEOPLE REMAIN PEOPLE

What all of these "just like you" examples convey is this: Creative people remain people. More than their words, their real-life experiences prove it true. If you think back across the many stories in this book so far, I feel confident you'll see it too. But this next story brings it home.

In 1983 Sara Lawrence-Lightfoot introduced her breakthrough idea of portraiture to a broad audience in her book *The Good High School: Portraits of Character and Culture*. As you may recall, portraiture broke with traditional sociology and developed an entirely new framework for understanding people—who they are, what they experience, and why they do what they do.

Before the book and her breakthrough idea of portraiture were first shared, however, there was no guarantee of how others would react.

More than that, potential risks accompanied her choice to even put her idea forth.

One clear risk for Sara related to being an untenured professor at Harvard University at the time. Typically, tenure doesn't go to those who cut against the grain. Being an African American female in a white male-dominated field didn't offer much risk insurance, either. Speaking about a dynamic that continues three decades later, Sara described it this way: "By the time you reach the level of the Academy as I have, you have been so socialized into the mindset that any boundary crossing—challenging the premises of the discipline—not only goes unrewarded but it's like shunning oneself."[260] In a word, putting her creative idea out there was frightening.

Yet she chose to walk briskly down an alternate path, crossing against all the lights and striding boldly into the intersection of her career and her "unprofessional" gut feelings. Martha would say she chose to trust her instincts.

When Sara's book debuted, *The Good High School* was honored with a number of awards, among them the *Outstanding Book Award* from the American Education Research Association (AERA). Interestingly, AERA members and leaders are known for being stringent empiricists. In layman's language, it would be fair to describe them as "stuck in their ways and views." Yet, they were giving Sara the group's top honor for breaking with those ways and views. In effect, her professional peers were acknowledging that her creative approach was valid *and* important in shaping the future of sociology.

It was like a hero's victory, as Sara explained. "I recall the moment when I received this award. The head of the [AERA] committee presided over the ceremony. I knew how he felt about people doing what I had done"—that is, cutting against the grain. "And I knew he couldn't have possibly voted for me to receive the award. So while I felt an appreciation for having redrawn the map, I was fully aware that what I had done was controversial. When this committee head came to the podium after I'd received my honor, he said to the audience, 'I think we would all agree that Sara Lawrence-Lightfoot's work is beautiful . . . but only she can do it.'"

Thus, even the moment of "making it" came with dismissal, pushback, and non-acceptance. "It was like he said the book had no validity or substance," Sara said about that moment. As she described the scene to me, it was clear this memory still had impact three decades later.

Her story teaches that even after the highest high, the journey continues; the hero must rise and be human all over again. If you want to create a breakthrough and see it made real, that's what you must do. It isn't simply part of being *creative*; it's part of being *human*. Sara hasn't backed away and neither should you.

REMEMBER: IT'S JUST YOU

In *Art & Fear*, the authors shared a story about the abstract landscape and figure painter Howard Ikemoto. "When my daughter was seven years old," Ikemoto said, "she asked me what I did at work. I told her I work at the college—that my job was to teach people how to draw. She stared back at me, incredulous, and said, 'You mean they *forget?*'"[261] It's time to remember.

A part of you has always guessed that *creative genius isn't heroic*. But consider two aspects you may not have suspected until now. The first: *You are closer to your own creative genius than you think*. The second: *You already know how to tap into your creativity—you've simply forgotten that you do*.

As if to punctuate the lessons of true geniuses, in *The Art and Science of Creativity*, George F. Kneller rhetorically asked, "Are there any noncreative people? It seems not. The genius and the average man may seem to have little in common," Kneller wrote, "yet the difference between them appears to be one of quantity. In the genius, imagination, energy, persistence, and other creative qualities are more highly developed, but fortunately he has no monopoly on them."[262] The creative "geniuses" who've revealed their true creative selves to you in *The Language of Man* would agree.

All geniuses begin as humans with a geni (a soul), a fox-hedgehog brain, and a capacity for creativity that waits to be tapped into. All humans also begin with the ability and inclination to be open, ask questions, challenge, play, and wonder about what could be. Like drawing, we do these things automatically with no measures. We don't even care how their output compares with that of others. *We just create*. It's in our nature.

Do people really forget their natural creative capacity? Ikemoto daughter incredulously thought it impossible. She was right, too. We don't forget; we just get rusty. We forget the "geni" that seeds the "genius" and withdraw from the practice of wonder. And when we do, the only thing we're left imagining is some pretend gap between creativity and ourselves.

As scary as standing at the edge of that gap can at first seem, closing it only requires taking a few refresher lessons in wonder plus one more thing: We have to be willing to come to the edge of and step into that gap. Here we go. . . .

SIMPLE TRUTH:

CREATIVITY

MEANS COMING

TO THE EDGE

CHAPTER TEN

SIMPLE TRUTH: CREATIVITY MEANS COMING TO THE EDGE

EDGING FORWARD INTO CREATIVE ACTION

It's wonderful to discover that creative geniuses are just like you. And it's empowering to realize that you, like everyone else, have a capacity for creativity built in, ready for use. But after these eye-opening good tidings, you've got to *do* something.

Like a creative idea, knowledge alone means little if it never manifests something new and better. Ultimately, creativity requires more than creative thoughts, it demands action. Yet the failure to act is the most common impediment to tapping into your uniquely human gift of creativity.

While there are many explanations we might give for not acting, underlying all of them is a little thing I've come to call the "edge." Though you may not always be conscious of them, your life has edges—invisible borders separating what you know from everything else. These borders help "contain" what you know. Your hedgehog builds them for you with the good intention of organizing your life and clarifying the boundaries of the space in which you feel most safe and secure.

It isn't just *your* hedgehog alone that defines these edges, it's all sorts of hedgehogs: parents, teachers, bosses, spouses, coaches, civic leaders, doctors, scientists . . . the hedgehog role call in each of our lives is long. By and large their intent is good. They not only do their part to help define your edges, they kindly provide you with "rules" of thumb to help you stay on your side and within the edges.

That's the upside. But there's a flipside too. Because those borders and the demand to heed them are so well reinforced, anything outside the edges of what you know feels distant, sometimes threatening, and even taboo. But the Simple Truth is this: In order to "act on" and actually tap that creative capacity of yours or to have any chance of manifesting something new and better, you must come to and move across those edges. Enabling you to see *why* and *how* is our goal in this chapter.

Even before I stated it here, you probably already sensed that **COMING TO THE EDGE** is important and inevitable. Such moments represent critical junctures in the creative process. They are opportunities for us to either open the door to the possible or inadvertently wall it off. The edge is a place of bold and necessary choice; it's also the deepest reflection of both the *challenge* and *reward* of being human.

But it turns out that the edge also represents a creative *advantage*, and several decades of science prove this to be true. In this chapter we'll explore this finding. Importantly, we'll also talk about you and the actions you must be aware of and take at the edge. (Spoiler alert: They're not nearly as daunting as you imagine.) We'll wrap up the chapter with a brief reminder of the upside of coming to the edge before gently but deliberately pushing you over it.

As with Chapter Eight and our exploration of the human question, the approach we'll take in this chapter targets *exposure* and *awareness*. You won't end this chapter as a master of moving from "idea to action" or suddenly become a fearless traveler of the unknown. Just as there's no one answer to the human question, the edge isn't a place where you can one day achieve a placid existence. If it were, there'd be no advantage in going there. That said, you will walk away more aware, informed, and confident about coming to the edge. You may even look forward to it.

Before we begin this exploration of the edge, I share with you the following story that wonderfully frames it all—the significance of the edge, the commonality of coming to it, the fear that often precedes the possibility, and the thing we must do when we arrive there. A promotional poster for an art show in the 1960s might seem an odd place to go for such a story, but that's exactly where we're headed.

TAKING FLIGHT

An English poet, playwright, and screenwriter, Christopher Logue was once asked to contribute the written copy for a simple public notice advertising an art exhibit. The exhibit actually featured the works of another artist, Guillaume Apollinaire, not Logue's own. The occasion called for short, pithy language, striking enough to give someone pause as they passed the poster in a shop window, for example, or perhaps on a subway wall while changing trains. It was, after all, an advertisement.

Even without knowing this story, we know the typical inclination of an ad's creator: to focus on the "thing" being advertised—the art to be seen or the product to be sold. And why not? If we want to get someone's attention fast and get a message across just as quickly, we cut to the chase: "Here's what you get." But Logue took a different path. In response to the challenge, he didn't write about Apollinaire's work directly or even about art. Rather than focus us on what we *get*, Logue turned us toward what we *feel*. He chose the universal human experience of coming to the edge—the moment, the feeling, the fear, and the answer to what to do when we arrive there. He wrote:

<blockquote>
Come to the edge.

We might fall.

Come to the edge.

It's too high!

COME TO THE EDGE!

And they came,

And we pushed,

And they flew.[263]
</blockquote>

Advertisement or not, what Logue wrote was poetic in every sense of the word. As with most poems and poets, there's no public record of him explaining the meaning of his words. In fact, if anything, he has spent more time explaining why his words have most often been misattributed to Apollinaire. (See Author's Notes: Chapter Ten-A.) The fact is he didn't need to explain; the power and accessibility of his words were self-evident.

We've all been there: a new experience, a walk on uncertain ground, and the mixed sense of curiosity and fear that can accompany such experiences. Such moments can present themselves as simply as the chance to experience new art, or as complicatedly as the call to change the direction of a project, a career, or our life. Whatever the circumstances, it's a shared knowledge of what it feels like to let go of something we know to explore something new, often based on little more than a hunch that something better just might be out there.

Since their first appearance in 1961, Logue's lines have been called forth many times by many people, a clear reflection of their universality and his eloquence. For those who've employed them, Logue's words simultaneously serve as a reminder of a recurring and unceasing need ("Come to the edge."), while equally acting in a call-and-response way that voices why we so often leave that need unattended ("We might fall; it's too high!") Importantly, Logue's brief verse further tells us what we must do when we encounter such moments (We must "come to the edge," even if as a result of a little "push.") and, encouragingly, reveals what that action can bring ("And they flew.")

Trying to describe this timeless pulse, actor Jeremy Irons is said to have remarked that "[Logue's poem] deals with risk and trust and the magic that occurs sometimes when you do either." Or both. (See Author's Notes: Chapter Ten-B.) There's something about the edge, and it has everything to do with creativity.

Joseph Campbell described the edge as a place of "creative incubation" where magic can happen, but *only*, he made clear, if we consciously steer toward it. Nobody knows this as well as those who practice creativity. And as it turns out, they don't just steer toward the edge consciously, they do so purposely and habitually—whether or not they are actively trying to create. Let's begin our exploration of the edge by looking at the science of the edge. Then we'll turn to how you can act on it. In both examinations, we'll lean on those who know the edge best: practitioners.

THE SCIENCE AT THE EDGE

There's a lot of scientific curiosity *about* creativity. But as professor of psychology and author Dean Keith Simonton noted, much of that science is focused on the wrong things.

Simonton, a prolific researcher in creativity, wrote in a January 2014 special issue of *Scientific American MIND* that most research is aimed at pinning down two things: 1) arriving at a profile defining "who" is most capable of creativity and 2) coming up with a means for predicting creativity's likelihood of occurrence.[264] The thinking behind this approach isn't hard to imagine. As one school of thought goes, "If I could identify a specific personality type that seems to align with some metric I could argue is associated with creativity, then in theory I could predict creativity." This reveals old thinking and methods in a search for something new—hardly creative.

In his own research, Simonton has chosen to take a different approach. Rather than search for traits that presuppose creative productivity, Simonton studies what creative practitioners actually *do.* He then looks for the patterns and commonalities *across* them, regardless of who they are or what their individual creative output looks like.

The Border Crosser Rises Again. Simonton's work builds on that of Donald Campbell who pioneered this research in 1960. Looking at the patterns across creative practitioners over decades, both have consistently arrived at this important finding: The most productive creators are habitual border crossers. Rather than having in common any single personality type, education, or background, they share the habit of coming to the edge.

You might wonder if other researchers have found a similar pattern. They have, Simonton says. But because they were so busy looking for a way to identify *who* was creative based on research methods and classifications familiar to them, they've tended to disregard or downplay the border-crossing finding. You might say it didn't fit the borders they'd set for themselves and their research.

The Pull of the Edge. Simonton and Campbell didn't just find a pattern of willingness among creative practitioners to come to the edge and cross over when in pursuit of a specific idea or goal. They found that the most productive creators were border crossing even when they weren't consciously creating something. Coming to the edge became not just their way of creating, but their way of being.

When Campbell pioneered this work, he dubbed this finding Blind Variation and Selective Retention, known by the acronym BVSR. Despite the fancy scientific name, it all begins with something quite simple. It seems the more that creators practice creating, the more they come to intuitively understand that "The creator must engage in trial-and-error or generate-and-test . . . to determine the worth of an idea."[265]

That part of the finding seems fairly straightforward. The creators studied understood that when testing a "specific" idea there was no guarantee that any specific action taken to try to make the idea real would actually work. What's striking is that the research indicated that creators were more generally in the habit of trying things—even when they didn't know exactly what they were. This is what the "blind" in Blind Variation refers to. As Simonton put it, "The 'blindness' of BVSR merely means that ideas are produced without foresight into their eventual utility."[266]

In short, the most productive creators know more than the Simple Truth that coming to the edge and choosing to cross over is a necessary act of creation. Most definitely they take this *action* when they are working on a specific idea. But importantly, they clearly further understand that the ongoing *practice* of coming to and crossing the edge benefits their creative habit in a broader sense.

Smoothing the Edges. Step back from the research for a moment and consider the implications of what you've just learned. If like the most productive creators you were in the habit of playing at the edges, how daunting would they actually be when you had to cross one? Probably not very, at least not in the way we often over-imagine the edge to be.

Coming to the edge isn't just a thing practitioners do or a step they take, in the more formulaic sense. Rather, it's baked into who they are. So busy are they playing at the edge that the fact of it being an edge becomes unimportant. What's important is the knowledge born of experience that tells them the edge is where it's at. They may not be able to put faith in a specific outcome, but they have full faith in the language, framework, and cycle that leads to breakthrough ideas.

Simonton and Campbell speak of this in terms of two common phenomena characterizing practiced BVSR thinking: superfluidity and backtracking. "Superfluidity means the creator generates a variety of ideas, one or more of which turn out to be useless. Backtracking signifies that the creator must often return to an earlier approach after blindly going off in the wrong direction."[267] Translation? The more habitual coming to the edge becomes, the less fear at the edge—of error, failure, or even just uncertainty, and the greater the openness to seeing something new.

Stepping back one step more from the science, as important as Simonton's research is, I encourage you to take note of the many others you already know who have not only echoed Simonton's conclusions, each in their own way, but more, have put those findings to effective use. Thinking back through *The Language of Man*, you'll quickly see further validation in the words and work of Koestler, Gardner, Kagan, Lanham, Ghiselin, Kneller, Streb, Nabhan, Bruner, Johansson, Lerman, Yukawa, Goldstein, and Churchland, to name but a few. Let's turn once more to Phil DeVries to understand just what you can and must do when you encounter the edge yourself.

COMING TO KNOW THE EDGE

Phil DeVries' example of coming to the edge will undoubtedly strike you as mundane. That's intended. Especially when you are in the practice of coming to the edge, you'll discover that most edges are like Phil's, remarkably ordinary. But within his simple example are important lessons about the nature of the edge, the critical actions that creativity requires you to take there, and insights as to how you can hone your ability to come to your own edges and advance. To organize the insights, I'll focus on the three critical actions necessary at any edge. Turns out, they too are remarkably everyday—it's choosing to take them that makes them powerful.

THE FIRST "ACT" OF CREATION: CHOICE

Choosing at the Edge. "My mother told me to stay away from bees and wasps," Phil told me in our conversation.[268] You may recall from earlier chapters that Phil grew up to be an insect biologist. But "young" Phil once faced a daunting prospect, one you can likely relate to.

Here you are a kid learning the ropes of life. Your own internal gyroscope says "explore," yet one of the most highly regarded teachers you have—your mom or dad—gives you a rule that comes head to head with your instinctive curiosity. You look at that bee or wasp and wonder: *What does it feel like? Is it soft? Could I hold one? If I did, would it keep buzzing? Can I teach bees tricks? What does one look like on the inside?* Your mother, on the other hand, follows your gaze and says, "Don't (wonder); stay back."

This is the thing about rules: They have the power to both help and hinder. It's accurate to see rules as handed out by parents (and later in life by teachers, bosses, and others) to help you to learn. But what exactly is the lesson we are meant to take away? Are the rules you're given intended to be your *guidelines for discovering and continuing to learn,* or are they intended to be your *immobilizing borders?* The rule-givers certainly have their own purposes. But then there's you—what's *your* purpose, and where do rules fit into realizing it?

Here's part of the lesson we most often overlook: Every rule, in every setting, and in every stage of life is forever imbued with a choice: Accept the rule as forever fitting, or wonder about its ongoing validity and relevance. "Rules," Phil explained, "are always things drawn from another time, from someone else's experiences, or from information that will inevitably change." That means that your first "job" at any edge is to *choose* how *you* see such rules in *this* time and place, and to decide their meaning and value from here forward.

A strange thing occurs when we look at rules and the borders they mark as recurring *choices.* Our typical response at a border is to *halt*—to stay put, not challenge, and definitely not transgress. It's that very response that helps give borders their edge. But seen as a choice, borders soften. Rather than default, we open ourselves up to the opportunity to reexamine—to look freshly at what we know and to reweigh the importance and value of the border. Recognition of choice awakens in us a willingness to explore.

Choosing to explore doesn't automatically imply change must follow. Sometimes when we reexamine our borders we conclude that they still have value and fit and choose to reaffirm them. And sometimes we don't. The important thing is to be conscious that each border always retains a choice, and the choice is pivotal.

Warning: Edges are Smaller Than They Appear. The choice to reexamine or explore beyond a border represents the first "act" of creation. It may sound familiar. The edge where that choice arises denotes that opportunity to "reconsider creativity," as Sarah Kagan so bluntly and beautifully described it in Chapter Two. Her bluntness was in the matter of fact way she expressed that the opportunity for a choice at the edge *must* be acted upon. If you don't, someone else will on your behalf. But the beauty of her description was in the opportunity she made clear that such moments offer. These moments at the edge are both big and little—big in the opportunity, little in that this first act of creation—consciously choosing—is typically far less dramatic and ominous than rumor has it. As Phil described about his choice to explore his curiosities, "I didn't listen to my mother and I got stung. But," Phil laughed, "it wasn't as bad as what the press said it would be."[269]

Edges are often billed as steep, sheer, and punishing. Rarely do they rise to such levels, especially when approached with thought rather than recklessness. As much as coming to the edge is about practice, it's also about perspective. "If you approach anything without fear and with a little cunning and you tell yourself, 'I'm not going to *do* anything here except *watch*,' you *see* that the rules are there as suggestions," Phil said. "True, I went beyond what other people said was acceptable or bad. But it wasn't to flaunt anything; it was to look first without seeking to boast or destroy. Doing this became an easy habit."

What you sense from Phil is balance—neither overplaying the fear of the edge nor disrespecting the unknown ahead of you. It's a balance born of time and practice. In seeing choice at your edges and exercising it, habit forms. Fear subsides. And creativity grows.

It's a funny thing. Habits *will* form. That's not up for discussion. It's the *direction* in which a habit forms that's open ended. When your habit is to see and make choices, eventually it becomes your way—of thinking, noticing, acting, and being. In truth, it's just as easy to consciously form the habit of choice as it is to form the habit of treating borders as impenetrable. But the former has far more upside than the latter. Rather than a place to fear, the edge becomes a place to take flight.

THE SECOND "ACT" OF CREATION: REACTION

As much as we have to adjust our mindset about *coming* to the edge, we must also adjust how we think *after* we've crossed over an edge. Consider this: Our choice to go forward at an edge frequently occurs under false pretenses of our own making. We sense the potential "good" in crossing, but too often, even if subconsciously, think in terms of a *guarantee*. We don't think too hard about what happens next because we expect it to be good. When we've allowed ourselves to inadvertently skip down this path, it can be particularly off-putting when the bee stings us.

Every outcome of a choice to explore that falls short of our expectations is another chance to reaffirm that we shouldn't mess with the way things are (read: reinforce the border and shut down our creative capacity). That's why what we do *after* we come to the edge and cross over matters just as much as choosing to test a border in the first place.

Creating is an ongoing series of choices and actions, not just a one-and-done. Returning to Phil, beyond his initial willingness to step over the edge, it was his *reaction to* the edge that shaped everything—what was possible to see and learn in that moment, but also how he approached edges in the future. When Phil chose to set aside the rule his mother had laid down, he got stung. But recall how he described his reaction: "It wasn't as bad as what the press said it would be."

Of course his reaction could just as easily have been a *"Damn, that hurt! I'll never break a rule again!"* kind of reaction. If he had reacted that way, few would question it; many might've applauded it. But that wasn't his reaction, and it's important to note what Phil actually did. Put simply, he repeated the very same creative element that helped him discover the edge in the first place: *He took notice.* As he put it, he crossed the edge to watch, not to judge. Because he did, when he crossed over, experienced, and noticed again, he wasn't looking to conclude anything in particular. He just wanted to see what was there. Rather than establishing *rules* that precluded further exploration when the bee stung him, he crafted *guidelines* that permitted him to continue exploring.

It doesn't matter that at that young age Phil probably wasn't conscious of all this, just as it doesn't matter that this example is derived from a simple childhood foray beyond the borders of a parent's "because I said so" command. What's important to see is that after choosing to cross any edge, a *second* choice immediately appears: Will I stay open to my fox, or call out to my hedgehog for reinforcements?

The biggest difference about coming to the edge as an adult, one tuned into the language of man, is that you know enough to choose consciously, one way or the other. Learning to do so isn't hard; it just takes practice. And for that to happen, you have to consciously act *and* re-act at the edge.

THE THIRD "ACT" OF CREATION: IMPROVISATION

Review with me for a moment the simple yet powerful actions you must take at the edge to allow "creative you" to flourish: First, you must see the choice in each edge. Then, you must allow yourself to make the choice to explore beyond the edge—to act. Whether the result of crossing is good or bad, you have to be aware and take notice—of the lessons and of what's possible. More, you must recognize these simple steps as cyclical and never ending. Just like creativity, the edge and what you do there is an unfolding.

What these actions at the edge are not is some kind of "recipe" for how to create. They are better seen as guidelines and checkpoints in an ongoing exercise in learning how to *improvise*. Improvisation is an important skill in creativity—it is, in fact, your third key action when encountering any edge or anything new.

While popularly associated with acting or performing before an audience, as on a theatre stage or in a comedy skit, improvisation applies everywhere creativity takes place. We improvise when we encounter the unexpected, or when we lack a ready answer. We improvise when we venture beyond our borders. Clearly we must do it when we test new ideas as well. There are countless circumstances presented by simply being alive that require us to be flexible beyond the script we know by heart.

Actor and world-class improviser Jason Mantzoukas described creating anything new as "a very loose improvisational process," one in which you have to develop "the spontaneity and flexibility to what happens once your ideas start landing." How could it be any other way? None of us can ever know what will happen once our ideas land—with a bounce, with a splat, or with some zigzag outcome in between. Still most often, we seem to assume it will be otherwise. To that point, Mantzoukas says people often ask how he came up with his great ideas (the FX comedy series *The League*, the film *The Dictator*, and contributions to critical successes like *Portlandia*), just as people ask Phil and other Fellows how they've made their creative discoveries. In a way, they're asking, "What are the steps?" What these wise practitioners tell us, however, is that rather than look for a step-by-step formula, we ought to rethink what we mean by steps.

About testing a new idea or a new audience, Mantzoukas said, "I loosely prepare what I want to do . . . kind of a macro version of the conversation." What proves most effective for him is letting people's responses as well as the flow of what happens once he crosses into new territories dictate how he proceeds. The "steps," such that they exist, are more along the lines of: Notice, act, notice, react, repeat. Like Phil, throughout this improvised dance Mantzoukas focuses not on good or bad but instead on what's possible, what's working, and what's valuable to each moment. About his process Mantzoukas said, "It's malleable. A lot of it involves reading the room. That's the important stuff."[270]

The Ongoing Struggle with Self. While on the surface it may seem that people like Jason Mantzoukas or Phil have this down and just flip some magic switch that allows them to go with the flow, the truth is they are simply in the practice of doing these things. That's it. No magic. But there's still challenge.

Even for the most practiced among us the edge can present what Hideki Yukawa described in *Creativity and Intuition* as a "struggle with self."[271] But importantly, what you hear from those who practice coming to the edge and improvising doesn't describe a struggle in which the goal is to declare a victor—boundary over boldness, hedgehog over fox, good outcome over bad. The struggle is in gaining increased comfort and applying improvised flexibility every time something you know encounters something you don't. It's an unending quest, but it's also the very one that moves you—and us—forward.

You might think of the quest this way: Creativity requires *additional* creativity at *every* phase of the journey—the journey to realize a single idea, and equally the journey across a lifetime of ideas. Staying open, noticing, border crossing, and questioning repeats. Edges are more a way of marking progress than a signal of having reached an end.

THE UPSIDE OF CROSSING THE EDGE

Christopher Logue's words at the beginning of this chapter tapped a universal truth about the edge. The popularity of his words over the last half-century speaks to the evergreen nature of that truth. Phil's story appeals because it moves the discussion of the edge from simply "relatable" to "real," and in the most everyday sense imaginable: the explorations of a child. His example further demonstrates that, while coming to and crossing edges can appear enormous from the outside looking in, the creative edges we face are far less precipitous than we imagine. More, his insights show us the simple steps needed to form the habit of coming to the edge.

All of this makes for a compelling reason to heed this Simple Truth. But what's the upside of coming to the edge, one large enough that we'd embrace the struggle with self, but more than that, the struggle often presented by the world around us? First let's cover the nature of that external struggle, then the upside of coming to the edge.

A Few Reminders About Humans. There is no progress without challenge and the disorder it temporarily brings. To make this point in *Creativity and Intuition*, Hideki Yukawa began with the obvious. "Anyone who carries on his studies for a long enough period of years becomes a mass of fixed ideas. And how could one not?" Yukawa said. He knew we could relate to that. On the one hand, it's true that, in any walk of life, agreements on ideas, methods, and ways of doing and being are indeed necessary to *produce*. But Yukawa wisely understood that, as humans, our internal gyroscope persistently reminds us that productivity is not enough.

Even more than being productive, we want to *progress*. As Yukawa continued, "What we know serves as a basis for discovering new things. But it also has a gradual immobilizing effect."[272] Inevitably, progress requires *challenging* the ideas, methods, and ways we've agreed on of doing things.

The Way of the Herd. It's a strange thing about us humans. Conceptually, we can relate to what Yukawa wrote. Individually, we might even form habits that build on his insight. But societally, our great tendency is to lean heavily off kilter toward keeping things the way they are. When we do, our "edges of opportunity" become our borders. And the habits, rewards, and messages we build around them make them feel vertical, steep, and something not to be crossed.

"At any given moment, the world offers vastly more support to work it already understands," wrote Bayles and Orland.[273] That means our social constructs are, by and large, oriented toward predictable models we hope will be productive. That creates an unnatural social pressure to stick with what we know. And yet, consistently, society also demands new, better, and more creative. The natural result? Struggle. The unintended result, however, is that "Society, nature and artmaking tend to produce guarded creatures"[274]—that is, until someone steps over the edge to remind us that's *not* what we want.

The Upside: Becoming You. In each of us occurs a fickle kind of arm wrestling between comfort and creativity. When we come to the edge, we address that conflict—not only at an individual level but at a societal level. That "struggle," as Yukawa dubbed it, is who we are. Embracing it is what allows us to *become*. We don't simply exist, we long to become. Knowing that makes us aware of the edge, that border defining who we are in *this* moment. But honoring that longing to become means coming to that edge and peering beyond. Whenever we do that, we find the upside, not simply the upside of the edge, but the upside of what it means to be human.

OVER THE EDGE TO CREATIVITY

When I wanted to share with you the actions you can take at the edge to move toward and not away from your innate creativity, I told you a story of childhood, Phil and the bee. There was purpose in doing so. I wanted you to feel what composer and MacArthur Fellow John Harbison describes so well. "The sense of an absolute jump off the cliff is pretty rare," John said about creativity and its edges. "There are many who, looking from outside, assume the view must be like that. There is a sense of a grand deed or gesture. But such moments are probably less frequent and fairly rough in their appearance—a passing moment perhaps, but not a perpetual state."[275] As simplistic as you might have regarded it to be, the bee sting is closer to the truth than initially thought.

Without question, you will face edges as you hone your creative capacity. But you're now better equipped to do so. You know the actions you must take. But you also know it's an ongoing improvisation, a perpetual trial and error. And while at times it may still *feel* like you're about to leap off the rim of the Grand Canyon, you'll find the height, trajectory, and consequences are far less severe than that. Either way, if you want to create a masterpiece or simply something beautiful, every path requires you to come to the edge in order to take flight. No doubt, it can feel frightening. "I have never *not* been terrified before a performance," Elizabeth Streb confided in *How to Become an Extreme Action Hero*.[276] But quitting or choosing not to engage? Not optional.

CONNECTING THE DOTS

While we perpetually face choices, in truth, as Brené Brown expressed in her book *Daring Greatly*, "Our only choice is a question of engagement. [This choice] determines the depth of our courage and the clarity of our purpose."[277]

That choice of how to engage also determines the degree to which we tap into our creative capacity. It plays a telling role in what it means to be human. It's a message that's simple and true, even if embracing it is hard. It reminds me of another story about how far simple engagement can take you if you want to "make a mark." Not surprisingly, the story comes back to childhood—that time when coming to the edge seemed less daunting and more about what it means to be you.

One of my young daughter's favorite books is *The Dot* by Peter H. Reynolds.[278] Vashti, the main character, begins the tale in her grade school art class with a blank canvas, a feeling, and a fear. Unwilling to edge into art and attempt to draw, her teacher tells her, "Just make a mark and see where it takes you." Stabbing the paper with her pen, Vashti says, "There!" "Now sign it," the teacher replies.

As Reynolds wrote, "That one little dot marks the beginning of Vashti's journey of surprise and self-discovery." That first dot leads to other attempts because, after making that initial mark and, by signing her name to it, owning it, Vashti immediately senses she can go further. It's as if by taking action the edge that held her back simply disappears. Soon single dots lead to many dots. Small dots grow into large ones. Vashti even makes dots without making dots. In this way, discovering a connection to things new becomes inevitable.

Artist Nathan Oliveira once advised, "See the first stroke as a start and everything after a recovery."[279] Both life and art require us to put down that initial mark with the purpose not only of *recovering* but *thriving*. But we must come to the edge to do so. True, you can't know for sure what will happen next.

"It's impossible to know if the idea will work out before you invest your time, money, reputation, and energy," wrote Frans Johansson in *The Click Moment*. "You are essentially placing a bet."[280] But as the old adage attributed to 3M's engineering group in its heyday goes: "If it's a dumb idea, you'll find out. You'll smack right into that brick wall, then you'll stagger back and see another opportunity that you wouldn't have seen otherwise."[281]

Go ahead, make your mark.

FRAMING

THE VIEW

TO SEE

BEYOND YOU

CHAPTER ELEVEN

FRAMING THE VIEW
TO SEE BEYOND YOU

One of the best ways to "reconnect" to your creativity capacity and *stay* connected is to be conscious of the things that can *impede* connectivity—among them, false impressions of genius and heroes, and misconceptions about the edge. Clearing out the hurdles is an important first step in moving you from *understanding* creativity to actually *applying* it.

To take the next step toward use, this chapter and Chapter Twelve focus on insights and actions that not only help you lever up your creative practice, but urge you to make that practice your habit.

Bit by bit, you've already been learning a central lesson of creativity and reconnection: habit. Applying your creative capacity with impact proves easiest when using it becomes habitual for two obvious reasons: 1) Habit makes each of the elements of the language of man more familiar. It's their habitual use that allows you to know which of them serves you best under what circumstances. 2) More, habit informs how you can connect the elements of the language of man to one another, and empowers you to do so in ever expanding and novel ways. In a word, habit facilitates fluency. And fluency in the language of man increases the odds of connecting your breakthrough ideas to the tangible value you dream they can bring.

The ability to generate breakthrough ideas and to create new value is part and parcel of our individual creative stories. We each want to tell our *own* creative story. We want our story to be a unique compilation of elements, ideas, and value, one that compels and advances us. But just as strongly, we want our story to move others forward too.

So in the same way you've learned to think of *language* in a larger sense, I invite you to think of *story* in a similar way—not story in the singular, one-time, one storyteller, one passive audience sense but story as cumulative, ongoing, and shared. To show you what I mean, let me tell you a story. I'm going to tell it to you in two very different ways. The first is a crappy version.

A STORY GREATER THAN THE SUM OF THE PARTS

A CRAPPY STORY

Once upon a time, there was an artist named Phil Hansen who was a pointillist. Pointillism is the art of making dots. (Think of Vashti in the story *The Dot* but juiced up a notch.)

Rather than being about single dots, pointillism is about making connections *between* dots. What's the reward? That the dots ultimately come together into something larger, grander—"a unified whole," as Hansen called it.

In his February 2013 TED Talk *Limits Spark Creativity*, Hansen confessed he was single-minded in his pursuit of his art, obsessive even. In fact, he'd narrowed in on that one way that produced that one result so much so that, after years of repetitively making countless tiny dots, he developed nerve damage in his hand. With the nerve damage came a shake. And the shake turned his precision dots into squiggles—less than ideal for a pointillist.

So what was Hansen's response? To double down. He grabbed the pen tighter, trying to *force* the annoying new reality of squiggles back into dots. "This progressively made the shake *worse*," Hansen said. "So I'd hold the pen *tighter still*."[282] It was like the old cliché that says insanity is doing the same thing over and over again hoping for a different result. According to Hansen, "This became a vicious cycle that ended up causing so much pain and so many joint issues, I had trouble holding anything. And after spending all my life wanting to do art, I left art school, and then I left art completely." The End.

WHY WE TELL STORIES AND HOW TO TELL A GOOD ONE

The preceding version of Phil Hansen's story, parsed from his larger story, just plain stinks, doesn't it? (That's one reason you should watch Hansen tell his own wonderful, more complete version on TED.com.)[283] But *why* does it stink? Among obvious reasons, it's depressing. It's also narrow, situational, and exclusively about him. And once we've heard it, it doesn't offer much value, does it?

Although this story stinks, it tells us a lot about creativity and connections. To see how, let's turn to Oscar-winning storywriter Andrew Stanton, the Pixar team member behind the highly successful *Finding Nemo* and *Toy Story* movies.

Describing the powerful gift and undeniable need for storytelling, Stanton said that, at its best, a good story confirms and/or sheds new light on some truth in a way that "deepens our understanding of *who we are* as human beings."[284] Of the dozens of "tricks of the trade" he's encountered for good storytelling, this insight tops his list. Take note that the key to good storytelling is also key to creativity—that connecting question of what it means to be human.

While it's an eyebrow-raising connection, Stanton's insight only describes the target we attempt to hit. What enables us to hit that target is what he calls, "The greatest story commandment of all: *"MAKE ME CARE."*[285] When listening to Stanton or watching his films, it becomes abundantly clear the "me" he refers to isn't one individual; it's a "universal" me. A story has to make "us" care—*all* of us—from the storyteller to the actors who help tell the story to each audience member. If the story fails to do that for any one of the people it's meant to reach, it's dead on arrival. (You might recall Deborah Meier's final question of her five habits of the mind. It pointed us to the same conclusion: "Who cares?")

In total, Stanton's hard-won insights teach this: Making people care means deepening their understanding of *who they are* as humans, but the impact is strongest when they go further to claim the story as their own. It's a crucial frame of reference when seeking to create something that matters, including your own creative story.

With that lesson in mind, let's go back to Phil Hansen's story.

A STORYLINE REFRAMED

What does Hansen's story convey to us about *who we are?* Well, in the first crappy version, not much. It fails in several ways, but mostly it fails because it's a *closed* story. It follows a bounded and linear path through the facts: Hansen had a passion and a talent; he pursued it to the point of obsession and injury; when faced with the limits his injury imposed, he doubled down and did more of the same; eventually this led to total collapse, failure, and his choice to abandon what he loved—end of story. This version offered no insights to help you understand it, and I doubt it made you care. You might say this version of Hansen's story got "stuck in the dots."

We all experience times when we become stuck in our own story. Typically this happens when we prematurely "conclude" our story, closing it off to new ideas and new possibilities. But creative stories, *human* stories, only close if we allow them to do so. They long to remain open. By reconnecting to our creative habit, we can reopen our story any time, which is precisely what Phil Hansen did.

When Hansen went to see a neurologist about his hand problem, the doctor confirmed he had nerve damage and the resulting shake would likely be permanent. But his doctor saw something more. "He actually took one look at my squiggly line," Hansen recalled, "and said, 'Well, why don't you just *embrace the shake?*'"[286] This simple observation went so beyond what Hansen had been able to come up with himself that it became the creative force behind an eye-opening new storyline. More than that, it reframed his world—something he simply hadn't been able to do on his own.

So Hansen took his doctor's advice. "I went home, grabbed a pencil, and let my hand shake and shake." The perspective reframed what and how he saw his art—but so much more. The spark from outside caused him to realize that his work was less about pointillism and more about *bringing fragments together into larger images*. What Hansen loved and sought to create, he realized, wasn't dots but *connections*. And with that insight, he was no longer stuck in the dots. "I discovered that, if I worked on a *larger* scale and with *bigger* materials, my hand wouldn't hurt," Hansen said. "I ended up having an approach to creativity that completely changed my artistic horizons."[287]

AN "OPEN" STORY

To give you a sense of what this breakthrough meant, let's compare the one-time "dot maker" with the "connector" by examining a few creative approaches Hansen took to rewriting his creative story.

In one project, Hansen threw away the pencil completely and dipped his feet in paint, then walked his way across a room-sized canvas to create an image. His feet replaced the pencil; his footprints became the dots and squiggles; the canvas became an entire floor. Firm borders became his enabling constraints.

In another project called Tesla, Hansen used two live electrical wires connected to the poles of a car battery to create "electrical burns" on a paper. This technique scorched, not drew, one tiny singed "dot" at a time until a portrait of the famed inventor emerged. We most often think of an artist's "medium" for creating as paint, pen, or clay (for example). For Hansen, his view expanded so much that "medium" became a relative element.

It isn't just the assumed limits of media that have dissolved for Phil Hansen; it's the permanence of his works as well. We most often regard art as permanent, something meant to last. And while Elizabeth Turk taught us in Chapter Four that such a view can be limiting and should be challenged, Hansen went further. He asked us to consider obliterating the idea of permanence altogether. One step in that direction was a project called Worms. Rather than using dots or footprints or burns to make lasting images, Hansen used 500 live, wriggling earthworms. As he shaped the worms, they also shaped themselves. Each "work of art," as we might typically think of it, was really a snap shot of a creative "moment." As soon as any one image took form, the worms would move. Each image or "piece" morphed into others, rendering permanence impotent but also unimportant. The video Hansen took of the entire project unfolding was far more telling than any single image he (and the worms) created within it.

Hansen pushed the boundaries further still in a series he called Goodbye Art. It began with this unexpected question: "What if instead of *making* art," Hansen thought, "I had to *destroy* it?"[288] Here's what that looked like to him.

Using more than seven thousand matches with dot-like heads of different colors, he stood them upright on the floor and connected them side by side to make an image (as seen from above) of the musician Jimi Hendrix. He then set the matches ablaze and videotaped the transformation and destruction that followed.

In his ongoing evolution, Hansen even made an image from something that effectively didn't exist. Slowly arranging candles into visual fragments, he captured on video each fleeting act of lighting and blowing out the candles over and over again so their flames' momentary existence appeared stitched together. In effect, he created "something" out of "nothing."

OPEN TO ALL

More than reflecting the "make me care" commandment, Hansen's awakened approach encourages us to dig deeper. Specifically, Worms and Goodbye Art cause us not only to care but to ask these key questions: Why *do I care? And is it the "thing" that I care about or* something deeper *that's only represented by that thing?* As you ask these questions, you realize that Phil Hansen has opened up the whole concept of "caring." More than that, his creative story causes each of us to reframe how we think about art, creativity, and the questions his works evoke. He's not only telling us his story; he's inviting us into it and even into our own.

To that very point, one of his most striking co-creation projects began with another question: "What if instead of relying on *myself,*" Hansen asked, "I had to rely on *other people* for the content of the art?" What he did next makes me smile at his openness and, dare I say, his "genius."

For nearly a week, he lived in front of a webcam aimed at a six-foot-wide circular canvas. This enabled anyone to watch him as he created. He then asked people to call him and share a life-changing moment in their lives—in short, to tell him *their* stories. Next, Hansen took elements of each of those stories and transferred them onto the canvas. By using different fonts, sizes, and spacing, his audiences' stories became the "dots" and their interconnection made a beautiful picture of a woman's smiling face framed by a ring of loving hands. Quite literally, "she" was manifested by many hands and many stories. In this valuable way, Hansen kept his own story open while at the same time opening up creativity to bring others actively into it.

LESSONS IN FRAMING THE VIEW

This time spent with Phil Hansen was a deliberate pause, and there were several important reasons for taking it. One was to help you see that each and every creative story is ongoing—something Hansen's story made clear many times over. This story also showed how easy it is to conclude that a single creative way of doing can last forever, in other words, that you can fix the framework through which you create into a static formula for all time. You can't. More powerful, we learned that story, in every sense of the word—yours, mine, ours—is about connecting. The more you understand that, the more capable you become of creating your own powerful story—or anything else for that matter.

At the start of this chapter, I laid forth the following logic: We all want to tell our own creative story—our own compilation of elements, ideas, and value that compels us and others forward. As noted, to do that, we have to develop fluency in the language of man. Fluency results, in part, from the habit of tapping into our creative capacity. But just as critical is having a creative framework through which to practice and form the habit of speaking creativity.

A FRAMEWORK TO BUILD ON

It's the framework—open, flexible, and habitually reconsidered—that makes possible all those "things" we want creativity to render. And while we each must create our own, Sara Lawrence-Lightfoot's framework, one she calls "portraiture," offers valuable principles to reference and guide each of us as we do.

Portraiture is unique in many respects, but one is that it was consciously developed as a framework for creating. It was also designed not just for use by Sara but by many people. In that sense it had to be anchored in core principles that were effective, versatile, and transferable—to anyone, anywhere.

To come to appreciate how Sara's insights can help any of us, in this chapter we'll begin by highlighting the basics of her framework. After that, we'll turn our attention to the creative frameworks of several other Fellows seeking to accomplish two things. First, we'll use these additional examples to note how the core tenets of portraiture appear in other productive creative frameworks. The fact that each practitioner we'll hear from arrived at a creative framework sharing the same principles without explicit knowledge of Sara's portraiture approach is a strong testament to the power and value of these principles. The second thing we'll be seeking is insight into what creative frameworks look like in actual practice and what they can teach us about using a framework anchored in the same principles in our own practice. While many important insights will be revealed, the most valuable is this: As you frame your view, you need to see beyond you. There is no more reliable way to create with value and impact.

FRAMING OUR POTENTIAL
THE PORTRAITURE WAY

Sara said that portraiture resulted from her deep desire to change the conversation around why people are who they are and do what they do, to explore how their lives might be better. That's the textbook definition of a sociologist's job. But Sara felt the typical conversation in her field was constrained, opaque, and esoteric—like seeing the dots, but missing the connections between them. To her way of thinking, the view needed to become more open, accessible, and shared.[289]

While portraiture was initially designed for use in sociology, its applications go further in large part because of its powerful underlying principles. First, portraiture is a "framework" methodology, not a formula approach—a principle you already appreciate but with important nuances we'll explore in a moment. Second, portraiture strives to facilitate a deeper, ongoing understanding rather than arrive at a single, permanent answer. And third and most important, portraiture assumes and facilitates a co-creation, an exchange by which individual ideas and creative stories quilt together.

Let's examine these three central principles one at a time.

FRAMEWORK OVER FORMULA

The first powerful principle of portraiture is that it's indeed a framework and not a formula. Now—if your immediate conclusion upon reading this is "that's old news," pause for a moment. True, you already know the general advantages of frameworks over formulas, but it's the subtleties that matter here. And to get at them, I want you to think about how a formula comes to be and how it can restrict the way we look at things thereafter.

We've all experienced that good specific answers that lead us to valuable results are hard to come by. Therefore when we arrive at a good one, it's not uncommon for us to become quite devoted—not only to the answer, but also to the way we came to it. That "way"— which we undeniably know developed as a way for getting that "one" answer in "one particular" set of circumstances—often becomes our "formulaic way," but in a broader sense. In other words, it leads to the habit of generalizing. At least when it comes to creativity, that's a problem—what author and sociologist Duncan Watts calls the "micro-macro" problem.

In his appropriately titled book *Everything Is Obvious: How Common Sense Fails Us*, Watts described that the macro part of the problem is that people don't just do this now and then. They try to generalize and categorize just about everything. That is, after arriving at a good answer, our dominant habit is to treat that answer as gospel, create formulaic explanations from it for why things are the way they are, and then use such formulas to categorize and sort everything we encounter thereafter.[290]

You can sense our hedgehog at work, and the results aren't all bad. But as Watts pointed out, generalizations, while certainly providing temporary aid to our thinking and learning, simply don't reflect reality. Each of us makes thousands of individual choices among hundreds of individual variables that in total define us in billions of different ways.

Generalizing and trying to put everything into preset categories certainly appeals to our hedgehog, but it leads to what Watts calls a "micro" problem, one with lots of negative implications. For example, categorizing based on generalizations inevitably yields poor descriptions of how things really work. Doing so also has limited predictive accuracy. But more directly related to creativity, such fixed generalizations often cause us to miss seeing new things. As you know, most often interesting ideas and possibilities are found not within the borders of a categorization, field, or formula, but outside those borders or where borders intersect and overlap.

After reading this far in *The Language of Man*, what Watts described should sound familiar. It's hard to see something different or discover something new if you expect that everything new you encounter will fit into an old mold. Thus, it's the degree of openness, flexibility, and ongoing development of a framework that makes it relevant when we think, learn, and—most important of all—create.

NOT AN ANSWER BUT A WAY

The second foundational principle that makes portraiture so powerful and versatile is that it strives not just to arrive at a single answer for all time but to facilitate a deeper, ongoing understanding. Where the first principle was concerned with *how* what we create is constructed, this principle has to do with *what* we are trying to construct.

To be clear, saying that portraiture isn't focused on arriving at a single answer doesn't mean it fails to produce answers and outcomes; it does produce them, and most often with a high degree of originality and value. But portraiture is primarily intended to cultivate a *habit*, facilitated by the use of an active and flexible framework for thinking, looking, and creating—one that guides rather than guarantees. As Sara told me, "It's not about being after one finite, dogmatic message. It's about identifying the thread running through something—an idea, a life, anything really. The goal of finding that thread is to deepen the conversation among all who touch it and, in doing so, inform it as no single answer or dogma can, at least in any lasting way."[291]

This is a difficult concept for many to get their minds around, as Sara acknowledged, because a truly creative framework is "referential, progressive, ongoing. It allows for and expects changing uses and responses. Its true power lies in the inverse of one view, person, or way. Its beauty is that it's collective, reciprocal, and co-created."

But it wouldn't be right to conclude that portraiture is "mushy" or lacking substance in either process or output. It simply seeks a different kind of outcome for a different set of purposes via a different path. Like Phil Hansen's work, it's an "art ongoing," and that's precisely what makes its value so rich.

The supporting data and the related process for gathering it necessary to portraiture serves as a good example of both the substance and the flexibility of this framework. Like any other science, portraiture applied to sociology involves the collection of data. The difference lies in the *reasons* for the collection, the source, and the intended use.

In sociology, portraiture focuses on in-depth interviews and observations rather than primarily relying on surveys, generalized data from media, or historical documentation, all sources to which sociologists frequently turn. The idea is to seek direct (not referential) relevance. Yes, such an approach can take more time. Also, it requires that the portraitist regularly go beyond her own borders to gather that data. Because of these differences, the portraiture process tends to reveal things unfamiliar or unexpected. All of these have at times been described by others as inconvenient and even as "interfering." But as you know, the "unfamiliar and unexpected" are often precisely where the *aha!* potential lies—that is *if* your frame and your habit are open and fluid and allow you to see an "intersection" where others see an "interference."

It's accurate to say that portraiture seeks the "simple truth" rather than the "convenient truth."

THE IMPORTANCE OF CO-CREATION

While the distinctions of "frameworks over formulas" (principle one) and "fluid stories over fixed answers" (principle two) make this framework powerful and versatile, the third principle of portraiture is the most compelling: **CO-CREATION**. Co-creation is the idea that, while one person may originate a single, even catalytic idea, it takes multiple ideas and many people to actually create the "tangible and valuable" out of the "possible." Here's what it looks like when applied in Sara's world.

Sara wanted to change the standard sociologist's conversation from a *mandate* to an ongoing *dialog* and from a language meant to *inform* to one that opened up *possibilities*.[292] To accomplish this, Sara decided that not only did the traditional approach need to change, but so too did traditional roles and assumptions about "expertise."

In traditional sociology, the "subject" is explicitly the focal point of a study and the roles in the sociologist-subject dynamic are unambiguous. Think of it as "I, the Ph.D. sociologist, come and analyze you, the subject, and thereafter dictate the findings of your life to you." It's strongly reminiscent of that pie drawing from Chapter Two. And traditionally, this dynamic dominated the thinking, the process, and the conclusions almost to the exclusion of the very person we'd rightfully expect to be at the center of that conversation: the subject, whose life is what any sociological study is trying to understand. Portraiture changed that.

In portraiture, the role of "expert" (a close kin to "genius" and "hero") is leveled to the same plane as the person being observed. Portraitists gain a different view by accepting they are only one of many participants in a conversation about the subject's world. And while they bring unique skills, they realize that they're not the most important or informed participants either. In fact, they serve much more as guides than experts.

"Portraitists not only listen to stories," Sara has said, they do what Sara calls "listening *for* a story, a process of co-creating compelling narratives *with* participants, complete with characters, metaphors, and a central narrative arc."[293]

Pause and recognize Sara is saying that combining and interconnecting the contributions of all participants is how the most distinct and valuable discoveries are manifested and also how the most compelling stories are told. This is co-creation and creativity at its most potent. It is also the very thing that brings a framework to life and enables it to remain open and valuable ongoing.

In total, these three principles underlying portraiture facilitate a powerful but ever-evolving creative framework. The proof is in their regular appearance across the creative frameworks of a wide range of practitioners. Let's turn to several examples to see this and learn more.

INSIGHTS FROM YOUR GUIDES: THREE CREATIVE FRAMEWORKS EXPLORED

Creativity comes alive when we allow our brains to connect in the expanded way that's exemplified by the portraiture framework. While Sara put a name to the framework that guides her, unnamed examples of similar open, fluid, and deeply creative frameworks appear across the creative landscape. Three examples—from Fellows Pat Churchland, Peter Pronovost, and Sarah Kagan—demonstrate how individualized these frameworks can be while sharing the same foundational principles.

PAT CHURCHLAND—QUILTED PORTRAITURE

One of the most interesting things about Pat Churchland's creative framework is that it doesn't simply *allow* for others, it *relies* on others to keep going and produce the creative results desired. Most certainly Pat had individually been employing a portraiture-like mindset in her earliest days of pioneering a new field. But what happened once she melded her view with like-minded thinkers offers a greater insight to why creative frameworks like hers and Sara's prove so effective.

Porting Portraiture into Community. Exploring the adjacent possible between philosophy and neurology, Pat was lucky enough to encounter others who'd taken similarly broad views in their creative practices and in their own fields. Two standouts were Francis Crick, the co-discoverer of the DNA double helix structure, and Jonas Salk, the polio vaccine pioneer. When she wondered aloud to them whether she should retreat to one field or the other to pursue her vision, both encouraged Pat to keep her frame wide open. But they suggested she expand it too—not only in her own mind but in tandem with others. They advised her to take her way of thinking into a broader community, even if she had to *create* that community.

Community from Scratch. Remember that neurophilosophy was virgin territory back then. Pat couldn't simply check her local listings for others interested in the field and then team up with them. In fact, for a long time it was hard to even convince anyone with overlapping interests to wonder and think as she was doing. So she went "parallel." Instead of trying to vet her ideas with potential converts or even with people sharing common knowledge, she vetted her ideas with others who thought in a similarly open and creative way *regardless* of their field.

After initial introductions from her mentors, Pat spent increasingly more time with a group of people who, while individually researching different topics, shared many of the same creative habits. Each understood what those creative habits had meant to their perceptions of the world around them, to their ideas, and to their sense of the possible. As Pat described it, "I began to move toward a community in which asking and challenging and constantly seeking to *expand* the view was the gold standard rather than something to be shunned. Independent of one another, we had discovered this kind of fluidity and the open view it characterized as being the keys to creativity. We wanted more of what we'd tasted on our own and sensed that a community of people sharing similar mindsets could give us that. I think, at a minimum, we each sensed it would be reinforcing to what we already were doing individually," Pat said. "But I had no idea how much I'd gain beyond the familiarity of like-minded thinkers."294

How to Merge Creative Frameworks. Pat had described an environment of smart, creative people, but people who knew little about one another's fields. In that sense, there was no one way of doing things, no single bank of knowledge, and no one creative "luminary" among them around which the exchanges would take shape. The latter point is worth expanding on.

All of them came to the group with big ideas. But just because an idea made sense to one of them didn't mean it got an automatic stamp of approval from others. When one person presented an idea to the rest, that person was expected to clarify his or her "genius" to a smart yet neophyte audience. They were forced to stand up to the baptism by fire of bringing their ideas out into public light. But it was more than that. Every time one of them put an idea on the table, others inevitably shaped it. They may not have been working on the same creative projects, but they were absolutely co-creating. Pat described what it felt like to both open up their individual creative frames and co-create a new shared one.

"Because it was a diverse group, we had to make sure everyone 'came along' as we explored. Our individual knowledge had to be broken down and explained across subcultures. We had to go back to the beginning of our own assumptions and understandings; we had to be clear and offer real explanations, ones that had meaning to everyone. The questions we asked would have sounded naïve to the 'experts' of our origin fields, but in our community, they felt natural and necessary. And the process put creativity in a whole new light. We made each other refine and reconfigure our assumptions, then added new perspectives to one another's ideas," Pat said.

"We had to convey more than our passion and do more than just follow our own way," is how Pat explained the creative evolution. "We had to communicate the logic and the value of our ideas and our stories so it was plain to others beyond our own fan club of one. And we had to learn to create in new and expanded ways. Really, it's hard to imagine many of our ideas ever advancing without being tested in this environment,"[295] Pat said. But if you reflect on her story, it could also be hard to imagine how this diverse group learned to speak to one another at this whole new level of creativity. Hard, that is, until you realize that their individual creative frameworks shared certain common principles, ones that as a group they built on.

Shared Principles Uniquely Applied. In Pat's description, you can hear clear parallels to what portraiture honors and allows. For one, she and her peers shared a similar "framework" mindset for creativity. Two, they saw one another as equals. Three, it wasn't a singular, one-time or for-all-time answer they sought from one another. Instead, it was a conversation leading to repeated advancements and insights they wanted. And four, inevitably, operating within this open, fluid, and shared creative framework led to not only co-creation but *better* creation. These are just some of the "sameness" elements that Pat's experience shares with Sara's.

Let's turn to another framework and a very different set of circumstances to see how these principles come into play and reveal other important principles to a creative framework with reach and longevity.

PETER PRONOVOST—PURPOSEFUL PORTRAITURE

By and large, Sara chose the people she engaged as participants in her studies. Similarly, Pat and her peers also selected one another. Yet this isn't always possible.

Often, we face a need to create within places and among people we already know and might even feel stuck with. Unfortunately, such environments can lead us to conclude that a creative framework with portraiture leanings isn't possible. Johns Hopkins School of Medicine doctor Peter Pronovost, however, has a habit of ignoring that conclusion.

Spreading a Mindset When You Lack the Power. Peter is perhaps best known for his "checklist idea," one made famous by doctor and best-selling author Atul Gawande (who just happens to also be a MacArthur Fellow) in *The Checklist Manifesto*. Peter's checklist idea was designed to save lives in hospital emergency and surgery wards by inserting "deliberate pauses" into well-worn healthcare routines. The point was to use a checklist of "questions" to trigger the habit of considering why things are the way they are and how they might be improved in the everyday patterns of providing healthcare—even where existing routines were commonly regarded as being just fine. And it worked. Where it's been tried, the checklist method has led to substantial declines in care errors and even patient deaths.

But as Sara and Phil Hansen taught us, the benefits of one idea or advancement can't be lasting if the creative construct from which it emerges is never reconsidered or built upon. In a way, the checklist embodies the same message. Even after it produced a powerful breakthrough idea, Peter had to figure out a way to further expand his creative framework in order to realize the true value potential of that idea. Core principles carried Peter forward—the portraiture ones plus a couple more.

Understanding what happened after the checklist idea's initial success helps us to see just how complex this challenge turned out to be. But, it also gives us a greater appreciation for the seemingly simple tenets of a creative framework that have allowed Peter and his colleagues to meet that challenge. Here's a short recap.

The Challenge of Spreading a Framework. Johns Hopkins is one of the largest hospital systems in the country, if not the world. Peter's checklist idea, as brilliant as it was, initially applied only to one part of one division of this massive hospital system. Also, as a leader in that subgroup, Peter had some degree of leverage to get his idea test-driven. Not surprisingly, that wasn't the case when he sought to spread the idea beyond his immediate borders. While it was absolutely clear that similar errors occurred throughout the system and caused the unwanted outcomes his checklist seemed to alleviate, Peter eventually faced a new challenge: How do you spread a creative framework elsewhere and to others when you lack the power and, at least at first, they seem to lack the interest?

A More Complex Problem. In seeking to spread his creative ways to the whole of the hospital system, Peter was doing what retired army four-star general Stanley McChrystal refers to as going from the *complicated* to the *complex*. In his book *Team of Teams: New Rules of Engagement for a Complex World*, McChrystal described the difference.

Things that are complicated—think of an internal combustion engine, a manufacturing line, or the interactions of a surgery room—"ultimately can be broken down into a series of neat and tidy deterministic relationships; by the end you will be able to predict with relative certainty what will happen when one part . . . is activated or altered."[296] By contrast, "Things that are complex— living organisms, ecosystems, national economies—have a diverse array of connected elements that interact frequently . . . fluctuate extremely and exhibit unpredictability."[297]

Reflecting this dynamic, Peter explained that what he'd already done in the OR to get his own department behind his creative idea was somewhat complicated. His new challenge, however, was far more complex. "Rather than innovating one issue, idea, or person at a time," Peter said, to develop a system-wide creative framework, "we had to shift our entire mindset."

Peter didn't mean his mindset or his department's, but a *collective* mindset—one formed not just from the dozens of divisions of the Johns Hopkins medical system, but from an amalgam of the thousands of individual ways of thinking and seeing that the system's employees represented.

He described the complexity of the necessary shift in thinking this way. "It wasn't only about 'what' we might create that was new or better. In the grand scheme, that was more like the 'thing' we might create. More than that, it came to be about what we were at Hopkins to do in the first place—all of us, in every department—and who we were there to do it for."[298] For the creative framework to evolve to handle the complex and not just the complicated, Peter and the Hopkins team needed to find their creative center: principles, you might say, that ran deeper than *what* they were trying to create to reflect more fundamentally *why* they were trying to create something new in the first place. You could see in Peter's existing framework all the vital features we've discussed. But this complex opportunity required more.

A Foundation of Purpose and Trust. McChrystal, too, faced a complex and unfamiliar challenge presented by Al Qaeda in Iraq. And it's worth a brief recap of his circumstances to appreciate Peter's situation and more, to see that while acting in entirely unique environments, both came to appreciate two more fundamental principles to their or any creative framework.

Al Qaeda in Iraq (AQI) represented a different enemy operating under completely new rules of engagement than any the U.S. and its allies had ever faced. The early and dramatic losses to AQI quickly made clear to McChrystal that the old ways didn't work. Formulaic approaches and rules, even rules of thumb, proved to be at best naïve, at worst, deadly. In his book, McChrystal described that his elite unit known as the Task Force quickly came to appreciate the value of a framework view over a more hierarchical and rigid approach. After adopting it, they became more flexible, more creative, and more successful. Yet while the challenge may have been complicated within his Task Force unit, it was almost unimaginably complex trying to get the many military and diplomatic divisions of the United States and its allies to even consider such an approach.

As McChrystal explained, to get others to see the value and open up the ways they thought and operated required gradually establishing two things: **PURPOSE** and **TRUST**.[299] Any framework details and any co-creation of better answers came out of shared purpose and trust.

It sounds so simple, so "mom and apple pie." But purpose and trust turn out to be central to creating anything, and they become exponentially more important when the environment in which you are trying to create is complex.

Peter arrived at similar conclusions at Hopkins. "Creating, even operating in such an environment," he said, "begins by establishing a collective sense of what's important to us and then building a framework in which to achieve those things. That collective sense of importance defined not just our priorities but truly our purpose.

"Priorities are fluid; purpose lasts far longer," Peter reflected. "Always pointing back to that purpose is what enables us to go beyond simply finding a solution to keep pressing for the *best* solutions and better ones after that. We trust each other because we know we're after the same thing, even if we see it in different ways."[300]

Trust and purpose are at the heart of what makes us willing to flex our framework. These are the things that give us the confidence to let go of the security of good answers, and peer over the edges once again to see if something better still might be out there. And without purpose and trust, there simply is no co-creating. With purpose and trust, however, even the impossible seems possible.

Paul Rogat Loeb, author and editor of the essay collection *The Impossible Will Take a Little While,* made a similar observation. He wrote about what can emerge from the most seemingly implacable environments when shared purpose and trust take hold. He referred to the collective mindset that emerges as "the alchemy of community," an environment in which "shared imagination leads outward to other people and new possibilities."[301] When this happens, it isn't just the ideas and solutions that break through; an entire space gets created where such breakthroughs can continue— or more accurately, be *co-created.*

SARAH KAGAN—THE PORTRAIT WITHIN THE FRAME

When we talk about creativity and forming a creative framework, it's important not to lose sight of the reason any frame matters in the first place: to allow individual pictures and stories to form within it. That's why Sarah Kagan's story is important to share. It might best be described as a "portrait" of what it means to be human and how any creative framework must enable that.

As with Sara, Pat, and Peter, some context about Sarah's world and work helps, so let's begin there and let Sarah be our guide.

Returning to the Beginning. To put the complex job of being a gerontological nurse in oversimplified terms, Sarah cares for elderly patients. As the number of aged people goes up both nationally and internationally, so does the complexity of caring for them. And as the complexity of this care rises, the tendency to focus disproportionately on the nuts and bolts of the "business" of healthcare does as well. An unintended consequence? The individual patient, the human, too often gets lost.

"Healthcare *is* a business," Sarah said, "but it's a business based on human lives."[302] While facilitative, the business of healthcare, Sarah explained, increasingly overshadows the *purpose* of care. Ironically, absent that purpose, the business of healthcare would cease to exist.

To help me understand this, Sarah took me back to the beginning, long before the complicated business came to be. "We think of 'health' as some amorphous thing in the background of our lives,"

Sarah stated reflectively. "When our health is good, we don't think about it much. When it's not good, we suddenly regain our focus. Healthcare doesn't simply exist within a larger realm called 'health.' In fact, what's forgotten is that it more accurately exists within the larger concept of 'care.' *Care*, however, is more about living. And living is something we do in the broader sense, whether our health is sound or failing," she said. Sarah then took this mind-opening insight and pointed it back to the business of healthcare to help me see the implications.

"As good as our healthcare systems are in many respects, true 'care' is often missing. These days, how we provide healthcare tends to follow rigid models and even tighter rules. But especially as the healthcare system grows bigger, the delivery of care within it starts to fall under a socially prescribed contract with business-like expectations of 'what I will do and when, what you will get, how much it will cost,' and so on," she said. "Actual 'living' becomes less clear in this environment. Whether or not such a system then delivers 'care' is up for discussion."

A Big Thought. How do we address such growing complexity? As Sarah said to me, one option is of course to turn our attention to changing the larger system as it exists today, and many who see the need for healthcare reform try to do exactly that. Some even do it well—at least as it relates to the business, the logistics, and the numbers.

But that isn't the only option, nor the one Sarah suggests we prioritize. She believes there's greater value in returning to *purpose*. Rather than think about purpose as "the purpose of the healthcare *system*," however, she suggests we think about the purpose of *each life* that system is in theory meant to serve.

"If we lose the link to the very reason the system came to be in the first place, then we also lose the point," Sarah explained. By choosing to focus our attention only on fixing the larger system, "We can continue to walk a slender, fragile thread that attaches our work, our ideas, and our ambitions to the purpose that makes any of those things meaningful. But how long can we do so before that thread unravels or breaks? And if it breaks, not much of whatever we create in its absence really matters."

A Story Ongoing. If you pause for a moment and reflect, it's possible to see what Sarah put forth as a breakthrough idea, maybe the very idea we need to address the growing challenges around care. Here at its beginning, however, that idea also appears a very tall order. Challenging as it may appear, somehow every creative practitioner that we hail as genius finds her or his own way to keep such breakthrough ideas in play until they become the thing for which we celebrate them. Remarkably, *story* is often the enabling tool for doing so. And Sarah Kagan clearly knows this.

"A lot of my time is spent listening," Sarah shared. "I try to understand as explicitly as possible patients' situations, their priorities, and their concerns. I want to know *their* personal stories—past, present, and only yet dreamed. I try to get at *who* they are and *how* they exist, but also how they live and dream. My work and how I do it is driven by *their* purpose."

With a tone of deep affection in her voice, she said, "What I've found is that more than anything, people want to be understood. They want you to know their story, and they want to feel that whatever happens next, their story won't get lost. Though they're often terrified to say it," Sarah added, "they don't want to lose the right to *author* their own story either."

There's a flip side to any such experience as well. "As much as they want to be heard, patients want an honest story and answers in return."[303] Our stories intertwine. It's what connects us. That knowledge too must be part of any creative framework. You might call it our *shared* purpose in the broadest sense. It's also the basis for our trust of one another. In every sense, it's how we co-create "the story of creativity"—one caring and considered action at a time.

"I see my job as looking to expand the view," Sarah stated. "When getting to know a patient, I ask 'what's close to my soul?' This helps me figure out how to understand what's close to their souls and how to connect with them as people. I keep their touchstones of care as references to guide me and reframe what I'm doing.

"I know this sounds strange," she said, "in these days of healthcare workers pushing care through for efficiency. But I see my purpose as beyond myself, to strive to be the person my patients and team need me to be. I look to enhance *how* they think but not tell them *what* to think. I endeavor to make their persona more powerful. This brings them more options and hopefully the ones they most need. It also makes me far more creative in delivering them."[304]

End of story . . . well, this one anyway.

SIMPLE TRUTH:

BEAUTY

FUELS

CREATIVITY

CHAPTER TWELVE

CHAPTER TWELVE

SIMPLE TRUTH: BEAUTY FUELS CREATIVITY

Simple truths. Noticing. Inquiry. Border crossing. A portraiture mindset. Even with all of this new understanding about creativity, doesn't it feel as if there's something more to it?

To some extent, that feeling won't go away until you actually tap into your own creative capacity and make using it your habit. But several elements have yet to be explored (value, learning, and mental locks among them). They will shed light on how our creative capacity ultimately generates what we desire—that "something more" we long for.

But before we explore these elements, consider these questions: What inspires you to want to be creative, to dig in and try? What helps you give shape and direction to your purpose and signals your progress toward it? What moves you past the edge and gets you to soldier on through trial and error to make an idea tangible? And after such a journey, what makes you want to do it all over again?

It might surprise you to learn the answers to all of these questions share a common element—one that reconnects us repeatedly to each other and to who we are. To begin to see it, let me share a beautiful story.

THE BEAUTY OF IT IS . . .

AN ACT OF GRACE

It took her fifteen years to write eleven pages. Fifteen years. And those eleven pages *included* the references and acknowledgments. Did you catch that? *Fifteen* years.

When I finally spoke with Fellow Sue Kieffer about her essay *The Concepts of Beauty and Creativity: Earth Sciences Thinking*,[305] I had to ask, *why* did it take fifteen years? *Why* did you stick with it? *Why* was it so important? And *why* take the risk? (More on that risk later.) Among a wealth of other talents, roles, and knowledge, Sue is a geologist. Her answer, not surprisingly, was a layered one.

Complexity. Of course, one response was obvious: She had a lot of other things going on. Understandably, she also needed time to incubate her thoughts. But on top of these things that could have dissuaded her to abandon her essay, she continued to have this strong sense, this "hunch." She kept seeing a pattern in her own work and also across the work of others. As a scientist, she knew hunches were only a start and also that such feelings were often dismissed by others—which brings us around to another reason her essay took time: her audience.

Sue was writing *Beauty and Creativity* for her scientist peers. When it was completed in 2006, her paper was published in the *Journal of the Geological Society of America,* a publication overwhelmingly read by (shocker) other geologists. Regarding this audience, Sue was direct. "Scientists and the institutions they tend to work for are focused on measuring, precision, and exactitude—something with a number attached, something reliable. That's different from many aspects of creativity (including hunches); it's therefore hard for *creativity* to merit attention, to say nothing of *beauty*."[306]

Yet deep in her soul, Sue felt creativity was vital to science and even to that precision scientists seek; creativity, she believed, gave *meaning* and *purpose* to that precision. More than a hunch, this sense became a *knowing* over time. It was a feeling so strong and visceral that Sue believed she had no choice but to break through to her audience— somehow and no matter how long it might take. She knew scientists habitually deferred to the boundaries of their knowledge, their methods, and their field. Theirs were borders unlikely to be crossed, let alone erased. But perhaps, Sue thought, passageways could be created within those borders.

Of Two Minds. To offer a better sense of the challenge in communicating what she saw and sensed, Sue explained that, "Most scientists are more deductive than inductive in the way they think." Reflecting a similar conclusion to our hedgehog and fox lesson, Sue continued, "The trick wasn't to suggest the elimination of one way of thinking for the other but instead to get them to see the necessity and interplay of both. You need to build a foundation and add guiding walls (deductive thinking), but you also need to have *holes* in those walls (inductive thinking)."[307]

To appreciate what Sue is saying, recall that *inductive* reasoning means arriving at ideas or conclusions by way of *observations*. This kind of thinking is about noticing, seeking new connections, and letting new and known data points intersect and inform one's thoughts and ideas. It's fox-like and fluid, with rules existing as points of reference; their importance is relative rather than absolute. That means sometimes the rules help us arrive at ideas and answers, and sometimes they do not.

The more dominant scientific mindset, Sue pointed out, is *deductive* reasoning. It relies on *previously known and agreed-upon facts*. Where inductive reasoning could be described as emphasizing possibility, deductive reasoning seeks hedgehog proof. And proof, deductive reasoning would have it, is most reliable when it points to what we already know. How then do we discover anything new?

The more Sue's work unfolded and the more she observed the breakthroughs of other scientists, the more emphatic her belief became: *Science needs both kinds of thinking to do what science is intended to do in the first place—explore, discover, and advance.* And that, Sue concluded, meant scientists needed to embrace creativity.

Oh, and One More Thing. You now have a sense of why Sue's essay took so long to craft and why it was important to complete. But that's only half the story. Another reason drove her all those many years too. Sue knew she must do more than convince her colleagues about the importance of a creative frame of mind; she needed to tell them about the vital role of *BEAUTY*. Yes, beauty.

I recognize that as open as you are becoming, this just might be one of those Simple Truths you find hard to accept. But before you dismiss it, pause and consider the wise insights our MacArthur Fellows have shared throughout this book. Recall the passion and beauty with which they consistently express their thoughts. Were you to go back and catalog their comments, you'd find a repeated pattern of pointing to beauty as a source of inspiration, motivation, and reward for creativity.

Sue felt this so deeply that even with the passage of fifteen years, she believed this insight had to be shared.

Exploring beauty's link to every step of the creative cycle provides a deep and necessary understanding of what's possible and how to realize it. And in a moment, we'll allow Sue to walk us through the evidence of beauty's recurring role in creativity, as well as some of the reasons we fail to see it or worse, choose to ignore it. But for the moment, consider these truths: Beauty points us to where and how we might discover breakthrough ideas. It shows us how to make them real. It clarifies the value that creativity enables us to produce and why we value it in the first place. And when that value is realized, beauty is part of the reward.

Knowing beauty's role takes our understanding of creativity to an entirely different and holistic level. It also allows us to reach a level of understanding about creativity that George F. Kneller so beautifully described in *The Art and Science of Creativity* as "recorded in the intellect but felt in the pulse."[308] On our journey, we've been seeking that blended understanding from the start. Now it's time to bring it to fruition.

A Beautiful Journey Ahead. With Sue's story as a backdrop, you're invited to think about what drives *you*. Don't only consider what *motivates* you to want to tap into your creative capacity; also focus on what *drives you forward* in every sense. I submit that once you realize your answer is *beauty*, your capacity to create will open wide and creativity will come into full bloom.

To move you that direction, in this chapter, we'll let the Simple Truth that *beauty fuels creativity* gradually reveal itself. First, we'll pause to refine how we talk and think about beauty. Next, with Sue and other Fellows as our guides, we'll take a look at evidence of its central role in creativity, consider some of the reasons we fail to see it or choose to ignore it, and also explore its function as a powerfully versatile tool. After that, author Dan Pink will help us see just how beauty points us toward the things we *really* want *and* even helps us to attain them. We'll then close the chapter by looking at different examples of how it manifests in creative practice.

A creative reminder before you continue: Treat this chapter like a border crossing. Its Simple Truth is a "compass reading," not a map dot. So don't expect that after reading about it, you'll have arrived at an endpoint and have an understanding of beauty for all time. Instead, recognize that exploring it gives you a chance to pause, reflect, and reconnect with something core to all of us and central to creativity—beauty.

PUTTING LANGUAGE AROUND BEAUTY

In an important way, beauty is analogous to language. Linguist and author Steven Pinker's description of language in his book *The Language Instinct: How the Mind Creates Language*[309] helps draw the parallel.

Pinker wrote that language, rather than being laid out uniformly and orderly like our grammar lessons in grade school, exists within each of us as an *instinctive* framework—one he calls *mentalese*. This language framework is an open one built to make an endless array of connections. It's powerful because the connections it enables are not predetermined; we make them as we go and as our circumstances and cultures require. Therefore, this framework functions as a reference point and an ongoing touchstone for what we seek, and not instead as a template for how we attain what we seek.

The problem, however, is that *this isn't the way we tend to think about language*. By and large, we regard language as equivalent to its "external" manifestations—English, Spanish, Swahili, or American Sign Language, for example. That is, after all, what those grammar lessons in school teach us to do. But as Pinker reminded, these are simply "applications" of something far greater—outputs of the frame and not the frame itself. In addition, Pinker made clear that this language framework is a universal one (there isn't, for example, a form of the framework for someone born in Japan that's different from the form of the framework someone born in Russia has).

Pinker's description of language and how we most often think about it similarly describes how we tend to think about beauty.

What we come to perceive on the outside as beauty—a beautiful painting, for example—isn't beauty in and of itself. Rather, it's a beautiful *outcome*. But as we do with language, our tendency is to truncate the robustness of beauty by coming to equate it with its expressions.

As an example, many regard Leonardo da Vinci's Mona Lisa as the most beautiful painting of the Renaissance. That may or may not be something you agree with, but even the idea of it being the most beautiful ignores the dozens (if not hundreds) of other beautiful paintings of that era by the likes of Michelangelo, Raphael, and even da Vinci himself, as if we could universally agree on one way to rank them.

Similarly, some view painting as the most beautiful expression in art. Taking it one step further, this can imply painting or even art itself to be the most beautiful output of creativity. But we know there to be countless beautiful outputs: a sculpture, a mathematical proof, even an act of kindness. And so, though we don't often reflect on it, intellectually we understand there's no common standard of beauty by which these outputs can be meaningfully compared to one another.

As with language, when we pause more deliberately and think about it, we know its individual "expressions" aren't beauty. Still, in our everyday lives, we often operate as if they are. When we do, we miss beauty's importance and power.

To open up our view, let's thoughtfully examine the "evidence": of beauty's central role, for why we miss or ignore the power and importance of that role, and for how we might shift our thinking to regard beauty as an important and versatile tool for speaking the language of man.

A PAUSE TO LOOK AT THE EVIDENCE

IMPORTANCE AND INHIBITION

Sue Kieffer has spent years thinking about the topic of beauty and has a beautiful way of explaining its power and importance, so let's return to her essay and her insights. Her experience, her research, and her gut led her to conclude that *beauty is central to human creativity* and even core to science itself. Here's how she built her logic.

A Fundamental Drive. "Communication of concepts, whether scientific, aesthetic, concrete or abstract, seems to be a fundamental drive of humans," Sue wrote.[310] Translation: We are a species of idea generators. And when we have ideas, we want to share them. More than that, we want to make them real. In doing so, we hope to realize the value promised by those new concepts, not only for ourselves, but for others as well. Instinctively, we understand that in multiple ways we need others in order to create. It was this premise that led Sue to consider two things: 1) If this is our fundamental drive, why we are less successful at conceiving and communicating big ideas than we'd expect to be, and 2) how we could change that.

What Inhibits Us? To the question of what drives but frustrates us, Sue wrote, "I think that the difference in perception, interpretation, and communication of world views is at the root of some of the problems that we currently have in perceiving the relationship among art, science, business and individual lives."[311] In other words, because we all do things so differently, we see, interpret, and therefore communicate in ways defined by our narrower, individualized perceptions (such as seeing language as only French or Japanese).

Most of us are aware of this problem. But we have a tendency to respond to it in this odd way: We turn up the volume on whatever "language" it is that we happen to perceive and communicate through. That is, if others don't understand what we're saying, we often choose to make the same point louder. Rather than back up from the narrowness to see the links across us, our work, and our ideas, our tendency is to dig in. But what if that doesn't work (which we all know it doesn't)?

That led Sue to her second question: *How can we change that?* Her answer was to seek a bridge, the use of which she sensed might be inconsistent or infrequent, but which could be increased, if only we were aware that bridge existed.

Beauty, Sue concluded, functions as that bridge—a common causeway that links ideas and people.

A Common Causeway to Our Progress. "Beauty as a concept, goal, and value is what links us, even with the differences that arise in application and perception," Sue concluded. "It's what allows us to understand one another, even when we're trying to communicate a previously unheard of idea."[312] This is what Sue arrived at through her observations. But over the years she discovered that others, even in her discipline of science, concluded the same thing. The most notable among them was Hideki Yukawa, the Nobel Prize-winning physicist.

In his book *Creativity and Intuition*, Yukawa made clear that bringing forth our fullest potential could not occur by focusing on facts or theory alone. As you know from Chapter Seven, it's an insight he was concerned that his peers in physics were increasingly dismissing and a driving reason for writing his book.[313] In *Creativity and Intuition*, Yukawa encouraged what he called an "open world view,"[314] one that would take us beyond the differences of East and West, physics and geology, or one spoken language versus another. The level of awareness that Yukawa believed such a view offered was precisely what would return us to what he believed had enabled our ancestors to advance: Not a pursuit of the "merely practical" but a striving "to create beauty, in every detail of their everyday lives."[315]

The Fear of "Feeling." Even though beauty's role had become obvious to Sue, something limiting still lurked in the background over those years it took to complete her essay—something we all immediately recognize, even if we haven't yet thought about beauty as much as Sue. Fellow and musicologist Susan McClary put her finger on that tenacious "something:" "We've been taught to feel shame if we think we hear affect, emotion, or meaning, or when we see or feel something beautiful," she said. "You're not supposed to admit that it knocks your socks off or moves your soul. As a professional, you're supposed to ignore all that."[316]

That unwritten "rule" implies that, as a geologist, musicologist, leader, professional, and person, talking openly about beauty is considered a risk. Rebecca Newberger Goldstein would say it might even be considered unprofessional. It's a strange thing to deny the element that made for a breakthrough in the first place for fear of being embarrassed. As Rebecca wrote about this too often prevailing sentiment, "You might think that, rather than being a criterion, the sense of beauty is a phenomenon to be *explained away*."[317]

What Sue, Susan, and Rebecca have found (and it seems clear Yukawa did as well) also appeared in the research for my first book, *A Deliberate Pause*. The book's focus was entrepreneurship, and to write it, I conducted over 200 interviews with a broad range of people. While they offered a variety of insights, a single pervasive one was shared with an odd discomfort. When I asked, "What more than anything else led to your success?" I was often met with silence. If the interview took place in person, the interviewees would often glance over their shoulders, as if to see if anyone else was listening. And then they'd tell me about "spirit"—a deeper sense they felt about what they were doing and what it might bring to others. Yes, they had a *plan* that the world saw, but they had a *vision* and a *feeling* and a *sense of what could be* that ran deeper than a plan—and was far more important.

To them, the feeling was beautiful, but it was also something they felt a danger in revealing. If something is that powerful and important, however, the risk is worth taking.

A POWERFUL UNDERLEVERAGED TOOL

Most of the time, we think of beauty as an output, a result. But consistently, MacArthur Fellows described beauty as a tool—one existing long before the output comes to be, and one taking many forms at many stages in the creative cycle. This is a thought worth reflecting on, and it provides a perspective we don't often get into beauty's importance and power. Here are some examples to shed light on this insight.

Beauty as a Cognitive Tool. "I think of beauty as one of our most important cognitive tools," Rebecca said.[318] Consider that for a moment: *beauty as a cognitive tool*. It's not a fluffy passing reaction to something or a descriptor of a "thing" we produce at the end of our work. Rather, as a cognitive tool, beauty is a powerful filter, a way of shaping thought.

As an example of what you might use this tool for, imagine connecting it to the creative element of inquiry. You might ask questions such as these: *Who is beauty? When is beauty? Where is the most unlikely place to find it?* Consider the shift in thought your answers to these questions would generate. Each prompts a whole new line of thinking.

You can imagine the effect would be even more profound were you to ask such questions, and indeed take the whole discussion of beauty outside the places we typically expect to consider it. As Rebecca noted, "It would be good if we taught beauty as a way to think in science and math and elsewhere, and not just where we tend to sanction it."

Beauty as the Goal. But there's more to it, and again Rebecca had some ideas. "What if we taught beauty as a critical *goal*, as a high *priority* . . . just think what might emerge." It's a nuanced thought that's important to consider.

Most often, beauty is regarded as the afterthought characterization of something, as in, "That was a beautifully written novel." Seen this way, beauty is just one of many adjectives we choose to describe something after the fact. That same novel, in other words, can be interesting, smart, challenging to read, and more. But what if beauty were considered first *before* the creating began and, as Rebecca suggested, sought as a critical goal? "We don't often recognize it," Rebecca said, "but as humans, we're in the business of beauty. For me, everything I see and do in my work is *beautiful* and interesting. But to make a goal of actually pulling out the beauty as part of the measure of the value of the outcome, it puts everything in a different view and place."[319]

As we spoke further about it, Rebecca suggested that rather than simply serving as an inspiration, *setting beauty as a goal* acknowledged that it's also a motivation for our creating. But she also suggested that, as a tool, it went one step further still: By considering it as a measure of value, beauty was a reward in and of itself.

Beauty as a Spark to the Creativity of Others. One of the most interesting references to beauty as a tool came from Fellow and founder of the Southern Mutual Help Association (SMHA) Lorna Bourg. What SMHA undertakes some regard as a daunting if not undesirable task: The organization develops communities. It sounds innocuous until you learn that the communities it works with are dying ones. "Beauty," Lorna said, "plays a key role in the ability of these communities to believe they can have goals to develop and become great once again, and then to accomplish them."

The economic drivers that once moved these places forward are fading or gone. Those in the younger generations are going as well, often feeling their place of birth has nothing to offer their futures. Even traditions and old ways are disappearing, all often leaving the residents of these communities with little hope to create a new spark of life and a path for moving forward.

Over the years of decline, people have come to such communities with ideas for improvement or change—outsiders, that is. As good or creative as they may be, the ideas they bring are *external*. And as anyone knows, if the idea isn't seen as one's own, it's tough to get behind it to make it real.

What Lorna realized was that only by fueling the creativity of the community residents themselves could change-inducing ideas be brought to bear. If that could happen, the residents, not some outsider, might change the downward direction and spark renewal—of hope, jobs, lives, sources of value, even themselves. For that to be a possibility, Lorna said, "Something must be put forth that can inspire people to undertake tasks so big they feel as if they're standing at the edge of a daunting cliff. That something must be important enough and felt deeply enough that it will also keep the tide rolling once it has begun."[320] But that "something" has to come from "within."

Here's the true challenge. Lorna knows what that "something" is . . . but she herself can't give it to the communities that need it. What is it that can help? Beauty. And so each time she begins to learn about a community and to earn the trust of its residents, she always asks, "What's beautiful about this place?" Something so simple often turns out to be the life-giving spark.

"Talk of beauty," Lorna said, "leads to talk of what matters to a community. People begin not to talk about their differences but about what they share. It doesn't take long for the conversation to be one of 'otherness,' a recognition that all of it—the beauty, the community, all the things they want again—they cannot achieve without one another."

What Lorna described is the rebirth of *purpose and trust*, those vital elements to a shared creative framework and process. She was also referring us to that "alchemy of community" Paul Rogat Loeb spoke of last chapter, that environment in which "shared imagination leads outward to other people and new possibilities."[321]

And it's inquiry about beauty that catalyzes it all. "When we talk of otherness and beauty," Lorna said, "we are really talking about imagining. Soon we begin to do just that—we imagine. Together. We ask questions. Then we talk about how we'd get there. Steps mount to bigger moves, and things emerge and expand. What starts as simple ideas are soon internalized and become missions. These beautiful concepts become inevitable—first within individuals, then within communities. It's a growing process. It's a creative process. It's a collective process. And always, it's a thing of beauty," Lorna told me, "because that's exactly what it helps them to see again: beauty."[322]

Something Worthy of a Pause. Freelance photojournalist Lynsey Addario was another who saw beauty's added power and importance as a tool. "Beauty," Lynsey said about her own use of this multifaceted tool, "is about making people pause. It's not to get them to say, 'Wow, that's beautiful.' It's to really *pause*—to come to a fully conscious stop in their thinking and the meaning of what they do. And to ask questions."[323] Through her description, you might begin to see that while beauty is its own important element of the language of man, it is furthermore embedded in other elements— pausing, inquiry, openness, and more. It should make you wonder: Could beauty actually be a way of increasing the potency and effectiveness of those other elements?

These thoughts of beauty as a tool are intended to get you thinking about it in new ways. Whether or not you agree with them or adopt beauty as a tool in these specific ways is beside the point. What stood out for me was the pattern across MacArthur Fellows of giving beauty more than a passing glance. They were putting beauty to work and in ways not often associated with it.

15 MILLION WEB VIEWS CAN'T BE WRONG

Counter-Hedgehog. So far we've talked about the insights of beauty as a common causeway and a Swiss army knife-like tool. Each has given us not only a new perspective of beauty but also evidence of its critical role in fueling creativity. And yet you may still have your doubts.

The fifteen years it took Sue to write her essay on beauty and creativity would suggest that even she, as certain as she was about beauty's importance, perceived doubts. While it's true that it influences every aspect of what Sue does, like creativity, beauty doesn't conform or acquiesce to the same kind of study, measure, and procedure that geology or any other science or field yields to. That's why our hedgehog tends to dismiss its importance.

What's interesting, however, is that beauty leads to, influences, or shapes many things our hedgehog finds extremely important. It's worth a little side trip to see how, and best-selling author Dan Pink makes a great guide.

Counter-Headline. Dan is the author of five terrific books, though it's his 2009 book *Drive: The Surprising Truth About What Motivates Us* that grabs our attention here. The pattern across Dan's books clearly shows his fascination with human potential; his approach to exploring it is unique. He isn't looking for a "headline" explanation or a formulaic answer for how we can rise to our possibilities. Instead, he wants to get at something we can fully relate to but maybe haven't taken time to pause and see. Yet it's something that, when pointed out, resonates with any of us.[324]

Dan knows people tend to focus on headlines, so in his 2009 TED Talk about *Drive*, he began with this headline: "If you want people to perform better you reward them, right? Bonuses, commissions, their own reality show. You incentivize them," Dan parroted. "That's how business works." (See Author's Notes: Chapter Twelve.) I can assure you that fourteen million people aren't watching his talk on YouTube because it echoes this conclusion. Instead, they listen because he says what we've been told motivates us—and by extension, what makes people most productive—is flat-out untrue. He's also telling us we're harming ourselves by continuing to adhere to the "extrinsic reward = motivation = productivity and creativity" refrain.

Dan looked through mountains of research on motivation, creativity, and even economics to understand why we're driven to create and what actually results in productivity. He found that, in the typical setup to motivate people in their work, "You've got an incentive designed to sharpen thinking and accelerate creativity, and it does just the opposite. It dulls thinking and blocks creativity." Dan made clear that such findings are "not an aberration. This has been replicated over and over again for nearly forty years." He called it "one of the most robust findings in social science, and also one of the most ignored."[325]

Okay, so where does that leave us? If what we think motivates us doesn't, what does? And how does it relate to beauty?

What We Really Want. "Rewards, by their very nature, narrow our focus and restrict our possibility," Dan said in his TED Talk. We don't like that. We naturally desire the freedom to look around, and when we are restricted in our environment, in our thoughts, or in what we are asked to produce, we turn off our creative brains.

According to Dan, what we want are undertakings characterized by three elements: *autonomy, mastery,* and *purpose.* In his talk, he described them as follows: "Autonomy: the urge to direct our own lives. Mastery: the desire to get better and better at something that matters. Purpose: the yearning to do what we do in the service of something larger than ourselves." (Note the incredible overlap with observations about beauty made by our guides and what matters to us.)

The Beauty of Getting What We Really Want. Evidence shows that when given tasks with these three elements, people not only become more creative but their creativity is driven by a desire to create something that matters, something shared, something larger than themselves, and something beautiful. That last finding is where my research and the experience of the MacArthur Fellows intersect with Dan's. As he emphasized in his earlier book *A Whole New Mind,* creating something meaningful and beautiful is what we hope that autonomy, mastery, and purpose will enable us to do.[326]

Seeing how deeply beauty goes in helping us create what we want enlightens lesser views of beauty that would tell us, "It's nothing more than a 'nice to have.'" But in a way, the news isn't so new, for as Dan said, "The science confirms what we know in our hearts."[327]

TWO EXAMPLES OF BEAUTY IN PLAY

We've talked about beauty's role and importance in creativity. We've shifted how we think about the language around it, and each part of the discussion has helped us reframe how we see it. But nothing substitutes for seeing something in practice (except, of course, our own practice). So let's look at two different examples of beauty in play—one from mathematician and Fellow Maria Chudnovsky, the other from Fellow and epidemiologist Lisa Cooper. Like all the examples provided by Fellows, these aren't blueprints. Rather, they're points of reference and pieces of the creative fabric from which we can quilt our own meaning.

THE CALCULUS OF BEAUTY

When the topic of beauty surfaces, the specific comments signal that a clear shift is taking place in discussions about creativity. It's as though the real heart of the subject had been eagerly lingering below the surface ready to burst forth. My conversation with Maria Chudnovsky was one poignant example of this.

A Balancing Force. To many, math appears rote and formulaic. Yet the way we are typically taught math differs from seeing mathematics in action, especially when it's being tested and expanded into new territory.

You might be surprised to know that Maria, an outstanding mathematician, sees the "beauty" aspect of math playing as important a role as the techniques and rules we memorized in school. "Beauty in math," Maria explained passionately, "is to distill an idea, to describe it in a way that's clear, and to show how it pushes through to the proof, to the importance, to the value others gain when they use it. Coming up with an idea like that requires being creative. Eventually, of course, you dress it up with detail and partner it with technique and technicality. But in my experience, that part is *supportive*. It's beauty and the possibility of rendering it that start it all, that propel us. And to arrive at beauty, at least in math, you must be capable of creativity."[328]

Notice the interchange Maria described—one between the need to create something useful and a sense that such a creation can be beautiful. There's a perceptible back-and-forth dance, each "partner" feeding off the other.

Sue Kieffer pointed to this as well. In fact, she believes beauty *precedes* creativity, which in turn precedes any form of creative output or value creation. But when that creative output comes and is regarded as beautiful, that ubiquitous "circle" in creativity makes the order less important than the interplay—a concept both Sue and Maria wholeheartedly confirmed.

The Beauty-Creativity "Equation." It's interesting to hear how Sue described beauty's role while considering how it actually comes into play in Maria's world of numbers and equations. To make the concept of beauty tangible, Sue called it "the *proper conformity of the parts* to one another and the whole."[329] In a similar way, she defined creativity as "the ability to *formulate* something that feels beautiful." To Sue, that feeling "implies elements of *simplification* and *unification*."[330] That almost sounds mathematical, doesn't it?

But the more you talk to people like Sue and Maria and hear how creativity unfolds in their everyday lives, the more you perceive it less as "math" and more as "calculus"—that is, a particular way of thinking and reasoning that leads to something beautiful.

By Sue's calculation, *beauty needs creativity* to make it real. But according to Maria, the reverse equation is equally true: *Creativity needs beauty*. It's a beautiful equation.

Beauty and the Arrow of Time. For the "equation" to work and for us to understand it, think about what Maria pointed out when she said, "Beauty is everywhere and plays multiple roles." Putting on her "math hat" for a moment, it's like saying "x" must be in every equation, but the value of "x" can change. She described beauty's multi-faceted role as sometimes inspiration, often motivation, and in the most fulfilling instances, it's remuneration. I love that description.

When thinking about beauty, our tendency (no matter how clear we are about it or its role) is to think of it in narrow terms. When we do, we can't help but "cap" its power. But one of the most important lessons Maria's example offers is a reminder that its impact and relevance go beyond the circumstances in which something beautiful is created.

In Maria's world, the ultimate realization of it is to produce the imagined proof *and* have that proof appear beautiful while also being *useful* to others. She imagines an ongoing cycle across history (and across mathematicians) in which what others have created doesn't only reward the creator, it also inspires and drives new generations to create. This humble statement reflects her thoughts: "My work stands on the shoulders of many before me. If I think of it in the context of legacy," Maria continued, "then what I seek in my work—what I hope to accomplish or create—is something simple, elegant, and beautiful enough to serve others in ways that those before me have aided and inspired me. In that sense, it's both my motivation and my reward."[331]

THE HUMANNESS IN BEAUTY

Something More Beautiful Still. Can you sense the change in tone when any one of the Fellows talks about beauty? Each time I took notice of that tone, I detected a hint of excitement, with a measured degree of caution, mixed with a wisdom and knowingness that not everyone appreciates beauty's magnitude. But there was something more.

As the Fellows spoke deeply and consistently about it being central to their ability to tap into their creative capacity, each one referred to something that went far beyond the obvious—beyond their profession, their personal sense of beauty, and the inherent reward in it for any one of them. Representative of this, after using the word "beauty" several times to explain creativity, epidemiologist Lisa Cooper took the thread and began to quilt something greater than her job, than creativity, than even herself.

"I don't believe ideas belong to any one person," Lisa said. "What makes an idea beautiful is sharing it. That happens to be the same thing needed to realize it as something more than an idea. What I've found is that what drives me is what ultimately drives creativity too—a *connection*, between the idea of something beautiful and people working together to realize it. People who create eventually realize that what they each see in any idea worth pursuing is something closer to the 'spiritual.' That reminds them we are part of a collective conscience, and that's where the beauty emanates from."[332]

You might recall Lisa from Chapter Seven. The context of her story there helps us understand her strong and bold comments. At Johns Hopkins where she works, Lisa has led the effort to change the way certain patient populations learn about their health options and receive care. Where once a "common causeway" between the patient population and the medical establishment didn't exist, it now does. Certainly sharing facts and information in both directions has helped a lot. But that part, like Maria's "techniques" in math, was ultimately supportive.

Lisa said something else played a far greater role. Can you take a one-word guess what it is?

"Once people could see each patient, regardless of the population they came from," Lisa described, "it was hard to consider any approach that didn't give equal care to everyone. But more than that, in the process of learning and creating a better solution together, we began to see people, not patients, to recognize them as *beautiful* and with needs and wants no different from our own."[333]

Much like Sarah Kagan's description in Chapter Eleven, once people see each other that way—not as say, "poor patients" versus "well-off patients" or "good doctors" versus "poor ones"—the entire equation of why these people interact shifts. The purpose is renewed and shared. Beautiful.

"A Beautiful Thing." As you reflect on the meaning of beauty and its force in creativity, remind yourself that it isn't about finding one beautiful thing, arriving at one definition, or settling on one form of expression. The draw, drive, and derivation of beauty are highly individual; the journey will always be unique and so will the expression.

Keep this in mind as well: While beauty's meaning is highly individual, we are driven to shape its meaning in ways that connect to others. We *want* to share it, and we hope it moves others as it does us.

When beauty is present, it serves as proof of what it can mean to be human. It's the reassurance of a pulse as we sort through what our intellect tells us. It is the soulful hub from which the spokes of creativity and progress and what it means to be human reach out and connect. But if you can believe it, to those who consciously pursue beauty, there's more still to its meaning.

"We all contribute to a more evolved and higher calling," Lisa told me about creativity. "What each of us does or sees in the moment might not be similar," she said, "but just the *possibility* we might make a new contribution advances us." It's where the difference lies between just "being" or simply "doing" and *creating*. It's where the opportunity for impact awaits. It's about the idea made more than real. It's about the impact being lasting.

"To me, that's a beautiful thing," Lisa said, "To me, it's *the* thing."[334]

A BEAUTIFUL LANGUAGE

Lynsey Addario said that, for her, beauty was a deliberate pause— not a pause to say, "Wow, that's beautiful" but a chance to actually *pause*, "to come to a full and conscious stop and ask questions" to reconsider meaning.[335]

When we're in the habit of taking deliberate pauses, we come face to face with the truth about what actually drives us and ultimately makes us creative. That knowing in our hearts (proven by science) conveys to us *what we do* and *why we do it*. When what we do revolves around something meaningful, something beautiful, and most of all, something shared, it creates the highest odds of actually realizing something tangible and valuable.

To be shared implies there must be a bridge. Beauty is a bridge— our common causeway, as Sue Kieffer called it—in all we seek to communicate or create. It's our reward too. It's a unifier between the polarities of pure method and pure emotion. It isn't stuck at one end of the spectrum any more than it's absent from the other. In all those ways and more, I submit to you that beauty may just be the most important element in the language of man.

Why is it important to declare it so? It isn't. More important is to be in tune with the elements of the language of man at any moment, to know which ones you lead with and why. In some rare elemental way, beauty helps us tune in. As John Harbison said to me, "With all the possibilities and plausible avenues to go down, it seems that the need to figure out what elements matter most has to be done first before anything else can follow. And people must decide that for themselves before they can ever tune in with their audiences."[336]

The reason I suggest that beauty is important enough that it should always be among the cards we're holding in our creative hands, is that we are constantly learning about the meaning and possibility of the elements of this language. And we ought to be in the perpetual practice of seeing how all of those "parts" can be strung together, reordered, and remade to forever create new meaning. Inevitably, we will shape and reshape how we use this language until it allows us to communicate what we need to express—ideas, love, desire, passion, to name a few. And then we'll use it all over again to reshape what we desire once more.

We repeat the creative journey because we believe, deep in our hearts, there are more ways to bring forth the beauty we unwaveringly know lies "out there." Whether it takes fifteen minutes or fifteen years, valuing a thing of beauty inevitably begets the chance to conceive something beautiful and new all over again. It's in such moments—those pauses in which the whole process of the search for beauty begins anew—that we see *who we are* and *what we still can be.* Beauty fuels us *and* the language of man.

The value in that lesson is incalculable. How we tap into that value is where we're headed next.

A

RENEWED SENSE

OF VALUE

CHAPTER THIRTEEN

CHAPTER THIRTEEN

A RENEWED SENSE OF VALUE

Each time I've introduced an element of the language of man, I've asked you to consider the meaning, use, and value you might have brought with you to the words that describe that element. Beyond being an intellectual exercise, you've learned that every time you use one of those elements, you *must* reconsider meaning, use, and value all over again if your creative actions are to have impact. More than a suggestion, this perpetual "return" is a prerequisite of creativity.

In this final section of *The Language of Man*, Return is our focus. And while return figures prominently in the use of all the elements of this language, the two elements that benefit most from perpetual return just may be *value* and *learning*.

Here in Chapter Thirteen, we focus on value; learning is our focus in Chapter Fourteen.

RETURNING OUR SENSE OF VALUE

Our fascination with creativity is closely tied to our desire to use it to produce something of value. This, however, presents a problem, one we rarely stop and think about: *What is value?* Without an answer to that question, it's hard to get very far in attempting to create it. An important way to return value from your creative endeavors is to reconsider how you look at value itself.

Making Room Anew for Your Value-Seeking Fox. To renew your sense of value, begin by recognizing that *VALUE* isn't its *measures*;

it's something far greater. A simple point of reference is *money*—a familiar measure of value. But money is only that: one form and one single measure within a far larger concept called value. There are in fact countless measures and forms of value—a product, a service, a social or environmental good realized, knowledge gained, kindness given, souls moved . . . the list is endless once you pause to think about value's true meaning.

It's a simple distinction, yet overlooking it is precisely what most often keeps us from recognizing new value and new opportunities to create it. This doesn't suggest we don't need tangible forms of value or that there isn't benefit in measuring it. But value rises above and encapsulates these forms and measures. And to truly understand and render it, we need to see value as much through the eyes of our fox as those of our hedgehog.

A Story of Value. The ideal way to see the nuanced meaning of value is to watch its form and function in practice and over time. Value is, after all, a living, breathing, moving thing because it's a product of the creatures who define and create it and also exhibit the same characteristics: human beings. Nothing reveals this point like a story, so we'll let the story be our guide as we return to and rediscover value's meaning.

With a nod to Walt Whitman's "powerful play," this story unfolds in five short "acts," complete with a prelude, back story, and intermission. Storytelling in this way allows us to move back and forth across time and across forms and meanings of value to see how it takes shape, why, and how easily we forget that this constant change is value's norm.

The goal is to help you expand your view of value and keep it open. Doing so is the surest way to increase your ability to "contribute *your own* valuable verse."

VALUE: A STORY IN FIVE ACTS

In the coming page, we're going look at the elastic nature of value in the United States over the course of roughly seven decades in the twentieth century. Though the tale begins before and continues after his time, at its heart lies U.S. President John F. Kennedy and his effort to reawaken the fox in American minds.

As this narrative unfolds, *another* will gradually reveal itself—how the meaning of value changes with time, and how, when we fail to recognize that it does, we can easily swing to extreme hedgehog or extreme fox and risk losing value. First, a prelude and bit of back story.

PRELUDE: A QUEST TO REVIVE THE FOX

When we talk about what we value, it's not unusual to speak in terms of 'things'—a smart phone, a vaccine, a new market for goods, or advanced weaponry. But those things aren't the value. The value comes in what those things represent, and what they represent are advancements—in technology, science, economic prosperity, or military might. While often far reaching, even those advancements have limitations. As far as they take us, each is temporal. Inevitably, something else will come along and advance us once more.

What is it then that we truly value that those things and advancements reflect? The answer is progress. It is, quite literally, built into who we are to value and seek it. Taken over the whole of our existence, "human progress" is what *moves* us in every sense of the word. Creativity is vital, not only to our individual and categorical advances but to our progress.

There is no doubt in my mind that John F. Kennedy sensed all this, and deeply. By the early 1960s, it's clear he also believed that Americans had forgotten these distinctions of value. So, over the course of a year spanning 1962 and 1963, Kennedy set out to remind us of what we valued most—as Americans and as human beings.

But something greater still was defining his mission. Kennedy wanted to help revive the *source* from which all advancement and all value springs: our creativity.

Beginning with a speech at Rice University in September of 1962 and ending with one at Amherst College in October of 1963, Kennedy gradually opened our eyes and set a new course for Americans. Before getting to the specifics of how he went about reviving our fox, it helps to know the back story and why he felt this deliberate return to value and creativity was necessary.

BACK STORY: WHY ALL THE FUSS?

To understand why Kennedy undertook this journey, it's important to know about the era in which he was living.

A Time of Audacious Ideas. When Kennedy's "year of the fox" speeches began in 1962, World War II's end was less than two decades old (it ended in September of 1945). That global conflict had reordered people's ideas of what was possible in both terrible and inspiring ways. There was of course the previously unimaginable idea that what began as a regional conflict could spread like wildfire to touch every continent of the world except Antarctica.

But of equal dissonance was the mind-boggling idea that the end of that conflict could come largely as a result of a single weapon (the nuclear bomb) and a single act (wiping out an entire city as happened with both Hiroshima and Nagasaki). The unimaginable wasn't only negative, however. Soon after the war came the audacious idea that the people of many nations could work together as one to heal the world and avoid future conflicts (the United Nations). The scale and speed with which these ideas came forth, both the inspiring and the terrible, were jarring to say the least, and sometimes difficult to accept as the "new order" of things.

The Idea of Certainty. When societies experience complex disruption, imagination plays on both sides of the coin, and fear runs neck and neck with hope. In such times, someone often steps into the dissonance with thoughts of how to settle the disruption in exacting ways. Feeling uneasy with the post-war ambiguity, U.S. Senator Joseph McCarthy offered his solution in the early 1950s. It was a very hedgehog-esque idea: To reorder the country into pure black and white with clear rules about right and wrong, valuable and not, American and un-American, with no allowance for ambiguity.

As much as McCarthy's dictates were clearly a grab for individual power, they fed off of a communal desire for certitude. With so many "unknowns" in the preceding decades, how tempting the thought of removing uncertainty must have sounded. As crazy and divisive as some of McCarthy's statements probably seemed, during much of the 1950s the implied orderliness of a black-and-white society proved attractive. (The Cold War between the United States and Russia played off a similar and reinforcing dynamic.)

The general effect was a shift to favor things that felt predictable, clear-cut, and within human control. Science, industry, and the military were among the sanctioned priorities, not expressly because of McCarthy but because they "appeared" to produce orderly tangibles that appealed to a country weary of uncertainty. The desire for predictability and rightness soon came to define the priorities and reflect the values of this era. And as they did, they inevitably defined value itself.

Value Defined One Way. No one ever accused Joseph McCarthy of being a genius. But he was astute enough to sense at least two things: The first was the attractiveness of certainty and order to our hedgehog brain. The second was some sense of the "conflict" that goes on between our fox and hedgehog, heightened by the opportunity to pit one against the other in some sort of competition (not dissimilar from two sides in a war).

So against the "clear" value perceived in the sciences, business, and the military, McCarthy pitted the arts and artists. He cast this creative lot as the enemy, played on human fears, and defined these people and their ways as more corruptive than creative. The artists and the arts were portrayed as being experimental and unpredictable rather than precise and productive. Bad versus good was implied. In short, to McCarthy and others caught up in this "ally versus enemy" storyline, "things creative" had no value; "things predictable" did.

The Extremes of Imbalance. It went beyond a simple difference of views about what was valuable. In this sad chapter of American history, McCarthy publically accused people of subversion or even treason if they held beliefs or took actions outside his norm. While others weren't immune, those in the arts were most overtly associated with creative thoughts and acts and the kind of "newness" that challenged the status quo. Consequently, artists took the brunt. McCarthy became famous for his black lists, an arbitrary roll call of screenwriters, actors, musicians, painters, entertainers, and other creative thinkers. Their outside-the-mainstream ideas were offered as proof of their intent to subvert the United States and undermine what it valued.

McCarthy's blacklists hung over Americans as an unyielding warning: *Step outside the borders of what's deemed in keeping with American values, and you too will be labeled shunned.* Fear dominated and careers and lives were badly damaged or destroyed. For much of the late 1940s and 1950s, America balled up and burrowed in, hedgehog-like, to defend the status quo and the known.

ACT I: A FEELING OF MISFIT

As many others eventually did, it's clear that Kennedy saw in McCarthyism a deep danger. Like others, he saw it explicitly in the blacklisting and public ridicule of some of our nation's greatest contributors. But Kennedy saw something bigger and more threatening yet.

The Fox Brain at Work. With the benefit of the Internet, it's now easy to dig into people's thinking in ways that, in the 1960s, we never could have. Today, we can access Kennedy's speech transcripts, his drafts, and his private notes. Looking at them, we see more fully his thoughts and how strongly he felt about the imbalance he sensed America had drifted toward from World War I to his time.

In the drafts for his Amherst College speech, for example, he initially wrote, "We take great comfort in our nuclear stockpile, our gross national product, our scientific and technological achievements, and our industrial might." His early notes make clear that to Kennedy, such "comfort" signaled an imbalance. It's telling of his larger mindset to learn that, in the final version of his speech, he struck the remark.[337] He similarly cut a reference to individual profiles considered heroic at that time—"statesmen, generals, magnates, inventors, men of notable courage in war, men of notable enterprise in peace"—along with the telling line, "A society betrays its innermost secrets by its choice of heroes."[338]

Without a doubt, Kennedy sensed Americans were out of balance, but notably it seems he also sensed that attacking our black-and-white-loving hedgehogs wasn't helpful. Indeed, it missed the point. Kennedy wanted to reawaken our foxes. Even though he ultimately chose to keep his more detailed thoughts to himself, his feeling that something was amiss still came through, and so too did his recognition of the importance of balance.

While he didn't use the words fox and hedgehog, his speeches of 1962 and 1963 clearly show he felt Americans had lost their creative way. Regaining it was his higher goal. But Kennedy appears to have realized that achieving that higher goal would require a gradual progression. To facilitate that, he first needed to reaffirm with the American people their sense of value and specifically the value of advancement. And that, Kennedy decided, had to happen in an inspiring, even dramatic way.

The broader push to revive the fox could only come after that inspiring affirmation of what we valued most.

INTERMISSION: A VALUE CONSIDERATION

Before continuing with our story, I want to take a brief intermission to absorb what we've already learned and to take note of a few important insights about value.

As we frame value in the context of creativity, we must embrace it as a "blended reality" and, equally, a moving target. Many variables influence value, each a product of time and circumstances. In other words, such variables change all the time. Conceptually we know this, but there are two variables we tend to treat as being relatively more stable and less changeable: individuals and societies. Our attitudes toward both have a significant impact on our ability to see value as something always in motion. They can also curb our creativity and our advancement. Let's consider each briefly.

Individual Value Shifts. At any point, we tend to think about a "value creator" not only as revolutionary for one time but as someone for whom that ability stretches to all times. A good near-term example would be Steve Jobs—specifically the Steve Jobs who, along with his Apple team, invented the first Macintosh computer in 1984.

More than a few people concluded in 1984 that what Jobs created would remain the future of computing. The "desktop" computer, many believed, would retain its crown as the preeminent personal device. It was also widely believed that devices as powerful as the Macintosh would likely only ever be accessible to a certain strata of the population (due to its price tag of close to $2,500).[339] And behind all of this advancement, Jobs was hailed as a new messiah, a genius-hero.

Well, things change, don't they? In 2015, it's estimated that nearly two-thirds of Americans (not a smaller, economically advantaged minority), own a smartphone[340] a device far more powerful than the first Mac desktop and one available for 1/27th of the price of the original Macintosh. Clearly the creative output could change in importance, value, and form, but so too could the creator. Jobs' "genius" was not guaranteed by the Macintosh. After 1984, Steve Jobs had as many failures as he did successes (recall that he was kicked out of Apple, the company he co-founded, or think about the failure of Jobs' NEXT Computer). Today, he's regarded in hindsight as an innovator, a showman and, to some, a bully.

The point is this: How we filter ideas, perceive the people who generate them, and rank the importance of the outputs that can come from both are constantly shifting as our sense of value shifts. It was as true of the times and ideas of McCarthy and Kennedy as it was of Jobs.

Value in Societies Changes Too. While the preceding example focused on an individual, we often regard companies and societies in similarly static ways as they pertain to value. One case in point is the way many talk about the United States as a creative and innovative nation, as though that's a birthright or a permanent reality rather than something to be renewed continuously.

This is not to say that the U.S. won't continue to be creative in the future. But the conclusion isn't foregone, and acting as though it is risks missing the indicators that would tell us when the variables, forms, or sources of value behind that creative reputation are shifting. At whatever level, individual or otherwise, value *moves*. And that movement can result in negative effects *if* the current measures or assumptions around value don't move as well. When they fail to, we find ourselves judging apples by the standard of oranges, sometimes without even recognizing we are doing so.

Equally true and related, value is a mixture of how we assign worth in any one moment and to any one thing. So when that mixture shifts, that too can make something that was valuable in the past more or less valuable going forward. If we're not constantly tuned into and reassessing value, we can easily miss its natural tendency to move. When we do, we risk missing the creative "opportunities" and "threats" as well.

Let's return to the story to see how true this is.

ACT II: REAFFIRMING OUR SENSE OF VALUE

Adhering to Our History. On September 12th of 1962, President Kennedy stood before a crowd of 35,000 at Rice University in Texas and challenged his fellow citizens in a stunning yet savvy fashion.

He began by setting forth a premise, the thrust being this: Yes, America and its citizens were great in many respects, but that only served as a warning not to become complacent. It was time to advance once more.

It wasn't a suggestion Kennedy was making; he called it "our duty," not only as Americans but as humans. "Fifty thousand years of man's recorded history," Kennedy said, proved both *continuous* advancement and rising to ever higher challenges to be our nature and our need.[341] He gave a fast-forward version of that history of continuous advancement reaffirming what we valued; all the while he deftly appealed to our desire for greatness and played to our sense of the possible.

And then he set the hook as he assigned us this task: *America must become the first nation to put a man on the moon.*

It's safe to say Kennedy turned heads with that statement but for widely different reasons. To some, his challenge immediately inspired. Others called him flat-out crazy. After all, it had been barely a half a century since man had taken to the skies in any form. And flying itself was an achievement made only after centuries of wonder, question, and outright disbelief that people taking flight was even possible. Yet there stood Kennedy confidently saying the U.S. must go to the moon—and do so in less than a decade.

Appealing to Our Purpose. The most important thing Kennedy was telling his country was not the "what" idea of going to the moon. As audacious as the proposal was, that was but a single form of advancement. More important was the "why." Kennedy wanted his audience to feel the distinction and embrace the idea of continuous advancement.

"[The] conquest [of such a goal] deserves the best of all mankind, and its opportunity for peaceful cooperation may never come again," Kennedy began. "But why, some say, the moon? Why choose this as our goal? And they may well ask, why climb the highest mountain?

Why, thirty-five years ago, did [Charles] Lindbergh fly [solo across] the Atlantic? Why does Rice [University] play Texas [in football]?[342]

After voicing the questions on everyone's mind, masterfully Kennedy then answered them, and his response was "Whitman-like" and powerful: "We *choose* to go to the moon. We choose to go to the moon in this decade and to do the other things, not because they are easy, but because they are hard, because that goal will serve to organize and measure the best of our energies and skills, because that challenge is one that we are willing to accept, one we are unwilling to postpone, and one which we intend to win, and the others, too."[343]

You can almost hear Walt Whitman chanting in response, "And the powerful play goes on, so that you may contribute a verse." With his immodest proposal, Kennedy had returned us to consider value in total. He'd shown us what it really meant to us, not just in one time but over the whole of our history; not just in single advances but in continuous advancement. Most of all, he'd established purpose, not simply for this particular challenge but a purpose in all things. Though he had made it specific to Americans, Kennedy planted the flag of purpose deep in the soil of what it means to be human, a terra firma on which to create once again.

ACT III: RECONSIDERING VALUE

Coming to the Edge. The Rice University address certainly put forth a specific idea (to land on the moon), but in truth, Kennedy had called us to the greater actions of reconsidering *what we valued* and *why*.

Still, he knew there was more. Kennedy realized that beyond "what" and "why" we had to remember "how": how to conceive and deliver what we valued. Rice was the warm-up. A year after his Rice University speech, Kennedy gave another at Amherst College meant to awaken our fox.

In his brief remarks—part of a larger ceremony dedicating a library in the name of poet Robert Frost—Kennedy covered broad terrain. As he did, his words purposely struck contrasts. He spoke, for example, of America as a strong nation and indeed "the leader of the Free World." Yet he made note of the problems the country faced at home and abroad, ones he characterized as "staggering."[344]

He talked of the great future he believed we could attain, but also suggested that that future could not be built solely on the country's obvious strengths in scientific advances, military might, and wealth. Gradually raising the stakes, Kennedy said we also needed and should "not be afraid of grace and beauty" as strengths. Deliberately and thoughtfully considered, each contrast marked extremes, purposely chosen, it seems—not to ask us to choose between them but to recognize the danger of embracing only one or the other.

Calling Out the Fox. Most strikingly, Kennedy spoke of the tradition among Americans of raising up heroes as examples to guide us in our choices and in our goals, and within that, the recent and disproportionate tendency to choose "men of large accomplishment." It's certain that everyone knew he meant those "generals, magnates, and men of war" he'd specifically noted in his earlier speech drafts, even though he consciously chose that day to leave them unnamed. But then he moved briskly forward to state that the time had come to honor more people like Frost—"a man," Kennedy said, "whose contribution was not to our size but to our spirit, not to our political beliefs but to our insight, not to our self-esteem, but to our self-comprehension. In honoring Robert Frost," Kennedy affirmed, "we therefore . . . pay honor to the deepest sources of our national strength."[345]

It's worth pausing to recognize that Kennedy was on the eve of his reelection campaign for 1964. In multiple speeches, he continued to emphasize this theme and build his case. Each time he did, his opinion of where recapturing our creativity ranked in his priorities as an American, a world leader, and as a person was unambiguous. Undoubtedly, Kennedy had many themes from which to choose to convince Americans to reelect him. And there's little question that emphasizing this particular one carried risks. But Kennedy undeniably sensed that recapturing our creativity was vital—in his time and in all times.

A Bigger Message About Creativity and Balance. Looking back and connecting the dots of Kennedy's comments over that period, I believe he intended to send these messages: Kennedy was saying value lies not simply in a moment or thing but in our continued advancement. As we advance, therefore, it follows that the things we value and how we value them will naturally shift as well. Our ability to advance requires creativity ongoing and a vibrant habit of engaging our fox.

But I also believe that Kennedy was saying that for any of this to happen requires balance. The tempering of his words between his speech drafts and his actual delivery is one indication. Also noteworthy is his encouragement of continued advancement in education and the sciences (the moon-shot challenge) alongside the arts. We can't imagine or achieve what we value in only one way, as either pure hedgehog or pure fox, Kennedy seemed to have been telling us. Rather, we needed both. We were *out of balance*, he made clear, and needed to regain it.

Though he'd been building the case publically for at least a year, many credit the Amherst speech in particular with providing the momentum to create the National Endowment for the Arts (NEA), a fund designed to direct public dollars to the arts. The NEA helped establish the arts—and with it creativity—as a national priority. But there's no doubt this was also a tipping point for how America as a country defined value.

ACT IV: VALUE CHANGES COURSE—AGAIN

A New Tipping Point. President Kennedy had used these speeches to shift the national palette out of its black-and-white mode toward a colorful balance. Of course, he wasn't the only or the first person to sense the imbalance. At the executive level alone, the shift began with President Eisenhower and continued to build with President Johnson, who took office after Kennedy. John F. Kennedy was simply the most passionately outspoken about it. He provided the crucial tipping point by asking us to pause and deliberately consider value.

The wave of value reassessment crested in 1965 with the government establishing the NEA. Rather than trying to quantify the precise value of the arts with a single measure or form, Kennedy had drawn attention to the greater concepts of advancement and worth that made room for the vast range of human undertakings and achievement. It was a broader view of value, and the United States Congress' choice to create the NEA symbolized its embrace. The rapid and dramatic shift in the meaning of value it led to is both breathtaking and instructive.

New View, New Value. More than a symbol, the NEA represented a major "investment." During the forty-three years in which the NEA thrived, it invested taxpayer dollars in the arts and individual artists in the form of unrestricted grants. From 1965 through 2008, the NEA gave more than 121,000 grants totaling in excess of four billion dollars. The expected "return on investment" was simply that grant recipients would experiment and explore their craft; no tangible or traditional financial return was outlined or anticipated. It was a remarkable statement. Thus, the whole idea of "value" associated with the NEA differed so markedly from the definition of value in previous decades that even more narrow measures of value changed. Support for this new and expanded definition of value was substantial.

In fact, at times, belief in and support for the arts was nothing short of effusive. "In 1968, Representative Robert O. Tiernan of Rhode Island, arguing for the annual reauthorization of the NEA, said, 'In the name of sensible economy, let us preserve not only for ourselves, but for all generations to come, that which is worthiest—the free, creative expression of a free people.'"[346] Even though the return on investment was difficult to pinpoint with a fiscal metric, it became, as Congressman Tiernan put it, considered part of a "sensible economy" and indeed "that which is worthiest." Joseph McCarthy would scarcely have recognized Tiernan's definition of value.

Lessons in Malleability. What's the real lesson of this story of value? It's not that Kennedy returned America to balance for good or that our nation's definition of value assumed a new and permanent form. Rather, it teaches us that the nature of value doesn't lie solely in one time or one thing, nor is it determined by one individual. History has continued to prove this to be true.

Fast-forward several decades when, inevitably, the value judgment of the United States government shifted once again. As vociferously as its proponents argued for the creation of the NEA in the 1960s, its detractors in a different generation argued to dismantle it. In the early 2000s, those anti-champions said the NEA was out of touch with American society's sense of value. They felt the return on its grants didn't justify the investment. The variables had changed once again. And, as with the comparison between McCarthy's time and Kennedy's, if you put the definition of value in the early 1960s side by side with that in the early part of the twenty-first century, you couldn't find more polar opposites.

ACT V: A CAUTIONARY TALE

Our story shows the challenge of value as a concept, an aspiration, or even a tangible end, especially when attempts are made to lock it in. It bears repeating: Value *moves*. And no area of human undertaking is immune to the changing winds of how it's perceived.

It should be obvious that, like value itself, this story has no fixed end. It rolls on unceasingly. But that doesn't keep us from taking note of a few evergreen insights crucial to our ability to create.

The first and most obvious insight is that value is something far larger than any one thing, person, or time. It's a simple insight, though one that seems hard to keep in mind at times. Yet keeping it in mind not only assures our ongoing human progress; it enables us to see new possibilities—no matter what form of value they may ultimately assume.

A second insight is the recognition that when we lock down value in narrow ways or to the extreme, we tend to fall out of balance. When we do, we risk pitting our fox and our hedgehog against one another rather than encouraging them to dance together.

The first two insights afford one last critical one: The relationship between creativity and value is deeply intertwined in every sense. When our view of value is open, so is our ability to see the possible, create, and advance. However, when our view of value becomes static and tightly bound, our creative capacity assumes similar limitations.

ADVANCING THE VALUE OF WHAT YOU ALREADY KNOW

Before we go forward to Chapter Fourteen, journey back with me for a moment to Chapters Five and Six. Among the lessons learned there was the insight that the breakthrough space—that place in which our creative ideas are formed—isn't a permanent place; it's one we continue to shape with time. In other words, it also moves.

You may not have been consciously aware of it, but by learning to define and create that space, you were also learning to define and create value. The news is better still: What you've learned about creativity in total by learning the language of man is precisely the knowledge you need to create value more often and more effectively.

If you want to change your value habit, practice "speaking" the language of man. *Notice* what and how things around you are being valued. *Connect* what you see with what's really happening, and *consider* if what once defined value has changed. Be willing to *flip the accepted view*, as John F. Kennedy did. In doing these things and others, you set yourself on the path toward a previously unimaginable source of value.

Oh and one more thing, . . . In all of this, don't forget the message upon which Kennedy built his case: Creativity, value, and advancement—all of it comes down to choice. As Kennedy said, fifty thousand years of our recorded history (and then some) prove it true.

LEARNING

TO

DISCOVER

CHAPTER FOURTEEN

CHAPTER FOURTEEN

LEARNING TO DISCOVER

One of the most frequently asked questions of creativity is this: *How do I learn to be creative?* The problem with this question lies in the assumptions that often accompany it—that the answer will take the form of an all-inclusive method, and that we can learn to be creative once and for all.

A November 2015 *Washington Post* interview with the revolutionary choreographer Twyla Tharp spoke to the truth about **LEARNING** when it comes to creativity. Tharp, who happens to be a MacArthur Fellow, was being interviewed on the occasion of her golden anniversary in dance—fifty years of border crossing and building a "legacy as a rule-breaker."[347] Over the course of the interview, one Tharp creation after another was referenced, each clearly unique in its own way. So too were the diverse awards she'd garnered as an innovator—two Emmys, a Tony, a Kennedy Center Honor, and of course that "genius" award. A full page and a half of newsprint later, the article left no doubt that Tharp was almost incalculably creative. It also left a visible trail of breadcrumbs to indicate that her form of creativity had been ever-changing.

After surveying Tharp's fifty years of dance and seventy-four of life, the interviewer asked her this final question: *What can you still find that inspires you?* "Oh, lots," Tharp quickly said, and then, as the article made a point to note, she paused. She "let that point hang for a moment," as if to make room for the real lesson and then added, "There's no need to fear that suddenly one has learned it all."[348]

How do you learn to be creative? Two answers: You learn creativity by returning to it repeatedly and by realizing that creativity isn't learning a prescribed methodology; rather, it's learning to discover.

WHAT'S POSSIBLE?

If Twyla Tharp is still learning so vibrantly after fifty years of creating, it makes you wonder: What is the scope of what's possible to learn about creativity? Gary Nabhan provided one of my favorite descriptions of what's possible.

DAUNTING OR DAZZLING POSSIBILITY?

The Enormity of It All. As a field biologist, Gary described the potential of what can be learned this way: "If I could distill what I've learned during a thousand and one nights working as a field biologist, waiting around campfires while mist-netting bats, running lines of traps, or pressing plants, it would be this: Each plant or animal has a story about a unique way of living in this world. By tracking their stories down to the finest detail, our own lives may be informed and enriched."[349]

To paraphrase the animated icon Bart Simpson, what we as humans *don't* know could fill a warehouse. Actually, that's lowballing it. What we *can* know might fill a warehouse, but what's potentially knowable overflows many warehouses a zillion times over. Be it learning creativity, learning to create value, or learning anything in any form, we face a potentially overwhelming opportunity. It can feel like an uncompromising hurdle.

A Movement "Toward" not "Away From." But consider this: Rather than running *away* from the enormity, Gary is actually running *toward* it. Not stopping at seeking to understand "species" or "ecosystems," he has set a goal to discover the stories of *each individual life form;* in other words, *each* member of *each* species. Yikes! And *why?*

Gary is creating a learning environment for himself, one quite literally without end. Similarly, by making his goal to track *all* those stories and "down to the finest detail," as he put it, he's ensuring that his learning will be as diverse, dynamic, and distinctive as possible—not to mention never-ending. (Quite the opposite of what you learned in school, isn't it?)

To be clear, Gary isn't attempting to solve every mystery of the universe or commit every one of its secrets to memory. That truly would make the possible warehouses of knowledge daunting. Instead, he's converting that bottomless storehouse from a potential impediment to his *creative advantage*.

A Learning Ongoing. Gary sees the world of "stories" and possibilities before him as a place to "visit" daily, not unlike an enormous library. It's a place not to conquer but to check out what he might learn next. He's quite certain that every time he goes to this resource center or into a new story, he'll come away with something he hadn't noticed before. The insight he gains each time comes not only from the "finding" of any particular lesson or idea, but from the "habit" of putting his proverbial library card to use. He'll never get to every volume in that library. He'll never be able to declare that he's "fully creative." And neither one is his learning goal. Like Twyla Tharp, Gary's goal is to stay engaged with creativity because he knows from experience it's the best way to "learn how to be creative." As if speaking for both of them, Tharp reflected, "Basically, I do what I do to make discovery [the goal] and to learn and to be surprised by something."[350]

A CEASELESS DANCE OF DISCOVERY

The Lesson is Discovery. If your senses feel overloaded, take a moment to set aside the scale of what there is to learn "out there" and reflect only on the approach that Gary and Twyla Tharp exhibit. Their approach to learning creativity is guided by discovery. Yet it's not discovery bound by the outcome—as in, "I want to discover this particular dance, this species, or this answer." And it's not discovery set on one single form of value either. Their form of learning is discovery as "the act" and "the habit." Their learning goal centers on refining the skill of discovery that can only be born of a state of perpetual practice.

"Anything that one does seriously," said Tharp, or with impact, "requires practice, and practice is habit. Rebellion, like creativity," she said, reflecting the border-shattering form of creation she continues to steep herself in, "doesn't just fly off the walls. It's pretty well studied and thought through."[351]

Far from an outlier's approach to learning creativity, this focus on discovery reveals itself as a norm and a touchstone to which practiced creators return.

Aimed at a Way Not a Thing. "I love discovery," Liz Lerman told me in speaking about the endless "possible" she believes, like Tharp, is still to be tapped.[352] But thoughtfully, Liz helped bring it down to an everyday scale. She spoke in the context of projects and dance pieces. Yet even when talking about a specific piece she's creating, Liz spends the most time talking about her *method* that produces the creative result rather than the result itself.

"Of course I'm producing dance pieces," Liz said bluntly, "that is to say, the 'thing' the audience sees once it's been packaged and put all together. But when talking about how I create—how I do what I do—to suggest that the end piece is what it's all about misses the point.

"My works don't just 'result' from a process of discovery, as though that process were like a journey from point 'A' to point 'B' or as if I somehow always knew the end I was headed toward. That's mythology. The real process and the true purpose of my work," Liz affirmed, "is to facilitate discovery itself. Works inevitably emerge *from* that process; but my true focus is on building a capability and a way of seeing that lets me discover many times over. It's funny how we (humans) always seem to lean toward the 'cart' and forget the 'horse' that drives and carries the load," she said. Then she added, "That's why when I engage in discovery, I work to make my process such that my collaborators and the audience discover too."[353]

Liz hasn't simply learned how to discover; she's learned the importance of teaching others to do the same. Most certainly *they* benefit, but Liz firmly believes *she* benefits as well.

A "Learning Intersection." Like Gary, Liz is concerned not only with the lessons but with building both a mindset and an environment of learning and discovery. And by opening up her method to others, she's allowing the dynamism, diversity, and distinction that's needed to discover something truly new and creative.

"That's what creativity is," Liz said in a way that made clear she didn't want me to miss the real "gold" in her insight. "It's perpetual discovery. And when you only think in terms of outputs or even your own capacity to discover, you end up weighing the value on those things alone and most of the time missing the true potential altogether."[354]

Liz put it all into context this way: "I look at what I do as a process of perpetually connecting. It's a continual testing, a never-ending experimentation. You hold and then you need to be willing let go to discover or to learn something new." And with that added insight, it's clear Liz is building more than a learning environment or mindset; she's creating a "learning intersection" a la Koestler—a perpetual meeting of the "known" and the "new."

When the point is intersection, nothing stays fixed for long. "The testing and the reengaging that comes in this environment don't let you get away with platitudes," Liz said. Too often, we cast learning as a recitation of past lessons and platitudes. We engage in an exercise of naming things and then narrow ourselves to the task of simply learning the names. Learning only in this way is the surest way to unlearn how to create.

"The act of naming things is of course vital," Liz continued, "but not for the reasons we'd assume." By "naming," Liz means identifying the lesson, the insight, or the fact. She's suggesting that the value in doing so doesn't come from treating any lesson as permanent once it's named. She explained the deeper potential by saying, "When you name something, you inevitably find that the name or thing alone is not enough. 'Not enough' is a sure sign of a deterioration of the value in the thing or of value yet to be tapped. For the lesson to stay relevant, you have to be able to imbue value into something ongoing. So when your process is driven by discovery, you go back into the world in which you first 'discovered' and once again push your way into things you hadn't previously known just to see what's revealed. In other words, you discover all over again. It's the learning and discovery process itself that's paramount."[355]

As I've watched my own children (currently an eighth grader and an eleventh grader) learn in school, I see not only a clear emphasis on the traditional "naming" conventions of learning but an increasing bent toward tradition over time. Is that wrong? A better question is: *What's the goal?* If the goal is to create and progress, we will have to discover new ways to think, name, and learn.

A RETURN TO SELF

One clear message Gary and Liz convey in their examples is that a world of possibility always lies before you. True, it may not always be presented as your formal education has trained you to expect it. But, as they suggest, you may learn the most by getting rid of the "packaging"—those expectations of set lessons, clear outcomes known in advance, and steady, linear courses to creating.

And the other message they don't want us to miss? That developing your own diverse, dynamic, and distinct environment for learning is something you *must do for yourself.*

In Chapter Three, Ken Robinson reminded us that humans are built for learning characterized by what I affectionately call the "3 Ds" (diverse, dynamic, distinct). He also made clear this isn't how the outside world is designed to teach us, and thus we must provide our own lead. True, it would be wonderful if the world comprising our schooling, our work, and every other place we learn would shift toward our natural way of thinking and doing.

Maybe someday, but *your time is now.* It's up to you and very much within your power to guide your own learning—about creativity and learning in total. Doing that means being aware of what things most inhibit your ability to learn and concurrently inhibit your creativity—that stuff in your head.

CREATIVE CONSTRAINTS IN OUR INNER ENVIRONMENT

In no small way, the difference between a learning style bent toward creativity and the style we're most often taught comes down to the learning *constraints* we place on *ourselves.* These constraints tend to frame everything else. Granted, adhering to them can provide advantages for getting by, but only for a short time. If we learn to stay attuned to these constraints, then our creative ability skyrockets. Along with it comes a way to see the world as our *advantage* rather than our *limitation.*

Mental Locks. In 1983, Roger von Oech, author of the appropriately titled book *A Whack on the Side of the Head,* identified a list of constraints to creativity.[356] He detected ten behaviors that he linked directly to the ways in which we severely limit our creative capacity. More important, he declared that these barriers were self-imposed. Among them were: believing there's a single right answer; screening out anything that's not logical; treating play as frivolous; emphasizing practicality; staying within one's area; and avoiding ambiguity and error. When put into this context, it seems obvious that these would effectively shut down our creative capacity.

Von Oech called these internal constraints **MENTAL LOCKS**. We gradually *acquire* most of these mental locks from the environments in which we learn—school, work, community, and even our own homes. They are not natural-born limitations to learning creativity. It's not surprising that we come to adopt many of them. In most settings, these constraints set the rules for productively participating in society and achieving the rewards offered by the "tribe." But allowing them to become our primary mode or our limitation is another matter.

Whether or not mental locks shape how you think and learn is a choice. *Your* choice. In truth, the choice of how you go about learning and thinking is a cumulative one. Many smaller choices—to screen out the logical or see play as frivolous, for example—add up over time. The constraints that bind you are built one link at a time. But taken together, von Oech said, these choices to "lock in" to a constrained way of thinking often grow into the biggest lock of all—a conclusion that *we are not creative.*[357] When that becomes our mental lock, we give up trying to learn creativity. In the most extreme case, we go further still to conclude that creativity *cannot* be learned—that it's accessible to a rare few.

UNLOCKING THE CONSTRAINTS

Mental Grazing vs. Mental Locks. If we give up the habit of mental locks, then what? One concept is replacing them with a new habit, what author Sarah Lewis calls **MENTAL GRAZING** in her book *The Rise: Creativity, The Gift of Failure, and the Search for Mastery.* It embodies what we know about forming the breakthrough space— "stepping outside of our borders, with no particular set agenda or schedule, with the simple intention of filling ourselves with new ideas, images, and concepts, most often ones we know little about."[358] It's precisely the approach that Gary and Liz take.

Examples, as you know, help. For one, imagine what an environment conducive to mental grazing looks like in a story you already know—the story of John Hunter and the World Peace game. Think back to John Hunter's fourth-grade class and you'll recognize an environment built to stave off the mental locks that limit creativity and instead encourage mental grazing. It's a vibrant example of a different path to learning.

Learning How to Learn. The learning environment in Hunter's classroom takes him out of the equation as "teacher," a move that doesn't simply open the locks but hands his students the keys. He creates an environment with the highest potential for students to learn *for* themselves and *about* themselves. And for both the students and Hunter, the challenge is completely different each time. Rather than learning to "answer," they're learning to "learn."

In his class, the target may be world peace, but the goal for his students is to learn to discover, each through his or her own potent, transferable, and unique style. Imagine the mental frameworks that approach can build. Rather than a "locking" rule, "right answers" become the ones that "fit the circumstances." Right answers are thus seen as temporal and fully open to reconsideration. Rather than "play" being considered a frivolous impediment to learning (another of von Oech's mental locks), it's taught to be the necessary avenue to "experimentation" and discovery. In Hunter's classroom, you could walk around and test each door von Oech suggests gets closed to creativity and you'd find each of them unlocked and thrown wide open.

Hunter's classroom represents a kind of balance often missing from learning environments. It's also emblematic of the power inherent in individual choice when it comes to learning. His approach reminds us how rarely we question and reconsider how we learn. And it potently points out the danger of mental locks.

But note that, rather than seeking to recreate our education system, Hunter teaches his fourth graders about their innate capacity for creativity and their ability to learn for themselves. At the same time, he shows them they possess an equally great *power of choice* to exercise that capacity. In every sense, his underlying "lesson" is this: It all comes back to *you*.

Relearning How to "Play." As Gary eloquently reminded us, we always have something more to learn. Play factors heavily in our ability to remember this. A "page from my own book" brings that lesson home.

At the time I spoke with MacArthur Fellow Pedro Sanchez, I was in a groove of doing interviews. With a whole range of questions filed in my brain, I asked many of the same questions to allow for points of comparison and direction across the conversations. But I was also in the habit of ending my conversations by asking this question: "Is there anything we didn't touch on or something important I didn't ask?"

To this question Pedro responded, "What do you do for fun?"[359] Admittedly, this caught me off guard. I hadn't thought I'd be asked to *respond* to questions, particularly this one. "Well," I began fumbling with my words, "I love time with my kids and coaching their sports. I like to kayak and hike with my wife. I read a lot. . . ."

"No," Pedro said. "*What do you do for fun? That's* the question you didn't ask me."[360] That was *my* "whack on the side of the head." Somewhere along the way, I'd discounted the importance of **PLAY**, not only in creativity but in learning.

Play and the "Purposeful Accident." The importance of play—as both a powerful means of learning and a creative catalyst—is stunningly self-evident (in addition to being backed by a growing warehouse of research). Think about it. Play frees our learning in any forum. Play *is* mental grazing.

When we play, we aren't intentionally out to learn. In fact, we think of play as an activity in which if we don't learn something conscious, specific, or earth-shattering, it's no big deal. Ironically, that frees us from attention to all those mental locks and opens us to learning something new and wonderful, even if "accidentally." Exploring, border breaking, changing scenery, noticing new things, making new connections, asking new questions—when we play, we do these things on purpose. And play not only facilitates them; subconsciously, we seem to know it *requires* them. When we play "purposefully"—both by choice and as part of our "habitual" practice—the discoveries may be "accidental," but they can also be grand.

Again, think of John Hunter and World Peace. It's a *game,* so its primary context is play. Hunter doesn't tell the students, "Heads up, you're about to learn something." Instead, the appeal to them is stated as, "How would you like to play a game for the next ten weeks, right here in class?" If you were ten years old again—heck, even right now—which method of learning would you choose?

Magically, you're doing your best learning when choosing the approach that your instinct wants you to choose anyway. As Hunter wrote about his students, "They learn right away that, if one thing changes [in the game], everything else changes along with it. I throw them into this complex matrix of conflicts and problems, and they trust me because we have a deep, rich relationship."[361] He's placing them in a world like Gary's and in a process like Liz's on purpose. But because it's "play" and because he's earned their trust, it doesn't matter that world peace is on the line. That thought would shut down even the most capable adult.

The need to change; trust; purpose; otherness; and a willingness to embrace and even lead change—who would have thought you could "teach" such things? But *before* his students open to learn any of this, Hunter asks them one question: "Do you want to play?" Every other lesson in creativity grows from that seed.

Consider *my* "whack on the side of the head" lesson to be *yours* now too.

RELEARNING WHAT WE "KNOW" TO BE TRUE

The Language of Man is providing guidance and ways to trigger a shift in your creative capacity. All the elements of this language (including value and learning) require returning to consider meaning and use as a matter of habit—that is, if you want to use creativity to progress.

The choice to engage in the relearning and reassessment of value is, as always, yours. Your quiver is full; you simply need to pull, nock, draw back, take aim, and shoot your creative arrows in the direction of what could be.

I leave you with the following story as a poignant reminder that this choice is eternal.

"THE EARTH IS BLUE . . . LIKE AN ORANGE"

In some views, a bat mitzvah is a time for a child to put away childish things and assume her role as an adult. That holds true if we believe that as we pass through the stages of our lives we actually substitute something "new" for something "known" and learn the "growing up" lesson as if for all time. A different view emerges by looking at each life phase as a *reconsideration* of the "known" *along with* an active *opening* to the "new." The bat mitzvah of our friends' daughter Regan powerfully reflected the choice of taking that alternate view.

A Self-made Rite of Passage. Though I'm not Jewish, I've attended many Jewish "rites of passage"—mitzvahs, weddings, funerals— each unique in its own way. And still, each ceremony borrows from a shared framework of traditions that have accumulated over the years. In a bat mitzvah, an important task is for the person being honored to choose for herself the lesson around which her year-long education and eventual ceremony will revolve. In other words, she *chooses* her own *learning*. I like that.

Regan's lesson was prompted at the start of her journey by this question she asked her rabbi: "Which traditions are more important, the old ones or the new ones?" The rabbi's response wasn't as simple as Regan might have presumed it would be. True, much of what she'd learn to prepare for her rite of passage was "written," as the expression goes. Her particular question, however, came down to a lesson in value and of choice. And both the rabbi and Regan took the better part of that preparation year to answer this guiding question—each for themselves.

A Shared Learning. As Regan later explained at the ceremony that ended her preparation year, the rabbi had expected Regan to learn the answer to her question for herself. Like John Hunter, the rabbi assigned herself the job of helping create the environment for Regan to do so. But during that year, an unexpected learning occurred as well. Regan's question caused the rabbi to reconsider what was most important and valuable. She too would be answering Regan's question—but for herself.

The rabbi knew what traditions mattered most to *her*. She was also aware that she had arrived at her ideas about tradition through the evolution of her own practice. As the rabbi told us that morning, she realized that her own answer of what was most important had actually *changed* many times—borrowing here, deemphasizing there, reinterpreting elsewhere—not always in major ways but in a constantly morphing forward motion. Each slight shift resulted in a set of values that fit *her*. So the traditions and practices she assigned the greatest value were, not surprisingly, those that fit her own values. But they also reflected the values of her congregation, her family, and her world.

Regan's rabbi knew deep within that her path to value had been and continued to be her own. More, she said that with Regan's question, for the first time she became fully conscious that the *real value* was in the journey, in the exploration and discovery. She also realized that while she recognized this in her own life, she'd also witnessed it in the "life cycle" of the temple's congregation. What had made the learning in total possible for her and her congregation was discovering how to *keep on learning and evolving and nurturing an environment in which she and others could do just that.*

A Valuable Symbol to Remember to Learn. On the day Regan celebrated by sharing with family and friends her own decisions, actions, and lessons, the rabbi gave her "answer" to Regan's question: "Which traditions are more important, the old ones or the new ones?" She told of her own journey and then offered something more: a symbol. Fittingly, she offered it through another story. Here, I pass it on to you.

The rabbi told the story of the significance of the orange placed on the Seder plate at the traditional Passover dinner. Passover is one of the most important Jewish holidays and commemorates the Jews' exodus from Egypt—itself a symbol of freedom, new beginnings, and possibility. To Jewish people, the exodus represented crossing a border into the unknown, yet a crossing made with the confidence of moving toward something new and better.

Traditionally, Passover is celebrated with a Seder, a ceremonial dinner. There are many traditions around this dinner, with some going back to the earliest days of the Jews. One tradition is to place an orange on the large serving plate used in these dinners—a tradition that, in the eyes of some, is as old as the exodus itself. Except it's not. But that isn't the point, as the rabbi helped her congregation understand.

The truth is that putting the orange on the Seder plate actually began less than twenty-five years ago with Dr. Susannah Heschel, a rabbi and scholar. She created this practice after reading a story about a young girl who asked her own rabbi this question: "Where in Judaism is there room for a lesbian?" Her rabbi apparently thundered back, "There is as much room for a lesbian in Judaism as there is for a crust of bread on a Seder plate." Because crust is not a feature of the Seder's traditional unleavened bread, the rabbi's declaration made clear that traditions and rules were unbendable, that the lessons around them were to be learned by rote, and that their value was in their constancy—in his view.

When Heschel heard this story, rather than judging the rabbi's statement as right or wrong, she sensed opportunity. For her, what lay in the story was a chance to reflect, to reconsider, and even to renew—not just one time, but perpetually. And that image of an out-of-place crust of bread on the Seder plate was the symbolic trigger. She just thought the symbol could use more "color." So rather than a crust of bread, she changed it to an *orange*. And she began placing one on her family's Seder plate every Passover.[362]

It was a creative act, and word of this "tradition" soon spread. Others adopted the orange as a symbol. It acquired added meaning and came to represent valuable lessons, "new" ones. For some, a "seeded" orange meant "rebirth"; to others, the same seeds symbolized the need to "spit out what limits us." For many, the bright orange color drew attention to "ideas at the margins" or things outside our borders we're taught to ignore or shun in favor of what we already know—even, it seems, within one's own "congregation."

The rabbi shared that, when the synagogue was renovated several years before, she unexpectedly found herself mediating a battle. The renovation was to include putting in new stained glass door panels, each depicting a different Jewish tradition. The panels themselves weren't the issue of contention. It was a single small image in one small part of one individual panel among a dozen or more. The image? An orange on the Seder plate—to some a tradition as "old" and important as the ones begun two millennia ago; to others, not so much.

Who was to say who was right and who was wrong? The rabbi apparently, but her answer wasn't about absolute rightness. It was about the *value* of the lesson—in this case, the lesson of traditions evolving to reflect the people who practice them. This became the most valuable lesson of all, and they'd helped each other to see it. The orange in the panel remained as a "symbol" of that creative lesson.

Finding Your Own Way. In a neat twist of serendipity, my personal reminder of this lesson reflected in the rabbi's story came from a single line borrowed from French poet Paul Éluard. I see it each day in a painting in our home. The painter chose to imbed a single written line in a work otherwise comprised of images. Doing so gave the line new meaning—perhaps not what Éluard originally intended but powerful in its own new way, at least to me.

I pause in front of that painting as I begin each day and read this line: "The earth is blue, like an orange." Within that line lie the seeds of creative possibility that inspire me for my day ahead.

SIMPLE TRUTH:

CREATIVITY

SEEKS

PERPETUITY

CHAPTER FIFTEEN

SIMPLE TRUTH: CREATIVITY SEEKS PERPETUITY

The preceding chapters returned you to a beginning, asking you to reconsider how we value and how we learn. In no small way, these two things shape whatever we create as well as our ability to create in the first place. But they are far from the only things we need to return to repeatedly so we can create to our fullest potential. In every sense, the Simple Truth is this: Creativity seeks perpetuity.

Some find this idea hopeful; others find it hard to abide. But this is how the story of creativity gets written. It's how you write your own creative story as well.

Here at the close of *The Language of Man*, let's acknowledge the *challenge* of creativity just as we've acknowledged its *promise* throughout this book. Most certainly, our guides would find me remiss if I did not address it.

But instead of ending on that, this chapter launches you toward perpetuity and, more important, the creation and contribution of your verse to the human story. To start off, Sara Lawrence-Lightfoot has one more gift to share.

JUST LIKE YOU

One More Gift to Share. Toward the end of our conversation about creativity, Sara broached this thought that may be on your mind right now:

What about the challenge that comes with building creativity into your life?

In my interviews with MacArthur Fellows, I sensed a palpable desire to share what they knew about creativity. Far from defending their given title of "genius," they were quick to point out that they are just like you and me. To Fellows like Sara, getting that message across meant sharing the "whole" truth about creativity—that is to say, the challenges and not just the excitement and possibilities. In this regard, Sara and others were abundantly clear: The pursuit of creativity is a braided journey in which the thrill and challenge intertwine. And that mix—as well as the changes wrought by it— is perpetual.

"Creativity takes different forms across the lifecycle," Sara said. "We change. Our work evolves. Other demands and responsibilities and joys take on different weights, shifting priorities. The entire human portrait, both what is in any one moment and what is still possible, is reframed and then recreated countless times over."[363] Her comments traced the edges of a Simple Truth.

Not Fancy, Simply "Every Day." It's not just that creativity is a perpetual thing; it's that creativity actually *seeks* perpetuity. It thrives on the next unknown and the future "what could be" that lies somewhere out there adjacent to what we know in this moment. And while it may seem counterintuitive, the challenge that accompanies that truth becomes remarkably reassuring—even encouraging— to those who practice creativity as a habit. The pull to cross our borders yields some strange but undeniable connection to the pulse of what it means to be alive. And the ways it tends to manifest are typically far more "every day" in nature than you might think. The pull to wonder, notice, and create exists constantly, even if it often comes dressed as the proverbial "opportunity in workman's clothes." This clear offering came from a lesson in Sara's own life.

The Birth of a New Way to Create. "When I chose to have kids and most assuredly when they arrived," Sara said, offering a familiar example, "I thought I'd never be able to write again. My previous creative process made me feel as though having children in my world would no longer accommodate creativity."[364]

It's a perfect example of creativity's perpetuity. But because it's so commonplace—the shift that comes with having children and becoming a parent—it doesn't look like a chance or a need to create again. More unexpected still, this was a moment when Sara, a practiced creator, actually believed she might no longer be capable of creating. In reality, hers was a "Phil Hansen" moment, a need to "embrace the shake" that is life's ever-changing nature. She had to reconsider what creativity could mean in her new circumstances.

"Mostly, I worried I couldn't be productive and creative," Sara said. "It's not as though I concluded I'd never have another creative thought enter my head. But it felt as if, overnight, the rules had changed, the game itself was different, and my ability to create had been seized from me. It was hard to know where to begin again or even if I could." It's remarkable to think this could happen to a person like Sara, but then again, she's just like you.

"It took a while to realize that the 'game' was of my own creation, and that it could be reset, restyled, even recreated—if I chose for it to be."

A Law to Go with a Feeling. As I listened to Sara, I was reminded of the telling yet maddening scientific law called the law of entropy. It says (in part) *the world and the entire universe is and will always be bent toward reordering and expanding.*

But this law goes beyond declaring that the universe has a strong "randomness element" that will inevitably upend any well-orchestrated plans we might try to grasp too firmly. It also says that when we try to control our slice of the universe in any permanent way—when we try to "close the system" and choose to believe it operates predictably—the universe responds by pushing harder to get us to open up. As science and humanities professor Alan Lightman wrote in *The Accidental Universe*, "Oblivious to our human yearnings for permanence, the universe is relentlessly wearing down, falling apart, driving itself toward a condition of maximum disorder."[365] Bummer. Or maybe not . . .

As I listened to Sara talk, I wondered if she believed in that law of entropy and, if yes, how she factored it in to her thoughts about creativity—especially when feeling self-doubt. In the same moment, I realized that, science aside, we see examples every day that the feeling Sara described is both universal and ubiquitous.

Unpredictable in the Everyday. One particular memory file of mine was of a February 2012 *Fast Company* cover story and its in-your-face headline "Modern Business is Pure Chaos" followed by the hopeful refrain "But Those Who Adapt Will Succeed." Seeking an enticing spin, the story included passages of dire bluntness. "Our institutions are out of date . . . career is dead . . . any quest for solid rules is pointless, since we will be constantly rethinking them . . . you can't rely on any established business model or corporate ladder to point your way . . . silos between industries are breaking down . . . anything settled is vulnerable."[366] Based on this analysis, it seems like the *only* "law" we can count on is entropy.

But stepping out of my mental files and back into that moment, I fine-tuned into the words that framed Sara's thoughts—"when I *chose* to have kids." In effect, she *chose* unpredictability, and I knew she knew it too. The anticipated beauty and joy of parenthood may have convinced her to border cross, but there was a scary part of that possibility as well—one filled with unknowns and change and threats to her modus operandi once she came to the edge and crossed over. What took time to see, even for Sara, was that it was simply a new edge she'd come to—and with it, a renewal of the creative journey.

This is Life. About that moment, Sara said this: "Instead of yielding, I engaged."[367] Rather than walk away from the creative game or resign herself to the new circumstances, she marched forward. It was her habit already; she just had to *change* the particulars within her habit—as we all must perpetually do the more adept we become at creating.

"By engaging in the messiness, you actually evolve and see other capacities," Sara explained. "Creativity is not a stationary thing. It's certainly not a simple or solitary thing. It's not something you escape to. It's not perpetual 'aha' moments. Rather, it's dealing with the demands and the joys." And then after a profound pause, she remarked, "It's life, isn't it?"

Yes, it *is* life—if we admit the thought. For "dealing with the demands" in our lives and still striding forward to seek the "aha" moments is what ignites our souls. Really, creativity means doing what we must do but with a different mindset. And though the world is perpetually in motion, we are still uniquely designed to deal with this reality. When we choose to engage, we in fact thrive on this dynamic—and progress through it.

A More Difficult "Truth" to Admit. So creativity—that uniquely human capacity we share—*seeks* perpetuity and all of life's fluxes. We are built for this. But do we *admit* this truth?

The word "admit" is not meant in the sense of declaring it true but in the sense of actually *allowing it in* to permeate our thoughts and actions. When we do "admit" it, that's when we give ourselves permission to go beyond the borders born of a "known" moment and into a "new" possibility.

THE POWER OF STORY

The Story in Our DNA. If creativity *is* life, as Sara said, w*hat gives it life?* More specifically, what pulls the pieces together from the messiness and into a larger whole with forward motion?

The answer is "story" or, more accurately, myriad stories into which elements of the language of man are woven, and which in turn are woven into your life. You now know "story" as it relates to creativity. Let's add to that knowledge about "story" itself—how you're built for it, how you need it, and how it helps you speak creativity as a habit.

In a 2015 essay for *aeon* magazine titled "The Power of Story," author Elizabeth Svoboda confirmed what many already know: "Our storytelling ability, a uniquely human trait, has been with us nearly as long as we've been able to speak."[368] Her own work and writing brought together decades of research and millennia of collective intuition to make the case for what this truth can and should mean to you.

"Whether it evolved for a particular purpose or was simply an outgrowth of our explosion in cognitive development, story is an inextricable part of our DNA," Svoboda wrote. "Across time and across cultures, stories have proved their worth not just as works of art or entertaining asides, but as agents of personal transformation."[369] When you set forth to learn and use the language of man, you seek transformation. Story facilitates that. It links the ideas with the outcome and the journey in between. It shows the path you've walked on. It reveals the lessons by forcing you to name them. But it also yields the reasons you care to take the journey in the first place—and care enough to share and repeat it.

One Final Story. When we tell our creative stories, we aren't simply applying the tool of narrative. We are transforming and shaping the stuff of our lives *consciously*, though as it turns out, we are programmed to storytell even when we aren't proactive and deliberate. As author David McRaney pointed out in *You Are Now Less Dumb*, telling stories is a pre-installed human practice that's likely been there long before our fox joined our hedgehog.

So deep in our makeup does it go that we rely on narrative even when we don't know we do, even when we're about to kick the bucket. "Narrative," McRaney wrote, "is so important to survival that it is literally the last thing you give up before becoming a sack of meat. Even as the brain is dying, it refuses to stop generating a narrative."[370]

McRaney's statement is based on numerous studies about near death, momentary death, and even simulated death experiences. These include jet fighter pilots who experience simulated death when their brains are artificially affected by the G-forces of flying at high speed and extreme altitude. It appears that when the brain senses the end to be near, its last gasp for survival involves pulling together thoughts running around loosely in the brain into some final narrative. People tell one last story to draw a conclusion about their lives. Perhaps it's one parting shot at answering the human question. Regardless, it's a remarkable validation of the hardwired power of story.

But while the primitive part of our brain might be satisfied with any story, what our complete, uniquely human brain wants is something more. It's not only our brain; it's our gut that constantly sends us signals of fit. It's our senses—what we see, of course, but also what we hear and feel. It's that "sixth sense" that tells us there could be more. It's our heart and our soul that tune us into beauty and other people. We seek a meaning that can be found at the intersection of all of this and more.

What Svoboda described is a power we seek that rises above biology—not the capacity *for* story but the desire and need to *be* a storyteller. We want the effect that story yields, an effect that's only possible when we engage it consciously. We want to tell our *creative* story, to contribute our verse and make ourselves and others *care*. That's what the language of man enables in us.

So how do you begin? To respond to that question, let me show how you already know the answer.

TELLING YOUR OWN CREATIVE STORY

To craft your own story, turn to the language of man. Practice using its elements. Draw often on the insights of your guides. And most important, use its Simple Truths to refresh and trigger and guide your creative thoughts going forward.

Beyond that, periodically return to these storylines in your mind:

I am creative. You now know this to be true. Only two things have made you feel less than creative: a lack of understanding and a lack of practice.

The "view" is long. Yes, the "here and now" and the tangible matter. But the view that carries you forward goes ever outward. That's where the *possible* lies. Conceiving and creating it—that's what your brain is built to figure out. *Go long.*

The "value" is wide. If you can begin to see value beyond its time and measures, it will appear in places and forms you've never imagined. Value through a wide-angle lens is imbued with endless possibility.

Meaning and beauty are what motivate and matter. You *know* why. You know also you'll have the highest odds of finding both beauty and meaning if you "frame the view to see beyond you." Remember: It's co-creation that moves you forward.

Come to the edge. There are always edges. What matters, as David Bayles and Ted Orland wrote in *Art & Fear*, is realizing that at such edges, "It is about committing your future to your own hands, placing free will above predestination, choice above chance."[371]

They wrote (and you now know), "In the end, it all comes down to this: you have a choice (or more accurately a rolling tangle of choices) between giving your work your best shot and risking that it will not make you happy, or not giving it your best shot—and thereby guaranteeing that it will not make you happy. It becomes a choice between certainty and uncertainty. And curiously, uncertainty is the comforting choice."[372]

The basic framework of the human story is a shared one. The choice of *how* and *where* you build your story within that shared framework is wholly yours. As Dan Gilbert wrote, "We are not merely spectators in this world but investors in it."[373]

Invest in your story and be creative as you do. As a human being, you are equipped to do exactly that. Life is movement. *Now, get going.*

IMPLICATION, ENGAGEMENT, AND ELOQUENCE

I asked Sara what she hoped would be her "return" on continuing to invest in her own creative capacity. What did she hope to reap from her narrative? What might others gain from it?

"I hope people see themselves in some aspect of my story and will feel implicated and engaged," Sara answered.[374] Her answer immediately took me back to Agnes, the woman in the front row at one of Sara's book events. Agnes was the first to put forth a question when Sara invited inquiries. And Agnes' questions and comments ended up teaching the teacher about her own work.

But an additional connection is layered into this story. Sara told me about her sister's reaction to the story of Agnes. "You know what's happening, don't you?" her sister told her. "Others are *finishing* your story." Yes, the story of creativity is a co-creation. When implication and engagement in one another's stories is allowed, creativity follows.

Make no mistake; you want to feel implicated in that larger story that is creativity. You want to feel *engaged* and *enmeshed* in the dance that is human progress. Your birthright not only affords it, but *commands* it. You have a part to play, a verse to add. And what might be the "return on investment" when you play your part? As Stu Kauffman suggested, "We cannot pre-state what will come. But why not dream of what we *might* become? The path is less important than the choice to actively participate."[375]

Choose to do so. See the language of man as a beautiful gift through which you narrate that journey. Give it meaning.

That's what makes life beautiful—and that's what it means to be human.

MACARTHUR FELLOWS

Following is a list of the MacArthur Fellows who generously spoke to me at length about creativity. They appear by order of the year they received the MacArthur award. Their chapter appearances in *The Language of Man* are noted in parentheses.

Also noted are their primary professional roles as they most often appear on their websites or in their biographies (as of the time of this writing). Note that these roles are points of reference indicating the diversity of the contributing Fellows. By no means are they meant to fully describe their areas of expertise, pursuits, or accomplishments.

1981	Howard Gardner (Chs. 3, 5, 6)	psychologist
	Elaine Pagels (Ch. 7, 8)	religion historian
	Michael Woodford	economist
1982	Francesca Rochberg	science historian
1983	Steve Berry	physical chemist
	Sylvia Law (Ch. 9)	human rights lawyer
1984	Ernie Cortés, Jr. (Ch. 9)	community organizer
	Bill Drayton (Ch. 8)	social entrepreneur
	Shirley Brice Heath	linguistic anthropologist
	Sara Lawrence-Lightfoot (Chs. 2, 7, 9, 11, 15)	sociologist
	Michael Lerner	environmentalist
	Matthew Meselson	geneticist
1985	Peter Raven	botanist
1986	Chris Beckwith	philologist

	David Rudovsky (Ch. 8)	civil rights lawyer
1987	Deborah Meier (Ch. 7, 8, 11)	education reformer
	Stuart Kauffman (Chs. 1, 4, 5, 7, 9, 15)	complex systems theorist
	Richard Wrangham	primatologist
	Peter Jeffery	musicologist
	Richard Kenney (Chs. 1, 4, 5, 7, 9)	poet
1988	Phil DeVries (Chs. 7, 10)	insect biologist
	Naomi Pierce	butterfly expert
1989	John Harbison (Chs. 5, 10, 12)	composer
	Pam Solo (Ch. 8)	arms control analyst
	Dan Janzen (Ch. 5)	evolutionary biologist
1990	Martha Clarke (Chs. 3, 9)	theater director
	Maria Varela	community organizer
	Gary Nabhan (Chs. 1, 3, 5, 6, 7, 8, 14)	ethnobotanist
1991	Pat Churchland (Chs. 1, 5, 6, 7, 9, 11)	neurophilosopher
1992	Joanna Scott (Chs. 5, 8)	novelist
	Lorna Bourg (Chs. 9, 12)	community developer
	Susan Meiselas (Chs. 2, 5, 7, 8, 9)	photojournalist
1993	Carol Levine (Chs. 8, 9)	family care specialist
	Heather Williams (Ch. 8)	animal behavior biologist
1994	Faye Ginsberg	anthropologist
1995	Susan McClary (Chs. 7, 12)	musicologist
	Nicholas Strausfeld (Chs. 1, 8)	neuroscientist
	Sue Kieffer (Ch. 12)	geologist
	Michael Marletta (Ch. 8)	chemist
1996	Rebecca N. Goldstein (Chs. 5, 6, 7, 8, 9, 12)	philosopher
1997	Kathleen Ross	education reformer
	Elizabeth Streb (Chs. 3, 7, 8, 10)	choreographer
1998	Ellen Barry (Chs. 7, 9)	human rights activist
	Gary Hill (Chs. 1, 3)	visual artist

	Edward Hirsch (Ch. 3)	poet
1999	John Bonifaz	election rights lawyer
	Ric Scofidio (Chs. 2, 3, 5, 9)	architect
2000	Carl Safina (Ch. 3)	marine conservationist
2001	Sandy Lanham (Ch. 6)	conservationist
2002	Liz Lerman (Chs. 2, 3, 7, 9, 14)	choreographer
2003	Sarah Kagan (Chs. 2, 5, 10, 11, 12)	gerontological nurse
	Pedro Sanchez (Ch. 14)	agronomist
2004	David Green	technology innovator
	Tommie Lindsey	high school debate coach
2005	Ted Ames (Ch. 9)	marine biologist
	Steve Goodman (Ch. 5, 6, 9)	conservation biologist
2006	Edie Widder	deep sea explorer
2007	Ruth Defries (Chs. 2, 6)	environmental geographer
	Lisa Cooper (Chs. 7, 12)	cardiovascular physician
2008	Peter Pronovost (Ch. 11)	critical care physician
2009	Peter Huybers (Chs. 4, 5)	earth and planetary scientist
	Lynsey Addario (Ch. 8, 12)	photojournalist
2010	Elizabeth Turk (Ch. 4, 8, 11)	stone carver
2011	Elodie Ghedin	parasitologist
2012	Maria Chudnovsky (Chs. 7, 9, 12)	mathematician
2013	David Lobell	agricultural ecologist

GLOSSARY OF "ELEMENTS"

This glossary is designed to be a convenient summary of the "elements" introduced to you throughout the book. Used in combinations of your own making, they help you increase your fluency in creativity. Their descriptions have far more meaning within the context of the chapters in which each is introduced and are therefore listed here by chapter and order of appearance so you may easily return to the larger story.

CHAPTER ONE: CREATIVELY FIGHTING OURSELVES

NEW VS. NEWTONIAN. There are two primary modes of human thinking. One (the new mode) is more heavily oriented toward the future and what could be; it's less rigid and less concerned with certainty. The other mode (Newtonian) is more focused on the here and now and favors predictability and certainty. Creativity requires a balance of the two.

NOW AND THEN THINKING. Coined by Liane Gabora, "now" thinking relates to being in this moment; "then" thinking is oriented to a time yet to be. Our unique human brains enable us to engage in both forms of thought and in ways no other species can.

FOX AND HEDGEHOG. These are simple metaphorical images for our open creative mindset (fox) and our more orderly, formulaic way of thinking (hedgehog). All humans have and need both mindsets.

CHAPTER TWO: SIMPLE TRUTHS

SIMPLE TRUTHS. In *The Language of Man*, Simple Truths are universal patterns that appear across creative practitioners and creativity. They offer valuable insights about how we can most effectively tap into our creative capacity no matter who we are or where we end up applying it.

CHAPTER THREE: WHAT CREATIVITY IS

THREE SALIENT FEATURES OF CREATIVITY. Though definitions and applications of creativity vary widely, those who've gone beyond a passing glance agree that all forms of creativity are characterized by three salient features: Creativity is *new*, can occur *anywhere*, and can be engaged and executed by *anyone*.

FRAMEWORK (VS. FORMULA). Frameworks are open, fluid, and allow for multiple "pictures" to be shaped within them. By contrast, formulas are fixed and favored for their ability to create the same picture, thing, or result over and over again.

QUILTING. A simple metaphor for creativity and how we create: The idea that creativity is a fluid accumulation of pieces stitched together many times over into a larger, more brilliant whole.

THE CREATION INSIGHT. The creation insight helps us to understand how breakthrough ideas materialize in that creative brain of ours. Simply put, breakthrough ideas most often take place at the intersection of things "known" and things "new." (See also: the intersection of the known and the new.)

THE MINDSET INSIGHT. All of our brains allow for a growth mindset (one that believes there's always more to learn and we are capable of learning it) and a fixed mindset (one that, in the extreme, concludes we are born with a limited capacity for what we can learn and do). This insight reminds us not only that we have both, but also that our orientation toward one over the other is something we *choose*. (See also: fixed and growth mindsets.)

THE LEARNING INSIGHT. The learning insight is as simple as this: Humans are built to *learn* in ways that are *diverse, dynamic, and distinctive*, but how we are *taught* does not always align with how we are built to learn. When there is a conflict, our ability to think, learn, or take action in a creative way is likely to be limited. (See also: three elements of human learning.)

THE OPENNESS INSIGHT. This fourth insight teaches that openness is both the key to tapping into our creative capacity and one of our core inclinations as humans. Openness works in tandem and in a back-and-forth fashion with our desire for order.

THE INTERSECTION OF THE KNOWN AND NEW. Arthur Koestler observed that breakthrough ideas occur at the intersection of two planes of thinking, one defined by what we know, the other by knowledge that's unexpected or new. At such intersections we are most likely to experience that *ah!* (or *aha!* or even *ha ha!*) sensation of discovery we so closely associate with creativity. Those sensations also serve as signals to take "notice" and "open up."

FIXED AND GROWTH MINDSETS. Inspiring "the mindset insight," these are Carol Dweck's terms for two very different ways to approach the world. With one, we believe that our ability to learn and grow is set from birth (fixed), and with the other, we see our capacity as ever-expanding (growth). Each of us operates using a combination of the two. How much we lean one way or the other is driven by choice—ours.

CHOICE. Choice is the defining factor in countless aspects of tapping into our creative capacity. Our choices can lead to a strengthening or a diminishing of our ability. Two pronounced examples are: 1) whether we choose a *growth* or a *fixed* mindset to lead our thinking, and 2) whether we come to the edge between things known and new or instead, avoid it.

THE YET FACTOR. This wonderful element is core to the growth mindset. It refers to the experience of arriving at the edge of something new, a place where we feel both trepidation and attraction. It reminds us that the discomfort of that place is most often tied to our not knowing what lies ahead of us . . . yet.

DIVERSE, DYNAMIC AND DISTINCTIVE. As described by Ken Robinson, all humans are built to learn in ways that are diverse, dynamic, and distinctive (what I think of as the "3Ds"). The more we create environments that allow us to learn in this way, the more creative we become.

THE LONG VIEW. Creativity is a gradual unfolding; it's also a perpetual one. Taking such a view helps us strike a balance between our eagerness to produce creative outputs right now and the reality of how the greatest breakthrough ideas actually materialize.

HIKING THE HORIZONTAL. A term borrowed from Liz Lerman, hiking the horizontal is a reminder that creativity is most likely to deliver its promise when these factors are present: We are open, unafraid to cross borders, framework-like in our thinking, and nonhierarchical in our views of where and how we can best learn and create.

CREATIVITY. Instead of a word to be defined, creativity is better seen as a mindset and a habit. For those who need a definition, *creativity is a human inclination to engage in a matchless human undertaking, one requiring us to tap into a unique human capacity. That internal predisposition is driven by the equally powerful outward desire to add to our collective human progress.*

CHAPTER FOUR: SIMPLE TRUTH: CREATIVITY IS THE LANGUAGE OF MAN

MEANING AND USE. Linguists agree that all languages have four features: meaning, use, structure, and sound. The first two are the most fluid and also the most important. Meaning and use are why we are drawn to language in the first place. The more fixed features of languages (structure and sound) can also be valuable, but they can also be overemphasized and end up limiting a language's true power.

ENABLING CONSTRAINTS. A term used by Stu Kauffman, it reminds us that those things we regard as limits, constraints, rules, or borders have the potential to instead give us leverage.

CHAPTER FIVE - WHERE BREAKTHROUGHS COME FROM

THE BREAKTHROUGH SPACE. This is a "place"—neither physical or field-dependent—that we can create anytime, anywhere. It's from this space that breakthrough ideas are most likely to come.

THE PRACTICED NOTICER. The practiced noticer is the person who habitually takes notice of what's around him or her in a way that increases the likelihood of making new connections, seeing new opportunities, and creating new value.

FOUR LUCK PRINCIPLES. As described by luck researcher Richard Wiseman, these are four principles to which so-called "lucky people" tend to adhere. They help us understand that luck, rather than being a unique genetic trait or the result of some random factor "out there somewhere," is a result of certain habits—habits that just so happen to align with the habits of those we regard as productively creative.

A DELIBERATE PAUSE. This term I coined in my first book of the same title. It describes "that conscious moment in which we open up our minds and ask, "Why are things the way they are?" and then we wonder aloud, "How could life be better?"

FIT. Fit is a two-way indicator that tells us both when something is off or doesn't fit and when a new combination of factors could allow for a better result. While everyone experiences feelings of fit, many people ignore them.

THE ADJACENT POSSIBLE. This is Stu Kauffman's term for the "place," just beyond the borders of what we know, where we most often discover the pieces we later quilt into breakthrough ideas. It's opposite to the "lightning strike" or "moon leap" view of where breakthrough ideas come from.

BORDER CROSSING. This refers to the act of going to and beyond the edges of what we know to explore "what could be." The habit of border crossing raises the odds of discovering breakthrough ideas.

CHALK LINES. This term was developed in *A Deliberate Pause*. In *The Language of Man*, it helps us remember that all borders of all kinds are temporary, permeable, and meant to be crossed.

THE "NO CHOICE" FACTOR. This factor is one consistently called out by practiced entrepreneurs and other creative thinkers. It aptly describes the point they reach when they realize no one else is noticing or pursuing what they see. It reflects a value calculation at that moment that leads to the conclusion that *not* choosing to go forward is the greater risk.

INTERSECTIONS. Intersections in the language of man are the place where the known and the new collide and where new ideas have the greatest odds of occurring.

CATALYST. A catalyst is a person who brings forth a new idea but is not to be misunderstood as the person who singlehandedly materializes that idea.

PURPOSEFUL ACCIDENTS. Patterns across creative practitioners reveal that most breakthrough ideas happen accidentally but occur as a result of a purposeful choice to border cross, take notice, and think creatively.

CHAPTER SIX: SIMPLE TRUTH: OPENNESS IS WHY BREAKTHROUGHS COME

GRAND CANYON MOMENTS. These are those moments when a whole world of possibility lies right before us, often in plain sight, and yet we just can't see it. In these moments, it's a good idea to tune into our creative habits anew.

OPENNESS. This is the critical factor for *why* breakthroughs come. A habit of openness honors and promotes many elements of creativity, including noticing, coming to the edge, border crossing, and inquiry.

FLIPPED VIEW. The flipped view refers to a perspective gained in a moment of choice (or the accumulation of many moments of choice) when we see things not just differently but the opposite of how we previously saw them.

CHAPTER SEVEN: THE PATTERN AND POWER OF QUESTIONS

THE FIVE HABITS OF THE MIND. Developed by Deborah Meier, the five habits of the mind are an example of a framework way of creating that relies on five mind-opening questions: *How do you know what you know? Is there a pattern? What if . . . ? Is there another way of looking at it? Who cares?* These habits prove particularly effective when shared inquiry is the goal.

THE 5 LAYERS OF WHY. Developed by Sakichi Toyoda and used companywide by Toyota in the 1980s, the 5 layers of why—the 5 Whys—is the practice of asking the question "why" five layers deep. It has proven a highly effective way to unearth more valuable and meaningful answers and, when used habitually, breakthrough ideas.

UNPROFESSIONAL QUESTIONS. Named for Rebecca Newberger Goldstein, these are any questions that fall outside the norm or the accepted standard of a job, field, or way of doing. Put simply, they question the accepted. They also have a tendency to ruffle the feathers of the status quo.

QUESTIONS OF FIT. These questions follow "a gut feeling," "sense," or "hunch" that either something doesn't quite fit (a misfit feeling) or that a new way of seeing or doing things might yield a better fit. They reflect a conscious choice to explore beyond the accepted answer, way, or view.

SELF-INTERVIEW QUESTIONS. Self-interview questions are questions turned inward to help us better understand who we are, what we care about, and what we are capable of. Absent that knowledge, it's hard to create anything new.

MISSING QUESTIONS. Missing questions are the questions no one is asking. They are often the flip side of typical questions asked.

PORTRAITURE QUESTIONS. Portraiture questions, named for Sara Lawrence-Lightfoot's revolutionary creative framework, are questions intended to reveal how individual parts relate to and shape the whole.

DEPTH-CHECK QUESTIONS. These questions help us assess the "depth" of our thinking, our ideas, or the meaning we attach to either. In other words they help us ask: "Are we digging deep, skimming the surface, or somewhere in between?"

REVERSE METAPHOR QUESTIONS. This is Gary Nabhan's practice and an example of the highly personal forms questions can take once inquiry becomes a mindset and habit. Gary's creative practice is to take any good metaphor he comes upon and flip around its transitive properties so they run the other way. The results can range from insightful to wacky.

CHANGE-THE-W QUESTIONS. This is the act of replacing one "who, what, where, when, why, or how" word that leads a question with a different "W" word. The goal is to shake up our assumptions and views linked to the initial question.

CHAPTER EIGHT: SIMPLE TRUTH:
THE HUMAN QUESTION DRIVES US

THE HUMAN QUESTION. The human question is this: *What does it mean to be human?* It is a question each of us asks and that our individual lives answer, whether we are conscious of it or not. There is no single or final answer to the human question; but being aware of it deeply enhances our creativity.

CHAPTER NINE: THE MYTH OF GENIUS

GENIUS. This word was derived from a belief that each of us has a "geni" or capacity within us to bring forth new, valuable, and highly creative things. From its original meaning, however, the word became a popular label for exceptional, productive, highly intelligent individuals who have exceeded the accomplishments of others.

THE HERO'S JOURNEY. As developed by Joseph Campbell, the hero's journey describes a pattern across hero mythologies in every culture that closely parallels the creative journey and, indeed, the human one. Though it consists of a dozen steps and is circular, in popular understanding, many of its steps are overshadowed or forgotten.

CHAPTER TEN: SIMPLE TRUTH:
CREATIVITY MEANS COMING TO THE EDGE

COMING TO THE EDGE. "The edge" is that border where "what we know" meets "what could be." If we aren't willing to come to our edges, peer over, and cross, there is no creativity. When we do, most often we discover that what we feared might be like stepping off a cliff is more like stepping off a curb.

CHAPTER ELEVEN: FRAMING THE
VIEW TO SEE BEYOND YOU

"MAKE ME CARE." According to Pixar filmmaker Andrew Stanton, this is the number one commandment of good story telling. Making the audience care typically confirms some truth or sheds new light in a way that "deepens our understanding of who we are as human beings." It is a key factor of any creative story as well.

CO-CREATION. This refers to the idea (and also the reality) that creativity takes many people, ideas, and iterations to become tangible, valuable, and real.

PURPOSE AND TRUST. They may seem like clichés, but these two elements are critical components in any form of creating, regardless of how many people are involved.

CHAPTER TWELVE: SIMPLE TRUTH: BEAUTY FUELS CREATIVITY

BEAUTY. It's a simple truth that beauty is what fuels creativity. Far more than an aesthetic feature, beauty is a powerful and multifaceted tool in creating. It functions equally as a source of inspiration, motivation, and reward.

CHAPTER THIRTEEN: A RENEWED SENSE OF VALUE

VALUE. Value is something far more than any one of its forms or measures, which can include: knowledge gained, a product, a service, a social or environmental good realized, kindness given, a soul moved. Value moves and is endlessly malleable. Understanding value in this way is key to our ability to see and create *new* value.

CHAPTER FOURTEEN: LEARNING TO DISCOVER

LEARNING. Learning creativity is something we return to over and over. At its core, it's about learning to discover something new. At least when it comes to creativity, learning doesn't take the form of some all-inclusive lesson or method we learn a single time.

MENTAL LOCKS. A term borrowed from Roger von Oech, mental locks are the artificial limitations we set up in our minds that limit our learning and creating. In combination, they can lead us to believe we are not creative.

MENTAL GRAZING. A term used by Sarah Lewis, mental *grazing* is the opposite of mental locking. She describes it as "stepping outside of our borders, with no particular set agenda or schedule, with the simple intention of filling ourselves with new ideas, images, and concepts, most often ones we know little about."

PLAY. Play is vital to how humans learn at every point in their lives. It's mental grazing, a powerful catalyst to creative thinking, and far from frivolous.

AUTHOR'S NOTES

The following offers additional context that some readers may want to explore—a sort of P.S. to the main story.

EPIGRAPH

Though often viewed as a religious treatise, Augustine's *Confessions*, the book from which this quote is drawn, was a work representing far more. More accurately, it was an exercise in inquiry, with the overarching questions concerning a search for answers to what it means to be human. For answers, he suggested we look not just at the "things" around us, but at ourselves. His work is also widely considered the first Western autobiography. (A side note: This quote has several translations. The wording varies slightly, but the meaning remains the same.)

REIMAGINING CREATIVITY-A

This book is both *for* you and *about* us. It's goal? To help you contribute your verse to the story of creativity so we may continue to progress. The words "of man" in the title symbolize that goal. I chose "man" as lyrical shorthand for *human, a person,* and equally for *the human race.* As you journey through *The Language of Man,* you'll see this intended meaning blossom. In every sense, creativity is a universal language shared by and open to use by all of us.

REIMAGINING CREATIVITY-B

My research project with the MacArthur Fellows ended in 2013. I considered seeking interviews with Fellows who received the award in years after 2013, but the patterns were already so strongly revealed that I determined more interviews, while enjoyable, would not significantly add to the Simple Truths shared in this book. It's also worth noting that references made to titles or roles of the Fellows are as of the time they were interviewed.

CHAPTER ONE

Most often, we regard the brain as a physical thing. But typically the references we make to it are really references to its functionality, not its physicality. Case in point, there is no single or set physical region of the human brain that one can call the "fox" brain. When I use that phrase, I am referring to a mindset, a mode of thinking that draws on countless physical regions of the organ that is the brain. Throughout the book you'll see others do the same. You can find an excellent and simple description of the distinctions of the physicality and functionality of the human brain in Susan Greenfield's book *Mind Change* (Random House, 2015), pp. 48-54.

CHAPTER TWO

Jefferson instructed that the inscription on his tombstone read this way: "Here was buried Thomas Jefferson, author of the Declaration of American Independence, of the Statute of Virginia for Religious Freedom, and father of the University of Virginia."

CHAPTER THREE-A

Howard Gardner has retained his connection to Project Zero over the years, in one form or another. At the time of this book's publication he was a Senior Director and Principal Investigator. The Project's site offers a wide range of media sharing the fascinating directions the Project has continued to take: http://www.pz.harvard.edu. (Last accessed April 22, 2016)

CHAPTER THREE-B

Alfred Binet did not create this test to identify intelligence but instead to distinguish different learning styles so that teaching might be adapted to better tap individual ability. He spent much of the twilight of his career traveling and speaking "against" the manner in which the IQ test came to be seen and used.

CHAPTER THREE-C

The multiple intelligences theory Howard developed concludes that, rather than having one form of intelligence, humans possess eight forms. We can think about them as *logic* smart, *word* smart, *people* smart, *body* smart, *music* smart, *picture* smart, *self* smart, and *nature* smart. (Telling, Howard believes that there are at least two more forms of intelligence: teaching intelligence and existential intelligence. The first closely aligns with the need to share and communicate our ideas, a concept Sue Kieffer taught us in Chapter Twelve, and the second refers to the importance of the "human question" in spades.)

It's not surprising that we humans can deliberate and ideate in many different ways. But here's the surprising part: Howard, his colleagues, and their many followers believe that *all* humans are innately equipped with *all* eight of these forms of intelligence. That doesn't mean we don't, over time, individually favor certain ways of learning, thinking, and creating. But the capacity for all of them is there from the beginning and throughout our lives.

CHAPTER THREE-D

The convention is to link Koestler's simple terms—*aha, ha ha,* and *ah* moments—to his seminal book *The Act of Creation*, and indeed he did give an expansive description of the meaning and context for those terms there. But he didn't actually use them until a few years later in his essay "The Three Domains of Creativity" (first published around 1967, but most often sourced to a 1981 collection of essays: *The Conception of Creativity in Science and Art*, edited by Denis Dutton and Michael Krausz for Martinue Nijhoff Publishing The Hague).

CHAPTER THREE-E

For a three-minute refresher on the origin of the Archimedes principle, watch the video, "How taking a bath led to Archimedes' principle" created by Mark Salata: https://www.youtube.com/watch?v=ijj58xD5fDI. (Last accessed April 22, 2016)

CHAPTER FOUR-A

An excellent three-minute video at http://aeon.co/video/health/ breath-a-short-video-about-the-essential-life-force/ shows how breath in myriad forms speaks a universal language. (Last accessed April 22, 2016) It's a nice eye-opening metaphor.

CHAPTER FOUR-B

While estimates and their criteria vary, more than a billion people speak Mandarin as their primary or secondary language. English speakers come in at 942 million followed by Spanish speakers at 518 million. See https://en.wikipedia.org/wiki/List_of_languages_by_ total_number_of_speakers. (Last accessed April 22, 2016)

CHAPTER FOUR-C

To see Elizabeth Turk's work, visit her website: http://www. elizabethturksculptor.com. (Last accessed April 22, 2016)

CHAPTER SIX

Though my version of this story is a compilation of similar stories, two of the best sources for learning more about it are Kevin Fedarko's *The Emerald Mile: The Epic Story of the Fastest Ride in History Through the Heart of the Grand Canyon* (Scribner, 2013) and Wallace Stegner's *Beyond the Hundredth Meridian* (Penguin Books, 1992).

CHAPTER SEVEN-A

To see what Elizabeth Streb does, check out this CBS *This Morning* video: https://www.youtube.com/watch?v=eUIaKbrZUI8. (Last accessed April 22, 2016)

CHAPTER SEVEN-B

This reference to Campbell comes from an article written by Maria Popova in her *Brain Pickings* enewsletter, April 12, 2015, titled "How to Find Your Bliss: Joseph Campbell on What It Takes to Have a Fulfilling Life." Her article draws on the book *The Power of Myth*, a transcript of interviews with Campbell by Bill Moyers in 1985—a truly remarkable record to explore. For information, go to:

https://www.brainpickings.org/2015/04/09/find-your-bliss-joseph-campbell-power-of-myth/. (Last accessed April 22, 2016)

CHAPTER EIGHT

Much of Williams' voiceover was borrowed from the script of the 1989 film *Dead Poets Society*. It's debated whether Apple had Williams rerecord the lines or the producers dubbed them from the film. To watch the spot, go to: https://www.youtube.com/watch?v=1mYCIKTX0ug. (Last accessed April 22, 2016)

CHAPTER NINE-A

Most of Kant's commentary on genius is found in Part I of his *Critique of Judgment*, first published in Germany in 1790. See https://en.wikipedia.org/wiki/Critique_of_Judgment.

(Last accessed April 22, 2016)

CHAPTER NINE-B

As referenced in Author's Note Chapter Three-B, Alfred Binet, the primary creator of the Binet-Simon Scale from which the IQ score is derived, intended the tests he created to be a way to distinguish learning styles. In later years, he spent his time fiercely arguing against the uses to which his scale and score had been applied. In *Ungifted*, author and psychologist Scott Barry Kaufman offers more context, pp. 21-28. For a brief explanation, go to https://en.wikipedia.org/wiki/Alfred_Binet. (Last accessed April 22, 2016)

CHAPTER NINE-C

Campbell's Hero's Journey is referred to as both eleven and twelve stages. Some include "return to the start" as a stage; others do not. I chose to include the *return* because Campbell consistently highlighted its importance.

CHAPTER TEN-A

The "poem" "Come to the Edge," has been borrowed, misquoted, and misattributed many times. The story and the confirmation of the accurate attribution are based on a 1995 Nigel Rees interview and noted on page 359 of his book *Mark My Words: Great Quotations and the Stories Behind Them* (Barnes & Noble, Inc., 2002).

CHAPTER TEN-B

Two notable examples when Logue's words were called forth to remind people of this fundamental human cycle and need were: Margaret Thatcher's use of Logue's lines in a 1980 address to Britain's Royal Academy of Arts; and Ireland's President Mary McAleese's choice to make them central to her first inaugural address to the Irish people in 1997. You can read a discussion of the poem at http://www.emule.com/2poetry/phorum/read.php?4,34313. (Last accessed April 22, 2016)

CHAPTER TWELVE

The video of Dan Pink's talk has been seen by more than 15.6 million viewers in forty-two languages. See Daniel Pink, The Puzzle of Motivation, TED Talk, July 2009: http://www.ted.com/talks/dan_pink_on_motivation?language=en. (Last accessed April 22, 2016)

ACKNOWLEDGMENTS

The most important thing to acknowledge is this: Creativity is a co-creation. Sometimes it's obvious; most often it's far subtler. So many things come together to formulate a breakthrough idea that oftentimes we don't even know, or too easily forget, what played a role. Those acknowledged and thanked here aided my creativity in a number of different ways, from the overt to the covert. And while I hope to acknowledge everyone who did, I nonetheless apologize if I fall short. At the very least, those noted here reflect the range that is the creative journey.

I would be remiss if I didn't begin by thanking those other passionate believers in the importance of creativity—the other writers and researchers who took the time to consider this topic in more than a passing way. They span centuries and fields of study, no two quite the same. Over many years now, I've read hundreds of works that have informed and inspired me. You will find the names and authors of some of the best of those works listed among the endnotes. More than suggesting you take note of them, I encourage you to read broadly across them, for I have no doubt you will discover unique insights of your own.

The choice to read most of those works came long before I even conceived of writing another book. So too did my interviews with the MacArthur Fellows who act as your personal guides here in *The Language of Man*. Initially, I approached them for broader reasons. You might say this book arose as a "purposeful accident." I am truly grateful to the Fellows who spoke with me and who shared their insights so willingly and passionately. Special thanks go to several who went further still—introducing me to their peers, sending me further works, or suggesting ways we could continue to learn more from each other: Howard Gardner, Ellen Barry, Kathleen Ross, Ric Scofidio, Ruth DeFries, Sandy Lanham, Liz Lerman, Phil DeVries, Gary Nabhan, and Pat Churchland. There were others who helped me in a similar regard, including connecting me to a Fellow or two: my thanks to Scott Miller and Barbara J. Culliton in particular.

Once I decided to write this book, new co-creators became a part of the effort. I'm grateful to Rick Toren, Paul Rogers, Jon Gould, and Brigid Schulte, among others, who worked to support my effort and did so fully and graciously.

Then came my earliest readers—the ones an author goes to when the manuscript can barely be called that. I am humbled by your willingness to invest in helping this work (and me) become better.

I extend what will forever be insufficient thanks to Tripp Eldredge who read the entire book three times, and at different phases of its development. Tripp, that you would do this is a daunting and humbling thought. The fact that you did it so willingly, honestly, voluntarily, and perceptively, is something for which I will be endlessly grateful—that and for your valued friendship over the past twenty years.

Any honest writer worth a damn knows that without good editors, your best writing remains in your head. My thanks to my editors— official and unofficial. To Barbara McNichol: I count on your wisdom and steadiness. Your willingness to go the extra mile—not simply to do the job but to make the product a quality one—is what sets you apart. My thanks also goes to Kai Robertson and Judy Davis. Though your editorial roles may not come with a business card, I am so grateful for your sanity-check reviews, your patience, your "tough love," and your unending support. Each of you is so very good at what you do, and this book and I are better for it.

Refinement follows editing, and for that, two individuals are important to acknowledge. The first is my proofreader Peggy Henrikson. Peggy, your care and attention to detail make the title of proofreader seem insufficient. What you offer is far greater, and it helped to make this book so much more. And then there's Vanessa Maynard—my co-creator in designing the book's cover and my layout specialist. How fortunate I was to discover you, Vanessa. This book is visually so much richer because of you, and I am richer to have had the chance to collaborate with you. Such a rare pleasure it has been.

As I suspect there are for all of us, for me there are those who too often don't get the acknowledgement they're due in a project of this magnitude. These are the "contributors" who, while they may not be directly involved in the work, enable it to come together. It will likely not come as a surprise that such important team members usually fall into the categories of family and friends. To my wife Kai, my daughter Ella (who tells me she's never listed first when I list my children), and my son Noah: I do this *for* you and am only able to do it *because* of you. The three of you are the wind at my back and the fuel for the fire in my creative soul. It *will* be great, Kai, some way, somehow. I *do* believe, Ella, and I will *always* strive to be bold. And Noah, as I work to make all of this true, you will never know how much you lift my spirits when I need it most. Your pride in and love for me—both of which you openly and graciously express—are matched only by your incredible example to me in your own undertakings. Each of you inspires me simply by being who you are.

As for friends: To my "breakfast boys" plus or minus a few—your repeated interest in "how the book was coming" buoyed me in ways you can't imagine. It's hard for me to tell you how much the laughter around this seemingly endless project—coupled with your efforts to provide quotes for it (more laughter), topped off by your steady commitment to our friendships—kept me moving. (One of you, at least, is scolding me right now for that lengthy sentence.) Oh, and regarding the quote that "made the cut," here it is (I'll leave it to you to guess which one of you said it): "Life may allude you, but only if you allow it." That message fits both this book and our friendships.

Creativity is indeed perpetual. And so to you, my reader, I thank you for pausing to explore this book. You represent a vital source for carrying the insights and ideas shared here forward and to ever-greater heights. In each conversation I had with the MacArthur Fellows, I viscerally felt their hope that I would take the conversation and the knowledge around creativity to "the next step." With this book, I pay it forward one more time and hope the same for you. I can't wait to see what your next step might be.

ABOUT THE AUTHOR

Larry Robertson is the 8-time award-winning author of *A Deliberate Pause: Entrepreneurship and its Moment in Human Progress* and the founder of two ventures, one for-profit and one non. He is a highly respected thought leader in creativity, innovation, and entrepreneurship, advising individuals and organizations across a broad spectrum.

Larry is a graduate of Stanford University and Northwestern University's Kellogg School of Management, and a former Adjunct Professor of Entrepreneurship at Georgetown University's McDonough School of Business. He lives in Arlington, Virginia with his wife and two children.

For more information please visit: larryrobertson.me

ENDNOTES

1.   *Confessions in Thirteen Books*, St. Augustine of Hippo, first published in Latin between 397 and 400 C.E. See Author's Notes.

2.   MacArthur Foundation website, July 29, 2015 (accessed April 22, 2016): https://www.macfound.org/programs/fellows/strategy/

3.   *Stanford Encyclopedia of Philosophy*, Newton's Philosophy, first published October 2006, substantive revision May 2014 (accessed April 22, 2016): http://plato.stanford.edu/entries/newton-philosophy/

4.   Nick Strausfeld, Interview, November 13, 2013.

5.   Daniel Gilbert, *Stumbling on Happiness*. Vintage, 2007. p. 4.

6.   Stu Kauffman, Interview, November 19, 2013.

7.   Liane Gabora, Home Page, University of British Columbia (accessed April 22, 2016): https://people.ok.ubc.ca/lgabora/

8.   Liane Gabora, Interview, December 3, 2013.

9.   Gary Nabhan, Interview, November 7, 2013.

10.   Heather Pringle, *The Origins of Creativity*, Scientific American Mind, Vol. 23, Number 1, *Scientific American*, p. 10.

11.   Liane Gabora, *The Power of Then: The Uniquely Human Capacity to Imagine Beyond the Present*, (blog for) PsychologyToday.com, March 10, 2010. Accessed April 22, 2016: https://www.psychologytoday.com/blog/mindbloggling/201003/the-power-then-the-uniquely-human-capacity-imagine-beyond-the-present

12.   Ibid.

13.   Heather Pringle, *The Origins of Creativity*, Scientific American Mind, Vol. 23, Number 1, *Scientific American*, p. 7.

14. Liane Gabora, Interview, December 3, 2013.

15. Philip Tetlock, *Expert Political Judgment: How Good Is It? How Can We Know?* Princeton University Press, 2005, p. 82.

16. Isaiah Berlin, *The Hedgehog and the Fox: An Essay on Tolstoy's View of History*. London: Weidenfeld & Nicolson, 1953, p. 2.

17. Accessed April 22, 2016: http://www.npr.org/ sections/13.7/2012/02/06/146464163/beyond-modernity-thoughts-we-might-consider

18. Gary Hill, Interview, October 3, 2013.

19. Pat Churchland, Interview, October 21, 2015.

20. Richard Kenney, Interview, December 16, 2013.

21. Sarah Kagan, Interview, July 23, 2013.

22. Ibid.

23. Ibid.

24. Accessed April 22, 2016: http://www.archives.gov/exhibits/charters/ declaration_transcript.html

25. Sara Lawrence-Lightfoot, Interview, October 11, 2013.

26. Susan Meiselas, Interview, January 9, 2014.

27. Ibid.

28. Ric Scofidio, Interview, October 10, 2013.

29. Liz Lerman, Interview, July 16, 2013.

30. Ruth De Fries, Interview, October 11, 2013.

31. Howard Gardner, *Creating Minds: An Anatomy of Creativity*. Basic Books, 2011, p. 7.

32. Ibid., p. 34.

33. Brewster Ghiselin, *The Creative Process: Reflections on Invention in the Arts and Sciences*. University of California Press, 1985, p. 2.

34. Ibid.

35. George F. Kneller, *The Art and Science of Creativity*. Holt, Rinehart and Winston, Inc., 1965, p. 18.

36. Ibid., p. 33.

37. Mihaly Csikszentmihalyi, *Flow: The Psychology of Optimal Experience.* Harper Perennial, 2008, p. 25.

38. Ibid.

39. Robert Paul Weiner, *Creativity & Beyond: Cultures, Value and Change.* State University of New York Press, 2000, p. 9.

40. Edward Hirsch, Interview, September 24, 2013.

41. Mihaly Csikszentmihalyi, *Flow: The Psychology of Optimal Experience.* Harper Perennial, 2008, p. 228.

42. Liz Lerman, Interview, July 16, 2013.

43. Ibid.

44. Ric Scofidio, Interview, October 10, 2013.

45. Gary Paul Nabhan, *Cross-pollinations: The Marriage of Science and Poetry.* Milkweed Editions, 2004.

46. Gary Nabhan, Interview, November 7, 2013.

47. Ibid.

48. Ibid.

49. Carl Safina, Interview, July 2, 2013.

50. Gary Hill, Interview, October 3, 2013.

51. Richard Florida, "America's Looming Creativity Crisis," *Harvard Business Review*, October 2004, p. 136.

52. Arthur Koestler, *The Act of Creation: A Study of the Conscious and Unconscious Process of Humor, Scientific Discovery and Art.* The Macmillan Company, 1964, p. 35.

53. Accessed April 22, 2016: http://www.flappytclown.com/eddy/ StevenWrightJokes.html

54. Accessed April 22, 2016: http://izquotes.com/quote/21069

55. Carol S. Dweck, *Mindset: The New Psychology of Success.* Ballantine Books, 2006, p. 6.

56. Ibid., p. 7.

57. Ibid., p. 16.

58. Ibid., p. 40.

59. Ibid., p. 12.

60. Ibid., p. 41.

61. Annie Paul Murphy, Jonah Lehrer, "On How to Preserve Kids' Creative Spirit" (blog post), anniepaulmurphy.com, May 4, 2012 (accessed April 22, 2016): http://anniemurphypaul.com/2012/05/jonah-lehrer-on-how-to-preserve-kids-creative-spirit/

62. Carol S. Dweck, *Mindset: The New Psychology of Success*. Ballantine Books, 2006, p. 29.

63. Ibid., p. 7.

64. Ibid., p. 10.

65. Accessed April 22, 2016: http://www.brainyquote.com/quotes/authors/k/ken_robinson.html

66. Ken Robinson with Lou Aronica, *The Element: How Finding Your Passion Changes Everything*. Penguin Books, 2009, pp. 46-51.

67. Ibid., pp. 12-13.

68. Fareed Zakaria, "We Can't All Be Math Nerds & Science Geeks: Our Obsession with STEM Education Will Make It Harder for America to Innovate," *Washington Post*, Outlook Section cover story, March 29, 2015.

69. Ken Robinson with Lou Aronica, *The Element: How Finding Your Passion Changes Everything*. Penguin Books, 2009, pp. 12-13.

70. Ibid., p. 14.

71. Accessed April 22, 2016: https://www.ted.com/talks/ken_robinson_says_schools_kill_creativity?language=en

72. Accessed April 22, 2016: http://mathforum.org/dr.math/faq/faq.mcdonalds.html

73. Ken Robinson, with Lou Aronica, *The Element: How Finding Your Passion Changes Everything*. Penguin Books, 2009, p. 49.

74. Ibid.

75. Ibid., back cover.

76. Accessed April 22, 2016: http://www.brainyquote.com/quotes/authors/k/ken_robinson.html

77. Ibid.

78. Accessed April 22, 2016: https://www.youtube.com/watch?v=sOnqjkJTMaA

79. Martha Clarke, Interview, October 18, 2013.

80. Elizabeth Streb, Interview, November 21, 2013.

81. Liz Lerman, *Hiking the Horizontal: Field Notes From a Choreographer*. Weleyan University Press, 2011, p. xv.

82. Ibid., p.xvi.

83. Ibid., p.229.

84. Edward Abbey, *Desert Solitaire: A Season in the Wilderness*. Touchstone, 1990, p. 36.

85. Ibid.

86. Jerome Bruner, *On Knowing: Essays for the Left Hand*. Belnap Press, Harvard University Press, 1997, p. 17.

87. Robert Paul Weiner, *Creativity & Beyond: Cultures, Value and Change*. State University of New York Press, 2000, p. 1.

88. Ken Robinson, TED Talk, Do Schools Kill Creativity? February 2006 (accessed September 22, 2015): http://www.ted.com/talks/ken_robinson_says_schools_kill_creativity

89. Jane Goodall, excerpted from *Reason for Hope*, in *Brain Pickings, Jane Goodall on Science, Religion, and Our Human Responsibilities* by Maria Popova, April 4, 2014 (accessed October 14, 2015): http://www.brainpickings.org/2014/04/03/jane-goodall-science-religion-responsibility/

90. Ibid.

91. Elizabeth Turk, Interview, October 2013.

92. Marilynne Robinson, "Beauty" Essay from *The World Split Open: Great Authors on How and Why We Write*, Tin House Books, November 11, 2014, from the series A Literary Arts Reader.

93. Peter Huybers, Interview, November 22, 2013.

94. Accessed April 22, 2016: http://www.goodreads.com/quotes/1227856-i-never-went-to-college-i-don-t-believe-in-college

95. Richard Kenney, Interview, December 16, 2013.

96. Elizabeth Turk, Interview, October 2013.

97.   Yoshiko McFarland quotes are from "Background of EL and the Founder Yoshiko McFarland" page (accessed April 22, 2016): http://www.earthlanguage.org/english/bg.htm

98.   Accessed April 22, 2016: https://en.wikipedia.org/wiki/Bombing_of_Osaka

99.   Yoshiko McFarland quotes are from "Background of EL and the founder Yoshiko McFarland" page (accessed April 22, 2016): http://www.earthlanguage.org/english/bg.htm

100.   Ibid.

101.   Ibid.

102.   Ken Burns, The 18th Annual Nancy Hanks Lecture on Arts and Public Policy, Americans for the Arts, March 14, 2005; transcript (accessed April 22, 2016): http://www.americansforthearts.org/sites/default/files/pdf/events/hanks/Hanks2005KenBurns.pdf. Note: Quote is Nancy Hanks Lecture + Twain description borrowed from writer Ron Powers.

103.   Ibid.

104.   Richard Wiseman, *The Luck Factor: Changing Your Luck, Changing Your Life: The Four Essential Principles.* Miramax Books/Hyperion, 2003, p. 165.

105.   Larry Robertson, *A Deliberate Pause: Entrepreneurship and its Moment in Human Progress.* Morgan James, 2009, back cover.

106.   Steve Goodman, Interview, October 2, 2013.

107.   Ibid.

108.   Ibid.

109.   Ibid.

110.   John Harbison, Interview, October 16, 2013.

111.   Susan Meiselas, Interview, January 9, 2014.

112.   Steven Johnson, *Where Good Ideas Come From: The Natural History of Innovation.* Riverhead Books, 2010.

113.   Ric Scofidio, Interview, October 10, 2013.

114.   Steven Johnson, *Where Good Ideas Come From: The Natural History of Innovation.* Riverhead Books, 2010, p. 28.

115.   Ibid.

116.   Stu Kauffman, Interview, November 19, 2013.

117. Ibid.

118. Ibid.

119. Frans Johansson, *The Medici Effect: What Elephants & Epidemics Can Teach Us About Innovation*. Harvard Business School Press, 2006, p. 143-145.

120. Ibid.

121. Ric Scofidio, Interview, October 10, 2013.

122. Ibid.

123. Pat Churchland Interview, October 21, 2013.

124. Rebecca Newberger Goldstein, Interview, October 28, 2013.

125. Pat Churchland, Interview, October 21, 2013.

126. Ibid.

127. Larry Robertson, *A Deliberate Pause: Entrepreneurship and its Moment in Human Progress*. Morgan James, 2009, p. 59.

128. Ibid. p. 47.

129. Pat Churchland Interview, October 21, 2013.

130. Howard Gardner, Interview, September 8, 2013.

131. Susan Meiselas, Interview, September 4, 2013.

132. Frans Johansson, *The Medici Effect: What Elephants and Epidemics Can Teach Us About Innovation*. Harvard Business School Press, 2006, p. 125-26.

133. Ibid., p. 126.

134. Gary Nabhan, Interview, November 7, 2013.

135. Gary Paul Nabhan, *Cross-pollinations: The Marriage of Science and Poetry*. Milkweed Editions, 2004, p. 12.

136. Dov Seidman, *How: Why How We Do Anything Means Everything*. John Wiley & Sons, Inc., 2007, p. 55.

137. Gary Paul Nabhan, *Cross-pollinations: The Marriage of Science and Poetry*. Milkweed Editions, 2004, p. 83.

138. Miles J. Unger, *Magnifico: The Brilliant Life and Violent Times of Lorenzo de Medici*. Simon & Schuster Paperbacks, 2008, p. 398.

139. Ibid.

140. Ibid., p. 57.

141. Irving Stone, *The Agony and the Ecstasy*. Doubleday & Company, 1961, p. 107.

142. Ibid.

143. Ibid., p. 110.

144. Miles J. Unger, *Magnifico: The Brilliant Life and Violent Times of Lorenzo de Medici*. Simon & Schuster Paperbacks, 2008, p. 137.

145. Robert Paul Weiner, *Creativity & Beyond: Culture, Values, and Change*. State University Press, 2000, p. 61.

146. Richard Kenney, Interview, December 16, 2013.

147. David Bayles and Ted Orland, *Art & Fear: Observations on the Perils (and Rewards) of Artmaking*. The Image Continuum, 2013, p. 21.

148. John Harbison, Interview, October 16, 2013.

149. Joanna Scott, Interview, November 11, 2013.

150. George F. Kneller, *The Art and Science of Creativity*. Holt, Rinehart and Winston, Inc., 1965, p. 36.

151. Ibid., p. iii.

152. Ibid., p. 36.

153. Accessed April 22, 2016: http://computationalcreativity.net/iccc2012/wp-content/uploads/2012/05/203-Gabora.pdf.

154. George F. Kneller, *The Art and Science of Creativity*. Holt, Rinehart and Winston, Inc., 1965, pp. 36-37.

155. Ibid., p. 36.

156. Ibid., p. 37.

157. Ibid., p. 38.

158. Richard Wiseman, *The Luck Factor: Changing Your Luck, Changing Your Life: The Four Essential Principles*. Miramax Books/Hyperion, 2003.

159. Ibid.

160. Ibid.

161. Ibid.

162.   Scott Barry Kaufman, *Ungifted: Intelligence Redefined*. Basic Books, 2013, pp. 260-61.

163.   Ibid.

164.   Sandy Lanham, Interview, July 8, 2013.

165.   Ibid.

166.   Ruth DeFries, Interview, October 11, 2013.

167.   Ibid.

168.   Ibid.

169.   Rebecca Newberger Goldstein, Interview, October 28, 2013.

170.   Ibid.

171.   George F. Kneller, *The Art and Science of Creativity*. Holt, Rinehart and Winston, Inc., 1965, p. 38.

172.   Ibid.

173.   David McRaney, *You Are Now Less Dumb*. Gotham Books, 2013, p. 24.

174.   George F. Kneller, *The Art and Science of Creativity*. Holt, Rinehart and Winston, Inc., 1965, p. 60.

175.   Accessed April 22, 2016: http://amorebeautifulquestion.com/einstein-questioning/

176.   Phil DeVries, Interview, October 2, 2013.

177.   Ibid.

178.   Gary Nabhan, Interview, November 11, 2013.

179.   Ibid.

180.   Hideki Yukawa, *Creativity and Intuition: A Physicist Looks at East and West*. Kodansha International, Ltd., 1973, p. 131.

181.   Jacob Bronowski, *The Ascent of Man*, 13-part documentary series developed by Sir David Attenborough, produced by the BBS and Time-Life Films; first aired on BBC2, 1973.

182.   Deborah Meier, Interview, November 18, 2013.

183.   Ibid.

184. John Hunter, *World Peace and Other 4th-Grade Achievements*. Houghton Mifflin Harcourt, 2013, p. 71.

185. Ibid., p. 1.

186. Ibid., pp. 1-2.

187. Ibid., p. 124.

188. David Bayles and Ted Orland, *Art & Fear: Observations on the Perils (and Rewards) of Artmaking*. The Image Continuum, 2013, p. 113.

189. John Hunter, *World Peace and Other 4th-Grade Achievements*. Houghton Mifflin Harcourt, 2013, p. 53.

190. Scott Barry Kaufman, "The Real Link Between Creativity and Mental Illness," Scientific American blog (accessed October 3, 2013): http://blogs.scientificamerican.com/beautiful-minds/the-real-link-between-creativity-and-mental-illness/

191. John Hunter, *World Peace and Other 4th-Grade Achievements*. Houghton Mifflin Harcourt, 2013, pp. 127-8.

192. Michele Root-Bernstein, *Inventing Imaginary Worlds: From Childhood Play to Adult Creativity Across the Arts and Sciences*. Rowman & Littlefield Education, 2014, p. 162.

193. Ibid.

194. John Hunter, *World Peace and Other 4th-Grade Achievements*. Houghton Mifflin Harcourt, 2013, p. 86.

195. Elizabeth Streb, Interview, November 21, 2013.

196. Elizabeth Streb, *How to Become an Extreme Action Hero*. The Feminist Press, 2010, back cover.

197. Elizabeth Streb, Interview, November 21, 2013.

198. Ibid.

199. James C. Abegglen and George Stalk, Jr., *Kaisha: The Japanese Corporation*. Basic Books, 1985.

200. Wikipedia entry for 5 Whys (accessed July 20, 2015): https://en.wikipedia.org/wiki/5_Whys

201. Elizabeth Streb, Interview, November 21, 2013.

202. Michele Root-Bernstein, *Inventing Imaginary Worlds: From Childhood Play to Adult Creativity Across the Arts and Sciences*. Rowman & Littlefield Education, 2014, p. 168.

203. Rebecca Newberger Goldstein, Interview, October 28, 2013.

204. Ibid.

205. Elaine Pagels, Interview, October 28, 2013.

206. Lisa Cooper, Interview, December 16, 2013.

207. Liz Lerman, *Hiking the Horizontal: Field Notes from a Choreographer*. Wesleyan University Press, 2011, p. 25.

208. Maria Chudnovsky, Interview, January 2014.

209. Richard Kenney, Interview, December 16, 2013.

210. Daniel Gilbert, *Stumbling on Happiness*. Vintage, 2007, p. 110.

211. Susan McClary, Interview, October 21, 2013.

212. Ellen Barry, Interview, September 26, 2013.

213. Ibid.

214. Liz Lerman, *Hiking the Horizontal: Field Notes from a Choreographer*. Wesleyan University Press, 2011, p. 22.

215. Ibid., p. 94.

216. Maria Chudnovsky, Interview, January 2, 2014.

217. Gary Nabhan, Interview, November 10, 2013.

218. Sara Lawrence-Lightfoot, Jessica Hoffmann Davis, *The Art and Science of Portraiture*. Jossey Bass, 1997, p. 25.

219. David Bayles and Ted Orland, *Art & Fear: Observations on the Perils (and Rewards) of Artmaking*. The Image Continuum, 2013, p. 114.

220. Susan Meiselas, Interview, January 9, 2014.

221. Ibid.

222. Liz Lerman, *Hiking the Horizontal: Field Notes from a Choreographer*. Wesleyan University Press, 2011, p. 3.

223. Ibid., p. 7.

224. Liz Lerman, Interview, July 16, 2013.

225. Stu Kauffman, Interview, November 19, 2013.

226. Sara Lawrence-Lightfoot, Interview, October 11, 2013.

227. Ibid.

228. George F. Kneller, *The Art and Science of Creativity*. Holt, Rinehart and Winston, Inc., 1965, p. 89.

229. James Nestor, *Deep: Freediving, Renegade Science, and What the Ocean Tells Us About Ourselves*. Houghton Mifflin Harcourt, 2014, p. 5.

230. Accessed April 22, 2016: https://www.youtube.com/watch?v=1mYCIKTX0ug

231. Walt Whitman, "O Me! O Life!" *Leaves of Grass*, first published 1892.

232. James Nestor, *Deep: Freediving, Renegade Science, and What the Ocean Tells Us About Ourselves*. Houghton Mifflin Harcourt, 2014, p. 9.

233. David McRaney, *You are Now Less Dumb*. Gotham Books, 2013, pp. 36-37.

234. Brené Brown, *Daring Greatly: How the Courage to Be Vulnerable Transforms the Way We Live, Love, Parent, and Lead*. Gotham Books, 2012, p. 10.

235. Joel Achenbach, "5 Big Questions Still Stump Science." *Washington Post*, February 11, 2014.

236. Twyla Tharp, *The Creative Habit: Learn It and Use It for Life*. Simon & Schuster Paperbacks, 2006, p. 234.

237. Rebecca Goldstein, Interview, October 28, 2013.

238. James Nestor, *Deep: Freediving, Renegade Science, and What the Ocean Tells Us About Ourselves*. Houghton Mifflin Harcourt, 2014, p. 97.

239. Ibid.

240. Jenny Volvovski, Julia Rothman, and Matt Lamothe, *The Who, the What, and the When: 65 Artists Illustrate the Secret Sidekicks of History*. Chronicle Books, 2014, back cover.

241. Accessed April 22, 2016: https://en.wikiquote.org/wiki/Arthur_Ashe

242. Sylvia Law, Interview, November 1, 2013.

243. Steve Goodman, Interview, October 2, 2013.

244. Richard Kenney, Interview, December 16, 2013.

245. Ibid.

246. David Bayles and Ted Orland, *Art & Fear: Observations on the Perils (and Rewards) of Artmaking*. The Image Continuum, 2013, Introduction.

247. Maria Chudnovsky, Interview, January 2, 2014.

248. Martha Clarke, Interview, October 18, 2013.

249. Stu Kauffman, Interview, November 19, 2013.

250. Susan Meiselas, January 9, 2014.

251. Lorna Bourg, Interview, December 11, 2013.

252. Ibid.

253. Ernie Cortés, Interview, October 10, 2013.

254. Ric Scofidio, Interview, October 10, 2013.

255. Martha Clarke, Interview, October 18, 2013.

256. Stu Kauffman, Interview, November 19, 2013.

257. Carol Levine, Interview, October 18, 2013.

258. Lorna Bourg, Interview, December 11, 2013.

259. Ted Ames, Interview, September 10, 2013.

260. Sara Lawrence-Lightfoot, Interview, October 11, 2013.

261. David Bayles and Ted Orland, *Art & Fear: Observations on the Perils (and Rewards) of Artmaking*. The Image Continuum, 2013, p. 79.

262. George F. Kneller, *The Art and Science of Creativity*. Holt, Rinehart and Winston, Inc., 1965, p. 14.

263. Nigel Rees, *Mark My Words: Great Quotations and the Stories Behind Them*. Barnes & Noble, Inc., 2002, p. 359.

264. Dean Keith Simonton, *The Science of Genius*. Scientific American Mind, Vol. 23, Number 1, *Scientific American*, p. 21-27.

265. Ibid, p. 27.

266. Ibid.

267. Ibid.

268. Phil DeVries, Interview, October 2, 2013.

269. Ibid.

270.   Joe Berkowitz, "7 Tips for Pitching Ideas From World Class
       Improviser Jason Mantzoukas" (accessed September 10, 2015):
       fastcompanycreate.com

271.   Hideki Yukawa, *Creativity and Intuition: A Physicist Looks at East and West.*
       Kodansha International, Ltd., 1973, p. 125.

272.   Ibid.

273.   David Bayles and Ted Orland, *Art & Fear: Observations on the Perils (and
       Rewards) of Artmaking.* The Image Continuum, 2013, p. 43.

274.   Ibid., p. 68.

275.   John Harbison, Interview, October 16, 2013.

276.   Elizabeth Streb, *How to Become An Extreme Action Hero.* The Feminist
       Press, 2010, p. 151.

277.   Brené Brown, *Daring Greatly: How the Courage to Be Vulnerable Transforms the
       Way We Live, Love, Parent, and Lead.* Gotham Books, 2012, p. 2.

278.   Peter H. Reynolds, *The Dot.* Candlewick Press, 2003.

279.   Accessed April 22, 2016: http://www.art-quotes.com/auth_search.
       php?authid=1808#.Vqpr-BGnDds

280.   Frans Johansson, *The Click Moment: Seizing Opportunity in an Unpredictable
       World.* Penguin Group, 2012, p. 138.

281.   Art Fry (quoting 3M mentor Dick Drew), *A Century of Innovation: The 3M
       Story,* 2002, 3M Company, p. 76.

282.   Phil Hansen, *Limits Spark Creativity,* TED Talk, February 2013. Accessed
       April 29, 2016: https://www.ted.com/talks/phil_hansen_embrace_the_
       shake?language=en#t-298650 filmed 2-2013.

283.   Ibid.

284.   Accessed April 22, 2016: http://www.ted.com/talks/andrew_stanton_
       the_clues_to_a_great_story?language=en filmed 2-2012.

285.   Ibid.

286.   Phil Hansen, *Limits Spark Creativity,* TED Talk, February 2013. Accessed
       April 29, 2016: https://www.ted.com/talks/phil_hansen_embrace_the_
       shake?language=en#t-298650 filmed 2-2013.

287.   Ibid.

288.   Ibid.

289. Sara Lawrence-Lightfoot, Jessica Hoffmann Davis, *The Art and Science of Portraiture.* Jossey Bass, 1997, pp. 9-10.

290. Duncan Watts, *Everything Is Obvious: How Common Sense Fails Us.* Crown Business, 2011, pp. 61-63.

291. Sara Lawrence Lightfoot, Interview, October 11, 2013.

292. Sara Lawrence-Lightfoot, Jessica Hoffmann Davis, *The Art and Science of Portraiture.* Jossey Bass, 1997, pp. 9-10.

293. Accessed September 14, 2015: http://isites.harvard.edu/icb/icb. do?keyword=qualitative&pageid=icb.page340906

294. Pat Churchland, Interview, October 21, 2013.

295. Ibid.

296. General Stanley McChrystal U.S. Army, Retired, with Tantum Collins, David Silverman, Chris Fussell, *Team of Teams: New Rules of Engagement for a Complex World.* Portfolio/Penguin, 2015, p. 57.

297. Ibid.

298. Peter Pronovost, Interview, October 28, 2013.

299. General Stanley McChrystal U.S. Army, Retired, with Tantum Collins, David Silverman, Chris Fussell, *Team of Teams: New Rules of Engagement for a Complex World.* Portfolio/Penguin, 2015, p. 100.

300. Peter Pronovost, Interview, October 28, 2013.

301. Paul Rogat Loeb, *The Impossible Will Take a Little Time: Perseverance and Hope in Troubled Times.* Basic Books, 2014, pp. 163-164.

302. Sarah Kagan, Interview, July 23, 2013.

303. Ibid.

304. Ibid.

305. Sue Kieffer, *Concepts of Beauty and Creativity.* The Geological Society of America, Special Paper 413, 2006.

306. Sue Kieffer, Interview, December 11, 2013.

307. Ibid.

308. George F. Kneller, *The Art and Science of Creativity.* Holt, Rinehart and Winston, Inc., 1965, p. 95.

309. Steven Pinker, *The Language Instinct: How the Mind Creates Language.* Harper Perennial, 2007.

310. Susan W. Kieffer, *The Concept of Beauty and Creativity: Earth Science Thinking*, Geological Society of America, Special Paper 413, 2006, p. 6.

311. Ibid., p. 7.

312. Sue Kieffer, Interview, December 11, 2013.

313. Hideki Yukawa, *Creativity and Intuition: A Physicist Looks at East and West.* Kodansha International, Ltd, 1973, pp. 54-55.

314. Ibid., p. 22.

315. Ibid., p. 85.

316. Susan McClary, Interview, October 21, 2013.

317. Rebecca Newberger Goldstein, "An Unresolved (and Therefore Unbeautiful) Reaction to the Edge Question," essay in *This Explains Everything.* Collection edited by John Brockman. Harper Perennial, 2013, p. 25.

318. Rebecca Newberger Goldstein, Interview, October 28, 2013.

319. Ibid.

320. Lorna Bourg, Interview, December 11, 2013.

321. Paul Rogat Loeb, *The Impossible Will Take a Little Time: Perseverance and Hope in Troubled Times.* Basic Books, 2014, pp. 163-164.

322. Ibid.

323. Lynsey Addario, Interview, December 31, 2013.

324. Daniel H. Pink, *Drive: The Surprising Truth About What Motivates Us.* Riverhead Books, 2009.

325. Daniel H. Pink, *The Puzzle of Motivation*, TED Talk, July 2009 (accessed April 22, 2016): http://www.ted.com/talks/dan_pink_on_ motivation?language=en.

326. Daniel H. Pink, *A Whole New Mind: Why Right-Brainers Will Rule the Future.* Riverhead Books, 2006.

327. Daniel H. Pink, *The Puzzle of Motivation*, TED Talk, July 2009 (accessed April 22, 2016): http://www.ted.com/talks/dan_pink_on_ motivation?language=en.

328. Maria Chudnovsky, Interview, January 2, 2014.

329.   Susan W. Kieffer, *The Concept of Beauty and Creativity: Earth Science Thinking*, Geological Society of America, Special Paper 413, 2006, p. 6.

330.   Ibid.

331.   Maria Chudnovsky, Interview, January 2, 2014.

332.   Lisa Cooper, Interview, December 16, 2013.

333.   Ibid.

334.   Ibid.

335.   Lynsey Addario, Interview, December 31, 2013.

336.   John Harbison, Interview, October 16, 2013.

337.   John F. Kennedy, "Annotated Draft of Kennedy's Convocation Speech Prepared by Arthur Schlesinger, Jr." Speech Date: October 26, 1963 (accessed April 22, 2016): https://www.amherst.edu/library/archives/exhibitions/kennedy/documents#Draft

338.   Ibid.

339.   Accessed April 22, 2016: http://www.cleveland.com/datacentral/index.ssf/2012/12/the_original_apple_macintosh_c.html

340.   Accessed April 22, 2016: http://www.pewinternet.org/2015/04/01/us-smartphone-use-in-2015/

341.   John F. Kennedy, "Rice University, 12 September 1962," September 12, 1962. John F. Kennedy Presidential Library and Museum (accessed April 22, 2016): http://www.jfklibrary.org/Asset-Viewer/MkATdOcdU06X5uNHbmqm1Q.aspx

342.   Ibid.

343.   Ibid.

344.   John F. Kennedy, "Remarks at Amherst Upon Receiving an Honorary Degree," October 26, 1963. John F. Kennedy Presidential Library and Museum (accessed April 22, 2016): http://www.jfklibrary.org/Asset-Viewer/80308LXB5kOPFEJqkw5hlA.aspx

345.   Ibid.

346.   Michael Benson, *Visionaries and Outcasts: The NEA, Congress, and the Place of the Visual Artist in America.* The New Press, 2001, p. 19.

347.   Sarah L. Kaufman, "Twyla Tharp's Nonstop Flight," November 8, 2015, *Washington Post*, Arts & Style, p. E6.

348. Ibid.

349. Gary Paul Nabhan, *Cultures of Habitat: On Nature, Culture, and Story.* Counterpoint, 1997, p. 12.

350. Sarah L. Kaufman, "Twyla Tharp's Nonstop Flight," November 8, 2015, *Washington Post*, Arts & Style, p. E6.

351. Ibid.

352. Liz Lerman, Interview, July 16, 2013.

353. Ibid.

354. Ibid.

355. Ibid.

356. Roger von Oech, *A Whack on the Side of the Head.* Creative Think, 1992.

357. Ibid., p. 11.

358. Sarah Lewis, *The Rise: Creativity, The Gift of Failure, and the Search for Mastery.* Simon & Schuster Paperbacks, 2014, p. 159.

359. Pedro Sanchez, Interview, October 7, 2013.

360. Ibid.

361. John Hunter, *World Peace and Other 4th-Grade Achievements.* Houghton Mifflin Harcourt, 2013, p. 7.

362. This story was first told in Dr. Susannah Heschel's 2003 book *The Women's Passover Companion* and recounted online (accessed April 22, 2016): http://www.juf.org/news/world.aspx?id=414773

363. Sara Lawrence-Lightfoot, Interview, October 11, 2013.

364. Ibid.

365. Alan Lightman, *The Accidental Universe: The World You Thought You Knew.* Pantheon Books, 2013, p. 26.

366. Robert Safian, "Generation Flux," *Fast Company*, Issue 162, February 2012, p. 71.

367. Sara Lawrence-Lightfoot, Interview, October 11, 2013.

368. Elizabeth Svoboda, "The Power of Story," *aeon Magazine* online, January, 2015 (accessed April 22, 2016): http://aeon.co/magazine/psychology/once-upon-a-time-how-stories-change-hearts-and-brains/

369. Ibid.

370. David McRaney, *You are Now Less Dumb*. Gotham Books, 2013, p. 28.

371. David Bayles and Ted Orland, *Art & Fear: Observations on the Perils (and Rewards) of Artmaking*. The Image Continuum, 2013, Introduction.

372. Ibid. p. 118.

373. Daniel Gilbert, *Stumbling on Happiness*. Vintage, 2007, p. 172.

374. Sara Lawrence-Lightfoot, Interview, October 11, 2013.

375. Stu Kauffman, Interview, November 19, 2013.

CPSIA information can be obtained at www.ICGtesting.com
Printed in the USA
BVOW06*1909150916

461771BV00003B/1/P